Cognitive Case Conceptualization

A Guidebook for Practitioners

The LEA Series in Personality and Clinical Psychology

Irving B. Weiner, Editor

Exner (Ed.) • Issues and Methods in Rorschach Research

Frederick/McNeal • Inner Strengths: Contemporary Psychotherapy and Hypnosis for Ego-Strengthening

Gacono/Meloy • The Rorschach Assessment of Aggressive and Psychopathic Personalities

Ganellen • Integrating the Rorschach and the MMPI-2 in Personality Assessment

Handler/Hilsenroth • Teaching and Learning Personality Assessment

Hy/Loevinger • Measuring Ego Development, Second Edition

Kelly • The Assessment of Object Relations Phenomena in Adolescents: TAT and Rorschach Measures

Kelly • The Psychological Assessment of Abused and Traumatized Children

Kohnstamm/Halverson/Mervielde/Havill (Eds.) • Parental Descriptions of Child Personality: Developmental Antecedents of the Big Five?

Loevinger (Ed.) • Technical Foundations for Measuring Ego Development: The Washington University Sentence Completion Test

McCallum/Piper (Eds.) • Psychological Mindedness: A Contemporary Understanding

Meloy/Acklin/Gacono/Murray/Peterson (Eds.) • Contemporary Rorschach Interpretation

Needleman • Cognitive Case Conceptualization: A Guidebook for Practitioners

Nolen-Hoeksema/Larson • Coping With Loss

Rosowsky/Abrams/Zweig • Personality Disorders in the Elderly: Emerging Issues in Diagnosis and Treatment

Sarason/Pierce/Sarason (Eds.) • Cognitive Interference: Theories, Methods, and Findings

Silverstein • Self Psychology and Diagnostic Assessment: Identifying Selfobject Functions Through Psychological Testing

Taylor (Ed.) • Anxiety Sensitivity: Theory, Research, and Treatment of the Fear of Anxiety

Tedeschi/Park/Calhoun (Eds.) • Posttraumatic Growth: Positive Changes in the Aftermath of Crisis

Van Hasselt/Hersen (Eds.) • Handbook of Psychological Treatment Protocols for Children and Adolescents

Weiner • Principles of Rorschach Interpretation

Wong/Fry (Eds.) • The Human Quest for Meaning: A Handbook of Psychological Research and Clinical Applications

Zillmer/Harrower/Ritzler/Archer • The Quest for the Nazi Personality: A Psychological Investigation of Nazi War Criminals

Cognitive Case Conceptualization

A Guidebook for Practitioners

Lawrence D. Needleman
Ohio State University

LAWRENCE ERLBAUM ASSOCIATES, PUBLISHERS
1999 Mahwah, New Jersey London

Lawrence Erlbaum Associates, Inc., Publishers
10 Industrial Avenue
Mahwah, NJ 07430

Cover design by Kathryn Houghtaling Lacey

Library of Congress Cataloging-in-Publication Data

Needleman, Lawrence D.
Cognitive case conceptualization: a guidebook for practitioners / Lawrence D. Needleman.
p. cm. — (The LEA series in personality and clinical psychology)
Includes bibliographical references and indexes.
ISBN 0-8058-1908-8 (alk. paper)
1. Cognitive therapy. 2. Psychiatry—Case formulation. I. Title. II. Series.
IN PROCESS
616.89'142—dc21 98-31852
CIP

Books published by Lawrence Erlbaum Associates are printed on acid-free paper, and their bindings are chosen for strength and durability.

Printed in the United States of America
10 9 8 7 6 5 4 3

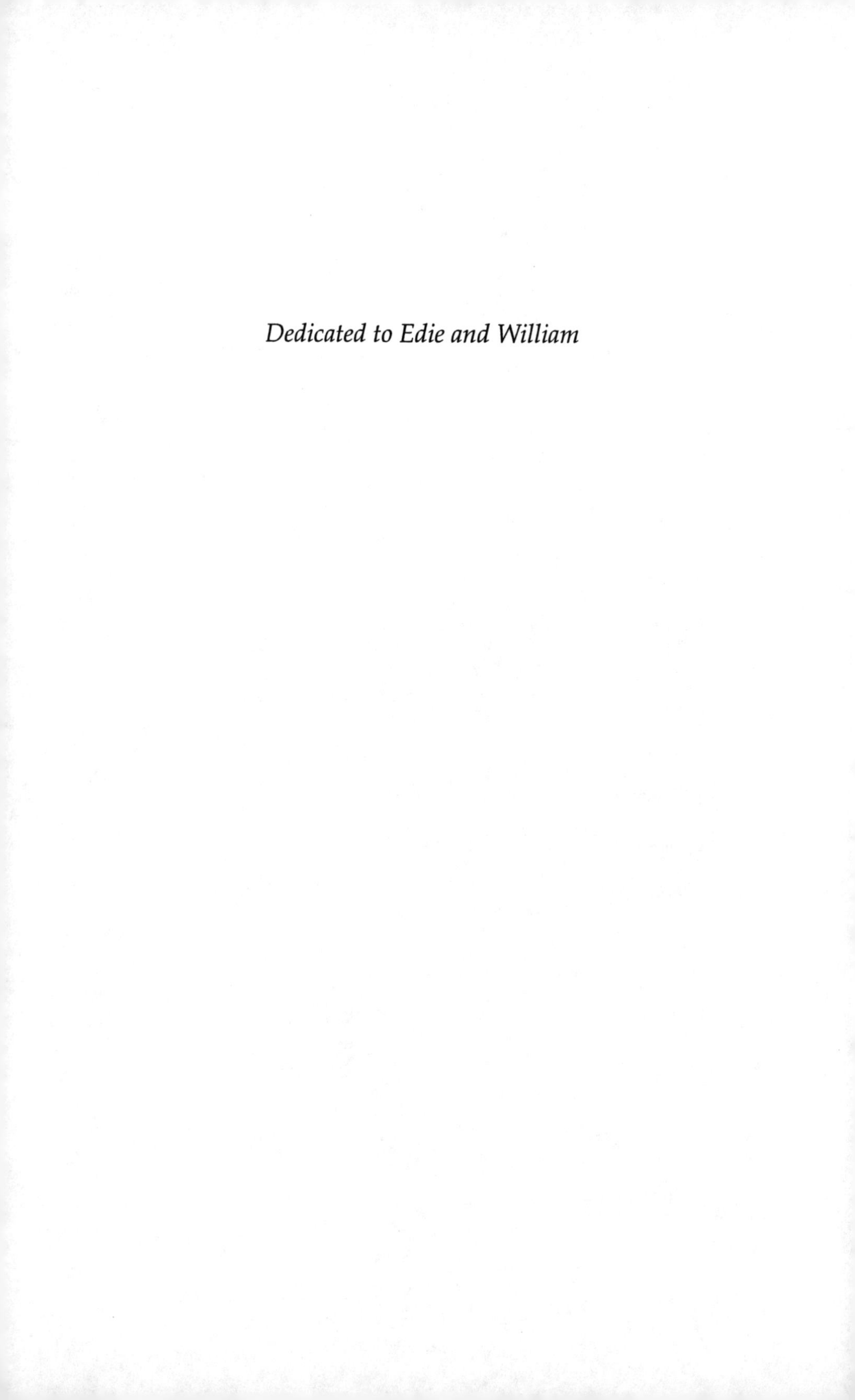

Dedicated to Edie and William

Contents

List of Cases

Chronic or Recurrent Major Depressive Disorder (MDD)

Foreword

Contemporary psychotherapy has taken a decidedly scientific turn as we enter the 21st century. The definition of the therapist as simply a good listener whose job it is to help the patient *feel better* has changed to the definition of the therapist as an active and directive participant-observer whose job it is to help the patient *get better.* Indeed, long before the advent of managed care, cognitive behavioral therapists were practicing an empirically based model of treatment planning and therapy.

All empirically based models of therapy are the product of an interaction between scientists and practitioners. They are developed and then tested, using standardized protocols. Psychodynamic models (e.g., interpersonal therapy [IPT]) and the cognitive behavioral therapy (CBT) model have several points in common.

They both call for a time-limited approach to therapy. Efficacy research protocols generally involve around 12 to 20 sessions, over a period of no more than 20 weeks. In clinical practice, however, the course of treatment is not limited to 20 weeks. For certain patients the length of therapy may be 6 sessions; for other patients, 50 sessions. The length of the therapy, the frequency of the sessions, and the session length are all negotiable. The problems being worked on, the skills of the patient and of the therapist, the time available for therapy, and the financial resources all have the potential to dictate the parameters of treatment. The goal is not simply to limit the number of sessions, but also to determine their most effective use so that even the patient who can come for unlimited sessions can best be worked with in a framework requiring that the therapy be "administered" in a pre-set modular fashion. The modular approach of working in 5- to 10-session blocks of time and effort keep the therapy, the therapist, and the patient on target.

The treatment protocols associated with empirically based models generally have been seen by some as negative and derided as "cookbooks." In point of fact, adherence to a treatment protocol has a positive impact on both patient and therapist in that it helps to maintain a focus in the therapy.

Therapists who advocate and practice a free-flowing, unfocused, boundaryless therapy seem to be hoping for change without specifying what change they are looking for and what will bring it about. I should note that the appellation of "cookbook" is not one that I shy away from. The use of a standard recipe helps ensure that the product will be predictable from one time to another. Once one knows the "recipe," he or she can start to customize the recipe.

We cannot assume that a single size fits all and that just because a model works with one disorder (e.g., depression), it will work equally well without modification on another (e.g., anxiety). Models must be tested in the treatment of each disorder.

The therapy must be proactive, not simply reactive. The reactive approach, so often seen as universal, involves the patient coming into the consulting room. The patient talks and the therapist responds. The patient talks and the therapist responds. The patient talks and the therapist responds. The patient talks and the therapist responds. The patient talks and the therapist responds by ending the session. The patient leaves and comes in next time at which point the patient talks and the therapist responds. The patient talks and the therapist responds. The patient talks and the therapist responds.

The proactive approach requires that the therapist conceptualize the problems, assess the patient's skills and motivation, assess the available time and resources for therapy, and choose the strategies and techniques best suited for the particular patient, given the time, motivation, and energy constraints, to deal with these problems.

There must be a structure to the therapy. First, at the outset, a discrete list of problems must be agreed on. This list helps both patient and therapist to have an idea of where the therapy is going and to know how the therapy is progressing. The content and the direction of the therapy are established early in the collaboration. Following the problem list, the individual sessions are then structured through *agenda setting* and *homework.*

Agenda setting is used by many groups to help the participants in meetings have a direction for the meeting, add to the agenda, become more active in the meeting process, and generally allow for maximum success in the minimal time often allotted to the meeting. In individual therapy as well, rather than let the therapy session meander, the therapist can work with the patient to set an agenda, help to focus the therapy work, and make better use of time, energy, and available skills. This is all accomplished (and is dependent on) the therapist's strong working conceptualization of the patient's strengths, weaknesses, resources, and pathology. Agenda setting at the beginning of the session allows both patient and therapist to put issues of concern on the agenda for the day. This structuring is important because the reason individuals often become patients is that they have lost their ability to organize and problem solve. By setting an agenda, the treatment model's problem-solving focus is modeled. Moving through the items on the agenda requires that the therapist be skilled at setting priorities and pacing the session, while taking into account the needs of the patient. This is a skill that is refined through practice and experience. However, even seasoned therapists may feel tense and anxious and be less effective when they are first learning how to pace a session that is built around a collaborative agenda.

Therapy cannot be limited to a session or two per week. Transfer and generalization of the skills developed within the session can be expanded through the use of intersession "homework." This systematic extension of the work of therapy to nontherapy hours results in faster, more comprehensive improvement. It builds the expectation that new skills, new cognitions, and new behaviors must be applied in vivo. Homework can be specifically cognitive or behavioral. Most often, it is both. Homework early in therapy focuses on helping the person to interrupt automatic patterns or routines (either cognitive or behavioral), and to observe the connections between thought, behavior, and mood. Thus, early homework tasks may include observing automatic thoughts through the use of DTR, activity scheduling, collecting evidence for and against the person's attributions and expectancies, and mastery and pleaure ratings. In the middle of therapy, homework includes trying out new behaviors through graded task assignments; acting differently in order to gather information about alternative hypotheses; noticing, catching, interrupting, and responding to negative thoughts and behaviors; and enacting a plan designed to lead to a specific goal.

Ideally, homework should be collaboratively developed and consist of tasks that the client is able to perform with reasonable time and effort. Furthermore, it should provide the client with choices that will enhance the individual's sense of control and self-efficacy.

The therapist takes an active and directive role in the therapy based on the treatment conceptualization. Rather than simply restating the patient's words, or reflecting the patient's mood, the active therapist will share hypotheses, utilize guided discovery, encourage the patient, serve as a resource person, be a case manager, and, in certain limited cases, be an advocate for the patient.

Therapy must be a collaborative endeavor. The therapist and patient work together as a team. The collaboration is not always 50/50, but may be 30/70, or 90/10, with the therapist providing most of the energy or work within the session or in the therapy more generally. The more severely depressed the patient, the less energy he or she may have available to use in the therapy. The therapeutic effort would be to help the patients to make maximum use of their energy and to build greater energy.

Therapy must involve skill building or the development of coping techniques. Rather than cure depression and anxiety, the therapist helps the patient to acquire a range of strategies with which to manage present and future exigencies of life. The focus of therapy is not on why patients act the way they do, but rather on what keeps them acting that way. Therapy addresses the question of how to make the necessary changes.

The plans for therapy, the types of changes that one can expect, and the path to reach the goals all derive from the therapist's formulation of the case conceptualization. Case conceptualization is, without a doubt, the highest order therapy skill. The novice therapist can be given a list of techniques and can then be taught, via a cookbook, about how to use the techniques. If enough techniques are thrown at a patient, something may work. But the skill that we would want the therapist to build and to have is the ability to develop a conceptualization that will then serve as a template for understanding the patient. If our conceptualization is accurate, it will do three things. It will account for the patient's past behavior. It will make sense of the patient's present behavior. And finally, it will allow prediction of the patient's future behavior.

The resources to draw on in teaching this crucial skill of case conceptualization have, to this point, been quite limited. I am both personally and professionally pleased that Lawrence Needleman has written the present text. It is the first breath of fresh air on this subject in almost 10 years. Whereas I have spoken of the importance of case conceptualization, stressed it in my workshops and lectures, and discussed it in various chapters and texts I have written, I have never given it the time and energy it deserves. Larry has done that.

This superb book has in its title two important terms. They are *guidebook* and *practitioners.* It is written for the practitioner of cognitive therapy. It is written in a manner that makes it usable from the first chapter. From that point it only gets better. It takes the therapist, novice or advanced, through the case conceptualization process in a guided discovery manner, typical of the cognitive therapy approach. The book starts with a thorough introduction to case conceptualization, followed, in chapter 2, by the basics of the cognitive model. What is of particular interest in this chapter is the use of Erikson's psychosocial model as a tool for understanding the development of core beliefs. It often seems that writers assume that everyone doing therapy understands the intricacies and elements of the therapeutic relationship, but this is, unfortunately, untrue. Chapter 3 reviews these complexities and discusses the socialization of the patient into the cognitive model of therapy. Chapters 4 and 5 offer an excellent introduction to the treatment planning approach, starting with the integration of the available information and leading to techniques for clinical intervention.

The second part of the book takes on the daunting task of applying the model to the most commonly seen disorders, including panic with agoraphobia (chap. 6), obsessive-compulsive disorder (chap. 7), and depression (chap. 8). The book is filled with rich clinical vignettes from Larry's clinical practice that illustrate the style and content of the necessary interventions.

My personal pleasure derived from this book is rooted in my narcissism. Larry was a former student of mine during his postdoctoral fellowship at the University of Pennsylvania's Center for Cognitive Therapy, directed by Aaron T. Beck. With this book Needleman has placed himself in the forefront of cognitive therapists. It is a text that I will use in my classes, recommend to others, and quote from in my workshops. I recommend that it be translated from English into any of the languages of the countries in which cognitive therapy has established itself over the last 12 years.

I would like to think that my work with Larry early in his career in some way helped him to reach this point. I am proud of him and incredibly pleased with this book. Without a doubt, this is the book that I wish I had written.

—Arthur Freeman
Philadelphia College of Osteopathic Medicine

Acknowledgments

Many people made this book possible. To them, I express my deepest gratitude.

I feel extremely privileged to have worked with Arthur Freeman, one of my clinical supervisors at the Center for Cognitive Therapy at the University of Pennsylvania. Learning from Art's insightful conceptualizations of clients and his incisive interventions profoundly influenced how I came to conceptualize and treat clients. In addition, at various times in my career, I have sought Art's counsel and benefited from his generosity, wisdom, caring, and enthusiastic support.

I also feel very fortunate to have worked with Aaron T. Beck. My time as a postdoctoral fellow and subsequently as a clinical associate at the Center for Cognitive Therapy was formative in my theoretical and technical development as a clinician. Besides creating an exceptional learning environment at the Center, Beck provided an extraordinary model of what it means to be a scholar and a lifelong learner.

To Ruth Greenberg, one of my clinical supervisors at the Center, I owe a great debt. Her wisdom, kindness, and dedication are of mammoth proportions. I also learned much from the supervision and teaching of Cory Newman, Marianne Layden, Bob Berchick, Judy Beck, and the late Fred Wright. Kevin Kuelwein, Norman Cotterell, Judy Washington, Andy Butler, Greg Brown, and Pamela Stimac were good friends and colleagues at the Center.

I feel enormous gratitude to Professor Scott Geller at Virginia Tech. He modeled an intense desire and commitment to making a difference in the world. In addition, he was an enthusiastic champion of my work.

At Case Western Reserve University, I had the opportunity to work closely with Jeff Janata. Jeff taught me much about the treatment of obsessive-compulsive disorder. He was kind, supportive, and encouraging throughout my training. Tina Zimmerman, Stan Altof, and Steve Levine taught me about psychodynamics. They opened my eyes to the role of what we cognitive therapists might think of as information processing, cognitive and emotional avoidance, and compensatory strategies that occur outside awareness.

Kim Breitenbecher, Tony Obradovich, and Jackie Schwartz, colleagues at Ohio State University, provided thoughtful feedback about portions of the text that helped shape the final product. I also appreciated the support of Ken Flannagan, Sandy Levy, David Soskis, Steve Stern, and Pete Zafirides. The University of the Sciences (formerly Philadelphia College of Pharmacy and Science) awarded me a summer grant, which provided me the opportunity to begin planning this project.

Many family members and friends were very supportive while I worked on this project. I owe the greatest thanks to my wife, Edie, who has been an ardent supporter of my ability, my career, and this project. She provided insightful suggestions and help with the organization and editing of the manuscript.

I am extremely grateful to my parents, Philip and Sima Needleman. They always have been enthusiastic, proud, and supportive of me. They modeled hard work, dedication, and an appreciation for excellence. My mother tirelessly and meticulously proofread several versions of the manuscript. My mother-in-law, Gloria Berkowitz, deserves special thanks. She visited numerous times to provide assistance of all kinds, which enabled me to focus on my writing.

William Needleman, my little boy, has been a source of joy, diversion, and perspective throughout the writing process. I am simply in awe of him.

Others who have been supportive since the inception of this project include my sister, Nina Needleman Swartz, who proofread the text and provided helpful suggestions. I've also appreciated the support of Lilly Needleman, Sadie Kolman, Haskell Goldstein, Jewel and Eddie Littenberg, Bet and Lou Berman, David Franklin, Jeff Zuckerman, Betty Gillespie, Wendy Brady, Deborah Rozansky, and Scott Swartz. Michael Berkowitz, my brother-in-law, provided advice, good cheer, and humor. Rachel and Stephen Berkowitz, niece and nephew, added sweetness and fun. Brenda and Marty Kramer were generous hosts in Rochester, New York, which enabled me to continue working during visits that coincided with important deadlines.

I am grateful to my clients from whom I have learned so much. Not only did they teach me about emotional problems and suffering, but they also taught me about strength, dignity, and resilience. It has been a privilege.

Finally, I thank the people at Lawrence Erlbaum Associates. Irving Weiner, the series editor, generously read over several versions of the manuscript and provided valuable suggestions. Susan Milmoe supplied a continual stream of guidance, insight, and encouragement. I also thank Dorothy Gribbin, Kate Graetzer, and Judi Amsel for all their help. The LEA staff was always professional, friendly, and most of all patient.

—Lawrence D. Needleman

Cognitive Case Conceptualization

A Guidebook for Practitioners

1

Introduction to Case Conceptualization

1. How Case Conceptualizations Facilitate Successful Treatment
   a. Conceptualizations Guide Selection of Interventions
   b. Conceptualizations Facilitate Intervention Implementation
      i. Conceptualizations Help Clients Understand Their Problems and Rationales for Interventions
      ii. Conceptualizations Help Therapists Predict Potential Obstacles to Treatment
      iii. Conceptualizations Help Clients Increase Their Motivation
      iv. Conceptualizations Help Therapists and Clients Establish an Effective Therapeutic Relationship
   c. The Conceptualization Process Can Help Therapists Further Their Understanding of Psychopathology
   d. The Conceptualization Process Can Help Scientist-Practitioners Develop Relevant Research Questions
2. Guidelines for Developing Case Conceptualizations
   a. Format of the Case Conceptualization
      i. Identifying Information, Presenting Problem, and Precipitants of the Presenting Problem
      ii. Exhaustive List of Problems, Issues, and Therapy-Relevant Behaviors
      iii. Relevant Beliefs
      iv. Origins of Core Beliefs
      v. Vicious Cycles/Maintaining Factors
      vi. Treatment Goals, Possible Obstacles to Treatment, and Treatment Plan
   b. Therapist's Perspective on Modifying the Conceptualization
   c. Client–Therapist Collaboration as Part of the Conceptualization Process
   d. Potential Threats to the Accuracy of Clinical Data
3. An Example of a Case Conceptualization Illustration
4. An Example of a Completed Case Conceptualization Summary Form
5. How This Book Is Organized

In brief, *cognitive case conceptualization* refers to the process of developing a parsimonious understanding of clients and their problems that guides effective and efficient treatment (Sacco & Beck, 1995). When developing a case conceptualization of a client, the therapist incorporates the following elements from the cognitive model:

1. the integrated cognitive, affective, and behavioral responses to triggering circumstances;
2. the client's underlying belief system that determines the client's responses;
3. the circumstances that activate maladaptive responses;
4. the environment's responses to the client's behavior;
5. the negative events that precipitated the client's problems; and
6. the learning history that contributed to the client's vulnerability to specific problems (Beck, Freeman, et al., 1990; Persons, 1989; Sacco & Beck, 1995).

To maximize a conceptualization's usefulness, therapists should attempt to find the fewest number of underlying beliefs and processes that can comprehensively explain the client's behavior and problems (Persons, 1989). By linking together relevant elements of the clinical material, conceptualizations enable therapists and clients to see the "big picture." Drawing an illustration that links various elements of the conceptualization and writing a summary of the relevant elements are invaluable methods for illuminating important connections. Without using these tools, therapists are more likely to miss some of these connections. Thus, case conceptualizations help therapists think about clients' problems clearly and efficiently.

When therapists develop individualized case conceptualizations, they integrate information from three sources. These sources are (a) knowledge of the intricacies of the cognitive model (see chap. 2), (b) a comprehensive assessment of the client (see chap. 4), and (c) research and theoretical literature related to the client's problems.

First this chapter describes how case conceptualizations facilitate the selection and effective implementation of interventions. Next, it presents guidelines for developing conceptualizations. Finally, it presents examples of conceptualizations.

HOW CASE CONCEPTUALIZATIONS FACILITATE SUCCESSFUL TREATMENT

An accurate conceptualization of the mechanisms that determine the client's problematic responses allows the therapist to predict the client's behavior and responses to interventions. By helping therapists make accurate predictions, conceptualizations facilitate successful treatment. Most important, for our purposes here, the conceptualization process guides therapists' selection and implementation of cost-effective interventions. However, the case conceptualization process also can help therapists further their understanding of psychopathology and can help scientist-practitioners develop relevant research questions that may lead to advances in clinical psychology.

Conceptualizations Guide Selection of Interventions

Beck, Emery, and Greenberg (1985) suggested that case conceptualization involves placing a psychological problem in its context. Understanding the context in which a problem arises permits appropriate selection of interventions. Although novice therapists may be aware of many techniques for addressing a particular clinical problem, they often choose inappropriate approaches. This results from failing to have a clear understanding of the underlying mechanisms that produced the problem.

Consider several individuals who had a common overt problem, chronic difficulties completing tasks in a timely manner. The first client, Latoya, believed, "Everything I do must be perfect." When she worked on projects, this belief resulted in anxiety, urges to check her work for errors, and repeated, overt checking behavior. Her repeated checking dramatically slowed her performance. Another individual with difficulties completing tasks was Byron. He held the belief, "I shouldn't have to do mundane tasks." He felt angry when people asked him to complete tasks. When they did, he had an urge to angrily refuse the request. However, this urge was tempered by his belief that he would be punished if he expressed his anger directly. As a result, he worked on projects, albeit slowly and carelessly. A third individual, Ava, believed, "I can't do anything right; I'll probably mess up." She felt anxious and had urges to escape. She avoided attempting tasks by feigning physical illness. A fourth individual, Jim, was depressed, had little energy, and believed, "Nothing really matters." When required to do a task, he wondered, "Why bother?" and did not attempt it. Clearly, understanding the idiosyncratic mechanisms responsible for a problematic response is necessary for selecting appropriate intervention strategies for the individual.

It should be noted that cognitive case conceptualizations are useful despite the availability of effective cognitive-behavioral treatment approaches for various disorders. Outcome studies have found that disorder-specific cognitive therapy approaches have been effective for several disorders. These include depression (Beck, Rush, Shaw, & Emery, 1979), panic disorder (Beck, Sokol, Clark, Berchick, & Wright, 1992; Clark, 1986; Clark et al., 1994; Sokol, Beck, Greenberg, Wright, & Berchick, 1989), agoraphobia (Hoffart, 1995; Marchione, Michelson, Greenwald, & Dancu, 1987; Sharp & Power, 1996), obsessive-compulsive disorder (Freeston, Rhéaume, & Ladouceur, 1996; Salkovskis, 1985, 1989, 1996; Salkovskis & Kirk, 1989; Steketee & Foa, 1985; Steketee & Shapiro, 1993; Turner & Beidel, 1988; van Oppen & Arntz, 1993), social phobia (Chambless & Hope, 1996), and bulimia nervosa (Fairburn, Marcus, & Wilson, 1993). Then, why bother developing individualized case conceptualizations for clients with these disorders?

There are several compelling reasons for doing so. First, even for clients with disorders for which effective interventions are available, successful implementation of treatment packages depends on the therapist's having an accurate understanding of the client's idiosyncratic cognitive, affective, motivational, and behavioral responses (Layden, Newman, Freeman, & Morse, 1993).

Consider how the treatment approach for panic disorder was tailored to two clients having this disorder. During his panic attacks, Jeff focused on feelings of dizziness and unreality and had the catastrophic cognition that he would lose control and "go crazy." To prevent himself from going crazy during attacks, he typically touched the ground to literally "feel grounded and make sure everything is still real." In contrast, Janie focused on her chest pain during her panic attacks and believed that she would have a heart attack and die. She believed the reason she had not actually had a heart attack was that she always lay down and tried to relax when she had panic attacks. Both clients received the same treatment components—cognitive restructuring, paced breathing, relaxation training, procedures for refocusing attention, and intentional exposure to the sensations of panic (see chap. 6 for a detailed description of the procedures for treating panic disorder). However, their treatment was individualized based on idiosyncratic features of their case conceptualizations.

For Jeff, cognitive restructuring targeted his belief that he was at risk for going crazy when he experienced panic attacks. Resulting from guided discovery (see chap. 3), Jeff generated compelling evidence that he was not in danger of going crazy (e.g., despite having hundreds of panic attacks, he never had hallucinations or delusions or exhibited grossly inappropriate behaviors; he had no family history of psychosis or mania). The therapist recorded the reasons on an index card that Jeff referred to during attacks. Regarding exposure to panic sensations, Jeff was exposed to dizziness by spinning around in a swivel chair and hyperventilating. He was not allowed to "ground" himself during these therapist-induced "attacks." The purpose was to teach him that even when pushed to the limit, he would not lose control and go crazy.

Based on Janie's cognitive case conceptualization, cognitive restructuring focused on her catastrophic belief that she was having a heart attack. To expose her to sensations of panic so that she could understand that her fear was unfounded, her therapist had her exercise vigorously during the therapy session. Janie was discouraged from resting and in fact was urged to exercise beyond the point at which she believed she must stop. (These procedures were cleared with her cardiologist first.) Frequently repeating this exercise helped her disconfirm her belief that she would have a heart attack. Although Jeff and Janie's therapists used the same basic approach for treating panic, individualizing the treatment was necessary for successful outcomes.

A second reason for developing individualized case conceptualizations despite the availability of effective cognitive therapy approaches is that clients often present multiple, clinically-relevant problems. Therefore, a treatment package designed for a specific clinical problem—even if the problem is primary or the most serious—may not take into account important features of clients that may affect outcome (Padesky, 1996). For example, Benjamin (a client presented in detail at the end of this chapter), had major depressive disorder, social phobia, and various problematic personality features. Simply treating his depression with a standardized treatment package, for instance, would have been unlikely to produce a successful outcome. Similarly, serially treating his various disorders would have been inefficient and probably ineffective.

Third, case conceptualizations allow clinicians to understand and treat problems for which there are no standardized treatments but that may respond well to cognitive therapy (Persons, 1989). A few examples of clinical problems for which there are not well-established, empirically proven psychotherapeutic interventions include hypochondriasis, bipolar disorder, depersonalization disorder, psychogenic itching, dyspareunia not due to a general medical condition, exhibitionism, and pathological gambling.

If a client either has multiple diagnoses or has a single disorder that has not been empirically investigated, the therapist must decide whether it is appropriate and ethical to treat the client. The following questions can help therapists make this determination:

- Is the person experiencing significant distress or impairment as a result of an emotional problem?
- Is there sufficient justification to believe that therapy can work?
  If the client has co-morbid problems, does the research literature suggest that the individual problems can be treated successfully?
  Does the therapist have a sound theoretical basis for believing that therapy could be successfully applied to the client's problems?
- What are the costs of not attempting to treat the client in terms of distress and impairment?

Conceptualizations Facilitate Intervention Implementation

Cognitive case conceptualizations can facilitate effective intervention implementation by helping (a) clients understand their problems and rationales for interventions, (b) therapists predict potential obstacles to therapy, (c) clients increase their motivation, and (d) therapists and clients establish an effective therapeutic relationship.

Conceptualizations Help Clients Understand Their Problems and Rationales for Interventions. A compelling case conceptualization presented to the client in diagrammatic form can be an excellent tool for helping clients understand their problems and helping them see convincing rationales for interventions. Through a pictorial representation, clients can see clearly how each intervention can impact the relevant factors that contribute to their problems. (At the end of the chapter, an example of a Case Conceptualization Illustration is provided. The end of the chapter also includes a therapy transcript in which a therapist presents the illustration to a client.)

Conceptualizations Help Therapists Predict Potential Obstacles to Treatment. Cognitive case conceptualizations help predict difficulties and obstacles in the therapeutic process that result from underlying psychological dimensions (Persons, 1989). Potential difficulties may relate to the therapeutic relationship or compliance with therapy. For example, the case conceptualization for Benjamin (presented at the end of the chapter) helped predict difficulties he might have had in the therapeutic relationship. His therapist anticipated that Benjamin would likely fear that she would be critical and unkind to him if he did not "perform" well in therapy. Anticipating this problem allowed the therapist to address this potential difficulty directly with Benjamin, possibly circumventing a problem that could have led to treatment failure.

Conceptualizations Help Clients Increase Their Motivation. Case conceptualizations can facilitate interventions by helping clients with low motivation and a sense of hopelessness improve their motivation to persevere in therapy. Low motivation for treatment is a risk factor for early drop out and treatment failure. Sharing case conceptualizations with clients can stop them from feeling confused, overwhelmed, and hopeless resulting from the complexity of their problems. Case conceptualizations allow clients with problems in multiple life domains to realize that their problems are related to a single core belief such as helplessness, mistrust, or unlovability. This realization, in turn, helps clients feel that their problems are finite and manageable. As mentioned previously, the conceptualization can help provide convincing rationales for interventions. This process helps clients realize that there are effective methods for solving their problems.

Another way that conceptualizations can help motivate clients is that they can identify the beliefs that contribute to hopelessness. Early in therapy, these beliefs can be targets of intervention. Some examples of cognitions that contribute to a sense of hopelessness include "I'll always be miserable" and "My situation will never improve."

If a client's social environment is interfering with the client's motivation, the assessment and conceptualization process can identify this issue and make it a target of intervention. A common example of how a client's environment interfered with her motivation is illustrated by the problems of Diane, an obese woman whose self-esteem and physical health were compromised by her excess weight. As Diane began to exercise and eat more sensibly, her husband, Jack, felt threatened. He worried that other men would become attracted to her and that she would ultimately leave him. As a result, Jack began bringing unhealthful food into the house and regularly pressured Diane to make unhealthful choices. He made comments such as "One pint of Ben and Jerry's ice cream won't kill you," "You've got to enjoy life more," and "Would you rather be skinny and miserable or let yourself enjoy life?" These comments activated Diane's feelings of sadness and decreased her motivation to follow her health regimen. By identifying this issue, the therapist and Diane decided to bring Jack into the therapy process. In therapy, Diane was able to allay Jack's fears and elicit his help, resulting in both weight loss and an improved marital relationship.

Clients who have personality disorders or other chronic psychological problems may have the expectation that therapy will result in their becoming "a completely different person" and their not knowing who they are. This expectation often results in apprehension and therefore can contribute to their resistance to therapy. Fears associated with change can be identified in the case conceptualization and then addressed directly.

Conceptualizations Help Therapists and Clients Establish an Effective Therapeutic Relationship. Another way that case conceptualizations facilitate successful implementation of interventions is helping to build the therapeutic relationship. Effective conceptualizations help clients see that their therapists have a sophisticated understanding of them. This often increases clients' confidence in their therapist and their therapist's ability to help. In contrast, intervening without an accurate conceptualization is likely to contribute to clients believing they are misunderstood and can lead to problems with rapport. Like shooting an arrow in the dark, a premature intervention is likely to miss the mark badly.

Case conceptualizations can also facilitate therapeutic relationships by positively influencing a therapist's attitudes and behaviors toward a client. Empathy, genuineness, positive regard, warmth, a nonjudgmental attitude, and expertise set the stage for a positive outcome (Egan, 1982; Raush & Bordin, 1957; Rogers, 1957). If clients do not respect and feel respected by their therapist, or if they do not like their therapist, they are not likely to invest in the therapeutic process. In addition, they are not likely to try to think, act, relate to others, and feel in new ways that could be helpful and healthy. Empirical studies have supported the positive role that therapists' empathy and warmth have on therapeutic outcome (e.g., Burns & Nolen-Hoesksema, 1992; chap. 3 discusses the therapeutic relationship).

Case conceptualizations can elicit therapists' compassion for clients who exhibit behaviors that most people would find highly aversive. It is often easier for the therapist to feel and express empathy toward a difficult client after developing a case conceptualization. Often in such cases, the conceptualization illustrates how the client's maladaptive responses originated from extreme pain or hardship and were initially reasonable responses to a horrific childhood situation. For example, Sally, a 42-year-old twice-divorced attorney, frequently exhibited demanding, rude, and entitled behavior (e.g., acting as if her needs were more important than everyone else's and getting angry when she did not get special treatment). The therapist was able to experience empathy for Sally after taking her social history. Sally was severely neglected by her parents and suffered malnourishment almost to the point of death. She learned early in life that the only way to get her needs met was to "be the squeaky wheel," a strategy that continued into adulthood. By realizing the origins of Sally's behavior, the therapist found it much easier to tolerate her actions and address them in a nondefensive and nonangry fashion.

The Conceptualization Process Can Help Therapists Further Their Understanding of Psychopathology

Therapists should continually work toward increasing their understanding of psychopathology. First, they must have a thorough knowledge of the literature related to their clients' problems and keep abreast of the latest developments in the field. In addition, therapists' understanding of psychopathology can be enhanced by systematic clinical observations and careful reflection. The case conceptualization can be instrumental in achieving these aims.

By providing concise understandings of clients who share common clinical problems, the cognitive case conceptualization process enables therapists to identify commonalities and differences among these clients. Therapists can collect Case Conceptualization Summaries and Case Conceptualization Illustrations of their clients and organize them by clinical problems. Such a collection of conceptualizations can help therapists identify common themes.

The Conceptualization Process Can Help Scientist-Practitioners Develop Relevant Research Questions

In addition to helping individual therapists improve their understanding of clinical problems, the case conceptualization process can help the field of clinical psychology do the same. As the next section describes, each element of an individualized conceptualization should be considered a hypothesis to be tested. The issues relating to such hypotheses may or may not have been adequately addressed in the literature. Therefore, scientist-practitioners who use the case conceptualization method when treating clients may generate important research questions that they wish to pursue empirically.

GUIDELINES FOR DEVELOPING CASE CONCEPTUALIZATIONS

Therapists should take into account several guidelines when developing cognitive case conceptualizations. These pertain to (a) the format of the conceptualization, (b) the therapist's perspective on modifying the conceptualization, (c) client–therapist collaboration as part of the conceptualization process, and (d) potential threats to the accuracy of clinical data. An example of a completed Case Conceptualization Summary Form and an example of a Case Conceptualization Illustration are also presented.

Format of the Case Conceptualization

Two theorists, Jacqueline Persons (1989) and Judith Beck (1995), developed single-page formats for readily displaying salient information as part of the cognitive case conceptualization process. Both approaches graphically depict various components of the cognitive model as they pertain to the particular client. Persons' (1989) Case Formulation sheet consists of the following: identifying information, chief complaint, problem list, hypothesized mechanism that underlies the client's various problems, relationship of the mechanism to the problems, precipitants of current problems, origins of the central problem, treatment plan, and predicted obstacles to treatment.

Beck's (1995) Cognitive Conceptualization Diagram provides the therapist with boxes for displaying the following: relevant childhood data, core beliefs, conditional assumptions/beliefs/rules, and compensatory strategies. In addition, the therapist can illustrate three problematic scenarios consisting of the situation, automatic thought, meaning of the automatic thought, emotion, and behavior.

The Case Conceptualization Summary Form proposed here is an integration of selected elements from the approaches just described. These elements are discussed in the following sections. (A blank copy of the form is presented in the Appendix.)

Identifying Information, Presenting Problem, and Precipitants of the Presenting Problem. Information about clients' current situations, the nature of their major problems, and events that preceded their psychological problems is important in developing sound case conceptualizations. More often than not, a client's presenting problem is the target of therapeutic intervention. In addition, identifying information, presenting problems, and precipitants of the presenting problems often are suggestive of the client's underlying belief system and vulnerabilities. Therefore, information pertaining to these dimensions should help the therapist hypothesize about the mechanisms that underlie the client's problems (Persons, 1989).

Exhaustive List of Problems, Issues, and Therapy-Relevant Behaviors. An exhaustive list of the client's problems and issues is important for two reasons. Repeatedly seeing a list of these reminds the therapist and client about topics that need to be addressed and monitored in therapy. Second, a list of problems, issues, and therapy-relevant behaviors—such as lack of compliance with self-help assignments, poor attendance, and dependent behavior during sessions—is often suggestive of underlying beliefs, long-term patterns, and vicious cycles.

Cognizance of therapy-relevant behaviors may help therapists modify therapy to best serve the client's needs. However, caution should be used in calling attention to problematic therapy-relevant behaviors because clients may find this threatening and therefore doing so may be detrimental to the therapy process. Therefore, clinical judgment is necessary.

Relevant Beliefs. As described in chapter 2, individuals' belief structures (schemas) and content influence all aspects of information processing. Specifically, belief structures and content influence (a) how individuals perceive and remember situations; (b) how they view themselves, the world, and the future; and (c) what rules and strategies they use for responding to situations. Core beliefs are the most central and enduring beliefs. Examples of core beliefs are "I'm weak," "Other people are to be used," and "Life is cruel." Other beliefs are less central but can still have an important impact on an individual's functioning (e.g., "If I work really hard at things, I might not fail" and "People must treat me with respect").

Origins of Core Beliefs. Learning the origins of clients' core beliefs can be important in designing interventions for changing the beliefs and can help identify other important issues. Chapter 5 describes procedures for using traumatic childhood events to modify core beliefs.

Vicious Cycles/Maintaining Factors. Vicious cycles and maintaining factors are hallmarks of psychopathology. In anxiety disorders, avoidance or escape behaviors often maintain anxiety-provoking cognitions. For example, a person with a phobia of dogs believed "All dogs will attack me." Consequently, he avoided dogs whenever he saw them from a distance. His avoidance behavior seemingly prevented him from disconfirming his anxiety-provoking belief and prevented the natural process of habituation from occurring. Clearly, interrupting vicious cycles and altering maintaining factors is a primary aim of therapy.

Treatment Goals, Possible Obstacles to Treatment, and Treatment Plan. Treatment *goals* should be realistic, focus on the most important problems the client is experiencing, and be agreeable to the therapist and the client. Therapists also should attempt to anticipate all *possible* *obstacles* to therapy for a particular client. Doing so helps prevent later difficulties and impasses. The treatment *plan* attempts to interrupt a client's vicious cycles and maintaining factors using relevant cognitive-behavioral techniques (presented in chap. 5).

Therapist's Perspective on Modifying the Conceptualization

Cognitive conceptualizations work best when they are considered processes of successive approximations that begin when the therapist first obtains information about the client and continue throughout the course of treatment. As early as possible in therapy, the therapist should begin to draw a Case Conceptualization Illustration linking together relevant information and should begin completing a Case Conceptualization Summary Form to provide structure and direction to assessment and treatment. However, it also is essential that the conceptualization be considered a working model that will be refined over time as more information becomes available.

It is helpful to think of each element of the conceptualization as a hypothesis to be tested (Beck, Freeman, et al., 1990; Carey, Flasher, Maisto, & Turkat, 1984; Persons, 1989; Turkat, 1990). Therapists should set up mini-experiments to test their formulation. Eliciting their clients' feedback provides another important source of information about the accuracy of the conceptualization.

When presented with new information, individuals—including therapists—respond most adaptively when they are neither excessively rigid nor excessively fluid regarding their beliefs. Therefore, therapists are more likely to provide effective treatment when they: (a) avoid rigidly and dogmatically holding on to their conceptualizations despite strong contradictory information, and (b) resist making major changes in their conceptualizations without sufficient justification (see chap. 2 for a discussion of assimilating and accommodating schemas).

Client–Therapist Collaboration as Part of the Conceptualization Process

Conceptualizations are most useful when they are generated within the context of a collaborative relationship. Through the assessment approaches described in chapter 4, the therapist and client jointly discover crucial information for the conceptualization. It is essential for the therapist to review the Case Conceptualization Summary Form and the Case Conceptualization Illustrations with the client who can suggest possible modifications.

Also, the therapist should be sure to use the client's own words for each component of the conceptualization. Consider the situation in which a therapist uses the word "helplessness" as a name for a core belief, but the client thinks of the same phenomenon as "weakness." Although the meanings of the words are fairly similar, if the therapist refers to "helplessness," the client may not feel understood and might not accept the conceptualization completely. In short, collaboration with the client increases a conceptualization's accuracy and the likelihood that the client will believe it.

Potential Threats to the Accuracy of Clinical Data

The final guideline for developing useful conceptualizations has to do with potential threats to the accuracy of clinical data. Although collaboration is highly desirable and usually possible, the therapist should be aware that clients at times are inaccurate reporters. Poor reporting may be the result of a host of factors including: difficulty introspecting, embarrassment or shame, suspiciousness, and resistance to therapy (e.g., as a result of a court mandate or coercion to attend therapy by significant others). If the therapist suspects that the client's report about a particular element in the conceptualization is inaccurate, the therapist should not insist that he or she is correct and the client is incorrect. Instead, the therapist might try one of several options. The therapist and client could generate several alternative explanations for that element of the conceptualization by brainstorming and then evaluating each alternative explanation. For some elements in the conceptualization, the therapist could corroborate the information with other sources (e.g., interviews with significant others, legal records). The therapist could ask the client to "try on for size" that aspect of the therapist's conceptualization for a week or so before forming a final opinion.

AN EXAMPLE OF A CASE CONCEPTUALIZATION ILLUSTRATION

Early in cognitive therapy, the therapist presents the client with a Case Conceptualization Illustration. The illustration graphically depicts the client's idiosyncratic experiences within the cognitive-model framework. A compelling case conceptualization presented to the client in diagrammatic form can be an excellent tool for helping clients understand their problems. Moreover, it helps them see convincing rationales for interventions. Over the course of therapy, the therapist and the client can expand and modify this illustration as they develop a more complete understanding of the client.

Figure 1.1 is an example of a Case Conceptualization Illustration for a client, Penny, whose presenting problem was anger. Penny was a bank executive and single mother who presented for difficulty controlling her anger both at home and at work.

Besides the illustration, an excerpt from the session, during which Penny's therapist presented the illustration to Penny, is included. The therapist presented the illustration to Penny as he was assessing her responses to a problematic situation. While he explained an element of the conceptualization to Penny, he drew the corresponding element on the illustration (see Fig. 1.1 for the Case Conceptualization Illustration).

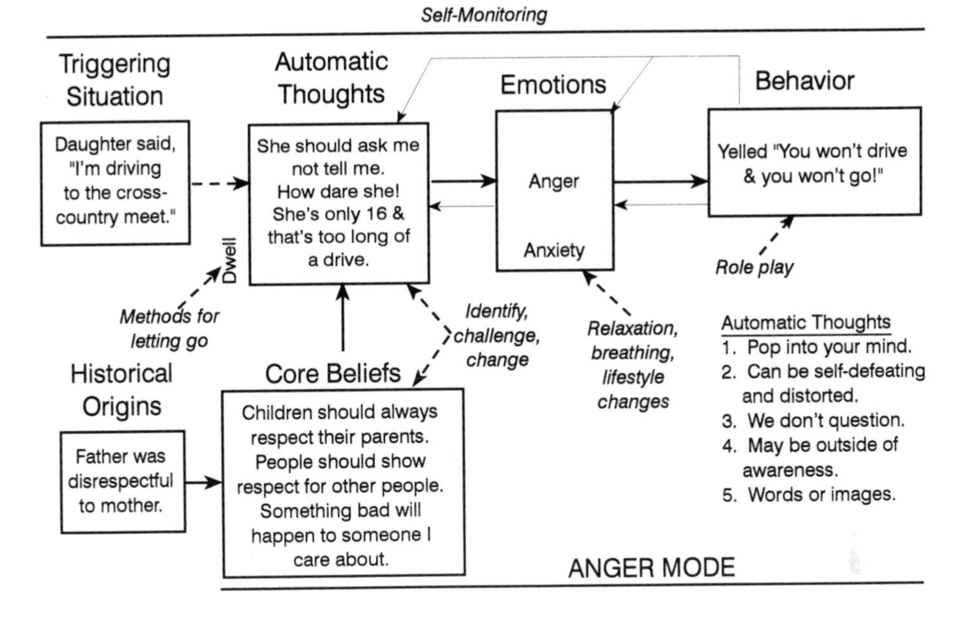

FIG. 1.1. Case Conceptualization Illustration for Penny.

Therapist: If it's all right with you, I believe it would be helpful to illustrate for you a framework for understanding and treating problems with anger.

Penny: OK.

Therapist: This framework is called the cognitive therapy perspective. To begin with, there may be a triggering situation, an external situation or internal experience that triggers your response. Should we use the situation that you described earlier, the one involving Estelle (daughter) this week?

Penny: That would be a good one.

Therapist: OK. So, the triggering situation for you was Estelle told you she was going to drive a friend to a cross-country meet that was several hours away.

Penny: Yes.

Therapist: The way you described it, your emotion was fairly intense anger. According to the cognitive therapy approach, a situation doesn't cause us to feel a particular way. It triggers it but doesn't cause it. What causes the emotion is what's going through your mind in the situation, what we call automatic thoughts. When your daughter told you she was driving to the cross-country meet, what went through your mind?

Penny: "She should ask me not tell me" and "How dare she."

Therapist: Any other thoughts or images in that situation?

Penny: Well, that "She's only 16 and that's too long of a drive for her."

Therapist: It sounds like part of your anger resulted from your concern about her.

Penny: Yes.

Therapist: OK, so you were having these thoughts and feeling really angry and concerned. Automatic thoughts and strong emotions often affect our behavior. How did what you were feeling and thinking affect your behavior?

Penny: I yelled at her, "You will not drive to any cross-country meet in Delaware, and you cannot go to the meet at all."

Therapist: Yes ... What questions or comments do you have about this model, so far?

Penny: None. But, I'll let you know if I don't understand something.

Therapist: Please do. Now, let me tell you more about automatic thoughts, characteristics that I think are important. First, automatic thoughts, as their name suggests, are automatic as opposed to being effortful or intentional. They just pop into your mind.

Second, automatic thoughts can be self-enhancing and rational or they can be self-defeating and distorted. Everyone has some self-defeating and distorted thoughts from time to time. But, when you're angry, your thoughts become dominated by distorted, maladaptive thoughts. In a little while, I'll show you a list of distortions that people often make.

Third, unfortunately, we tend to believe automatic thoughts are true without questioning them. If someone else says something, we may question it in our mind. However, when we have automatic thoughts, they're just kind of there, and we tend to accept them without really thinking about them.

Fourth, automatic thoughts can be fully in our awareness and long-lasting. Or, they might be only at the fringes of our awareness, or they may even be completely out of our awareness. That makes them particularly difficult. They're really important in contributing to our emotions and behavior. But, we may not even be aware we're having them. Even if we are aware, we may tend to not question them. Fortunately, there are ways to become aware of automatic thoughts and begin to evaluate them to see if they are appropriate and useful. To begin with, we need a signal that we are having an automatic thought. From this illustration, do you have any idea of possible signals?

Penny: Yes. When I'm angry, that's a pretty clear message.

Therapist: Exactly. Are there ever any other signals that anger might be on its way and that you might have some important automatic thoughts to address?

Penny: Yes. If I feel like yelling or carrying on.

Therapist: What about other emotions as signals?

Penny: Oh, yes. Like in this case, anxiety. Also, feeling like my daughter doesn't respect me.

Therapist: When you suddenly have a change in either your emotions or behavior and you don't know why, you can ask yourself one of several questions that can get at the automatic thoughts. You can ask yourself "What's going through my mind right now?" or "What does this situation mean to me?" or "What's the most upsetting part of this situation?" One of those questions almost always will help you find the automatic thought. Let me make one final point about automatic thoughts. Automatic thoughts can either be words, as the ones we identified for this situation with your daughter, or they can be mental pictures or images. Are you aware of having any mental pictures or images—for example, daydreams, fantasies, video clips in your head or a snapshot of a person's face?

Penny: Yes. Sometimes I see in my mind Estelle getting hurt in a car accident.

Therapist: Mm hm. That sounds really scary … Any questions or comments about what we've discussed so far?

Penny: No, I've got it.

Therapist: Good. I've drawn this illustration as if the processes are linear. Situations cause automatic thoughts, cause emotions, cause behaviors. In fact, they're not linear. When you become angry for example, you're more likely to have angry thoughts; that is, the emotions contribute to the thoughts. When you engage in angry behaviors, it contributes to having angry thoughts and feelings. All these factors probably interact.

In fact, when a person becomes angry in the way you described, they sometimes go into an angry mode. All their systems can be affected by anger, their thoughts, their emotions, their motivation, their blood pressure and heart rate, and their behavior. But, I think it's clearer to draw it in this simplified way because it helps show the ways we can intervene on these components. I'll show you that in a few minutes.

So far, I've been talking mostly about cognitive content. However, the process of thinking is important, too. When people are angry, they often ruminate or dwell on upsetting things. Are you aware of doing this?

Penny: Yes. I can't stop thinking about it, sometimes for days afterwards. Also, I become angry at myself for getting angry.

Therapist: What are your automatic thoughts there?

Penny: That I shouldn't get so angry and that I should have better control of myself.

Therapist: I see ... Another thing that is important is that these automatic thoughts don't just come out of the blue. Not only are they triggered by situations but also they come from deeper beliefs. What cognitive therapists call core beliefs. These are long-standing, deeply held beliefs about ourselves, other people, the world, and the future. Do you have a sense for what core beliefs might have been triggered in the situation with your daughter?

Penny: "Who knows what can happen with two 16-year-olds driving all that way?" and also "She doesn't respect me."

Therapist: Do you have a rule about that? Like, "Children should always respect their parents" or "People should show respect for other people?"

Penny: Both of those.

Therapist: Any other underlying beliefs that may have become activated in that situation, such as beliefs about safety?

Penny: I do tend to expect bad things to happen. I'm not consumed by worry about them. But, I do think about them fairly often.

Therapist: So, how would you phrase the belief?

Penny: "Something bad will happen to Estelle or someone else I care about."

Therapist: Now, these core beliefs tend to come from somewhere, too. They often come from our personal history. Often these are things that happened in our childhood. Are you aware of things that happened in your past that may have contributed to being vulnerable to feeling like people don't respect you?

Penny: My father was very disrespectful toward my mother. I felt angry for her and ashamed.

Therapist: Yes. That's exactly the kind of historical event that I was talking about. Now, let's discuss the kinds of things we can do to decrease the frequency and intensity of your anger.

Penny: Good.

Therapist: First, you can begin to monitor the situations that trigger you or even get you a little annoyed, irritated, or frustrated. From this information, you can become more aware of what the triggering situations are and your thinking that contributes to acting angrily. Second, once you identify the automatic thoughts and beliefs, we can begin to challenge and change them. Third, we can practice in imagery or we can role play typical difficult situations. This can give you opportunities to practice responding in an adaptive way and try out new strategies that we develop together. Fourth, we can work on ways to decrease your anger while you're angry. Focusing on breathing, for instance, can help there. Fifth, we can look at ways to let go of the anger after you are angry, ways to decrease your rumination. Finally, there may be some lifestyle issues that we can look at. For example, you drink a lot of caffeine, which can contribute to anger. In addition, you've mentioned that you are more likely to get angry when you've overextended yourself, and you mentioned this happens fairly often. That may be helpful to look at as well. Any concerns, questions, comments?

Penny: Nope.

Therapist: How does this sound as an initial plan?

Penny: It sounds very promising.

AN EXAMPLE OF A COMPLETED CASE CONCEPTUALIZATION SUMMARY FORM

This section shows how case material can be integrated effectively. It provides a written description of the client and is followed by a completed Case Conceptualization Summary Form (Fig. 1.2).

Benjamin was a 44-year-old, married, middle manager in state government who lived with his wife and two teenage children. Throughout his adult life, he had been depressed, either in a full depressive episode or in partial remission.

During depressive episodes, Benjamin experienced daily sadness, anhedonia, irritability, difficulty with concentration and memory, terminal insomnia, low energy, psychomotor retardation, feelings of worthlessness, and passive wishes to die with no intent or plans for suicide. His symptoms were worse in the morning, especially after sleeping poorly, which was most nights. His first few episodes of depression followed major life stressors, whereas subsequent episodes appeared to occur spontaneously. Between major depressive episodes, Benjamin experienced low-grade depressed mood, low self-esteem, and difficulty sleeping.

Benjamin chronically had activated depressogenic beliefs. His negative core beliefs about himself included "I'm a failure," "I must be perfect," and "I'm out of control." His depressogenic beliefs that related to the world included "People will reject me," tempered by the conditional belief, "If I'm perfectly nice and competent, I might be able to fool people into liking me." Another negative belief relating to the social world was "If I make a mistake, people will be cruel and critical." His negative future-related beliefs included "Life will always be hard for me" and "I'll always be miserable and a hopeless failure." An example of an external situation that triggered a worsening of his mood was making a minor mistake. Internal triggers included feeling irritable or impatient with his wife or children and dwelling on his imperfections, mistakes, and shortcomings.

In response to his depressed mood and his depressive cognitions, Benjamin engaged in a variety of disorder-maintaining behaviors. He engaged in these behaviors to punish himself and to prevent himself from making similar errors in the future. When he became impatient with his family, he isolated himself for hours, and sometimes days, to prevent himself from acting inappropriately. As a result, he often felt like a failure for not being able to control his behavior well enough to be a part of the family. Isolating himself also prevented him from engaging in family activities that might have taken his attentional focus away from himself. In addition, isolating himself contributed to his wife's being angry with him. Her anger further confirmed his beliefs about himself and other people.

A second disorder-maintaining (covert) behavior was intentionally berating himself for mistakes. He believed he must criticize himself to teach himself a lesson. In addition, he believed that if he punished himself, he would experience less hurt if other people criticized or punished him. Berating himself strengthened his negative beliefs about himself.

To prevent mistakes at work, Benjamin employed a third disorder-maintaining strategy. He reviewed his work repeatedly and excessively often resulting in staying long past quitting time. Excessively reviewing his work prevented him from learning that others typically would not criticize him for making minor mistakes. Also, because it contributed to long hours and less time with his children, he considered excessively reviewing his work as evidence supporting his belief that he was a terrible father and husband.

Several factors and life events were likely to have predisposed Benjamin to depression. His mother was chronically depressed. As a result, he may have inherited a genetic predisposition for depression. In addition, she modeled depressive behavior, and she was less responsive to his needs than she might have been if she were not depressed. In addition, his parents divorced when he was in elementary school. His biological father had little contact with him after the divorce. His mother remarried a man who was highly critical and who often verbally and emotionally abused Benjamin and his mother. Benjamin's mother had neither the energy nor the assertiveness skills to defend Benjamin against her husband. Benjamin had low-grade depression for most of his childhood. His first depressive episode occurred when he was 17 years old after his mother died of cancer.

HOW THIS BOOK IS ORGANIZED

This chapter introduced (a) the cognitive case conceptualization process, (b) the ways that conceptualizations facilitate the selection and effective implementation of interventions, and (c) procedures for developing conceptualizations.

For therapists to develop effective case conceptualizations, they must integrate a sophisticated understanding of the cognitive model with a thorough understanding of their individual clients. Chapter 2 describes the intricacies of the contemporary cognitive model. Specifically, Beck's Modal Information Processing Model is presented in detail. A *mode* is an integrated network of cognitive, affective, motivational, and behavioral systems that works in concert to mobilize an individual to achieve a particular aim. Psychological problems result from modes being activated in inappropriate circumstances.

The therapeutic relationship is widely considered to be necessary for achieving therapeutic success. Chapter 3 describes important issues regarding the therapeutic relationship in cognitive therapy. The following relationship factors are addressed in detail: (a) the therapist's attitude and behavior, (b) the collaborative nature of cognitive therapy, and (c) the process of socialization into cognitive therapy.

Chapter 4 describes effective assessment procedures. During the assessment process, therapists elucidate the various elements of the cognitive model that relate to their individual clients. The chapter provides detailed guidelines for various aspects of assessment. These include guidelines relating to preintake questionnaires, the intake interview, and ongoing assessment during therapy.

The ultimate purpose of the case conceptualization is to guide therapists' selection and implementation of effective interventions. Therapists should, therefore, have skills in using various empirically proven interventions. Chapter 5 provides the reader with procedures for using numerous state-of-the-art cognitive therapy interventions.

Chapters 6 through 8 focus on specific disorders. Each of these chapters describes a specific cognitive model for the disorder. The chapters also provide disorder-specific procedures for assessment, conceptualization, and treatment. Finally, they demonstrate the assessment, conceptualization and intervention processes with multiple case examples. The disorders include panic with agoraphobia (chap. 6), obsessive-compulsive disorder (chap. 7), and chronic or recurrent major depressive disorder (chap. 8).

CASE CONCEPTUALIZATION SUMMARY FORM

Client's Name: Benjamin

Identifying Information: 44-year-old, married with 2 teenage children, middle manager in state government.

Presenting Problem: Depression, social isolation, and anxiety.
Precipitant(s): Most recent exacerbation of symptoms occurred spontaneously.

Exhaustive List of Problems, Issues, and Therapy-Relevant Behaviors:

1.	Self-punitiveness, guilt, and self-directed anger.	6.	Works excessively.
2.	Depression.	7.	Fears punishment and cruel treatment.
3.	Insomnia.		
4.	Generalized social phobia.		
5.	Marital discord.		

Diagnoses (Axis I): Major Depressive Disorder, Recurrent (Chronic) Moderate; Social Phobia.
Personality Characteristics: Obsessive-Compulsive, Paranoid, and Avoidant Personality Features.
Relevant Beliefs:

1.	I have to criticize myself to prevent mistakes from happening again & lessen the pain if others are critical.	5.	I must be perfect.
2.	I'm dumb, a failure, inadequate, bad.	6.	People will reject me; people will be cruel and critical.
3.	I'm a terrible father and husband.	7.	People won't be there to meet my needs.
4.	I'm a loose cannon and out of control.	8.	Life will always be impossible for me; I'll always be miserable and a hopeless failure.

Origins of Key Core Beliefs: Mother failed to meet Benjamin's needs ==> *I'm inadequate* and *People will reject me;* and mother modeled depressive behavior for him.
Biological father had little contact with him after divorce ==> *People will reject me.*
Stepfather was highly critical, demanding of perfection, and often verbally and emotionally abusive==>*People will be cruel, especially if I perform imperfectly* and *I have to criticize myself to prevent mistakes from happening again.*
His mother failed to defend him against her husband ==>People won't be there to meet my needs.

continued on next page

WORKING MODEL

VICIOUS CYCLES / MAINTAINING FACTORS:

Makes small error==>*I must berate myself to prevent future errors*==>*I'm stupid, incompetent; someone's going to find out*
==>anxiety==> urge to hide==> avoids others==>*I'm inadequate and a failure*==>depressed mood

Perfectionistic behavior prevents him from learning that if he does less than a perfect job, others usually will not be critical. Similarly, avoiding people when he makes a mistake prevents him from learning that the consequences of making a small error are minimal.

People will be cruel and critical ==> hypervigilance to making errors and chronic anxiety
==>social isolation==>*I'm a (social) failure.*

Insomnia <==> depression and anxiety.

TREATMENT:

Goals:

1. Improve sleep.
2. Improve mood, self-esteem.
3. Increase self-acceptance, increase acceptance of mistakes and errors; increase contact with other people after he has made errors (i.e., reduce isolation).

Possible Obstacles to Treatment: Fear of being criticized by therapist for doing an imperfect job.

Plan:

1. In the first session or two, assess and, if required, address the client's fear that the therapist will criticize him.
2. For insomnia, teach progressive relaxation, stimulus control, and sleep restriction skills.
3. Cognitive restructuring that focuses on self-punitive beliefs, perfectionism, expectations that people will be cruel to him.
4. Graded experimentation with less than perfect work performances and with staying in the presence of family after he acts irritably.
5. After he has made progress toward these goals, reassess the appropriateness of marital therapy.

FIG. 1.2. (*cont'd*) Example of a completed Case Conceptualization Summary Form (Case 7.B, Benjamin).

2

The Cognitive Model

1. Cognitive Content
   a. Core Beliefs
      i. Cognitive Triad
      ii. Erikson's Psychosocial Stages of Development as Core Beliefs
      iii. Culturally Shared Core Beliefs
      iv. Disorder-Specific Core Beliefs
   b. Intermediate Beliefs
      i. Conditional Assumptions
      ii. Central Goals
      iii. Implicit Rules
   c. Automatic Thoughts
2. Information Processing
   a. Characteristics of Cognitive Schemas
      i. Activation and Deactivation of Schemas
   b. Modes
      i. Modes Show Distinct Patterns but Are Not Invariant
      ii. Description of the Systems That Comprise a Mode
         (1) The Cognitive System
         (2) The Affective System
         (3) The Physiological System
         (4) The Motivational System
         (5) The Behavioral System
         (6) The Conscious Control System
      iii. Modifying Modes
      iv. Characteristics of Psychologically Healthy and Psychologically Disordered Individuals
         (1) Appropriateness of Settings in Which Primal Modes Are Activated
         (2) Assimilation and Accommodation
         (3) Ability of the Conscious Control System to Deactivate a Primal Mode
         (4) Number of Activated Primal Modes and Their Duration of Activation
         (5) Core Beliefs

        (6) Attentional Deployment
        (7) Cognitive and Behavioral Strategies and Responses
        (8) Interpersonal Functioning
3. Development of Cognitive, Affective, and Behavioral Response Patterns
    a. Innate Response Tendencies
    b. Learning
        i. Triggering Stimuli
        ii. Behavioral Responses
        iii. Beliefs
        iv. Traumatic Events
4. Factors That Maintain Self-Defeating Response Patterns

The cognitive model provides the framework for understanding clients from a cognitive therapy perspective. Knowledge of the model's intricacies is a necessary starting point for developing cognitive case conceptualizations that guide effective treatment. Consequently, cognitive therapists should be well versed in the cognitive model.

In the mid-1950s, as a result of his research on depressed subjects, Aaron T. Beck began developing a revolutionary and parsimonious theory of depression. His cognitive model of depression suggested that depressed individuals systematically distort their thinking in a negative manner to conform to their negative views of themselves, the world, and the future. According to the model, negative thinking plays a crucial role in the various affective, motivational, and behavioral manifestations of depression. As a result of this model, Beck developed methods for helping depressed clients modify their thinking. These methods included teaching clients to apply logic and rules of evidence to their thoughts and teaching them to adjust information processing in a self-enhancing direction. In addition, Beck and colleagues began teaching depressed clients to set up systematic experiments to test their self-defeating cognitions. By the late 1970s, evidence was beginning to mount supporting the efficacy of this approach in the treatment of depression. (For descriptions of Beck's early theorizing, see Beck, 1963; Beck, 1967; Beck, Rush, et al., 1979; for a biographical account of Beck's life and work, see Weishaar, 1993.)

Since the model's inception more than 40 years ago, Beck has authored or coauthored nearly 400 articles. His research has focused on the role of cognition in psychopathology and the effectiveness of cognitive therapy for various psychological disorders. As a result of Beck and colleagues' prolific research and theorizing, the cognitive model has evolved into a sophisticated, integrative, and comprehensive theory of psychopathology. For a variety of specific disorders, cognitive formulations have been developed. These formulations delineate the specific types of cognitive content and processes that initiate and maintain these specific disorders. Effective treatment approaches for each of these disorders have arisen from these formulations. Treatment manuals for many of these disorders are available (e.g., depression, see Beck, Rush, et al, 1979; personality disorders, see Beck, Freeman, et al., 1990; substance misuse disorders, see Beck, Wright, Newman, & Liese, 1993; inpatients, see Wright, Thase, Beck, & Ludgate, 1993; social phobia, see Chambless & Hope, 1996).

This section of the chapter presents a detailed description of the various elements of the cognitive model. The first part discusses cognitive content—core beliefs, automatic thoughts, and intermediate beliefs (conditional assumptions, central goals, and implicit rules). The second part focuses on information processing, the processes and structures that are responsible for people's psychological responses. Specifically, properties of schemas (hypothetical structures in which beliefs reside) and their activation are described. Also, a detailed examination of modes is presented. Modes are higher order organizations consisting of cognitive, affective, motivational and behavioral systems that work in concert to mobilize an individual to achieve a particular aim. In addition, characteristics of psychologically healthy and disordered individuals are discussed as functions of modes and schemas. The next part of the chapter discusses the development of cognitive, affective, and behavioral response patterns. Finally, the chapter describes the factors that maintain self-defeating response patterns.

COGNITIVE CONTENT

The cognitive model posits the existence of structures referred to as *cognitive schemas.* Within cognitive schemas reside various cognitions. These cognitions all relate to a central theme or meaning involving the self, the world, or the future (Beck, 1996). At any moment in time, particular cognitions may or may not be accessible to an individual's awareness. Indeed, individuals often are unaware of important cognitions, such as beliefs, that shape their reactions to situations.

Cognitions are categorically and hierarchically organized (Beck, Freeman, et al., 1990). The *core belief* is considered the deepest or most central category of cognition. It represents the theme or meaning of the cognitive schema (e.g., "The world is a dangerous place"). Residing within cognitive schemas are less central cognitions that are derivatives of core beliefs. These cognitions are referred to as *intermediate beliefs.* Examples of intermediate beliefs are conditional assumptions (e.g., "If I'm brilliant, people might accept me"), implicit rules (e.g., "I should never get angry"), and central goals (e.g., "Having a lot of money is extremely important"). The most situationally specific and least central cognitions derived from core beliefs are *automatic thoughts* (e.g., "She thinks she's too good for me").

Before discussing cognitive content, a further elaboration of the differences between cognitive schemas and beliefs is warranted. Beliefs refer to the cognitive *content* of a cognitive schema. In contrast, cognitive schemas refer to cognitive *structures* in which the beliefs reside (Beck, Rush, et al., 1979). (Important structural characteristics of schemas are described later in the chapter.) To use a vivid (but unpleasant) analogy, the cognitive schema can be likened to a disease vector, such as a mosquito, that transmits a virus; the core belief can be likened to the virus itself, such as malaria. An individual cannot develop malaria symptoms without viral transmission via a vector. Rainfall, temperature, the presence of insecticides, and characteristics of the potential host animal can affect the probability of infection. Similarly, a core belief cannot influence an individual's subjective experience and functioning without the activation of the relevant schema, which also depends on environmental conditions and the state of the individual. When the schema is quiescent, the core belief has no effect on the individual. When the schema is highly charged, it can have a profound effect on information processing and behavior.

Core Beliefs

Cognitive therapists benefit from awareness of the range of core beliefs individuals may experience. This section presents various helpful methods for categorizing core beliefs. These include the cognitive triad, Erikson's psychosocial stages as core beliefs, culturally shared core beliefs, and disorder-specific core beliefs.

Cognitive Triad

According to Beck and colleagues (Beck, Rush, et al., 1979; Beck, Freeman, et al., 1990), people's core beliefs involve the *cognitive triad*: beliefs about the *self, the world, and the future*. Some examples of clinically relevant core beliefs about the self include "I'm helpless/powerless/out of control," "I can't manage on my own," "I'm a failure/incompetent," "I'm unlovable," "I'm bad," "I deserve special treatment," and "I'm in danger of sudden death." Problematic core beliefs about the world could include "Danger (in the form of potential accidents or crime) lurks around every corner," "People are to be used," and "People will hurt me." Self-defeating core beliefs about the future might include "My life is hopeless," "I'll always be miserable," and "Things will never get better."

Erikson's Psychosocial Stages of Development as Core Beliefs

Freeman (personal communication, October 5, 1992) suggested that each theme that Erikson (1950) described as a psychosocial stage of development can represent core beliefs. The following are some examples of clinically relevant core beliefs with relevant Eriksonian themes: "People are not trustworthy" (basic trust vs. mistrust), "I need a strong person to take care of me" (autonomy vs. shame and doubt), "I must feel like doing something before I put effort into it" (initiative vs. guilt), "I'm incompetent" (industry vs. inferiority), and "I've got to look out for number one because nice guys finish last" (generativity vs. stagnation). Clearly, each theme that Erikson identified represents issues that can profoundly affect individuals' information processing, emotional responses, and behavior.

Culturally Shared Core Beliefs

Within cultures, people often share important beliefs. Several theorists have suggested that culturally shared beliefs, as with core beliefs in general, can provide important benefits in terms of teaching important lessons and providing direction and meaning to people's lives (e.g., Bettelheim, 1975; Campbell, 1972). However, culturally shared core beliefs also can contribute to problems for individuals, as well as the larger culture. Three examples of core beliefs shared by members of traditional U.S. culture that may contribute to psychological problems include "living happily ever after," "the rugged individual," and "material wealth defines worth."

Many children in traditional U.S. families are read fairy tales in which a poor, mistreated, pure, kind, innocent, beautiful, young girl/woman is swept off her feet by a prince (initially in the guise of a frog). They overcome some extraordinary hurdles and then ride off into the sunset to live *happily ever after*—to an easy life with no conflict, no dirty dishes, and unmitigated joy. A related myth is that somewhere in the world, each person has a "soul mate" waiting to make that person whole. Dan was a 35-year-old never-married professional who sought therapy for the disappointment and emptiness he felt in his search for what he called a "mythical mate." Each year, he slept with dozens of different women searching for the one who would make him feel fulfilled.

Another traditional U.S. myth that many children grow up with is that the U.S. cultural forbearers were *rugged individualists* who singlehandedly defended themselves and then prevailed against "Indians," staked out their claims for land, and thrived in the face of adversity. That is, they "did it on their own." Consequently, there is a commonly shared belief in traditional U.S. culture that people should be strong and independent. This belief is especially true for males for whom asking for help can be a sign of weakness and worthlessness. This culturally shared core belief often leads to isolation and a failure to use available resources when overwhelmed with stress.

A third culturally shared belief has to do with *material wealth, possessions, and prestige* that are thought to represent a person's worth. Many people have low self-esteem because they believe they do not measure up with respect to these characteristics. Alternatively, there are subcultures for which this is not so. For example, most environmental groups believe that accumulating material wealth is extremely destructive to the planet and represents an unhealthy way of life. In fact, some ecopsychologists attempt to help clients work through their general sense of alienation by having them get in touch with and help restore the environment (e.g., Roszak, Gomes, & Kanner, 1995).

In addition to being aware of the traditional U.S. culture's prevalent beliefs, therapists should be aware of beliefs shared by clients' ethnic groups, religious/spiritual communities, family cultures, and peer group cultures. Clearly, these reference groups can have a profound effect on how individual clients view the world.

Disorder-Specific Core Beliefs

The *cognitive-content specificity hypothesis* suggests that every psychological disorder has a unique belief structure (Beck, 1967, 1987; Beck, Freeman, et al., 1990). For example, in depression, core beliefs reflect themes of loss, failure, or deprivation (Beck, Rush, et al., 1979). Core beliefs in anxious individuals relate to being in danger and having inadequate coping resources (Beck et al., 1985). Clients suffering from panic disorder believe that they will experience a medical catastrophe (e.g., stroke, heart attack) or a mental health catastrophe (e.g., go crazy, lose control; Beck et al., 1992; Clark, 1986; Clark et al., 1994; Sokol et al., 1989). Those who have obsessive-compulsive disorder believe that they might be responsible for harming themselves or others, unless they take action to prevent it (Salkovskis, 1989, 1996). Socially phobic individuals expect to fail publicly and be rejected, criticized, or humiliated (Chambless & Hope, 1996). Substance abusers seem to hold two types of core beliefs that maintain their substance misuse. These are anticipatory beliefs and relief-oriented beliefs (Liese & Franz, 1996). Anticipatory beliefs involve expectations that using a substance will provide gratification, increased self-efficacy, and heightened sociability (e.g., "Cocaine will make me feel powerful"). Relief-oriented beliefs refer to the expectation that an abused substance will provide relief from unpleasant physical and emotional states (e.g., "I won't feel like a nervous wreck if I have a drink").

Intermediate Beliefs

Intermediate beliefs are beliefs that are intermediate between core beliefs and automatic thoughts in terms of their effects on information processing and emotion. The intermediate beliefs that reside in cognitive schemas are closely related to each other because they share common themes or meanings. That is, they are derivatives of common core beliefs. As is the case for core beliefs, individuals are often not aware of their intermediate beliefs. Intermediate beliefs include conditional assumptions, central goals, and implicit rules.

Conditional Assumptions

Conditional assumptions take the form of if–then statements (Beck, Freeman, et al., 1990). For example, Sally had a belief that she was unlovable that was moderated by the conditional assumption, "If I always put other people's needs first and I anticipate and meet their every need, then they may start to love me a little." Thus, her unlovability belief was not absolute.

When conditional assumptions exist, they emerge directly from a core belief. However, the converse is not necessarily true. Clients may have core beliefs that are not moderated by conditional assumptions. These beliefs are absolute; clients believe they can do nothing to change some highly unpleasant "truth" about themselves, the world, or the future.

Central Goals

Central goals are goals that people use to guide their behavior in order to accomplish what is most important to them. Although goals frequently are beneficial, when taken to an extreme, central goals can result in problems for the person and others. For example, Richard was a child during the Great Depression. As a child, he often went to bed hungry and constantly worried about getting enough to eat. Stemming from this experience, he considered material possessions to be one of the most important goals in life. He compulsively hoarded anything that could possibly be useful to him later. In fact, he threw very little away and accumulated enormous quantities of food, newspaper, junk mail, free samples, and the like. As a result, his house was unlivable, infested with insects and rodents, and was a serious fire hazard. Not surprisingly, his hoarding and the condition of the house had great personal costs for him. Specifically, his wife left him, the city gave him a stiff fine and threatened to condemn his house, and he spent an enormous amount of his time looking for things among the refuse.

In another example, Martita, a 30-year-old woman with an avoidant personality disorder, considered tranquility and safety to be her most important life goals. She avoided all situations, behaviors, thoughts, and feelings that she thought might upset her. As a result, she led a very constricted life. She was single, friendless, living with her parents, and working in a job that was far below her capabilities. She sought therapy for depression when she realized, "Life is passing me by." Thus, pursuit of her tranquility and safety goals at the exclusion of other important aspects of her life eventually caused her to feel dissatisfied with her life.

Although life goals often seem to be derivatives of core beliefs, it is not always possible to determine clients' life goals by knowing their core beliefs. In fact, two people with the same core beliefs may have disparate goals. For example, Hank had an unlovability belief and placed being loved as his most cherished goal. Similarly, Al had a constantly hypervalent unlovability belief, but he foreswore love altogether and placed work achievement as his most important goal.

Implicit Rules

Implicit rules are beliefs people have regarding how they and/or others "should," "must," or "ought to" think, feel, or behave. People may benefit from implicit rules, if they consider rules as simply guidelines. However, when rules are dogmatic and unconditional, they appear to contribute to distress and problematic behavior (Ellis & Dryden, 1987). An example of a dogmatic and unconditional rule is "I must always excel in everything I do."

Many implicit rules are the products of the person's schemas. For example, "I should use every moment productively" could be part of a failure schema or a perfectionism schema. "I shouldn't ever show unpleasant emotions to people" might be a constituent of social undesirability or defectiveness schemas. "People should always be nice to me" might be part of an entitlement schema. However, implicit rules may also be learned directly from parents, peers, teachers, and cultures. Implicit rules developed in these ways may or may not be central to an individual's life.

Automatic Thoughts

Automatic thoughts represent the least durable and least central cognitions. Automatic thoughts are thoughts or images that may enter awareness. They influence how a person feels and behaves in a particular situation. In addition, automatic thoughts have a variety of characteristics that are worthy of mention. Their duration is from a fraction of a second to hours. A person can be completely aware of the thoughts, or the thoughts can be more or less outside awareness. The thoughts can be self-enhancing and accurate or they can be distorted. People with psychological problems often believe their self-defeating automatic thoughts are true without subjecting the thoughts to reality testing. Automatic thoughts are often cryptic as in "Here we go again" but represent some complete thought such as "I'm going to make a fool out of myself in front of the whole class again."

INFORMATION PROCESSING

Information processing refers to the mechanisms by which an individual perceives, consolidates, stores in memory, integrates, and accesses information. This discussion describes information processing as it relates to characteristics of cognitive schemas as well as activation and deactivation of schemas.

Characteristics of Cognitive Schemas

To begin the discussion of cognitive schema characteristics, a brief description of automatic and controlled information processing is warranted. Automatic information processing occurs rapidly and outside awareness. It requires little cognitive capacity and therefore can occur in parallel to other cognitive processes. In addition, automatic information processing involves highly practiced tasks executed stereotypically or habitual ways of thinking. It is difficult to interrupt and modify automatic information processing (Schneider & Shiffrin, 1977; Shiffrin & Schneider, 1977).

Automatic information processing can be contrasted with controlled information processing. Controlled information processing occurs fully in awareness, requires effort, and is slow and sequential. As compared to automatic processing, it involves higher level processing and can deal with unique and complex tasks or problems. Controlled processes consume a great deal of cognitive capacity and therefore cannot occur concurrently with other cognitive processes (Schneider & Shiffrin, 1977; Shiffrin & Schneider, 1977). The various processes that comprise psychological functioning (outlined later in this chapter) involve some combination of automatic and controlled processing (Beck & Clark, 1997).

Cognitive schema activation involves mostly automatic information processing, although the cognitive products of the schema—interpretation, predictions, and images—are often in awareness (Beck, 1996). When cognitive schemas are activated, they influence all aspects of information processing. They color perceptions, affect inferences, influence recall of information, and shape the formation of new memories (Beck, 1996; Beck & Clark, 1997; Beck, Freeman, et al., 1990; Fiske, 1993; Fiske & Taylor, 1984, 1991; Hastie, 1981). In short, cognitive schemas help people assign meaning to their immediate experience, understand themselves and the social and physical world, predict events, and plan their behavior.

Activation and Deactivation of Schemas

Schemas appear to exist on a *continuum of activation.* At one extreme, a schema is *dormant* and has no current influence on information processing. At the other extreme, it is *hypervalent* (most activated) and colors all aspects of information processing, including perception; recall of schema-consistent memories; coding new memories; emotion; motivation; and behavior (Beck, Freeman, et al., 1990). Thus, a hypervalent schema may result in information processing errors, such as dichotomous thinking, overgeneralizing, personalizing, and blaming (Beck, 1967).

Priming refers to the condition in which some event brings a schema closer to its threshold of activation. When a schema is primed, it might be activated by minor events. The primed schema might require less evidence or a less tight fit between the current circumstances and the template for activating the schema. *Triggering* refers to activating a schema by bringing it above its threshold.[1]

According to Beck (1996), schemas may be deactivated in two ways. The first is that the external situation may change. For example, Wendy's helplessness schema was activated when her husband became depressed over his work and she was unable to help. The next day, he was feeling better, and therefore her helplessness schema became deactivated.

---

[1]Schema activation and deactivation are analogous to the firing of a neuron influencing the likelihood that other neurons will fire. More specifically, the axon of each neuron synapses with the dendrites of many other neurons. The firing of the presynaptic neuron can have either excitatory or inhibitory effects on the postsynaptic neurons. The firing of an excitatory presynaptic neuron increases the likelihood that postsynaptic neurons will fire by bringing them closer to threshold. Conversely, the firing of an inhibitory presynaptic neuron decreases the likelihood that postsynaptic neurons will fire by bringing them further away from threshold.

A second way that a schema can be deactivated is through metacognition. People can think about their thinking. After a schema is activated, individuals can sometimes reexamine the triggering situation to see if their initial appraisal of the situation was accurate and helpful. The realization that they misinterpreted the situation deenergizes the schema. For example, even if Wendy's husband continued to feel depressed, she may have been able to reinterpret the situation. Over time, she may have become more objective and thought something like the following:

> Although I wished he felt better, a person cannot make another person feel better. I'll be supportive and hope he feels better soon. I'm not truly helpless; there are many important things I'm capable of doing. However, directly changing how another person feels is not one of them.

As shown later in the chapter, the two ways by which schemas can be deactivated also represent ways that modes can be deactivated.

Properties of a cognitive schema can have profound effects on an individual's functioning, as can be inferred from the following questions. What specific circumstances activate the schema? Is there a wide range of circumstances that can trigger the schema or are there just a few triggers? What is the threshold of activation? In general, does it take major or minor events to trigger the schema? How energized is the schema? Is it close to threshold due to prior activation? Does activation of this schema create conditions that increase the likelihood that other schemas will be activated, deactivated, or inhibited? How intense is the individual's emotion when the schema is triggered? What behaviors does the individual exhibit when the schema is activated, and are the behaviors self-enhancing or self-defeating for the particular situation? How modifiable is the schema?

Schema activation can be either *adaptive* or *maladaptive*. Cognitive schemas are necessary, and they frequently result in adaptive responses (Beck, 1996; Beck, Freeman, et al., 1990; Kagan, 1984; Piaget, 1952). Clearly, the world is exceedingly complex and humans' cognitive capacities are limited. As a result, people need cognitive schemas to simplify and summarize information to a manageable level. In addition, individuals need schemas to guide their behavior in the world. Without cognitive schemas that automatically become activated in response to immediate events, people would be lost in a world of chaos. Alternatively, individuals would respond to situations in a painfully slow and inefficient fashion. They would have to deal with each situation anew without the benefit of prior experience and reflection.

Therefore, humans develop vast numbers of schemas for construing situations and guiding their behavior. For example, most adults have schemas for behaviors as simple as conducting personal hygiene. They also have schemas for behaviors as complex as handling stress, recognizing danger, understanding other people's motives, and relating to significant others. These schemas often serve them well. Schemas can mobilize individuals to physically protect themselves when situations are objectively dangerous. They can elicit a sense of safety and trusting behavior when involved with others who are likely to live up to their expectations. In short, schemas can motivate people to respond in ways that help them achieve adaptive goals.

Unfortunately, cognitive schemas also can cause serious difficulties. Any approach to summarizing data or simplifying information results in a loss of information and possible errors or distortions in interpreting experience. Cognitive schemas can result in stereotyping (e.g., "All men have one-track minds"). Moreover, schema activation in inappropriate situations can result in unnecessary distress or maladaptive behavior. For example, consider Jerry, a physically healthy person who had the following hypervalent cognitive schema, "I am at risk for medical catastrophe." With every ache, pain or unfamiliar sensation, he became terrified and called the rescue squad. In contrast, activation of that same schema and the associated affect and behavior could serve an adaptive function if it were triggered when an individual truly was at high risk (e.g., vomiting blood, extreme fever).

Parenthetically, mental health professionals have schemas for understanding clients. Diagnostic systems, such as the *Diagnostic and Statistical Manual of Mental Disorders* (*DSM*), define diagnostic categories in which clients with particular symptom clusters can be identified. The categories, it is hoped, share other important features such as etiology or response to treatment. The borderline personality disorder illustrates the advantages and disadvantages of using such schemas. This label can provide an invaluable heuristic that informs mental health professionals that the individuals they are treating are likely to experience particular responses—emotional lability, intense interpersonal relationships, and identity disturbances. The danger of such a label, however, is that it can contribute to distorted information processing in the form of negative stereotyping that adversely affects treatment. Therapists are more likely to provide effective treatment when they strike an appropriate balance between assimilation and accommodation when developing case conceptualizations (i.e., schemas). This balance helps maximize the usefulness of a conceptualization and helps minimize the chances that it will result in unhelpful stereotyping.

Difficulties can arise from schemas being too rigid or too flexible. Piaget's (1952) well-known work on schemas suggests that people have two methods of adaptation with regard to schemas. *Assimilation* refers to fitting new information into preexisting schemas, whereas *accommodation* refers to modifying schemas to fit new information. In most cases, a balance between the two processes appears to be most adaptive. According to Kagan (1984), "The key tension in every problem is the initial preference for using knowledge and abilities that have worked in the past, pitted against the recognition that old habits are not adequate and must be altered (p. 192)." When individuals habitually overrely on assimilation, they rigidly hold on to cognitive schemas despite much contradictory information. On the other hand, when individuals habitually overrely on accommodation, they can have problems because their cognitive schemas are so fluid that they sacrifice structure, organization, and predictability.

Modes

Beck and colleagues expanded the cognitive model to incorporate the concept of modes (Beck, 1996, Beck & Clark, 1997; Beck et al., 1985; Beck, Freeman, et al., 1990). The reason for elaborating the model was that a linear schema model was unable to explain several phenomena adequately. Beck (1996) described the following phenomena that were inadequately explained: (a) systematic bias across cognitive, affective, motivational, and behavioral systems suggesting that a more global and complex organization of schemas is involved in intense psychological reactions; (b) the findings of a specific vulnerability to specific circumstances that are congruent with a particular disorder; (c) the low threshold for symptom formation in vulnerable individuals; (d) the progressive sensitization to activating events ("kindling"); (e) the apparent continuity of many psychological problems with personality; and (f) the relationship between automatic and controlled processing of information.

According to Beck's Modal Processing Model, a *mode* is defined as an integrated network of cognitive, affective, motivational, and behavioral components. These components work in concert and serve to mobilize an individual to achieve a particular aim. For *primal modes,* the aims of the modes relate to the survival or procreation of the individual. For example, when an individual's danger mode is activated, the goal of the mode is to protect the individual from danger.

Although clients' psychological problems for which they seek therapy are related to mode activation, activated modes per se are neither maladaptive nor adaptive. When driving on the highway, activation of the fear mode can mobilize a driver to quickly respond if a truck in front of the driver's car drops debris on the road. However, if the fear mode is strongly activated when the same individual is giving an important presentation, that person's performance may be compromised resulting in unfortunate consequences for the individual's career. Thus, what determines whether mode activation is adaptive or maladaptive is the situation in which the mode is activated and how the mode affects the individual and his or her interactions with the environment.

Modes Show Distinct Patterns but Are Not Invariant

As mentioned earlier, modes are oriented to achieve particular aims. Therefore, the products of a mode—the associated conscious thoughts, affects, urges, and behaviors—always follow patterns that are congruent with the mode. In addition, many of the processes occur automatically. Nonetheless, the products are not necessarily invariant. Individuals often have a repertoire of mode-consistent responses. Selecting a response on a particular occasion depends on the circumstances and on controlled processing. Take for example Ken, a man whose hostility mode was activated frequently in response to behaviors exhibited by his wife, Jessica. Each time his mode was activated, Ken believed he was wronged, experienced anger, and had an urge to get revenge. However, he responded with different hostile behaviors. On some occasions, he yelled and belittled Jessica; other times, he locked her out of the bedroom at night. On rare occasions, he physically pushed her or shook her.

A metaphor for possible response variability within a mode relates to the game of chess. If a player is in "chess mode" while playing a game of chess, he or she would neither "jump" other pieces, as in checkers, nor attempt to eat the opponent's pieces. These would be mode-inconsistent behaviors. However, on some occasions, the player might capture the opponent's piece, whereas on similar occasions, the player might place an opponent in check. Which move is selected on a given occasion is likely to be influenced by subtleties of the environment, the positions of the player's and the opponent's pieces. How the player moves also depends on the goal of the mode (i.e., to win) and on the cognitive chess schemas (i.e., beliefs about how to best gain position, capture opponents' pieces, and protect his or her own key pieces).

Description of the Systems That Comprise a Mode

As mentioned earlier, modes are comprised of cognitive, affective, physiological (peripheral), motivational, and behavioral systems. Each system is described in this discussion.

The Cognitive System. Beck (1996) described the cognitive system as follows:

> [It] ... accounts for the functions involved in information processing and assignment of meanings: selection of data, attention, interpretation (meaning assignment), memory, and recall. This system is composed of a variety of cognitive structures relevant to persons' constructions of themselves and other people, their goals and expectations, and their storehouse of memories, previous learning, and fantasies. The processing often extends to the secondary elaboration of complex meanings relevant to abstract themes such as self-worth, social desirability, and causal attributions. (p. 5)

Information processing begins with what Beck (1996; Beck & Clark, 1997) referred to as an *orienting schema,* which can be thought of as a gatekeeper for the mode. When a stimulus is initially perceived, the orienting schema compares it to a template to determine whether there is a "match."

If there is a match, the orienting schema is activated and spreads activation to the rest of the mode.

The logic of the orienting schema follows if–then rules. *If* the individual perceives the conditions to match the mode, *then* the mode will be activated. This process exclusively involves automatic information processing. With respect to anxiety disorders, Beck and Clark (1997) suggested that this processing also may be undifferentiated. Specifically, the only information it may provide is the valence of the stimulus (positive, negative, neutral) and its personal relevance (relevant or not relevant).

A mode becomes activated when the orienting schema identifies a current circumstance as a match for the mode. There appears to be a threshold of activation that depends on the "energy level" of the mode. If a mode has been primed (energized) as a result of prior activation, the mode may be closer to its threshold of activation, or possibly, the threshold for activation may be lower. It takes less evidence or a less tight fit between the current circumstances and the template to activate the mode.

If this is the case, it could help explain a variety of clinical phenomena, including sensitization, "kindling," and personality disorders (Beck, 1996). When an individual becomes sensitized, a relatively low-level stressor may trigger a mood or anxiety episode after an individual has experienced other recent stressors. Initially, the low-level stressor probably would have been insufficient to trigger an episode. Similarly, the concepts of mode energies and thresholds may account for the "kindling" phenomenon described in the depression literature. After experiencing prior depressive episodes, an episode can be precipitated by relatively minor events or may even be untriggered. Finally, personality disorders may be viewed as constantly hypervalent primal modes or primal modes that are easily and inappropriately triggered (Beck, 1996). These hypervalent modes result in subjective distress and maladaptive behaviors. This line of reasoning is an extension of the cognitive diathesis-stress hypothesis of psychological disorders. The hypothesis suggests that cognitively vulnerable individuals—those with an energized primal model—who are exposed to congruent stressors (i.e., mode-consistent stressors) are at increased risk of developing mode-related symptomatology.

A brief aside about *exposure therapy* is warranted. For a variety of psychological disorders, systematic and intentional exposure to triggering situations—rather than increasing the fear that an individual associates with a triggering circumstance—is a crucial component of effective treatment. According to the cognitive model, the effectiveness of this approach is likely the result of mode activation under controlled circumstances. As a result, clients can learn coping strategies for deactivating the relevant mode while they are experiencing their naturalistic responses. In addition, intentional exposure can provide evidence that disconfirms core beliefs and may change the relevant schemas. Take for example a cardiovascularly healthy, panic client who was afraid that she would have a heart attack. Her therapist exposed her to a highly elevated heart rate through vigorous exercise. Repeated, intentional exposure of this kind helped disconfirm her belief that she was vulnerable to a fatal cardiovascular event.

Characteristics of *cognitive schemas* have been described in detail. It is important to note, however, the differences between cognitive schema activation and mode activation. When a mode is activated, the constituent cognitive schemas—as well as the relevant affective, motivational, and behavioral schemas—are activated. The converse is not necessarily true. When a schema is triggered, a mode may not be triggered. As compared to schema activation in isolation, when a mode is activated, all systems are activated and the duration of activation is often longer.

The Affective System. The affective system determines the affective state of the individual when a mode is activated. For example, when a hostility mode is activated, the affective state is anger, and when a depressive mode is activated, the affective state is sadness.

The Physiological System. The physiological system to which Beck (1996) referred is:

> ... not the central nervous system activation (or inhibition) that underlies all psychological processes but ... the innervation of the peripheral systems such as the autonomic nervous system, the motor systems, and the sensory systems. The physiological symptoms, accompanying anxiety or anger, for instance, are important not only because they enhance the impulse to flee or fight but also because of the interpretations ("I'm going to faint," "I can't stand this") placed on them. The physiological feedback from the muscles when the person is mobilized for action add to the feeling of being "charged up." (p. 6)

The Motivational System. Regarding the motivational system, Beck (1996) defined motivation as "... the automatic and involuntary impulses and inhibitions that are tied to the primal strategies" (p. 6). He contrasted motivation with conscious intention, which is in the domain of the conscious control system and is discussed later in the chapter.

The Behavioral System. Within the behavioral system reside procedural memory and behavioral strategies. Procedural memory refers to "learned connections between stimuli and responses, including those involving complex stimulus patterns and response chains" (Tulving, 1985, p. 387). Behavioral strategies are plans for overt or covert behavior that are consistent with the aim of the mode. For example, a panic client held the belief, "If I lie down when I'm having chest pain, I may not have a heart attack." Therefore, her behavioral strategy was to lie down whenever she had chest pain.

As is the case for all constituents of a mode, the *behavioral strategies and responses* are dictated by the aim of the mode (e.g., survival in anxiety, holding on to a powerful other in dependency). Behavioral strategies and responses are a combination of automatic and controlled information processing. They can be completely outside awareness resulting in impulsive behavior. At the other extreme, behavioral responses can be the result of careful planning. Whether a behavioral response is adaptive or maladaptive depends on its appropriateness to the situation and the flexibility of its use.

Conditional assumptions often determine behavioral strategies. For example, a businessman spent 30 hours per week lifting weights as a result of his belief, "If I get huge (i.e., muscular), I'll be attractive and may be able to find a partner." In addition, implicit rules suggest how individuals "should" behave and therefore can dictate behavioral responses. For example, the implicit rule, "I should always make other people feel good and laugh," resulted in Tom consistently trying to be "on" and entertain others.

Most behavioral responses are neither solely advantageous nor solely detrimental. Fran was a highly successful economist who had a chronically hypervalent failure mode with an associated conditional assumption, "If I don't work every conscious moment, I'll fail and that would be terrible." Her mode drove her to work extremely hard (behavioral strategy). Clearly, hard work can be quite adaptive. Fran's behavior contributed to extraordinary professional success.

However, Fran's excessive reliance on this behavioral strategy was associated with her developing psychophysiological disorders (i.e., ulcer, chronic headaches) and feeling "burned out." Moreover, she deeply regretted her decision to forego marriage, children, and other close personal relationships in pursuit of her career.

Beck, Freeman, et al. (1990) suggested that people with personality disorders overdevelop some strategies and underdevelop others. Thus, clients with schizoid personality disorder have overdeveloped their ability to act autonomously and live in isolation but have underdeveloped their ability to be intimate and reciprocal. Histrionic clients have overdeveloped their use of exhibitionism, expressiveness, and impressionism but have underdeveloped their ability to reflect, control, and systematize.

Young and colleagues (e.g., Young, 1990; McGinn & Young, 1996) suggested that the reason personality disordered individuals with similar core beliefs can behave in opposite fashions is that they have different behavioral strategies for coping with unpleasant cognitions and feelings. Young suggested that there are three main ways that people deal with what he referred to as Early Maladaptive Schemas: *maintenance, avoidance, and compensation.* In schema maintenance, a person with a helplessness schema, for example, surrenders to the schema by thinking, feeling, and acting as though he or she were indeed helpless. A person engaging in schema avoidance might use drugs or alcohol, shopping, gambling, watching television, working, eating, having sex, or dissociating to distract himself or herself from pain. Finally, in schema compensation, individuals act in opposition to their core beliefs and how they are feeling. For instance, if a person feels worthless and defective, he or she might become demanding and aggressive and act as if the opposite of the schema were true—that he or she is special, superior, perfect, or infallible.

The Conscious Control System. Although the conscious control system is separate from the modes (Beck, 1996), it is relevant to modal responses and therefore is included in this section. It involves controlled information processing exclusively. The conscious control system can deactivate modes by reinterpreting the triggering event in a manner opposed to the mode. After the mode is activated, an individual may continue to appraise a situation to determine whether the initial interpretation of the situation was correct. If the individual decides that it was not correct, the mode becomes deenergized.

Take for example the case of Tony whose rejection mode was activated, but after a day, his conscious control system deactivated it. The event that triggered the activation of his rejection mode was that his partner, Alex, informed him that he wanted to delay moving in together for a month. This event matched Tony's template for rejection. His automatic thought was "He doesn't want to live with me, and he'll probably break up with me." His relevant core beliefs were "I'll always be alone" and "I'm unlovable." Tony experienced powerful feelings of sadness (affective schema) and was overcome with an urge to sleep (motivational schema). As a result, he stayed home from work and slept for 14 hours that day (behavioral schema). The next day, however, Tony began thinking about the event more objectively and considered other possible reasons why Alex may have wanted to delay moving in together. Tony remembered that within the next month, Alex had an important assignment due at work and Alex's mother was scheduled to have major surgery. Tony realized that these events may have been the reason why Alex wanted to delay moving in together. (Besides the conscious control system deactivating modes, modes may be deactivated as a result of external situations changing.)

Modifying Modes

Not only can modes be deactivated (as a result of changing circumstances or reappraisal), but also some may be modified. The naturalistic modification of a childhood fear provides an illustration of how modes can be modified. When Julio was 2 years old, his danger mode was activated by all insects. However, by the time he was four, this mode had changed. He stopped experiencing fear when exposed to many types of insects. Seeing a worm, for instance, no longer matched his danger template, and his cognitive beliefs about insects had changed. Instead of believing, as he did when he was two, that "All bugs will bite me," his belief at four was "Some bugs like wasps might bite or sting, but most bugs won't hurt me." This change appeared to have resulted from several factors. Julio's parents educated him about various harmless insects (e.g., gnats, fireflies, worms). His parents also modeled nonfearful responses to benign insects, and Julio naturalistically experienced repeated exposure to benign insects. Chapters 5–8 of this book provide therapeutic approaches for both deactivating and modifying modes.

Characteristics of Psychologically Healthy and Psychologically Disordered Individuals

Psychologically healthy and psychologically disordered individuals differ in several important ways. These individuals differ in terms of the appropriateness of the settings in which their modes are activated. Moreover, psychologically healthy and psychologically disturbed individuals differ regarding the appropriateness of their cognitive, affective, motivational, and behavioral responses in various settings. Specifically, these individuals differ in terms of (a) assimilation and accommodation, (b) the ability of their conscious control systems to deactivate primal modes, (c) the number and duration of primal-mode activation, and (d) the ways they deploy attention. Further distinctions between psychologically healthy versus psychologically disordered individuals include the content of their core beliefs, their cognitive and behavioral strategies and responses, and their interpersonal functioning.

Appropriateness of Settings in Which Primal Modes Are Activated. When individuals are psychologically healthy, their modes are triggered in appropriate settings and result in adaptive responses. Primal modes typically are only activated when vital interests are at stake rather than as a result of misconstruing situations. For example, a danger mode is activated when the person is in actual danger (e.g., a car barreling toward the person after it jumped the curve) but not otherwise. In healthy individuals, the cognitive schemas in which self-defeating beliefs reside are rarely activated, activated briefly, and their activation often is not associated with full mode activation. That is, schema activation is associated with a limited number of other activated systems. Consequently, self-defeating core beliefs do not play a prominent role in their lives.

On the other hand, when individuals have psychological disorders, their modes are triggered frequently in inappropriate settings and result in maladaptive responses. Primal modes that are specific to their disorder are often activated as a result of misconstruing situations. For example, a danger mode of an anxiety-disordered individual is activated in benign situations (e.g., when being out in public). The cognitive schemas associated with self-defeating beliefs are frequently activated, activated for extended periods (perhaps chronically), and their activation often is associated with full mode activation. Thus, the negative beliefs of psychologically disturbed people play a prominent role in their lives.

Assimilation and Accommodation. With respect to the processes of assimilating information to preexisting schemas or accommodating schemas to account for novel situations, psychologically healthy individuals exhibit a flexible balance. They can recognize when a situation fits with prior experience for which they have adaptive ways of responding. For example, Jewel's boss began asking her to do personal errands for him like picking up his dry cleaning. She held the following beliefs: "People shouldn't take advantage of me; if they do, I will try to call it to their attention and stick up for myself in a calm and firm manner." As a result, she appropriately asserted herself with her boss who responded favorably. He promptly stopped making inappropriate requests and started treating her with greater respect. Psychologically healthy individuals are also able to recognize when a situation has important novel features. In such cases, they frequently can appraise the situation attentively and objectively, resulting in adaptive ways of understanding and responding to it.

In contrast, psychologically disordered individuals may exhibit deficits in accommodation or assimilation. For example, as a result of primal mode activation in inappropriate settings, these individuals may have difficulty accessing adaptive skills; that is, they may have problems assimilating a situation. Thus, an individual may be able to assert herself or himself with loved ones but not with a boss (or other authority figures) as a result of a danger mode being activated.

Individuals with psychological problems also may have difficulty recognizing when a situation has important novel features to which they should modify their responses (i.e., accommodate). As a result, these individuals are more likely than psychologically healthy people to misconstrue situations and act stereotypically and maladaptively. This is particularly the case with severely personality disordered individuals. An opposite problem with accommodating schemas can occur when individuals' schemas are too fluid (too accommodating). Individuals who meet criteria for borderline personality disorder provide an extreme example of this. Their identity confusion is likely a product of their constantly and dramatically changing view of themselves. Their schemas being too fluid also can account for their dramatic and rapid oscillations in how they perceive others. Based on a single interaction, they can change their beliefs and feelings about a person instantaneously and radically (e.g., from idealizing to devaluing).

Ability of the Conscious Control System to Deactivate a Primal Mode. If a mode is activated in an inappropriate situation, the healthy individual's conscious control system is likely to deactivate it in short order. For example, Salvadore was a happily married man who felt intense attraction to a single woman with whom he worked. His conscious control system was able to decrease mode activation. Salvadore reminded himself that this coworker was off limits, that he loved his wife and children, and that if he had a lapse of control and permitted himself to be unfaithful, he would likely feel intense guilt and anger at himself. He also strategized about decreasing unnecessary contact with his coworker to decrease temptation.

On the other hand, the conscious control system of an individual with psychological problems is less likely to deactivate a mode that was activated in an inappropriate situation. Take for example Beatrice, an individual who had anger control problems. A representative problematic scenario for Beatrice was that her teenage son used a swear word in front of her. She became infuriated and had the following cognitions: "How dare he," "He doesn't respect me," "He's a bad kid," and "People should treat me with respect." She had an urge to teach him a lesson and slapped his face. Only hours later did she regret how she had behaved. A second example involved Eleanor, who was depressed. Frequently, when she made even a trivial mistake (e.g., forgetting to take out the garbage the previous evening), her core beliefs, "I'm a loser" and "Life sucks!" were strongly activated. She then typically plunged into a severely depressed mood with serious suicidal urges. Because she did not consciously reappraise her mistake, Eleanor's intense depressive responses lasted for days after the occurrence of the small mistake.

Number of Activated Primal Modes and Their Duration of Activation. For many clients with *acute psychological disorders,* a single primal mode is hypervalent for a limited time. Before or after the episode, the primal mode is quiescent. For example, Bob, a college student with a single, 6-month episode of depression had a "worthlessness" schema that was hypervalent during the episode. However, before the episode and when the depression remitted, he considered himself worthwhile. In contrast, the inappropriately activated modes of people with *personality disorders or chronic psychological disorders* remain in a hypervalent state for sustained periods. The sustained activation of maladaptive modes accounts for the persistence and pervasiveness of their problems.

Individuals with personality disorders or chronic psychological disorders are more likely to experience activation of several primal modes simultaneously or in rapid succession. Herb was a client whose danger and depression modes were activated simultaneously when he was given a new and challenging assignment at work. Activated beliefs included "I'll screw up, and my boss will fire me," "My girlfriend will leave me when she learns that I messed up," "I can't do anything right," "I am a loser," and "I'm defective." Opposing beliefs, to which he sometimes had access, were inhibited. These beliefs included "I'm capable" and "I'm a good person." Similarly, his access to positive memories relating to his abilities, other people's devotion to him, and his positive attributes were entirely cut off. He felt intense anxiety and depression. At times, he had no energy and felt deflated. At other times, he had an urge to escape from work.

Individuals with borderline personality disorder represent an extreme case of multiple primal modes that are easily and inappropriately activated. For example, these individuals often have intense activation of abandonment, dependency, and hostility modes.

Core Beliefs. The core beliefs of psychologically healthy adults mostly are self-enhancing and balanced. Psychologically healthy individuals generally like, respect, and have confidence in themselves. They derive a sense of fulfillment and satisfaction from their lives. They have mostly positive but balanced views of others (e.g., "Most people can be trusted; however, I should be somewhat cautious until I've known a person for awhile"). Also, emotionally healthy people tend to be optimistic about the future but not in a pollyannaish fashion (e.g., "Things will ultimately work out for me, but there may be bumps along the way").

In contrast, many core beliefs of disturbed individuals are self-defeating and, especially for chronically disturbed individuals, absolute (e.g., helpless, incompetent, unlovable). People suffering from chronic disorders frequently lack cognitive schemas for the converse, self-enhancing responses—or, at least, the converse responses are underdeveloped (Beck, Freeman, et al., 1990). For example, they may never believe they are good, worthwhile, lovable, or competent. In addition, they lack conditional assumptions that temper their core beliefs (e.g., "If I do everything perfectly, I won't be abandoned"). Individuals with psychological problems may also have negative and unbalanced views of others (e.g., "People cannot be trusted"). People with mental illness may feel unfulfilled and dissatisfaction with their lives. Also, they may be pessimistic about the future. Again, the more chronic and the more personality disordered individuals are, the less likely they are to have balancing or moderating beliefs about themselves, their lives, and their future.

Attentional Deployment. Healthy individuals deploy their attention adaptively. They can focus on unpleasant cognitions, emotions, behaviors, and situations. However, they are also able to find healthy respite from their pain. They generally do not "overattend" to their problems; that is, they do not ruminate or dwell on them. Their flexible balance of attention allows them to resolve their problems without being overwhelmed by them. Even when faced with extreme pain, they find a way to work through their problems without being overcome.

Bowlby's (1980) description of processes that occur in normal grief represents an example of healthy and flexible attentional deployment. According to Bowlby, the bereaved "may oscillate between treasuring ... reminders and throwing them out, between welcoming the opportunity to speak of the dead and dreading such occasions, between seeking out places where they have been together and avoiding them" (p. 92).

Individuals with psychological problems, on the other hand, often maladaptively deploy their attention. They may use one of three unhelpful strategies. Some habitually avoid unpleasant emotions, as well as situations, cognitions, and behaviors they associate with unpleasant emotions. Others ruminate or dwell on unpleasant issues or situations. A third group seems to alternate between the two extremes of avoidance and rumination or cognitive intrusions. For example, individuals with posttraumatic stress disorder generally avoid situations, thoughts, feelings, and conversations that they associate with the trauma. They also persistently reexperience the trauma. Many experience intrusive thoughts or images of the event and nightmares (APA, 1994).

Cognitive and Behavioral Strategies and Responses. Psychologically healthy people's cognitive and behavioral strategies and responses are generally adaptive. Most of the time, people who are emotionally healthy are flexible and can keep things in balance. When they experience negative events, they have and implement adaptive coping skills. Intrapsychically, they often can soothe themselves when they are upset. People who are emotionally healthy can accept in themselves and others a wide range of unpleasant (as well as pleasant) emotions and can nurture themselves despite shortcomings. They also have a capacity to accept the various situations in which they find themselves. They typically do not attempt to fight reality. In terms of ability to delay gratification, psychologically healthy individuals generally have this ability. However, they also are able to have fun, play, and be "present in the moment."

On the other hand, psychologically disturbed people's cognitive and behavioral responses are maladaptive in the areas in which they have chronic difficulties. People who have chronic psychological disturbances exhibit inflexible and rigid cognitive and behavioral responses in their problem areas. When they experience negative events in their vulnerable areas, they lack adaptive coping skills. Intrapsychically, they may have difficulty soothing themselves when they are upset. They generally have difficulty accepting their own responses, the behaviors of others, and their environments. In terms of their ability to delay gratification, individuals with chronic psychopathology may exhibit impairment. Alternatively, they may have trouble enjoying themselves and being in the moment.

When they find themselves in situations that are unhealthy, psychologically healthy individuals can explore ways to change the situation or select other environments for themselves. Typically, they have skills for effectively solving problems. They often are able to be objective regarding situations and relationships in their lives. On the other hand, when individuals with psychological problems find themselves in situations that are unhealthy, they may have difficulty with the problem solving necessary to alter the situations. Also, these individuals may have difficulty selecting healthier environments for themselves. In their problem domains, they have difficulty being objective regarding situations and relationships.

Interpersonal Functioning. In terms of interpersonal functioning, psychologically healthy adults are able to establish and maintain mutually satisfying relationships. They can give and receive love, share their sorrows and joy, and ask for what they need. When they need help or support, they have the skills to elicit it from those in their social environment. Often, psychologically healthy adults get satisfaction and meaning from making the lives of others better in a generous but not self-sacrificing way. Regarding their work, psychologically healthy adults are able to initiate and sustain productivity and often can derive pleasure or satisfaction from their work.

In contrast, emotionally disturbed individuals may have difficulty establishing or maintaining mutually satisfying relationships. They may have trouble giving or receiving love, confiding and sharing their sorrows and joy, or asking for what they need. When they need help or support, they may have deficits in the skills necessary to elicit it from those in their social environment, and they may lack social supports. Often, chronically disturbed individuals are self-absorbed and ruminate about their problems. As a result, they often have difficulty being generous with others. Regarding their work, chronically disturbed individuals may have difficulty initiating and sustaining productivity and often fail to derive fulfillment from their work.

DEVELOPMENT OF COGNITIVE, AFFECTIVE, AND BEHAVIORAL RESPONSE PATTERNS

The probable mechanisms by which cognitive, affective, and behavioral patterns are likely to develop appear to be complex and interacting. In this section, innate response tendencies are described. This is followed by a discussion of how stimuli come to trigger responses (i.e., Pavlovian conditioning). The focus then shifts to how individuals learn behavioral responses through operant conditioning, observational learning, verbal instruction, and feedback. Next, the probable mechanisms by which beliefs develop are detailed (i.e., messages from significant others, direct experience, comparisons of self to others, identification with significant others, and reasoning). Finally, the role of traumatic events in the development of problematic response patterns is described.

Innate Response Tendencies

Several response tendencies appear to be innate. Timberlake (1984) suggested that "the organism [including the human] comes equipped with organized stimulus sensitivities, processing proclivities, response structures, and integrative states evolved to produce adaptive behavior in particular environments" (p. 324). Similarly, Beck (1996), drawing on the theorizing of Pinker (1994), suggested that:

> the initial formulation and development of the mode depends on the interaction of innate patterns ("protoschemas") and experience. These protoschemas simply provide the basic structures that respond selectively to congruent experiences and evolve into cognitive schemas in a way analogous to the development of specific language structures from the undifferentiated primitive language structures. Thus, learning how to recognize and respond to real threats depends on the availability of the protoschemas and their exposure to relevant life experiences which then interact to produce differentiated schemas. (pp. 11–12)

Some protoschemas are probably common to vertebrates in general, others appear to be specific to human beings, and still others seem to be specific to each individual person. Protoschemas that are common to vertebrates probably relate to self-protection and procreation and, once differentiated and integrated, become primal modes. For example, vertebrates tend to fight, flee, or freeze in response to perceived danger.

In terms of protoschemas that are specific to humans, a clear example is the innate ability to learn language (Brown, 1973; Chomsky, 1965). In the domain of cognitive processes, Kagan (1984) suggested that humans have several basic cognitive competencies that "are prepared to be actualized given proper experience" (p. 187). Kagan suggested the following as likely candidates: (a) the world consists of discrete objects that exist over time, (b) appearances of objects may be deceptive, (c) alterations in the appearance or position of an object must have been produced by a preceding event, (d) things can symbolically represent other things, (e) objects can be categorized, and (f) a prior state of affairs can be reconstructed by reversing thought or action.

Regarding emotional responses, investigators from many different theoretical orientations taking disparate methodological approaches have discovered what they consider to be *basic emotions*. Neural approaches (e.g., Izard, 1971; Panksepp, 1982; Tomkins & McCarter, 1964), facial expression approaches (Ekman, 1993), empirical classification approaches (e.g., Shaver, Schwartz, Kirson, & O'Connor, 1987), and developmental approaches (e.g., Trevarthen, 1993) have been used to investigate the existence of basic emotions. Although these investigators have proposed slightly different lists of basic emotions, the lists share many commonalities. For example, each list includes fear, anger, and pleasure. Most lists include sadness, and some lists include shock or surprise.

Besides inherited response tendencies that are general to vertebrates and those that are specific to humans, some tendencies appear to be unique to an individual's genetic inheritance. Extreme cases include individuals with Down's syndrome and individuals with sickle cell anemia. People with Down's syndrome have an extra piece of a chromosome (i.e., chromosome 21) that typically influences their appearance, their intelligence, and their longevity. Those with sickle cell anemia have a point mutation in a single DNA base that results in distorting the shape (i.e., sickling) of red blood cells (Linker, 1991). In both cases, despite genetic defects, environmental conditions play important roles in the functioning of people with these conditions. For example, specialized education can significantly raise the intellectual functioning of individuals with Down's syndrome (Willerman & Cohen, 1990). In sickle cell anemia, high altitudes, for example, precipitate acute disease episodes (Linker, 1991).

In addition to these exceptional illnesses, genetic transmission clearly plays an important role in psychological functioning. Familial studies of intelligence, mental health and illness, and personality show that genetics account for a large portion of the variance in these dimensions. On the other hand, environmental factors alone and the interaction between genetic and environmental factors also contribute to these dimensions (Davidson & Neale, 1994).

Learning

The specific way that individuals develop patterns of responses is a combination of their innate tendencies and learning. This discussion focuses on how triggering stimuli, behavioral responses, and core beliefs may be learned. The discussion ends with a brief description of the mechanisms by which traumatic events may contribute to psychological problems.

Triggering Stimuli

According to many cognitive-behavioral theorists, the mechanism by which stimuli come to consistently trigger an individual's response is Pavlovian conditioning. In Pavlovian conditioning, a previously neutral stimulus acquires the power to elicit a response that was originally elicited by another stimulus. The change occurs when the neutral stimulus is followed by the effective stimulus. Thus, Pavlovian conditioning can be thought of as a process of stimulus substitution; the same response is elicited by a new stimulus.

Pavlov (1927/1960) suggested that this process of conditioning was necessary for an animal to adapt to its environment. He stated:

> Under natural conditions the normal animal must respond not only to stimuli which themselves bring immediate benefit or harm, but also to other physical or chemical agencies—waves of sounds, light, and the like—which in themselves only *signal* the approach of these stimuli. (p. 14)

In general, Pavlovian conditioning probably plays a significant role in the development of people's emotional responses. For example, when Jan met John for the first time, her feelings for him were neutral. However, each time she interacted with him, she enjoyed the interaction; she perceived him as cheerful, interesting, and friendly. After Jan spoke with John on several occasions, the sight of him elicited in her feelings of excitement and anticipation. In another example, Pavlovian conditioning resulted from a couple's ongoing disagreement about whether to send their toddler to child care. During the first several discussions about the topic, the husband, Harry, initially was not angry. However, each time they had the discussion, it became heated. Over time, if Harry's wife even mentioned the issue, he became extremely angry. In these examples—and probably in many conditioning circumstances—Pavlovian conditioning and higher cognitive processing are likely to have jointly contributed to learned emotional responses.

In a clinically relevant example, many cancer patients become nauseated when they near the hospital where they are receiving chemotherapy. Similarly, in the development of anxiety disorders, a previously neutral stimulus evokes fear in individuals. For example, Ed developed a fear of storms after being hit by lightning. Likewise, Carol developed a fear of large men with blond hair after being raped by a man who had these characteristics.

A controversial issue centers on whether there are species-specific constraints on Pavlovian conditioning. For example, humans seem to develop specific phobias to a very finite number of stimuli, including: spiders, snakes, tunnels, bridges, heights, darkness, enclosed places, and blood, injection or injury (APA, 1994; Beck et al., 1985; Rachman, 1990). In contrast, people rarely develop fears of electric outlets, guns, clothing, high speed driving, flowers, or snow. Seligman (1971) theorized that this is because humans are evolutionarily *prepared* to become phobic to the former but not latter groups of stimuli. Although there has been extensive research investigating the issue of preparedness—using both human subjects and laboratory animals, the results have been mixed (e.g., Davey, 1992, 1995; Foa, McNally, Steketee, & McCarthy, 1991; Garcia & Koelling, 1966; Honeybourne, Matchett, & Davey, 1993; Hugdahl & Johnsen, 1989; Lovibond, Siddle, & Bond, 1993; Öhman, Fredrikson, Hugdahl, & Rimmo, 1976; Regan & Howard, 1995; Soares & Öhman, 1993).

Behavioral Responses

Behavioral strategies and responses are probably acquired in three main ways: *operant conditioning, observational learning,* and *verbal instructions and feedback.* Through *operant conditioning,* particular behaviors become more or less probable as a result of the consequences of those behaviors (Skinner, 1953). Behaviors that are reinforced increase in frequency, whereas those that are punished decrease. For example, when children are repeatedly praised for polite behaviors and scolded for impolite behaviors, the ratio of polite to impolite behaviors generally increases.

Two clinically relevant examples of operant conditioning follow. First, as a young child, Joey was slapped (punished) every time he disagreed with his parents. Apparently, as a result of this learning history, when he reached adulthood, he never voiced disagreement. Second, when Helene felt bored or depressed and went shopping, she felt better. Subsequently, she began shopping more frequently when she was feeling bored or depressed.

In addition to influencing the frequency of relatively uncomplicated behaviors, operant conditioning can facilitate learning complex behaviors. Through a process of reinforcing successive approximations of some desirable behavioral sequence, people can learn complex behaviors. Skinner (1953) referred to this process as *shaping*. He suggested that,

> through the reinforcement of slightly exceptional instances of his behavior, a child learns to raise himself, to stand, to walk, to grasp objects, and to move them about. Later on, through the same process, he learns to talk, to sing, to dance, to play games—in short, to exhibit the enormous repertoire characteristic of the normal adult. (p. 93)

Observational learning is a second way that individuals learn behaviors. Observational learning, also known as modeling, can teach individuals how to perform particular skills and what consequences to expect from their performing observed behaviors. In addition, modeling can increase observers' self-efficacy expectations regarding performance of behaviors and inform observers about appropriate emotional responses in situations (e.g., Bandura, 1973, 1986; Bandura, Blanchard, & Ritter, 1969). Parents of young children know how closely children imitate parents' and siblings' behavior.

People can learn adaptive coping strategies from observing others (e.g., how to confront their fears and how to deal effectively with people). Alternatively, observational learning may sometimes contribute to maladaptive behavior patterns (e.g., how to convert distress into somatic complaints and how to abuse substances or people).

In addition to learning specific behaviors or skills, individuals appear to learn broader classes of behaviors. For example, they may learn how to behave as a male or female, a member of an ethnic community, and so on. At a broader level still, individuals may model much of their personality to be like that of significant persons in their lives. The ability to internalize some behaviors of a beloved person in an integrative way is considered a sign of mental health. In contrast, someone having a severe identity disturbance, for example, who "swallows another person's personality whole" is often a very disturbed person (e.g., Vaillant, 1993).

Finally, people can learn behaviors from *verbal instruction and feedback* about their performance. This process is straightforward and therefore is not elaborated in the text.

Beliefs

Beliefs probably can develop through an integration of the following: (a) messages from significant others, (b) direct experience, (c) comparisons of self to others, (d) identification with significant others, and (e) reasoning. Individuals can develop beliefs about themselves, the world, and the future from direct and indirect messages from parents, teachers, peers, or the culture. Some examples of verbal messages that can contribute to people's views of themselves might include "You're a wonderful kid," "You're so smart," "I love you," "You're a bad kid," "You're a loser," "You're stupid," "You can't do anything right," "I wish I never had you," or "Why can't you be like your sister?" Even when these messages are expressed nonverbally, they can have a profound effect on how individuals come to view themselves. Significant others, especially those who are influential in early life, can also convey messages about the world (e.g., "Life's a blast!" "The world is dangerous," or "People are inherently kind and helpful"), or the future (e.g., "You'll always be a failure" or "You'll be a wonderful father and husband"). Individuals may develop central goals from a desire to please some early significant other.

Many implicit rules are directly related to particular core beliefs. However, other implicit rules appear to be learned directly from parents, peers, the larger culture, the mass media, or from childhood events. For instance, the implicit rule that "A husband should never get angry at his wife" may be a rule that a client learned from his parents' statements and modeling.

Direct experience is a second way that people develop beliefs. For example, before language develops, infants learn that when objects are released, they fall to the ground and that objects that are out of sight continue to exist. They may learn from their experiences with caregivers whether people in general can be trusted. Individuals also may develop beliefs about themselves from conscious awareness of their internal experiences—feelings, thoughts, intentions, standards—as well as their overt behavior and their ability to achieve goals (Kagan, 1984). For example, if individuals frequently experience anger (and come from social environments that disapprove of anger), they may conclude that they are "bad," "evil," or "abnormal."

Another type of direct experience that can influence people's beliefs about themselves comes from observing others. Many social psychologists have demonstrated that people develop beliefs about themselves as a result of social comparisons (see, Brown, 1990; Kruglanski & Mayseless, 1990; Pyszcynski, Greenberg, & LaPrelle, 1985). Presumably, conclusions from repeated comparisons with others, especially early in life, can result in stable beliefs about one's attributes. For example, Consuela compared her attractiveness to others and usually concluded that she was prettier. She developed the belief, "I'm pretty." Roger compared his emotional stability to others and frequently concluded that his moods were more labile than most; he developed the belief that "I'm a moody person."

People may also develop beliefs about themselves by identifying with others.[2] According to Kagan (1984), "An identification begins with the belief that some of the distinctive qualities of another person belong to the

[2]The identification process is closely related to the process of modeling much of one's behavior after another person's behavior.

self" (p. 139). He suggested that the assumption that one has important psychological similarities to the person with whom one identifies may have no objective evidence. He further suggested that identification results from a universal tendency to overgeneralize information. Children often identify with parents—but also may identify with older siblings, peers, or teen idols—and view themselves as having many psychological similarities to the person with whom they identify.

For some people, identifications can contribute to self-esteem and self-efficacy. However, other individuals' identifications contribute to distress. For example, often people who have severely mentally ill parents assume that there must be something very wrong with themselves despite a lack of objective evidence for this belief.

Reasoning also appears to be another important source of beliefs. For example, when young children's parents die, they often conclude that they caused the loss (because of developmentally appropriate egocentrism). As a result, they frequently conclude that they are "bad." Another example of reasoning resulting in the development of important beliefs is shown in the case of Lois. Lois was a college student with depressive tendencies who became severely depressed soon after the onset of the Bosnian war. She attributed how she was feeling to the development of a belief "If atrocities like these could happen, there must be no God, and life is meaningless."

Reasoning may also contribute to the differentiation of beliefs within a cognitive schema. For example, if a person believes that he or she is fundamentally "selfish" (core belief), he or she may think extensively about ways to lessen the selfishness. Resulting derivative beliefs may include: "If I spend as much time and effort as possible giving to other people, I might not be so selfish" (conditional assumption), "I must give to others" (implicit rule), and "It is very important to me to be a generous person" (central goal).

Traumatic Events

Traumatic events can contribute to psychological problems in several ways. First, traumas can result in primal mode activation that causes acute symptoms. Second, traumas often condition individuals to respond to benign circumstances as if they were threatening; traumatized individuals develop maladaptive triggers for primal modes. Third, if a trauma is sufficiently severe or chronic, it might result in chronically hypervalent modes leading to chronic difficulties. Finally, traumas can shape people's beliefs about themselves, the world or the future.

FACTORS THAT MAINTAIN SELF-DEFEATING RESPONSE PATTERNS

Once established, a particular self-defeating response pattern may be maintained by one of several different mechanisms. First, individuals may be *unaware of adaptive strategies* relating to their problems. High levels of physiological arousal can contribute to their failure to find adaptive strategies. Extreme arousal hinders clear thinking, creativity, and effective problem solving (D'Zurilla, 1988). Alternately, high levels of physiological arousal, because aversive, may also result in cognitive, emotional, or behavioral avoidance that contributes to individuals' problems.

Self-fulfilling prophecies (Snyder, Tanke, & Berscheid, 1977) represent a second mechanism that contributes to maladaptive-pattern maintenance in some people. Frequently, individuals have expectations that negatively influence their responses; their responses in turn result in their expectations being fulfilled. For example, Jenny expected to have difficulty sleeping and considered insomnia to be a "horrible affliction." At bedtime each night, she typically became so anxious that she had difficulty falling asleep, which reinforced her initial expectation. Another example of a self-fulfilling prophecy relates to depressed individuals' tendency to view themselves and the world negatively. Their thinking helps maintain their depression, which in turn maintains their negative thinking.

Third, *ongoing negative treatment by others* can maintain individuals' maladaptive responses. Each time an individual receives a negative message, it may activate a primitive mode that results in maladaptive responses. In addition, the repeated negative messages can eventually lead individuals to forming negative core beliefs that perpetuate their distress.

A fourth mechanism that seems to maintain self-defeating response patterns in some individuals relates to their *anxiety resulting from a belief that they would become an entirely different person* by giving up a long-term, pervasive strategy. As a result of their fear, they strongly resist attempting new approaches to their difficulties. This anxiety is most commonly seen in individuals with personality disorders.

Fifth, individuals who have ongoing problems may feel *hopeless* with regard to their ability to change self-defeating patterns. They may have unsuccessfully attempted to change patterns numerous times in the past. As a result of hopelessness, they often lack motivation for attempting to change.

A sixth mechanism that helps maintain some self-defeating patterns is that the patterns result in *immediate reinforcing consequences*. For example, John suffered from extreme anxiety. The predominant strategy he used for coping was drinking alcohol to excess. Immediately after he drank, he felt relief, although in the long run, his alcohol dependence cost him his family and his job. Consequences that follow immediately after a behavior tend to have a more powerful effect on subsequent behavior than do consequences that are delayed (e.g., Logan, 1965).

Seventh, maladaptive behavior patterns are often *reinforced intermittently*. When people are continuously reinforced for a behavior, reinforcement termination results in rapid extinction of the behavior. In contrast, a behavior that is intermittently reinforced tends to take much longer to extinguish (Skinner, 1953). For example, pathological gambling is a highly tenacious problem despite profound costs to the afflicted individuals; gambling is intermittently reinforced.

Eight, individuals' *social environments can unintentionally reinforce maladaptive behavior patterns.* For example, a wife gave her husband more attention and support when he was depressed than when he was not depressed, which reinforced his maladaptive behavior pattern.

Finally, some self-defeating response patterns are *encouraged and reinforced by society at-large.* For instance, Western society's strong preference for extremely thin women is widely considered to contribute to eating disorders, its preference for work achievement has resulted in "workaholism," and its hunger for material possessions has encouraged thousands to live beyond their means.

3

The Therapeutic Relationship

This chapter discusses the importance of the therapeutic relationship, the foundation on which cognitive therapy assessment and intervention is based. The following relationship factors are addressed in detail: (a) therapist attitudes and behavior, (b) the collaborative nature of cognitive therapy, and (c) the process of socialization into therapy.

THERAPIST ATTITUDES AND BEHAVIOR

The relevant attitudes and behaviors that set the stage for a positive treatment outcome are empathy, an accepting attitude, warmth, genuineness, and positive reinforcement (Egan, 1982; Kanfer & Schefft, 1987; Kolenberg & Tsai, 1987; Persons, 1989; Raush & Bordin, 1957; Rogers, 1957). If clients do not like, respect, and feel respected by their therapist, they are not likely to invest in the therapeutic process. Nor are they likely to try to think, act, relate to others, and feel in new ways that potentially would be helpful and healthy. Empirical studies have supported the positive role that these therapists' attitudes and behaviors have on the therapeutic outcome (e.g., Burns & Nolen-Hoesksema, 1992; Rogers, 1953, 1957). The current discussion focuses on three of these—empathy, acceptance, and positive reinforcement—because the other attitudes and behaviors generally follow from these three.

Empathy

A common pitfall in cognitive therapy is that novice cognitive therapists—in their enthusiasm for helping clients find and modify distorted cognitions—appear unempathic to clients. As a result, rapport is often compromised, and clients can feel alienated. Therefore, it is important for therapists to first accurately reflect the quality and intensity of their clients' pain as well as the subtleties of what clients are thinking about a situation or themselves. Only then should therapists attempt to facilitate changes in their clients' thoughts, beliefs, and feelings (Greenberg, Rice, & Elliott, 1993). Clients generally need to believe they are understood and accepted before they are willing to change. Thus, insightful case conceptualizations can improve therapeutic relationships by helping clients believe that they are understood and by facilitating therapists' covert and overt empathy for their clients.

The therapist attempts to convey that he or she is listening carefully and understanding the client's perspective and emotional experience. To accomplish this, the therapist should exhibit appropriate eye contact, receptive body language, and nonverbal listening vocalizations. Therapists should also paraphrase what the client says, gently ask questions for clarification, and reflect feelings (e.g., Layden et al., 1993).

Acceptance

Theorists and researchers from a wide range of traditions recognize the importance of the therapist embodying an *accepting attitude* toward the client. Rogers (1961) defined acceptance as:

> a warm regard for ... [the client] as a person of unconditional self-worth—of value no matter what his condition, his behavior, or his feelings. It means a respect and liking for him as a separate person, a willingness for him to possess his own feelings in his own way. It means an acceptance of and regard for his attitudes of the moment, no matter how negative or positive, no matter how much they may contradict other attitudes he has held in the past. This acceptance of each fluctuating aspect of this other person makes it for him a relationship of warmth and safety, and the safety of being liked and prized as a person seems a highly important element in a helping relationship. (p. 34)

Linehan (1993a) suggested that therapists attempt to maintain the *paradoxical stance* of (a) accepting clients as they are, problems and all, while (b) concurrently working toward change. This becomes increasingly important for clients who are severely personality disordered. Linehan (1993a) described this paradoxical stance as follows:

> By "acceptance" here, I mean something quite radical—namely acceptance of both the patient and the therapist, of both the therapeutic relationship and the therapeutic process, exactly as all of these are in the moment. This is not an acceptance in order to bring about change; otherwise, it would be a change strategy.[3] Rather, it is the therapist's willingness to find the inherent wisdom

[3]Inevitably, therapists lapse into acting in an accepting manner *in order to* effect change and help their clients. Therapists can attempt to be mindful of these lapses. Each time they become aware of a lapse, they can gently bring themselves back to truly accepting clients as they are in that particular moment. In other words, acceptance is not a one time decision but rather an ongoing process requiring mindful attention.

> and "goodness" of the current moment and the participants in it, and to enter fully into the experience without judgment, blame, or manipulation. ... however, reality is change, and the nature of any relationship is that of reciprocal influence. In particular, a therapeutic relationship is one that originates in the necessity of change and the patient's wish to obtain professional help in the process of changing. An orientation toward change requires that the therapist take responsibility for directing the therapeutic influence, or change, to the advantage of the patient. Such a stance is active and self-conscious; it involves systematically applying principles of behavior change.
>
> From the perspective of acceptance versus change, DBT[4] represents a balance between behavioral approaches, which are primarily technologies of change, and humanistic and client-centered approaches, which can be thought of as technologies of acceptance. In DBT, the therapist not only models a change-acceptance synthesis but also encourages such a life stance to the patient, advocating change and amelioration of undesired aspects of herself and situations, as well as tolerance and acceptance of these same characteristics. (pp. 109–110; footnotes not in original)

Positive Reinforcement

To facilitate further a positive therapeutic relationship, cognitive therapists should praise clients' behaviors that are difficult or painful but are likely to have positive long-term benefits (Kanfer & Schefft, 1987; Kolenberg & Tsai, 1987). Some examples of these include: being assertive, resisting the urge to take an alcoholic beverage, doing self-help work outside sessions, or contacting a potentially supportive person. The therapist attempts to encourage and reinforce the client's *effort* for positive change and new behaviors that are *early approximations* of the desired outcome (shaping). In addition, therapists attempt to *validate* their clients as people even when—perhaps especially when—clients are having difficulty changing responses.

COLLABORATION

In cognitive therapy, the therapeutic relationship is collaborative, with the therapist and the client being full partners in the therapeutic enterprise (Beck, Rush, et al., 1979; Beck et al., 1985; Beck, Freeman, et al., 1990; J. Beck, 1995). One way that therapy is collaborative is that the client and therapist each make a *unique contribution.* Clients provide the "raw data" for therapeutic work. This is because only they have direct access to their inner experience, the events that occur outside sessions, and their personal history. The therapist provides expertise, skills, guidance, and a supportive interpersonal context, all of which encourage positive change.

---

[4]DBT refers to Dialectical Behavior Therapy, Linehan's brand of cognitive behavior therapy for clients with borderline personality disorder, which is a therapeutic approach that has shown efficacy with this difficult client population (see Linehan, Tutek, Heard, & Armstrong, 1994; Linehan, Heard, & Armstrong, 1993, for outcome studies).

Another way that therapy is collaborative is that the therapist and the client work jointly on the various therapy tasks. For instance, together the therapist and the client select therapy goals. Therapy goals should be specific, measurable, and, preferably, positively framed. Common goals for cognitive therapy include: (a) improving mood states (e.g., improving mood, increasing mood stability, increasing relaxation or calmness, increasing ability to cope with stressful interpersonal situations), (b) decreasing symptoms (e.g., the frequency and intensity of obsessions and compulsions, suicidal ideation, and panic attacks), (c) understanding the subtleties of one's maladaptive responses, (d) increasing social activities, (e) increasing motivation, (f) learning social skills such as appropriate assertiveness, and (g) developing a sense of purpose in life—to name a few.

Therapists and clients also collaboratively select the frequency of sessions, what to work on in each session, and what tasks clients will attempt as self-help assignments before the next session. The pair works together to objectively analyze situations and the client's reactions to them, solve problems, and design mini-experiments to test beliefs.

At various times during each session, the therapist and the client jointly summarize and review skills that the client has learned and insights gained during the session. In addition, they collaboratively evaluate the therapy process for what has been helpful and what needs to be modified. For example, at the beginning of sessions, the therapist may ask the client to "bridge from the last session, that is, summarize the major things we discussed, what you got out of the session that was worthwhile, as well as anything that you found upsetting or confusing in the session."

At the end of the session, the therapist may ask "How did we do today? Was there anything that was particularly upsetting, unhelpful, or confusing? Were there things we discussed that were particularly helpful?" In fact, some cognitive therapists—including those at the Center for Cognitive Therapy at the University of Pennsylvania and at the Beck Institute for Cognitive Therapy and Research—ask clients to complete a written feedback form at the end of each session (for an example of a therapy feedback form, see Burns & Auerbach, 1996). By frequently and collaboratively discussing the therapy process, the pair can shape therapy to best meet the client's needs.

Guided Discovery

Guided discovery (Beck, Rush, et al., 1979; Beck, Freeman, et al., 1990), also known as Socratic Questioning, is an important tool for collaboration and therefore deserves special mention. In guided discovery, the therapist asks the client a systematic series of questions.

When using guided discovery, therapists carefully select questions with a direction in mind. The series of questions is based on the therapist's case conceptualization of the client and the client's responses to earlier questions in the dialogue. Therapists use guided discovery to accomplish two aims: (a) to assess clients' responses and the situations that trigger them and (b) to help clients change their self-defeating thinking. Regarding the first aim, careful questioning helps the client and the therapist gain greater understanding of the client's belief system and automatic responses to a situation. Information derived from guided discovery often helps fine-tune the conceptualization. The client's answers support, clarify, correct, disconfirm, or add new information to the conceptualization.

The second aim of guided discovery is to help the client modify his or her thinking. What follows is an excerpt of a session with Jill, a 35-year-old depressed woman. The transcript demonstrates the use of guided discovery.

Jill: I've been really disgusted with myself for the last few days.

Therapist: Would you mind rating how disgusted you've been with yourself, on a scale of 0–100, where 100 is the most disgusted you've ever felt and 0 equals not disgusted at all?

Jill: I'd have to say about 90.

Therapist: Would you like to focus on your disgust for yourself now?

Jill: Yes.

Therapist: What have you been disgusted with yourself about?

Jill: Everything.

Therapist: Did anything in particular happen a few days ago that might have contributed to this?

Jill: Yes . . . I treated my six year-old awfully.

Therapist: Tell me more about what happened.

Jill: I screamed at him about something stupid, and he started to cry.

Therapist: Did you do anything in addition to screaming?

Jill: No.

Therapist: About how long did you scream at him?

Jill: A minute or two.

Therapist: What in particular did you scream at him about?

Jill: He jumped down about 10 steps at once. I've told him a million times not to do that! But, he's six, and he doesn't realize the consequences, and he's really a great kid.

Therapist: To the best of your recollection, what exactly was the content of what you screamed?

Jill: Don't do that! You're going to get killed! Do you want to give me a heart attack! Don't ever do that again! I can't believe you did that!

Therapist: Before, you said, "He's a great kid."

Jill: Yes.

Therapist: Do you believe that even after he jumped down those steps?

Jill: Yes, of course.

Therapist: Good. Some parents I work with don't have a good sense for what is age-appropriate behavior. Unfortunately, they take behavior like this as evidence that their children are bad or defiant in a global way.

Jill: Oh, no! He's really a great kid!

Therapist: Yes. In general, do you think he knows that you think he's a great kid?

Jill: Yes, definitely.

Therapist: Do you think your screaming at him changed this or didn't change this?

Jill: I guess it didn't change it. He's been acting fine since then, and we've continued to be affectionate.

Therapist: Good ... Back to the incident. What was so upsetting about his jumping down all of those steps?

Jill: I'm afraid some day something terrible will happen.

Therapist: You're afraid that he'll be seriously injured or killed?

Jill: Yes. He could break bones, get brain damage, or break his neck.

Therapist: Is that a good reason to get upset with him when he jumps down a lot of stairs?

Jill: I guess so, but I shouldn't get hysterical with him. I was overreacting.

Therapist: Is it possible that he could have gotten hurt jumping down those stairs?

Jill: Yes. I guess it wasn't even unlikely that he could have been hurt. The foyer door is right near the bottom of the stairs.

Therapist: So, do you think this was or was not a legitimate thing to be upset about?

Jill: Put that way, it was legitimate.

Therapist: OK. What messages do you think he got from your reaction to his jumping down the stairs?

Jill: That I'm a loose cannon!

Therapist: You clearly don't want to respond like that on a regular basis in the future, right?

Jill: Right.

Therapist: However, you did this time. Might anything positive have resulted from doing it this one time?

Jill: Well, he clearly got the message that he shouldn't jump down the stairs.

Therapist: Anything else?

Jill: It shows him that I care about him and want him to be safe.

Therapist: Can you think of other parents who you think do a good job with their children but once in awhile yell or scream at their children?

Jill: My husband is one.

Therapist: Has he ever blown up at Jerry Jr.?

Jill: Rarely … But, yes a few times.

Therapist: How often would you say you blow up at Jerry Jr.? Rarely or frequently or somewhere in between?

Jill: Rarely. You're right! And, I know other parents who are good parents who sometimes blow their stacks at their kids. I feel much better thinking of it that way.

Therapist: Approximately, how disgusted do you feel with yourself now about this, 0 to 100?

Jill: About 10.

In the situation described in this dialogue, the therapist used guided discovery first for assessment. He asked questions to learn about the problematic situation and the client's response to it. He also was assessing her responses to determine whether she was acting in ways that may have been damaging to her son. That is, he probed about whether her unpleasant affect was a signal to be listened to that something was wrong. To these ends, the therapist asked "Did you do anything in addition to screaming?" "How long did you scream?" and "What exactly was the content of your screaming?" The therapist discovered that the client's son was not at risk from her behavior. Then, the therapist focused his questions on helping Jill discover that her behavior with her son on that occasion did not reflect that she was a bad mother. Rather, she was human and in fact was a caring mother who perhaps went a little overboard.

Presumably, guided discovery is effective for two main reasons. First, people are often more convinced by something they discover themselves than something that others impose on them. Second, as therapy proceeds, clients learn to internalize this method of questioning as a skill that can help them deal with future problems or upsets. That is, guided discovery helps clients "become their own cognitive therapists" by gaining skills for independently improving the way they feel and for solving their own problems.

SOCIALIZATION INTO COGNITIVE THERAPY

During the first psychotherapy session or two, therapists socialize clients into the cognitive therapy process (Beck, Rush, et al., 1979; J. Beck, 1995).

Socialization into cognitive therapy involves educating clients about: (a) their problem through an individually tailored case conceptualization, (b) the collaborative nature of therapy, (c) an important therapy goal, which is for clients to learn eventually to solve their problems without the therapist's help, (d) the session format, (e) the fact that improvement occurs nonlinearly, and (f) the parameters of therapy. (Because the first two items have been discussed previously, they are not repeated in the present discussion.)

An important goal in cognitive therapy is for clients to learn the skills and gain the confidence necessary to improve their mood and *solve their problems without the therapist's help*. In other words, the ultimate goal of therapy is to make the therapist obsolete. Toward these ends, therapists encourage clients to gradually take more responsibility and a larger role in deciding how to select solutions to their problems. (A large variety of intervention strategies that clients can learn as skills are presented in chap. 5.) As clients master therapy skills, the therapist's role should decrease and the emphasis should be on *generalization*. Clients should master and maintain self-enhancing behaviors in a range of situations outside the therapy session. They may, for example, first practice assertiveness during role plays during the session. When their skill and confidence increase, they should then attempt assertiveness outside the session. Preferably, they should begin at the bottom of a hierarchy of perceived threat and work their way up to more challenging situations.

Toward having clients gradually become more in charge of solving their own problems, it is often helpful for termination from cognitive therapy to occur gradually. For example, sessions can "taper" from weekly to biweekly to monthly to every 3 months. This allows clients to get practice solving their problems independently and to check back with their therapists for feedback and fine-tuning. The tapering process also gives clients greater confidence about dealing with issues and problems on their own.

Also, during the socialization process it is helpful for therapists to suggest a typical *session format*. Beck, Rush, et al. (1979) suggested the following format. First, the therapist reviews with the client relevant questionnaires, logs, and self-monitoring forms that measure symptoms or progress toward therapy goals. Second, the client briefly updates the therapist on significant events and internal experiences since the previous session. Third, the client (and if necessary the therapist) "bridges" from the previous session. They summarize the previous session and identify therapy activities that were helpful as well as those that were confusing, not helpful, or upsetting. Fourth, the pair review previously assigned self-help work. Fifth, the client and therapist select specific topics or skills to work on in the current session. Sixth, they work on the selected topics or skills. Seventh, they jointly choose self-help assignments that the client can work on prior to the next session. Finally, the client, with the therapist's help, summarizes and reviews the session.

Clients also benefit from being educated about *nonlinear improvement* that typically occurs in psychotherapy. For example, therapists can show them a graph similar to the one in Fig. 3.1. The therapist can explain the nonlinear nature of progress in a manner similar to the following.

Therapist: Therapy rarely occurs linearly. Improvement usually comes in fits and starts with three steps forward and one back. It's important to remember that there may be times when you feel worse, like here (points to the frowning face on Fig. 3.1). At those times, you may think "I feel as bad now as when I started therapy," and you may even consider quitting therapy. But, this is just a blip in the graph. At other times, you will feel better (points to the smiling face). You may think, "I feel great; I don't need to continue with therapy," but that may just be a blip in the curve, too. You probably won't be quite done with therapy yet.

The fact that progress comes in fits and starts, I think, is quite useful. If you feel particularly bad one week, we can learn what happened and what you were thinking or doing that may have contributed to your feeling worse. Similarly, when you feel better, we can learn from that. Another reason that I think it's good that there is fluctuation in the curve has to do with when you finish in therapy. At that time you will have reached your therapy goals, and overall you will be feeling a lot better. However, there probably will be days and even weeks when your mood is a little blue. That's normal, everyone experiences it. However, since you've been ______ (targeted problem) before, you may tend to overreact. You may assume that your ______ (targeted problem) is coming back when really it is probably just a normal fluctuation in the curve. Seeing fluctuations in here can help remind you later.

Regarding *parameters of therapy,* therapists inform clients about confidentiality and its limits, the length and frequency of sessions, the expected duration of therapy, and the cancellation policy.

SUMMARY

Cognitive therapists work at experiencing and exhibiting empathy, genuineness, positive regard, warmth, nonjudgmental attitude, and expertise. In addition, therapists attempt to maintain the paradoxical stance of (a) accepting clients as they are, problems and all, while (b) concurrently working toward change.

The therapeutic relationship is collaborative, with therapist and client being full partners in the therapeutic enterprise. A major tool of collabora-

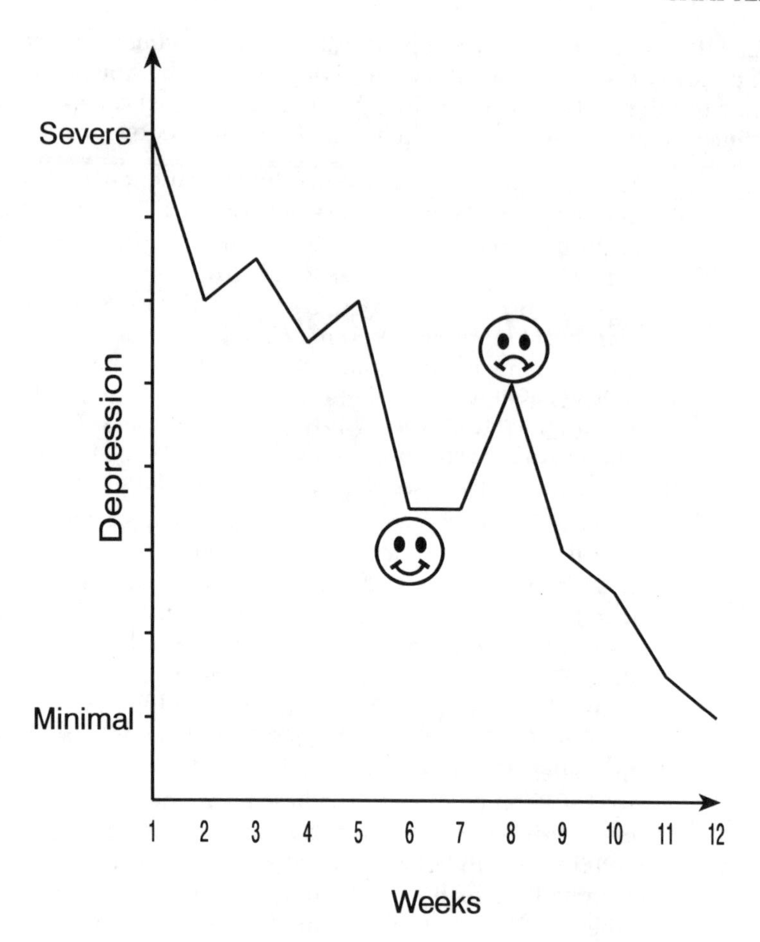

FIG. 3.1. The nonlinear progress in cognitive therapy.

tion is guided discovery, in which the therapist systematically asks questions that help clients gain greater understanding of a situation or their reactions to a situation. Insights derived from guided discovery often pave the way for positive change.

A positive therapeutic relationship is necessary for effective assessment and treatment. The next chapter provides the reader with detailed guidelines for assessing clients within a cognitive framework. Assessment guided by the cognitive model sets the stage for developing useful cognitive case conceptualizations.

4

Assessment and Information Integration

1. Pre-Intake Questionnaires
   a. Multimodal Life History Inventory
   b. Questionnaires for Screening Clinical Disorders
   c. Questionnaire for Screening Personality Disorders
   d. Procedures Pertaining to the Pre-Intake Interview Questionnaire
2. Intake Interview
   a. Presenting Problem
      i. Stressors That Appear to Have Precipitated the Presenting Problem
         (1) Interpersonal Stressors That May Contribute to the Maintenance of the Presenting Problem
   b. Strengths and Resources
   c. Neuropsychological Deficits
   d. Diagnostic Interview
   e. Behavioral Observations During Intake Interview
3. Ongoing Assessment During Therapy
   a. Fine-Grained Analysis of Problematic Responses
      i. Behavioral Assessment Test
      ii. Role Play
      iii. Moment-by-Moment Functional Analysis
      iv. Case Conceptualization Worksheets
      v. Downward Arrows Technique
   b. Behavioral Observations During Ongoing Therapy
      i. Therapeutic Relationship
      ii. Intense Emotional Reactions
   c. Other Approaches for Elucidating Information for Case Conceptualizations
      i. Assessing the Origins of Core Beliefs
      ii. Intermediate Belief Elucidation
      iii. Using Previously Obtained Information to Generate Hypotheses and Guide Further Interviewing
   d. Questionnaires for Tracking Progress in Therapy

To develop an accurate and effective case conceptualization, a high-quality, comprehensive assessment is necessary. During the assessment process, the therapist attempts to elucidate the various elements of the cognitive model as they relate to the individual client. Specifically, the elements of the cognitive model include:

- the integrated cognitive, affective, and behavioral responses to triggering circumstances,
- the client's underlying belief system that determines his or her responses,
- the circumstances that activate maladaptive responses,
- the environment's responses to the client's behavior,
- the negative events that precipitated the client's problems, and
- the learning history that contributed to the client's vulnerability to specific problems.

This chapter discusses various aspects of assessment including pre-intake questionnaires, the intake interview, and ongoing assessment during therapy.

PRE-INTAKE QUESTIONNAIRES

Unfortunately, in this era of managed care, the amount of time allowable for assessment typically is exceedingly brief. Having clients complete an initial packet of questionnaires prior to the initial intake session can reduce the time needed for assessment. This saves precious therapy time, while not compromising assessment quality. The packet suggested in this book takes approximately 1½ hours for the average client to complete. It consists of the Multimodal Life History Inventory, the Prime-MD Patient Questionnaire and other *DSM–IV* screening questions, and the SCID II (Personality) Screening Questionnaire.

Multimodal Life History Inventory

The Multimodal Life History Inventory (Lazarus & Lazarus, 1991) is a 13-page questionnaire that assesses the following information: general information, personal and social history, description of presenting problems, and modality analysis of current problems (i.e., behaviors, emotions, physical sensations, mental images, thoughts, interpersonal relationships, biological factors). Although the Life History Inventory does not yield quantitative scores and does not give normative information, it often is quite helpful in developing case conceptualizations. It provides therapists with a great deal of information about their clients. The information often helps therapists generate hypotheses about elements of the cognitive model that are specific to their clients.

Questionnaires for Screening Clinical Disorders

Establishing an accurate diagnosis is another important task in the development of case conceptualizations. Having an accurate diagnosis often allows the clinician to tap into an extensive literature on treating clients with a particular diagnosis.

Careful assessment of a range of disorders conveys a second advantage. Doing so can provide a therapist with much information about the cognitive model as it relates to the client. This is because the *DSM–IV* (APA, 1994) diagnostic criteria often include items related to activating circumstances, cognitive content and processes, affects, motivations, and behaviors. For example, the *DSM–IV* diagnostic criteria for social phobia (pp. 416–417) includes items related to the activating circumstances (i.e., "person is exposed to unfamiliar people or to possible scrutiny by others"), cognitive content (i.e., the phobic individual expects to "act in a way or show anxiety symptoms that will be humiliating or embarrassing"), affective response (i.e., anxiety), and motivational and behavioral responses (i.e., "social or performance situations are avoided or else are endured with intense anxiety or distress").

A thorough diagnostic assessment often helps uncover other problems for which the client is *not* seeking help. These unreported problems may play an important role in maintaining the client's problems. Alternatively, unreported problems may be more serious than the problems for which the client is seeking help. A common example of this is substance misuse. Often clients do not present with alcohol- or drug-related problems. Instead, substance abusers present for problems with anxiety, relationships, or sustaining work—all of which often are secondary to their substance misuse.

The Structured Clinical Interview for the *DSM–IV* Axis I Disorders (First, Spitzer, Gibbon, & Williams, 1997) and the Prime–MD (Spitzer et al., 1994) are structured clinical interviews constructed by the authors of the *DSM–IV* (APA, 1994).[5] The instruments exhibit good reliability and validity. The SCID was designed for mental health professionals to establish comprehensive fine-grained diagnoses. Part I of the SCID assesses for clinical disorders (Axis I), whereas Part II assesses for personality disorders (Axis II disorders, which are described in the next section). As the name suggests, the Prime–MD was designed for use by primary care physicians to detect the most common mental illnesses—depression, somatoform disorders, generalized anxiety, panic attacks, and alcohol misuse.

Both the SCID–I and the Prime–MD include screening questions. The Prime–MD's screening questions are in the form of a paper-and-pencil Patient Questionnaire, whereas the SCID uses a brief clinical interview. To save interview time, this book suggests using the Prime–MD Patient Questionnaire. In addition, it recommends that a paper-and-pencil adaptation

[5]The Prime–MD can be obtained from Pfizer Inc.

of the SCID–I screening questions be used for disorders not covered by the Prime–MD. (Included in the adaptation of the SCID–I screening interview are questionnaire items that assess for recreational drug use, misuse of prescription drugs, panic disorder, agoraphobia, social phobia, specific phobia, OCD, anorexia, and bulimia.)

If a client endorsed a screening question for a disorder, then during the intake interview, the therapist should ask SCID interview questions to thoroughly assess for that disorder. Conversely, when a client does not endorse the screening item for a disorder, further assessment of that disorder is not necessary.

Questionnaire for Screening Personality Disorders

The Structured Clinical Interview for the *DSM–IV*, Axis II Personality Disorders (SCID–II; First, Gibbon, Spitzer, Williams, & Benjamin, 1997) is a clinical interview that assesses for each feature of each *DSM–IV* personality disorder. Included in the interview is a paper-and-pencil screening questionnaire. Clients' responses to the screening questions help therapists decide which personality disorder categories they can omit during the SCID–II clinical interview. (Omitting categories from the SCID–II can save a great deal of interview time. When clients answer a SCID–II question in the affirmative, their therapists ask them to provide examples from their lives to support their answer.)

Procedures Pertaining to the Pre-Intake Interview Questionnaire

In a telephone conversation prior to the intake, the therapist or the intake coordinator should describe the questionnaires, provide a strong rationale for their importance, and ask the client if he or she is willing to complete the questionnaires prior to the scheduled intake. If the client is willing, the therapist can send the questionnaires to the client prior to their first meeting, or the client can arrive early.

Despite the advantages of having clients fill out questionnaires prior to the intake, therapists should carefully consider the appropriateness of questionnaires for their specific, prospective clients. From an initial phone contact with clients, therapists can learn about some of the major problems and difficulties that the client is experiencing. Clients with particular problems or characteristics—for example, vegetative depression, passive resistance to demands of adequate performance, disregard for the rights of others, or extreme suspiciousness—may respond adversely to being asked to complete questionnaires prior to the scheduled intake.

For example, Jen was severely depressed and vegetative. If she were provided with a large packet of questionnaires prior to therapy, she probably would have had insufficient motivation to complete it. Her failure to do so might have further confirmed her negative view of herself, the world, or her future (including her prospects in therapy). Sandeep had a pattern of passively resisting demands for adequate performance. Were he asked to complete the questionnaires, he likely would have failed to do. Perhaps, he would have claimed that he forgot or failed to realize that he was supposed to do this before the intake interview. Alternately, he may have filled out parts of the questionnaires but responded to items in a way that provided little useful information (other than about his personality style). Stan tended to disregard others' rights and enjoyed "getting people's goat." Were he asked to complete the questionnaires prior to therapy, he may have seen this as an opportunity to defy authority. Susan tended to be quite suspicious. She most likely would not have felt safe enough to answer the questionnaires honestly.

Giving questionnaires to clients having any of these types of presentations may result in their decision to not proceed with therapy. Alternatively, they may proceed with therapy but may begin with negative feelings and beliefs toward the therapist. For example, had Jen been given the questionnaire, she may have assumed, "This therapist must not understand depression since he gave me this questionnaire despite my low level of motivation."

It should also be noted that regardless of the type of assessment, many clients initially will be guarded about sensitive and painful information. This information is likely to emerge as a positive therapeutic relationship develops.

INTAKE INTERVIEW

Prior to or during the intake, the therapist should thoroughly review the client's pretreatment questionnaire packet to reward the client's compliance and to guide the intake interview process. During the interview, the therapist should (a) further explore important questionnaire responses that the client omitted or answered vaguely, (b) gather information about the presenting problem, its history, and stressors that may have precipitated the problem, (c) learn whether the client had a complete physical examination since the onset or exacerbation of his or her problems,[6] (d) identify the client's strengths and resources, (e) conduct a Mini-Mental Status Exam to identify gross neuropsychological deficits, (f) establish *DSM–IV* diagnoses, and (g) collect as much information as possible about the various components of the cognitive model as they relate to the client.

---

[6]The overlap between symptoms of general medical conditions and psychiatric disorders is great. Symptoms that are the direct physiological effects of general medical conditions are often similar to those of psychological disorders (e.g., stroke, hypothyroidism, multiple sclerosis can resemble major depression; hyperthyroidism, hyperparathyroidism, pheochromocytoma, vestibular dysfunction, seizure disorder may resemble panic disorder).

Therefore, at the onset of cognitive therapy, it is often advisable for clients to have a complete physical examination to rule out any general medical conditions that may be mimicking psychological problems.

Realistically, it is usually not feasible to collect information regarding all of the cognitive model elements during the intake interview because third party payers rarely allow more than 1 hour or 1½ hours for the initial session. As a result, information that is not obtained during the intake interview can be obtained during ongoing assessment during therapy proper.

Presenting Problem

Besides representing a problem that the client wants to resolve, the presenting problem can provide important clues regarding other elements of the conceptualization. These elements may include core beliefs, behavioral strategies, and diagnoses. For example, consider a client who presents a litany of how people have been cruel and undependable. The therapist may make the following hypotheses about the client: (a) she may have a core belief relating to mistrust, (b) she may be hypervigilant to interpersonal threats, and (c) she may have features of paranoid personality disorder.

During the intake evaluation, the therapist should attempt to obtain as much information as possible about the client's experience of the problem and the factors that elicit and maintain them. Specifically, therapy benefits from having a detailed understanding of the nuances of repetitive patterns in which triggering stimuli elicit cognition, emotion, and overt behavior, which in turn elicit a response from the environment (e.g., social consequences). In addition, therapists should conduct a detailed history of the presenting problem. Realistically, due to time constraints, assessment of much of this information often must wait until subsequent sessions.

Stressors That Appear to Have Precipitated the Presenting Problem

Stressors that appear to have precipitated a presenting problem are important for two main reasons. First, the events that precipitated the problem might have continued and therefore may be contributing to the maintenance of the problem. As a result, developing coping strategies for dealing with these continuing stressors can be a focus of therapy.

Second, the nature of the precipitant sometimes provides clues for the client's cognitive vulnerabilities. For example, a client developed a major depressive episode following a promotion at work. When the therapist asked the client for the meaning of this event, the client admitted that he believed he was "incompetent and would fail miserably."

Therapists should ask clients open-ended questions about what was happening in their lives in the months preceding the onset or exacerbation of their problems. If clients fail to mention any negative events during the time period in question, therapists should inquire explicitly about any significant changes or losses. Therapists may need to continue their inquiry by asking about specific life areas. These areas should include clients' work or school, physical health, love relationships, family, and finances. In addition, the therapist should inquire about whether the client experienced legal problems or was the victim of a crime or natural disaster. (Examples of major stressors are provided in Box 4.1.)

Interpersonal Stressors That May Contribute to the Maintenance of the Presenting Problem. Interpersonal relationships play an extremely important role in individuals' psychological health and problems. Therefore, this section provides procedures for assessing current relationship difficulties and long-term relationship deficits.

Regarding *current relationship difficulties,* therapists should assess for the presence of healthy, supportive relationships, as well as evidence of overt or covert conflicts with significant others. For significant people in the client's life (e.g., spouse/partner, parents, each child, boss), the therapist can ask for descriptions of the client's relationship with them in an open-ended fashion. The therapist should ask about each relationship preceding the onset or exacerbation of the client's problems as well as currently. When necessary, the therapist can ask follow-up questions regarding the specif-

Social

- Death of a loved one
- Divorce
- Separation from partner
- Relationship discord
- Having a child with health, psychological, or conduct problems
- Being infertile
- Having a new child

Health/Mental Health

- Having a serious and/or chronic health or mental health problem
- Developing a new health problem

Work

- Being downsized or fired
- Being unemployed
- Being harassed by supervisor or coworkers
- Having little control of working conditions
- Major changes in responsibilities
- Large workload
- Job dissatisfaction

Traumas

- Being the victim of a violent crime, serious accident, or natural disaster
- Seeing a loved one seriously injured or killed

Other

- Financial difficulties
- Legal difficulties
- Changing cities

Box 4.1. Stressors that may precipitate psychological problems in adults.

ics of each relationship. For example, therapists can ask about the following: (a) satisfying and unsatisfying aspects of the relationship, (b) areas of conflict and how they are dealt with, (c) resentments or disappointments, (d) what each party's expectations are for the relationship and whether these expectations are being fulfilled, and (e) what the client would like to be different in this relationship. Klerman, Weissman, Rounsaville, and Chevron (1984) suggested that insufficient or overidealized descriptions of seemingly important current or recent relationships may be clues to difficulties that the client is unwilling to recognize, explore, or discuss.

The therapist should explore whether the client has any current supportive relationships.

- Does the client have people who care about him or her?
- Does the client have people who encourage him or her to talk about private problems, cognitions, and emotions?
- Does the client have people who give practical help with his or her problems?

As part of the assessment of factors that maintain clients' difficulties, it can be helpful to identify *long-term relationship deficits*. This provides therapists with an understanding of the client's ability to initiate and maintain relationships (i.e., skills) as well as deficits in these areas. Therapists can use the same sorts of questions to assess significant past relationships as they use to assess current significant relationships.

Strengths and Resources

Strengths and resources—which may be internal or external—can help clients adapt to stressful situations, solve their problems, and have a fulfilling life. Some examples of strengths and resources include: supportive friends and family, the capacity to form and sustain healthy interpersonal relationships, high intelligence, common sense, optimism, education, charm, sense of humor, engaging personality style, creativity, financial resources, and a supportive employer.[7]

Neuropsychological Deficits

Therapists should conduct a Mini-Mental Status Examination to rule out gross neuropsychological deficits (Folstein, Folstein, & McHugh, 1975). If

[7]Clients often fail to recognize the strengths and resources that they possess or have access to that could help them to solve their own problems. Thus, an important way that therapists can help clients is by identifying their clients' strengths and resources and showing clients how to apply them advantageously to their present situation. In addition, explicating their strengths and resources may help clients shift from a helpless psychological framework to a coping framework. Finally, recognizing and explicating a client's strengths can help build rapport between the client and therapist by helping the therapist experience and show liking and respect for the client.

clients appear to show significant deficits, therapists should refer them for a full neuropsychological assessment.

Diagnostic Interview

If a client answers a SCID or Prime–MD screening question in the affirmative, the therapist should use the SCID interview questions to thoroughly assess for the relevant disorder.

Behavioral Observations During Intake Interview

The sample of behavior in an intake evaluation is limited (single setting, single point in time). Nonetheless, remarkable behavior in the initial meeting helps the therapist generate hypotheses about a client's maladaptive responses and his or her belief system.

Frequently, cognitive, affective, motivational, and behavioral symptoms of psychological disorders are readily apparent during intake interviews. This is because clients often present to mental health clinics when primal modes are activated. For example, clients suffering from major depressive disorder often discuss loss and beliefs that they are worthless, defective, or unlovable (cognitive schema). They admit that their affect is sad or depressed (affective schema). Depressed clients often exhibit extremely slow speech and movement (motivational schema), and they may act in a socially inappropriate fashion (e.g., excessive complaining, frowning, poor eye contact; behavioral schema). During a manic episode, clients often discuss grandiose ideas (cognitive schema), exhibit elation or irritability (affective schema), report urges to engage in goal-directed activities and stand up and pace (motivational and behavioral schemas).

Strategies that clients use in relationships with other people also may become apparent to the therapist during the intake evaluation. For example, a client arrived 50 minutes late for an intake evaluation stating that he knew that their appointment was earlier. He indicated that he was "a busy man and therefore if you [the therapist] want to work with me, you will just have to be accommodating." This behavior provided the therapist with strong evidence suggesting that the client had an entitlement schema. If a client flirts with the therapist, this may indicate how she behaves in general when she meets certain people, such as male authority figures. A client who exhibited hostility toward a therapist during an intake assessment may treat other people similarly.

ONGOING ASSESSMENT DURING THERAPY

The line between assessment and treatment is an artificial one. Questions that therapists ask during assessment can begin to elicit changes in the client. For example, when therapists assess for the various elements of the cognitive model related to clients' problems, clients often become more cognizant of the role of various factors in establishing or maintaining their problems.

Conversely, throughout the entire therapy process, assessment should continue. The therapist should continue to ask about and gather new information about the client and the situation. Ongoing assessment of this kind helps fine-tune the therapist and client's conceptualization of the client's difficulties.

This section is divided into four parts. The first part discusses conducting a fine-grained analysis of the factors that maintain the targeted problems. The second describes the role of behavioral observations in gleaning information about the client's core beliefs and behavioral strategies. The third part discusses other methods for elucidating information for the case conceptualization. Specifically, it describes procedures for assessing the origins of core beliefs, elucidating intermediate beliefs, and using previously obtained information to generate hypotheses and guide further interviewing. The final part of the section describes the importance of tracking progress in therapy with questionnaires.

Fine-Grained Analysis of Problematic Responses

As a result of time constraints, intake evaluations frequently are limited to a "broad strokes" assessment of the client's problems. During ongoing therapy, once the therapist and client choose a problem on which to work, a fine-grained analysis should be conducted. Therapists should conduct a fine-grained analysis of the factors that elicit and maintain a targeted problematic response. Understanding the subtleties of the client's problems permits highly targeted and effective interventions.

This section presents several approaches to conducting fine-grained analyses of clinical problems including (a) Behavioral Assessment Test, (b) role play, (c) moment-by-moment functional analysis, (d) downward arrows technique, and (e) Case Conceptualization Worksheet.

Behavioral Assessment Test

Assessment information often is most accurate when the therapist can observe the client's responses in as naturalistic a situation as possible. When clients are not in naturalistic situations, they often do not have access to the subtleties of the factors that elicit and maintain their problematic responses. Specifically, they may not be aware of the details of the external environment that elicit responses or that reinforce or punish their behavior. In addition, they often are unaware of aspects of their own cognitive, affective, motivational, or behavioral responses. This can be because the information never entered their awareness. Alternatively, clients often may quickly forget aspects of their response as a result of "information overload" during the situation or a lack of stimuli that might trigger recall after the event.

As a result, whenever possible, therapists should thoroughly assess clients' responses in problematic situations. The procedure for doing so is known as the Behavioral Assessment Test. With respect to the problematic situation that is being observed, therapists observe their clients' behavior and what is happening in the external environment. Watching the sequence of interactions between clients and the environment can provide invaluable information for understanding clients' problems.

In addition, therapists should ask their clients what is happening internally moment by moment as the problematic situation unfolds. Specifically, they inquire at various intervals about clients' thoughts and images, affects, and urges.

Cognitive-behavioral therapists often use Behavioral Assessment Tests to assess clients suffering from phobias. Therapists ask phobic clients to get as close as they can to the phobic object or situation and stay in the exposure situation for as long as possible. Therapists then observe the clients' behavior. In addition, therapists should ask clients about their internal responses, as well as their Subjective Units of Distress ratings (from 0–10, where 0 represents *not at all distressed,* 5 is *moderately distressed,* and 10 is *extremely distressed*). Consider a client whose phobic situation was meeting attractive persons of the opposite sex. The therapist arranged a Behavioral Assessment Test that consisted of having the client meet an attractive colleague while the therapist observed. (The use of Behavioral Assessment Tests for clients with agoraphobia is described in chap. 6.)

Often, therapists are not present during Behavioral Assessment Tests. Sometimes, therapists' presence interferes with clients' naturalistic responses to situations. This may occur, for example, with agoraphobic clients because therapists are often considered safe people. Therefore, their presence often results in reducing the clients' anxiety in the phobic situation. Alternatively, it may not be possible or cost-effective for therapists to be present in problematic situations that clients experience (e.g., difficulties with supervisors). In such cases, it may be useful to have someone in the client's naturalistic environment—such as a partner or trusted coworker—observe and take careful notes about the client's behavior in the problematic situation. In addition, immediately after the event, the client should record the cognitions and feelings experienced moment by moment in the situation. (Over the course of therapy, therapists can repeat the Behavioral Assessment Test to track progress.)

Role Play

When it is not possible to assess clients' interpersonal difficulties in a naturalistic setting, a useful method for conducting a fine-grained analysis is role playing. Some clinical problems for which role playing may be useful as an assessment tool include difficulties with assertiveness, anger, or social anxiety.

During role-play assessments, therapists observe the content of clients' speech as well as nonverbal behaviors. In addition, therapists assess clients' cognitions, affects, impulses, and inhibitions that occur during the role play. It is important that the therapist ask the client how similar the client's responses were during the role play to responses he or she has in the naturalistic situation. If a client reports that the response was different from ones that occur outside of sessions, the therapist should ascertain why. Then, the therapist should attempt to modify the role play or add imagery to better recreate the client's naturalistic responses. Finally, therapists should assess clients' perceptions of clients' own behavior because unawareness of maladaptive behavior can contribute to its maintenance.

Moment-by-Moment Functional Analysis

Another method of assessing the subtleties of a client's problems when the therapist's presence in the naturalistic environment is not possible is a moment-by-moment functional analysis (e.g., Linehan, 1993a). In short, therapists can use guided imagery to help clients recall subtleties of problematic situations and their reactions to them. Box 4.2 lists questions that therapists can use to obtain a moment-by-moment functional analysis.

Here is a transcript from a moment-by-moment functional analysis conducted with a bulimic client. The therapist gave the client several minutes to call forth a detailed image of a typical situation in which she ultimately binged and purged. In addition, he instructed her to experience the situation as if it were happening in the present.

Therapist: Where are you, who are you with, and what are you doing leading up to binging and purging?

Client: I am alone, reading a magazine, and I see an advertisement with a casually dressed attractive woman.

Therapist: What goes through your mind?

Client: I could look like that; she looks good, and she's tiny. I looked like that before, but I don't anymore.

Please describe in detail what you noticed first in the external situation (Who? What? Where? How?)
With regard to your reaction, what did you notice or do (being sure that they are reporting cognitions, affects, bodily sensations, urges, and overt behavior)?
(Repeatedly ask the following:)
What happened or how did you react next?

Box 4.2. Questions for conducting moment-by-moment functional analyses of problematic situations.

Therapist:	What do you experience next?
Client:	Frustration … defeat … sadness … annoyance.
Therapist:	Do you have any physical sensations?
Client:	Yes. Tightening in my neck and like I am going to cry.
Therapist:	What do you experience next? It could be a thought, image, emotion, or behavior.
Client:	I think, "I can't; why bother?"
Therapist:	What happens next?
Client:	I tell myself "Don't eat!" but I also am feeling so defeated.
Therapist:	What do you experience next?
Client:	I think, "To hell with you; I'm going to eat anyway."
Therapist:	What do you experience next?
Client:	I think, "I'm going to eat it; I'm going to screw it up; I'm going to do what I've always done."
Therapist:	What happens next?
Client:	I numb out.
Therapist:	Numb out?
Client:	I stop feeling anything.
Therapist:	What happens next?
Client:	I slowly walk to the fridge.
Therapist:	What do you experience next?
Client:	I'm not hungry, so I am thinking "I don't know what to eat."
Therapist:	And then?
Client:	I grab cake and begin eating.
Therapist:	What do you experience next?
Client:	Mixed emotions. Part of me is feeling relief: "At least it's over."
Therapist:	What else?
Client:	I feel stupid and say to myself "You screwed up again."
Therapist:	Then what do you experience?
Client:	I feel totally defeated; my emotions are back on. Then part of myself is saying to myself "get rid of it" and part is saying "OK, you binged but don't throw up."
Therapist:	And then what?
Client:	I think, "I'm going to put on weight; get rid of it."
Therapist:	What do you experience next?
Client:	I go to the bathroom, throw up, and feel relief.
Therapist:	Then what?
Client:	I fall asleep.

Case Conceptualization Worksheets

Case Conceptualization Worksheets are presented for various disorders (see Appendix for blank worksheets). The worksheets were designed to provide therapists and clients with detailed information regarding problematic situations.

These worksheets are tailored to specific disorders that have a well-developed formulation in cognitive-behavioral theory. For example, in chapter 7 on obsessive-compulsive disorder, the Case Conceptualization Worksheet includes sections that describe intrusive cognitions, catastrophic misinterpretations of the intrusive cognitions, and overt and covert compulsions. The worksheet for panic disorder contains columns for internal and external triggering stimuli, benign physical symptoms and sensations, catastrophic misinterpretations of physical sensations, and disorder-maintaining behaviors.

Clients can use the worksheets as a self-monitoring tool for keeping track of and analyzing problematic events that occurred between sessions. Therapists should keep copies of clients' completed worksheets as well as record situations that arise during sessions.

The worksheets serve several functions. First, having Case Conceptualization Worksheets that are tailored to specific disorders reminds the therapist of the specific cognitive model for the relevant disorder. As therapists collect data for their clients' conceptualizations, the categories shown on the worksheets prompt therapists for relevant information.

Second, as a self-monitoring tool, the Case Conceptualization Worksheet helps clients become more cognizant of the subtleties of what they experience during problematic situations. It also helps them recognize the range of situations that elicit their problematic responses. Self-monitoring helps clients become more objective about their problems.

Third, a list of problematic situations and reactions often helps therapists and clients detect themes, such as core beliefs and behavioral strategies. For example, Jose described several social situations and his responses to them on worksheets. His automatic thoughts reflected his concern about what others thought of him (e.g., "I know I'm going to say something stupid," "They think I'm weird," "They'll laugh at me"). Based on this information, Jose's therapist hypothesized that Jose held core beliefs that he was socially undesirable and defective. Jose confirmed these hypotheses.

Besides providing useful information about his beliefs, Jose's behavior in the situations—which he described on the worksheets—reflected long-term, problematic behavioral strategies. Specifically, he attempted to escape the situations as quickly as possible. If he was unable to escape, he attempted to avoid social contact by averting his eyes or pretending to do something else (e.g., read a book). Finally, if he was forced to talk to another person, he avoided talking about himself by asking multiple questions about the other person.

(The Dysfunctional Thought Record and the Thought Evaluation Worksheet are effective therapeutic tools for modifying automatic thoughts. Reviewing either of these forms completed for a variety of situations helps therapists and clients detect patterns of thinking that cut across situations. These patterns of thinking often represent core beliefs. These tools are described in detail in chap. 5.)

Downward Arrows Technique

An invaluable method for uncovering core beliefs is the downward arrows technique (Beck et al., 1985; Burns, 1980). Beginning with an automatic thought, the therapist queries the client for the "meaning of that thought" or "the worst or most upsetting part of it, if it were true." Once the meaning of the thought is reported, the therapist asks the meaning of the second thought, and so on, until the client can go no further or until the client exhibits intense affect. Below is a brief transcript in which the therapist uses the downward arrows technique.

Therapist: What was going through your mind when you were meeting with your boss and feeling anxious and sad?

Client: I thought, "It's all over."

Therapist: What did you mean by that?

Client: He's going to know I'm anxious.

Therapist: Suppose that were the case, what would have been the worst part of it?

Client: He'll think I'm a "loser" and incompetent.

Therapist: What would it mean to you, if he thought you were an incompetent "loser?"

Client: He might give up on me.

Therapist: What would be the worst part of that?

Client: He might not give me more responsibility, or he may fire me.

Therapist: What would it mean to you if he fired you?

Client: I'm a failure (begins to cry).

Seemingly, the client has a hypervalent failure schema.

Behavioral Observations During Ongoing Therapy

As during the intake, behavioral observations during ongoing therapy can provide essential information about clients. Behavioral observations can provide information about the circumstances that activate a client's problematic responses, behavioral strategies, and social skills. In fact, as therapy progresses beyond the intake, the therapist has a larger sample of behaviors from which to draw conclusions. Over time, the therapist can see patterns (e.g., inconsiderateness) emerging across sessions that may hint at hypervalent core schemas (e.g., entitlement). Because clients frequently feel more comfortable and less guarded as time passes, they may disclose information that they were reluctant to share earlier in treatment.

Therapeutic Relationship

The therapeutic relationship provides special opportunities for behavioral observations. The relationship provides a valuable source of hypotheses concerning core beliefs, intermediate beliefs, and behavioral strategies.

In transference reactions, clients respond to an interpersonal situation, such as the therapeutic relationship, in an automatic manner that does not reflect the realities of the situation. Importantly, these responses in sessions are often representative of clients' responses to particular interpersonal triggers outside the therapy context. (Psychodynamic theorists dating back to Freud have argued that these responses frequently represent unresolved issues related to significant others, usually parental figures, from clients' childhoods.)

A transference reaction is illustrated by the case of Sam, a client who agreed with everything his therapist said and excessively asked her for advice. The therapist gently pointed this out to Sam and asked if there were other people with whom he responded similarly. Sam indicated that when he was around authority figures, he felt extremely uncomfortable, inadequate, and self-doubting. He attributed this response to how he was treated by his father and older brother, who was 5 years his senior. Sam's older brother frequently mocked him in front of other people including his father who laughed along with the older brother.

Conversely, a therapist's emotional response to a client can be an important source of information about the client (as well as about the therapist). Often, therapists become aware of an important therapeutic issue through their own emotional responses. When a therapist notices an emotional reaction in himself or herself, he or she should carefully observe the client's behavior for hints of why the therapist was affected. Frequently, therapists' reactions to their clients parallel the reactions of other people in the clients' life (Kiesler, 1979). However, the therapist has the difficult task of trying to understand the countertransference. How much of the therapist's response reflects the client's pathological tendency to elicit certain strong responses from most others he or she meets versus how much reflects the therapist's own unresolved issues? When in doubt, it is important for therapists to consult with trusted colleagues.

Intense Emotional Reactions

Therapists' observations of intense emotional reactions represent a special case of behavioral observations. When clients exhibit intense emotional responses not explicitly connected with the present situation (or the situation they are describing), they are usually experiencing strong schema activation (Young, 1990). Such situations are ideal for identifying core beliefs. This is because "hot" cognitions (i.e., activated schemas) tend to be readily accessible to awareness. At such times, therapists should use the standard *cognitive therapy probe,* "What's going through your mind right now?"

During a session, a therapist asked his client, Keisha, to write a list of implicit rules derived from her family of origin. After several minutes of working on the list, Keisha began sobbing and hid her face. When asked what she was feeling and what was going through her mind at that time, Keisha admitted to feeling deeply ashamed and thinking, "I'm pathetic." Patheticness was thus one of her core beliefs.

Another example of a schema being activated during a session occurs when a client experiences a panic attack during a relaxation induction. (This occurs in a small minority of clients suffering from anxiety disorders.) When this happens, the therapist might discover that the client has a history of being sexually assaulted and, during the assault, was told by the perpetrator to "just relax." For a client with this history, relaxing represented intense danger. Schema activation—besides providing ready access to belief content—provides an excellent opportunity for determining triggering events.

Other Approaches for Elucidating Information for Case Conceptualizations

Other approaches for developing a clearer understanding of clients and their problems deserve mention. First, methods for assessing the origins of core beliefs are described. Next, methods for developing hypotheses about two types of intermediate beliefs—major goals and implicit rules—are described. Then the discussion focuses on using previously obtained information to generate hypotheses and guide further interviewing.

Assessing the Origins of Core Beliefs

Knowledge of the origins of core beliefs is often important in developing a complete picture of the client and, later, in effectively modifying these beliefs. Therefore, therapists should ask clients how they think each core belief developed.

In addition, therapists should assess important events in their clients' personal and social histories that may have influenced their view of themselves, the world, and the future. Some of this information can be obtained from the Multimodal Life History Inventory. Information that is important for therapists to obtain about a client's childhood includes:

- the client's relationships with parents or caregivers;
- characteristics of parents (e.g., disposition, health and mental health status, employment status);

- relationships between the client's parents;
- significant separations from parents;
- the nature of the home environment;
- how the client was disciplined;
- the client's relationships with siblings;
- whether the client was abused, the nature of the abuse, the identity of the perpetrator, the time frame for the abuse;
- relationships with peers and friends;
- dating and relationship histories;
- academic performance and attainment;
- moves; and
- family rules.

Intermediate Belief Elucidation

Intermediate beliefs—conditional assumptions, implicit rules, and major goals—can be uncovered in a variety of ways. This section discusses elucidation of implicit rules and major goals, and the next section illustrates how knowing core beliefs can help the therapist assess for conditional assumptions.

When assessing for *major goals,* it can be helpful for therapists to consider a variety of possible goals. Ford (1992) suggested the following categories of goals:

- *self-assertive social relationship goals,* such as individuality, superiority, and resource acquisition;
- *subjective organization goals,* such as unity and transcendence;
- *affective goals,* such as entertainment, tranquility, happiness, bodily sensations, and physical well-being;
- *cognitive goals,* such as exploration, understanding, intellectual creativity, and positive self-evaluation;
- *integrative social relationship goals,* such as belongingness, social responsibility, equity, and resource provision; and
- *task goals,* such as mastery, task creativity, management, material gain, and safety.

To elucidate *implicit rules,* therapists should keep in mind that clients' anger or guilt often signifies that an implicit rule has been violated. Therefore, when clients experience these emotions, therapists should attempt to determine what rule they or others violated. Specifically, they should discover what the offending party *should* or *should not* have done differently in the triggering situation.

McKay and Fanning (1991) suggested another useful method for elucidating what they referred to as basic rules. They developed a checklist that probes for rules related to a variety of topics. The checklist is reproduced with permission in Box 4.3.

Dealing with other people's ...
  Anger
  Needs/desires/requests
  Disappointment/sadness
  Withdrawal
  Praise/support
  Criticism
	Trusting others
	
	Making friends
	  Whom to seek
	  How to act
	
	Finding a sexual partner
	  Whom to seek
	  How to act

Dealing with mistakes	
Dealing with stress/problems/ losses	Ongoing romantic relationships
Risk taking/trying new things/ challenges	Conversation

Expressing your ...
  Needs
  Feelings
  Opinions
  Pain
  Hopes/wishes/dreams
  Limits/saying no
	Sex
	
	Work/career
	
	Dealing with children
	
	Health/illness

Asking for support/help	Recreational activities

Being...
  Alone
  With strangers
  With friends
  With family
	Traveling
	
	Maintaining your environment/ self-care

Box 4.3. Implicit rule checklist. (From McKay & Fanning, 1991. Reproduced with permission of New Harbinger Productions, Oakland, CA 94605, www.newharbinger.com.)

Using Previously Obtained Information to Generate Hypotheses and Guide Further Interviewing

Clinical information relating to one element of the conceptualization often provides clues for other elements of the conceptualization. When a client has a conditional assumption (e.g., "If I can't get everyone to like me, I don't deserve to be happy"), therapists should evaluate whether the second clause represents a core belief (e.g., "I don't deserve to be happy").

Conversely, a therapist should assess under what conditions a client believes a core belief is true and untrue. This can help reveal conditional assumptions. Take for instance Andy, a client who had an "I am a weak person" core belief. When asked, Andy admitted that he felt most weak when he was anxious, sad, or needed help from others. His conditional assumption was "If I'm anxious, sad, or need help, I'm weak." On the other hand, Andy indicated that when he was feeling self-assured or was controlling other people, he felt strong.

Knowing both a core belief and a behavioral strategy can often suggest conditional assumptions. For example, a client is a "workaholic" and has the core belief that she is a failure. It is worth exploring whether she has a conditional assumption along the lines, "If I work extremely hard, I may not fail." Another client has a hypervalent unlovability schema and has a behavioral strategy of acting in a histrionic fashion. The therapist should examine whether these elements are connected. The client may have a conditional assumption that if she is sufficiently entertaining, people may love her.

Previously identified core beliefs or conditional assumptions can provide hypotheses about behavioral strategies. Behavioral strategies are attempts to positively influence conditions. When Andy's therapist asked him how he tried to prevent himself from feeling weak, Andy admitted that he "always tries to get the upper hand."

Finally, therapists should consider how clients' personal history might have influenced the development of core beliefs and behavioral strategies. For example, Ronny's mother deserted the family when Ronny was a toddler. Assessing the effects of this event on Ronny's life revealed that he had a hypervalent abandonment schema. In addition, he learned several strategies for protecting himself from being hurt by others.

Although therapists often can fruitfully use previously obtained information to hypothesize about clients' beliefs and strategies, therapists should use clients' feedback to corroborate these hypotheses.

Questionnaires for Tracking Progress in Therapy

Systematically tracking progress with reliable and valid instruments provides important feedback about how a client is progressing or failing to progress over the course of therapy. As a result, on an ongoing basis, therapists should give their clients questionnaires that focus on the specific symptoms or problems targeted during therapy. Over the course of therapy, if clients are improving, therapists should maintain the initial treatment approach. Alternatively, if clients are not improving, therapists should evaluate the factors that may be impeding process, consider modifying the case conceptualization, and modify interventions accordingly.

Whatever the clinical problem therapists are treating, they should familiarize themselves with the literature on reliable and valid assessment instruments before selecting appropriate questionnaires. Ideally, clinicians would have time to read original research articles that present the psychometric properties of questionnaires. However, when this is not possible, consulting a text that evaluates questionnaires can be helpful. For example, *Measures for Clinical Practice: A Sourcebook* (Fischer & Corcoran, 1994) is a useful resource. It provides psychometric information including internal consistency, test–retest reliability, sensitivity to change in psychotherapy, norms, and concurrent and discriminant validity. The text also gives instructions on scoring the questionnaires. In addition, it presents the actual questionnaires, many of which are not copyrighted. Chapters 6, 7, and 8 of this volume suggest relevant questionnaires for tracking panic attacks, agoraphobia, obsessive-compulsive disorder, and depression, as well as problems that relate to these disorders (e.g., phobias, perfectionism, unassertiveness).

Not only are the total scores of questionnaires helpful, but also knowing how an individual responds to particular items can be particularly useful. For example, a panic client, who was not improving in therapy, endorsed the following item on the Beck Depression Inventory, "I feel that I am being punished." When her therapist asked who was punishing her, she admitted that she believed that God was punishing her with panic attacks as a result of her past sins. In addition, she admitted to believing that she deserved punishment and that having panic attacks was a way that she could be purged of her sins. Addressing these beliefs directly and involving her pastor in the discussion resulted in dramatic progress in therapy.

5

Cognitive Therapy Interventions

1. Deactivating Maladaptive Cognitive, Affective, Motivational, and Behavioral Responses
   a. Dysfunctional Thought Record
   b. Thought Evaluation Worksheet
      i. Completing the Thought Evaluation Worksheet
         (1) The Front Side of the Thought Evaluation Worksheet: Describing the Triggering Situation, Automatic Thoughts, and Emotions
         (2) The Second Side of the Thought Evaluation Worksheet: Alternative Responses and Rerating the Thought and the Emotion
      ii. Tips on Teaching and Using Worksheets
   c. Coping Cards
   d. Externalization of Voices
   e. Problem Solving
      i. Problem Definition
      ii. Brainstorming
      iii. Evaluating Potential Solutions
      iv. Selecting the Best Solution(s)
      v. Implementing the Solution(s) and Evaluating the Outcome
   f. Refocusing Attention
   g. Self-Management
      i. Goals and Feedback
      ii. Stimulus Control
      iii. Incentives and Self-Rewards
   h. Relaxation Strategies
   i. Guided Imagery to Deactivate Maladaptive Responses
      i. Interrupting Unpleasant Moods
      ii. Decreasing Anxiety
   j. Activity Scheduling
2. Modifying Psychological Structures
   a. Fostering an Accepting Attitude
   b. Establishing Life Goals and Life Meaning
      i. The Importance of Life Meaning
      ii. Sources of Meaninglessness

- iii. Sources of Meaning
  - (1) Work
  - (2) Loving Relationships
  - (3) Unavoidable Suffering
- iv. Cognitive Therapy Can Foster a Sense of Meaning

c. Cost-Benefit Analysis of Beliefs
d. Historical Test for Modifying a Core Belief
e. Rewriting Implicit Rules
f. Guided Imagery for Modifying Psychological Structures
- i. Desensitizing Clients to Situations They Find Upsetting
- ii. Modifying Core Beliefs

g. Intentional Exposure to Avoided Emotions, Cognitions, and Situations
h. Designing Behavioral Experiments
i. Mindfulness Meditation
- i. Benefits of Mindfulness
- ii. Teaching Clients to Become Mindful

j. Social Skills Training

Cognitive case conceptualizations provide concise representations of clients' problems and therefore enable the therapist to select intervention points and effective interventions. This chapter presents an array of cognitive therapy interventions. These interventions are referred to in later chapters to illustrate how the interventions are applied to specific clinical problems based on case conceptualizations.

Here, interventions are characterized as belonging primarily to one of two categories. The first category involves methods for *deactivating* maladaptive cognitive, affective, motivational, and behavioral responses. The second category includes methods for *modifying* psychological structures.

DEACTIVATING MALADAPTIVE COGNITIVE, AFFECTIVE, MOTIVATIONAL, AND BEHAVIORAL RESPONSES

Clients usually seek therapy because they are having marked distress or functional impairment resulting from primal modes being activated in inappropriate circumstances (see chap. 2). Therefore, clients benefit from interventions that deactivate these modes. Ideally, however, these interventions do not just help clients respond more adaptively at the time of the intervention. Rather, the goal of therapy is for clients to learn these interventions as skills for independently and successfully coping with future difficulties. The specific interventions addressed in this section include: (a) the Dysfunctional Thought Record, (b) the Thought Evaluation Worksheet, (c) coping cards, (d) externalization of voices, (e) problem solving, (f) refocusing attention, (g) self-management, (h) relaxation strategies, (i) guided imagery, and (j) activity scheduling.

Dysfunctional Thought Record

Identifying, evaluating, and changing automatic thoughts are critical cognitive therapy skills that greatly benefit most clients. As a result, Beck, Rush, et al. (1979) developed the Dysfunctional Thought Record. It is an invaluable tool for teaching clients these critical skills. The Dysfunctional Thought Record has columns for objectively describing triggering situations and associated automatic thoughts and emotions. It also has a column for generating alternative, self-enhancing responses.

Because Beck et al. described the Dysfunctional Thought Record elsewhere, it is not duplicated. (The interested reader should see Beck, Rush, et al., 1979; Sacco & Beck, 1995.) Instead, the Thought Evaluation Worksheet is presented. The Thought Evaluation Worksheet is a variation on the Dysfunctional Thought Record that is helpful for clients who like a highly structured format.

Thought Evaluation Worksheet

Like the Dysfunctional Thought Record, the Thought Evaluation Worksheet is a tool for teaching clients to: (a) detect self-defeating automatic thoughts, (b) identify cognitive distortions, (c) become more objective about triggering situations, and (d) change their self-defeating thoughts, emotions, impulses or inhibitions, and behaviors. After much practice with the worksheet, many clients find that the evaluation process itself becomes automatic. Whenever they begin to experience hints of unpleasant emotions, they can quickly think through the situation (often without writing it out) and dissipate the feelings. In addition, some clients report that as a result of diligent use of the worksheet process, the ratio of pleasant, self-enhancing automatic thoughts to unpleasant, self-defeating automatic thoughts increases.[8] (The Appendix provides a blank Thought Evaluation Worksheet.)

Completing the Thought Evaluation Worksheet

To demonstrate how to complete the Thought Evaluation Worksheet, each section of the worksheet is described and an example of a completed worksheet is presented in Fig. 5.1. The worksheet was completed by Michelle, a 25-year-old woman who presented for anger and difficulty keeping a job and who was diagnosed with passive-aggressive personality disorder.

The first side of the worksheet guides the client in accurately recording the triggering situation, automatic thoughts, and emotions. The second side of the worksheet provides steps for evaluating and modifying the automatic thought that the client selected.

[8]The mechanism by which the ratio changes is unclear. On the one hand, it might result from deactivating the maladaptively activated schema and activating adaptive schemas with no change in the cognitive structures. On the other hand, it may be the result of schema modification.

THOUGHT EVALUATION WORKSHEET (side 1)

Name: Michelle
Date: November 23
Time: 1:15p

TRIGGERING SITUATION (objective description of environment or events; who, what where, when, how, but not why)

Boss asked me to a do a project that I thought would be boring and tedious.

EMOTIONS (Rate intensity of each, 0-100)

Anger 85%

AUTOMATIC THOUGHTS: What is/was going through my mind when I felt that emotion?

Please make sure there are thoughts or images corresponding to each emotion. Also, be sure there are emotions that correspond to each thought.

Are there Automatic Thoughts that account for the intensity of the emotions? If not, search for and record other Automatic Thoughts that may be present and causing the emotion. Rate how much you believe each thought is true (0-100%).

I shouldn't have to do this g -- @x#!!!
The S.O.B. gives me all the crummy jobs and gives everyone else more interesting ones (99%).
He sits on his duff all day making small talk while I do all the work.
If I were male, I would have his job, and he would be working for me.
I'm going to do a slow and sloppy job to serve him right!

Select one key Automatic Thought above that you want to work on. Select the above Emotion that corresponds to the key Automatic Thought. Write these on the reverse side of the page and use the questions for evaluating the automatic thought.

FIG. 5.1. Example of a completed Thought Evaluation Worksheet.

THOUGHT EVALUATION WORKSHEET (side 2)

AUTOMATIC THOUGHT: The S.O.B. gives me all the crummy jobs and gives everyone else more interesting ones. 99%
EMOTION: Anger 85%

1. **Is this a thought that I can DISREGARD without further consideration (e.g., is it absurd or is it one I've already worked through effectively)?** No.

2. **Circle any DISTORTIONS that apply to the key thought:**
   All-or-Nothing; Over-Generalization; Mental Filter; Discounting Positives; Mind-Reading; Fortune-Telling; Emotional Reasoning; Magnification/Minimization; "Should's"; Labeling; Personalization

3. **What's the EVIDENCE FOR the Automatic Thought?**
   He gave me these projects: A (tedious) B (tedious).
   He gave Sally C (interesting).

   What's the EVIDENCE AGAINST the Automatic Thought?
   He gave me D & E (fairly interesting projects).
   He gave Sally F (tedious) & G (neutral).

4. **What are ALTERNATIVE PERSPECTIVES of the situation?**
   Sally has been here 2 years longer than me and has a good track record here. I have more expertise with the graphics programs and that's why John gives me these projects. It's not that he's trying to give me boring projects. Plus, he might not think they are boring projects--boredom is very subjective.

   What would I tell a FRIEND if s/he were having the thought in the situation?
   Hang in there and do a good job. Then he may start giving you more interesting projects.

5. **What's the WORST that could happen given the situation?**
He'd keep giving me the jobs I find boring.

Could I live through it? Yes
What's the likelihood that this will happen (0-100%): 40%
What would happen over time?
I'd probably look for and find a job that I found more interesting.

What's the BEST that could happen given the situation?
From now on, he'll give me all interesting projects.

What's MOST LIKELY to happen given the situation?
Over time, he'll give me more interesting projects.

6. **What are the ADVANTAGES, if any, of having the Automatic Thought?**
None.

What are the DISADVANTAGES of having the Automatic Thought?
Makes me angry and makes me want to do a bad job which will hurt me in the end.

7. **What constructive PLANS can I make given the situation?**
Do the best job I can. If he doesn't start giving me more interesting jobs, talk to him about it. If he still doesn't, start looking for a new job.

8. **After re-reading answers to questions 1-7, please CIRCLE numbers of the above questions that were most convincing.** #4, 5, 6, 7
RE-RATE Belief in key Automatic Thought (0-100): 50
RE-RATE Key Emotion (0-100): 20

FIG. 5.1. *cont'd*

The Front Side of the Thought Evaluation Worksheet: Describing the Triggering Situation, Automatic Thoughts, and Emotions. After recording on the top of the form the date and time at which the problematic situation occurred, clients should objectively describe and record the *triggering situation.* When recounting the situation, clients describe "who," "what," "where," and "how" (but not "why") without judgment or assumptions. For some, it helps to think of the situation as if the client were an observer with no vested interest in it. Alternatively, the client may think of the situation as if she or he were an anthropologist from another culture describing an unfamiliar phenomenon. In the example of Michelle, the triggering situation was that her boss asked her to work on a project that Michelle perceived as boring and tedious.

Next, clients should record their *emotions* on the worksheet. The reason it is helpful to record emotions before automatic thoughts is that people are typically aware of changes in how they are feeling before they recognize their automatic thoughts. Indeed, the appearance or intensification of an emotion is often the signal that makes clients aware that they are having an automatic thought that may require evaluation.

In the emotions section, clients are instructed to record all of the emotions they are experiencing in response to the triggering situation. It is important for clients to spend sufficient time detecting all of their emotions. This is because emotions can provide clients with clues for detecting the key automatic thoughts they are having. Next, clients rate the intensity of each emotion from 0 to 100, where 100 represents the *strongest they have ever felt that emotion,* 0 represents *none of that emotion at all,* and 50 represents *moderate intensity of the emotion.* The purpose of rating the initial intensity of the emotion is that the rating serves as a basis for later comparison. At the end of the worksheet process, clients rerate the emotion (and the level of their belief in the targeted automatic thought) to determine whether the process was effective in decreasing their distress (and changing their thinking). In the demonstration worksheet, Michelle felt extreme anger, which she rated at an intensity level of 85%.

In the next section, clients record the *automatic thoughts* they are having in the situation. Box 5.1 illustrates helpful probes for identifying automatic thoughts.

- What is going through my mind right now in this situation?
- What does this situation mean to me or to my life?
- What is most upsetting about this situation?
- What thoughts or images make me feel _______ (sad, anxious, angry, etc.) in this situation?

Box 5.1. Cognitive probes.

After considering these questions, if clients continue to have difficulty recognizing their automatic thoughts, it often is fruitful for them to "free associate" about the situation—that is, say anything that comes to mind without censoring, no matter how embarrassing or improbable. After clients generate many associations, they often recognize one or two as important automatic thoughts relevant to the situation.

When generating automatic thoughts, clients are instructed to make certain that for each emotion there is a corresponding thought or image. Conversely, clients should make certain that for every thought there is a corresponding emotion. It is very important to identify all of the cognitions and emotions in the triggering situation. If clients miss some, they are less likely to benefit from the worksheet.

Automatic thoughts frequently are in forms that are difficult to evaluate. Therefore, clients often benefit from learning how to record automatic thoughts in a form that facilitates evaluation. For example, if the automatic thoughts take the form of a question, the question should be transformed into a statement because questions cannot be evaluated but statements can. The thought "Does she think I'm a buffoon?" becomes "She thinks I'm a buffoon." If automatic thoughts are cryptic, they need to be elaborated and clarified to be analyzed. For example, a depressed adolescent who looked in the mirror thought, "Same thing every day!" by which he meant, "I'm always ugly." The former would have been difficult to evaluate productively whereas the latter was conducive to productive evaluation.

After thoroughly generating automatic thoughts for a triggering situation, clients then pick a single automatic thought that they think is most upsetting and circle it. (In the sample Thought Evaluation Worksheet, the selected automatic thought is in bold typeface.) It is important to pick a single automatic thought because it often is difficult to respond to more than one upsetting thought simultaneously. Next, clients rate how much they believe the automatic thought is true from 0% to 100%. As with rating the intensity of emotions, rating the degree of belief in an automatic thought serves as a basis for comparison when the Thought Evaluation Worksheet is completed. Similarly, clients should circle the emotion with which the automatic thought was associated.

Michelle experienced a variety of automatic thoughts in the triggering situation. The one that she found most upsetting was "The S.O.B. gives me all the crummy jobs and gives everyone else more interesting ones," which she believed was 99% true.

The Second Side of the Thought Evaluation Worksheet: Alternative Responses and Rerating the Thought and the Emotion. At the top of the second side of the worksheet, clients should recopy the selected automatic thought and corresponding emotion.

Figure 5.1 illustrates the *alternative responses* that Michelle generated with her therapist's help. The first evaluation question is, *Is this a thought that I can disregard without further consideration?* Often, clients ruminate about highly unlikely, even absurd, negative topics. For clients who ruminate, carefully evaluating the same thought repeatedly, even within the Thought Evaluation Worksheet structure, can be counterproductive. As a result, the first question of the worksheet can help these individuals interrupt the rumination process. This was the case for a client who had the thought that "If I make a minor mistake, I will be fired," despite knowing that this was extremely improbable. He was a valued employee and had excellent relationships with his boss and coworkers. Reminding himself that his expectation was farfetched helped him reduce his anxiety.

Similarly, clients who successfully worked through a self-defeating thought in the past and therefore do not need to rethink it can benefit from this worksheet question. In either of these circumstances, it is helpful for clients to simply remind themselves that they have already thought this through completely or that the thought is not worthy of consideration. Then they should attempt to refocus their attention on something that is more productive or enjoyable. Such an approach can help clients see a healthier perspective without going through an extensive evaluation process. (On the other hand, as shown later, sometimes it is helpful for clients to read over completed worksheets several times to help the healthy perspective "sink in.")

If clients decide it would be helpful to proceed with evaluating their thought, they should respond to the remainder of the questions on the worksheet. When considering these questions, it is important for clients to remember that alternative responses must be reasonable ways of looking at a situation to help them change their thinking or help them select a useful action plan. The alternative responses only improve clients' mood or lead to constructive actions if they are supported by convincing evidence—not Pollyannaish affirmations or the "power of positive thinking."

The next question on the worksheet asks clients to determine whether their automatic thought is distorted and, if so, record the type of *distortion.* Beck, Rush, et al. (1979) and Burns (1989) developed typologies of cognitive distortions that people often make. For example, Burns (1989) described 10 forms of distortions: all-or-nothing thinking, overgeneralization, mental filter, magnification/minimization, jumping to conclusions, labeling, personalization and blame, should/must statements, discounting the positives, and emotional reasoning. It frequently helps to refer clients to the list of distortions in Burns (1989) and encourage them to learn to identify and categorize their own distortions. Clients generally find it helpful to have a system for identifying distorted thinking that enables them to become more objective.

Often clients find it useful to create additional distortion categories that describe their own idiosyncratic patterns of thinking. When clients who procrastinate tell themselves, "I don't feel like doing it (task they are avoiding)," "I'll do it later," or "I'll just spend 10 more minutes on the (Inter)net," they can remind themselves they are engaging in procrastination thinking.

For some clients who experience much interpersonal conflict and difficulty with empathy when they are in the midst of an argument, they can benefit from asking themselves, "Am I engaging in self-centered thinking?" Clients who ruminate can benefit from labeling their process of thinking as ruminating. Then they can remind themselves to shift their attention away from these unproductive thoughts or distract themselves with something else. Michelle was able to recognize that the automatic thought she was evaluating was distorted. Specifically, she identified the thought as falling in the categories of overgeneralization, personalization, and labeling.

The next questions on the worksheet ask the client to examine the *evidence for and against the automatic thought*. Examining the evidence for automatic thoughts is a fundamental cognitive therapy skill. The evidence clients consider to support their automatic thought is often weak and is fraught with distortions. It is important that the evidence both for and against the automatic thought be solid. It often helps clients to ask themselves, "Would this evidence stand up in a court of law?" In addition, clients can be encouraged to act the part of the prosecuting attorney and then the defense attorney to generate solid evidence for and against the thought. If the therapist is present, he or she can play the part of the judge who, when necessary, rules that evidence is hearsay or inadmissible. In the demonstration worksheet, the evidence Michelle gave for and against the automatic thought were specific tasks that her boss asked of her and her coworker, Sally.

Often situations can be construed in many different ways, each of which fits the evidence. Therefore, considering *alternative perspectives* for the situation is extremely important in helping clients feel better and/or act more constructively in problematic situations. Therefore, this represents the next question on the worksheet. Often people stop evaluating a situation as soon as they have an explanatory automatic thought. In addition, the explanation they generate is often schema driven. For example, a person with an activated mistrust schema frequently construes situations as threatening and other people's intentions as malicious despite inadequate evidence to support these conclusions.

Generating alternative perspectives is akin to brainstorming, generating as many alternative explanations as possible without rejecting or judging the solutions. Next, the client evaluates the evidence for each, decides which explanation is most self-enhancing and functional, and uses that explanation as a working hypothesis that can be changed later if compelling evidence to the contrary arises. In the demonstration worksheet, Michelle was able to generate the alternative view that her boss may have made project assignments based on her and her coworkers' differing levels of experience and skills. In addition, she was able to consider that perhaps her boss did not realize that she found the projects that she had been assigned boring.

The use of humor can sometimes help clients provide useful alternate perspectives. Humor can (a) provide new views of triggering situations; (b) provide objectivity, including helping clients realize that they are taking themselves too seriously; (c) improve therapeutic rapport; (d) quickly dissipate unpleasant affect such as anxiety, anger, shame, or sadness; and (e) elicit pleasant affect (Beck, Rush, et al., 1979; Beck et al., 1985; Ellis & Dryden, 1987; Nathanson, 1992; Persons, 1989). Albert Ellis suggested numerous ways of helping clients learn to see the humor in their situation (e.g., Ellis, 1977a, 1977b, 1981).

However, a word of caution is indicated regarding the use of humor. Although humor is healthy, close relatives of humor—such as sarcasm and ridicule—are shaming and damaging (Beck, Rush, et al., 1979). When therapists use humor, they should look carefully for clients' reactions and ask them for feedback to be sure that they are taking the joke in the helpful manner that it was intended. In addition, therapists should not use humor if they cannot comfortably, spontaneously, and good-naturedly do so.

A question that often helps clients generate useful alternative responses is, *What would you tell a friend if he or she were in the situation and having the same thoughts and feelings?* People are typically more objective about other people's situations than their own. As a result, they tend to give more helpful advice to friends than to themselves in difficult situations. Therefore, considering what they would tell a friend can help them step outside their situation and become more objective. Variations on this question that are helpful for some clients are, *What would ______ (respected other) tell you to do in this situation if they knew what you were thinking and how you were feeling?* or *How would _____ (respected other) respond to this situation if he or she were in it?* For individuals who routinely engage in harsh self-criticism but are loving parents, it is often useful for them to consider the following question: *What would you say to _____ (loved child) if he or she were in a comparable situation and having the same thoughts and feelings?* In the demonstration worksheet, considering what she would tell a friend helped Michelle generate encouraging and useful self-statements such as "Hang in there and do a good job; then he [her boss] may start giving you more interesting projects."

When people are distraught, they frequently believe "in the back of their minds" that the outcome of the situation will be catastrophic. These thoughts are often extremely unrealistic given the situation. In addition, when people think catastrophically, they often stop the thoughts or images at the worst moment, rather than continuing until they see some livable resolution. Therefore, it often helps for clients to make their negative expectations explicit. As a result the next worksheet question for evaluating automatic thoughts asks, *What's the worst that can happen?* Making negative expectations explicit can help clients see how unrealistic their expectations are. Alternatively, they can see that even if the worst case scenario occurs, they would survive it. In addition, over time the negative event would not interfere with their ability to have a meaningful, fulfilling life. Michelle decided that the worst case scenario was that her boss would continue to give her boring jobs. Although she thought that this scenario was fairly unlikely, she realized that if it did happen, it would not be terrible. She would look for another job, would probably find one, and the new job might be more interesting than the old one.

The worksheet also has clients consider, *What's the best that can happen given the situation?* Besides explicitly considering the worst case scenario, it often helps to think about the best case and the most realistic case scenarios. Considering the best case allows the client to consider positive outcomes and can help break the client out of a pessimistic cognitive set. Michelle thought that the best that could happen in the situation was that her boss would give her interesting projects immediately. Another best case that she considered was that she would become extremely happy regardless of the tasks he gave her. She indicated that the *most realistic outcome* was that after she had more experience, her boss would give her interesting tasks more frequently.

Other helpful questions included on the worksheet address the *advantages and disadvantages of the automatic thought in the situation.* When asked for advantages and disadvantages, clients frequently realize that there are no advantages and many disadvantages to their automatic thought. Disadvantages often include that they become upset or they act in ways that are contrary to their ultimate goals. If this is so, realizing that there are only disadvantages can help clients let go of the automatic thought. In the demonstration worksheet, Michelle saw no advantages to her automatic thought.

However, sometimes upsetting automatic thoughts do have advantages. For example, Jorge, a college student with an obsessive-compulsive personality disorder, had the belief, "I must do everything perfectly." He reported that advantages of this belief for him were that when he completed a task, the quality was excellent. However, the disadvantages were that he failed to complete many assignments and experienced much unnecessary worry. When clients view automatic thoughts as conveying some advantages despite strong disadvantages, it is often helpful to determine whether there are healthier ways to think about the situation that confers the same advantages. Jorge decided that the following perspective was likely to be optimally functional for him: "Within my time constraints, on important tasks, I'm going to try to do an excellent job; for moderately important tasks, I'll strive to do a good but not great job; and for unimportant tasks, I'll just do a good enough job."

The next useful question for generating alternative responses is, *What constructive plans can I make given the situation?* This question may help clients access helpful problem-solving skills. Often, emotions provide important signals suggesting that action (or inaction) is needed to respond to and change a problematic situation. (Of course, in therapy, therapists often see emotions conveying misinformation that misleads clients; for example, panic attacks are false alarms that signal "danger.") Take for example, Murray, a young man who was extremely anxious about being the victim of a violent crime; he in fact lived in a neighborhood in which violent crimes were common. For Murray, anxiety provided a useful signal that resulted in his changing residences (which he fortunately could afford to do).[9] Examples of other potentially useful actions include preparing for an upcoming performance, engaging in activities that are enjoyable, engaging in assertive behavior, or selecting a different, healthier situation. Sometimes unpleasant situations are unchangeable. Fighting an unpleasant, unchangeable situation results in increased distress and is therefore counterproductive. As a result, in such situations, the most constructive plan is to work on accepting the situation and keeping in mind the perspectives generated from the worksheet.

Michelle decided that a promising plan involved performing her job to the best of her ability and talking to her boss about her concerns. She also planned to look for other employment if he did not start giving her more interesting jobs within a reasonable time frame.

The next statement on the worksheet asks clients to reread answers to questions 1–7 and circle the numbers corresponding to the answers that they found most compelling. It also asks clients to rerate their belief in the targeted automatic thought and rerate the intensity of the corresponding emotion, both rated on scales from 0 to 100. If the intensity of the emotion and the belief in the automatic thought decrease substantially after going through the worksheet, it suggests that the worksheet was used successfully. Michelle's level of anger decreased dramatically from 85% to 20% and her belief in the automatic thought decreased from 99% to 50%.

If belief in the automatic thought decreases substantially but the intensity of the emotion remains unchanged, it suggests that one or more additional automatic thoughts are probably more important in generating this emotion. As a result, it may be helpful to select another automatic thought to work on. If neither the belief in the automatic thought nor the intensity of the emotion changed significantly, it suggests that the alternative responses generated in the worksheet were unconvincing to the client. In such cases, it often is helpful for therapists to review the worksheet with clients to help them generate more helpful responses. Finally, it is possible that the client was viewing the situation realistically and his or her level of upset was appropriate to the situation and not amenable to change with a worksheet.

Tips on Teaching and Using Worksheets

Initially, when therapists teach clients to use Thought Evaluation Worksheets, therapists should help clients select an upsetting situation. A

---

[9]In this case, Murray's decision to escape the situation appeared to be sensible. Obviously, in other cases, clients' tendencies to avoid or escape unpleasant situations represent self-defeating strategies that maintain their problems.

therapist should make this decision based on an assessment that a particular thought of the client's has good potential for change and is a repetitive or representative situation. Selecting such situations for worksheets increases the likelihood that clients will have an early success experience with the worksheets and that they will immediately experience a positive impact.

Clients often benefit from learning to use the Thought Evaluation Worksheet as a two-stage process. The first stage involves clients learning to use the first side of the worksheet—that is, the sections for identifying the triggering situation, automatic thought, and emotions. The goal of this stage is to help clients get in the habit of viewing situations objectively and recording the situations and their automatic thoughts and emotions. Clients generally benefit from doing this for 1 or 2 weeks and recording 10–15 situations with their associated automatic thoughts and emotions.

After clients have become proficient at using the first side of the worksheet, they proceed to the second stage—learning to generate and record alternative responses. Clients benefit from memorizing the capitalized words on the worksheet questions for easy cognitive access. After generating alternative responses on a worksheet, it is often helpful for clients to use a highlight marker to accent the cognitive responses that were most helpful in making them feel better or giving them direction in how to address the situation. The more clients practice using the worksheet, the more effectively they are able to use the process when they are in potentially problematic situations.

Clients tend to benefit significantly from using Thought Evaluation Worksheets for recurrent problematic situations. When clients use worksheets in these situations, they often do not have to repeat the process of writing out answers to their automatic thoughts when situations subsequently arise. Rather, they can read over the relevant completed worksheet. In addition, they can carry completed worksheets with them in their pocket or purse to provide them with easy access to helpful responses when faced with a recurrent problematic situation.

Coping Cards

Rather than reviewing an entire worksheet, clients frequently benefit from selecting a few of the most helpful alternative responses and copying them onto an index card. These index cards are often referred to as *coping cards.* Coping cards can provide clients with self-statements that remind them about healthy ways to view a particular difficult situation and useful strategies or self-instructions for dealing with the situation. Therefore, coping cards can deactivate inappropriately activated schemas or modes and activate more appropriate ones.

For example, Jerry was a graduate student with a public speaking phobia. He was afraid of "going blank" when giving a presentation in class. His coping card included reassuring self-statements, such as "I know this material well," "Even if I look a little nervous, this is a good talk, and I can convey some useful information; even if I go blank, I have an outline and can refer to it—that's what it's there for," "Often, I'm nervous at the beginning but quickly I forget about my nervousness and do fine," "I've given lots of good presentations in the past," "Even if it goes badly, it's not the end of the world," "I can still get a good grade in the class," "I know most of my classmates would still respect me," "The professor knows my work and has seen examples of my thinking in papers I've written," and "It won't matter how the talk goes, in a month from now." The coping card also reminded him to take slow breaths and, that if all else fails, to make a joke about being nervous (a technique that had worked well for him in the past).

As shown in chapter 6, coping cards can be particularly helpful for clients suffering from panic disorder. This is because during a panic attack, individuals typically have great difficulty remembering reasonable, benign explanations for the physical sensations they are experiencing.

Externalization of Voices

When learning to dispute dysfunctional automatic thoughts, many clients benefit from externalization of voices, that is, vocalizing their automatic thoughts and having the therapist provide strong alternative responses that challenge these automatic thoughts (Freeman & Reinecke, 1993). After the therapist has modeled effective responding, the therapist and client change roles. The therapist expresses the dysfunctional automatic thoughts and the client voices healthy alternative responses. The therapist provides feedback and assistance with responses if the client has difficulty.

The *cognitive-emotional role play* is a specific type of externalization of voices that is helpful for clients who report that "rationally" they recognize that a particular view is self-defeating and distorted, but "emotionally" it seems true. In the cognitive-emotional role play, the therapist plays the self-defeating and distorted side and the client forcefully provides cogent responses. This often helps the client believe self-enhancing, undistorted beliefs more fully.

Problem Solving

The ability to solve complicated problems is important for navigating through life. Clients often have difficulty solving problems either because they feel overwhelmed or depressed or because they lack the necessary problem-solving skills. For clients who are feeling overwhelmed or depressed, often techniques for improving their mood or lessening their anxiety can help them access their own problem-solving skills.

If clients lack problem solving skills, an important task in therapy is for them to learn the skills. Problem solving consists of the following steps: (a) defining the problem, (b) brainstorming to generate potential solutions, (c) evaluating potential solutions, (d) selecting a solution, (e) implementing the selected solution, (f) evaluating the outcome, and (g) if the outcome is nonoptimal, repeating steps b–f (D'Zurilla, 1988; Layden et al., 1993).

Problem Definition

The first step in problem solving is defining the problem clearly and specifically. For example, Betty, a 35-year-old, married, professional woman with two young children, formulated her problem as follows:

> After coming home from a long day in the office each day, I have five or six hours of childcare and household responsibilities. I'm exhausted, feel burned out, and am very angry at my husband, John, who provides little help. In brief, my problem is too much work, too little help, and not enough time for R&R.

Brainstorming

The second stage in problem solving is generating possible solutions through brainstorming. When brainstorming, it is important to produce as many potential solutions as possible, intentionally including some extreme or outlandish ones (e.g., Hawton & Kirk, 1989). Including extreme options encourages people to be open minded and nonjudgmental, qualities that encourage generating numerous and creative solutions. Therapists can help by suggesting farfetched solutions and encouraging clients to do the same to decrease censoring.

Betty and her therapist generated the following potential solutions:

1. Go on strike—do no more housework or childcare responsibilities in order to coerce John into becoming involved.
2. Quit my job at the brokerage.
3. Run away—abandon the family, move to Alcapulco.
4. Take care of the kids but do no more housework and accept the dust, dirt, and clutter.
5. Do all the housework and leave the kids entirely to John.
6. Beg, coerce, demand that John helps more.
7. Feign a nervous breakdown.
8. Relax my standards for housework somewhat.
9. Give John an ultimatum—"You do your equal share, or I'll divorce you."
10. Hire an *au pair* to do all of the housework and childcare responsibilities.
11. Hire someone to do some of the housework (e.g., one time every 2 weeks).
12. Hire a babysitter once or twice per week.

Evaluating Potential Solutions

The third stage of problem solving is evaluating each potential solution.

Often potential solutions are clearly not viable and can be immediately discarded without further consideration. Other solutions require careful consideration. Often it is helpful for clients to consider, and even list, advantages and disadvantages for potential solutions. Therapists can help a client learn to evaluate solutions by providing the individual with feedback regarding whether a particular advantage or disadvantage that the client generated was realistic and nondistorted.

Betty immediately eliminated solutions 1–4 and 7 as not being viable. Regarding the other potential solutions, she realized that attempting to persuade or coerce John to help more would not likely be effective. Neither of these strategies had worked before, and they resulted in unpleasant consequences. She decided against divorcing him because she loved him, and she felt some empathy for him. He was depressed, his motivation for activities outside household responsibilities was also low, and therefore she believed he was not maliciously "loafing." Because she felt uncomfortable with having someone live in their home, she eliminated the *au pair* idea.

Selecting the Best Solution(s)

The fourth stage is selecting the best solution or combination of solutions. Betty selected: relaxing her standards, getting someone to babysit one day per week, and hiring a cleaning service to clean twice per month. Hawton and Kirk (1989) suggested that once a solution is selected, it is often helpful for clients to rehearse the solution in guided imagery. This can help clients and therapists discover and avoid potential obstacles to executing the solution. Similarly, it is sometimes necessary to teach clients skills for successfully implementing the best solution. For example, sometimes clients benefit from learning assertiveness skills to implement a solution to a problem related to other people.

Betty had the necessary skills for finding babysitters and cleaning services. In therapy, she and her therapist discussed her housework standards, which were rather perfectionistic. As a result, she was able to modify them resulting in a decrease in her workload.

Implementing the Solution(s) and Evaluating the Outcome

The two final steps in problem solving are implementing the solution(s) and evaluating the outcome. If implementation of the solution results in an undesirable outcome, the therapist guides the client in selecting another solution based on the previous problem-solving steps. The outcome for Betty was that hiring a babysitter and a cleaning service and relaxing her housework standards freed up approximately 20 hours per week for her. As a result, she felt better rested, happier, and less angry with her husband. Over time, John's depression began to lift and their relationship began to improve. In addition, he began participating more in household responsibilities further freeing up time for Betty—although the division of labor continued to be far from even.

Refocusing Attention

As described in chapter 2, individuals with psychological problems often maladaptively deploy their attention. One form of this is rumination or dwelling on negative cognitions, emotions, or situations. It is well known that individuals suffering from emotional disorders—including depression, obsessive-compulsive disorder, social phobia, panic disorder, generalized anxiety disorder, somatoform disorders, and sexual dysfunction—often engage in self-focused rumination. (These same individuals also may engage in cognitive, emotional, or behavioral avoidance. Therefore, exposure interventions for treating avoidance are discussed). Depending on the disorder, negative self-focused attention centers on themselves, their problems, their symptoms, their performance, or anticipated negative consequences of their behavior. Moreover, rumination appears to worsen and prolong emotional problems, whereas refocusing attention tends to lessen it (Beck et al., 1992; Blagden & Craske, 1996; Frankl, 1959/1984; Kaplan, 1989; Masters & Johnson, 1988; Morrow & Nolen-Hoeksema, 1990; Nolen-Hoeksema, 1987, 1991; Nolen-Hoeksema & Morrow, 1991, 1993; Nolen-Hoeksema, Morrow, & Fredrickson, 1993; Nolen-Hoekseman, Parker, & Larson, 1994; Salkovskis & Campbell, 1994; Wincze, & Carey, 1991).

It is often therapeutic for psychotherapy clients to refocus their attention on pleasant or fulfilling thoughts or activities to interrupt pathological self-focused attention (Beck, Rush, et al., 1979; Beck et al., 1985; Beck et al., 1992; Frankl, 1959; Freeman & Reinecke, 1993; Gupta, Banerjee, & Nandi, 1989; McCabe, 1992). Depending on the clients' problems, therapists can teach them one of several refocusing techniques. For example, depressed clients often benefit from focusing their attention on activities that are potentially pleasant or that could potentially elicit positive self-efficacy beliefs (see Activity Scheduling section below). For clients with anxiety disorders or physical pain, mindfully focusing attention on their breathing or other bodily sensations has been shown to result in symptom reduction (see Mindfulness Meditation section). Clients with panic disorder benefit from focusing their attention on the mechanics of a task they are performing. (Chapter 6 describes at length refocusing procedures that are helpful with panic clients.) Although not the preferred approach, as a last resort, they can focus on complex puzzles or other tasks that demand much cognitive capacity and interrupt their panic attack (see Panic Disorder with Agoraphobia chapter).

Self-Management

Any skill learned in therapy or any behavioral or cognitive strategy a person attempts to use can be considered self-management. However, three forms of self-management interventions merit explicit mention. These are goals and feedback, stimulus control, and incentives and self-rewards.

When successful, each of these types of interventions activates individuals' motivation.

Goals and Feedback

Goals and feedback are well-established facilitators of performance (e.g., Bandura & Cervone, 1983). Clients benefit from setting goals for themselves and monitoring their performance and progress toward their goals. Goals are most effective when they are specific and challenging but realistic. In addition, breaking down goals into subgoals improves motivation and performance (e.g., Ford, 1992). Clients and therapists should collaboratively develop therapy goals. However, clients benefit also from learning the process of making goals for themselves, which they can use for the rest of their lives.

Stimulus Control

Presumably through classical conditioning, stimuli begin to increase the frequency of particular self-defeating responses, such as overeating, using tobacco products, using recreational drugs, or misusing alcohol. Stimulus control procedures involve clients learning to set up their environments in such a way to elicit their desired responses. Researchers have used stimulus control procedures in the treatment of a variety of habit disorders or addictive behaviors (e.g., Azrin, McMahon, Donohue, Besalel, 1994; Becona & Garcia, 1995; French, Jeffery, & Wing, 1994).

Stimulus control has also been shown to be effective in the treatment of primary insomnia (e.g., Morin, Culbert, & Schwartz, 1994). The general approach is described here. The mechanism by which stimulus control presumably helps individuals with insomnia is that it helps them learn to associate their beds and bedtime with sleep and relaxation, as opposed to worrying and alertness (Lacks, 1987). When therapists use stimulus control procedures in the treatment of insomnia, they instruct clients to engage in the following stimulus control procedures (presented here in the format that therapists could use with clients):

1. Stop consuming caffeine at least 5 hours before bedtime.
2. Develop and follow a new bedtime ritual—an invariable sequence of behaviors that you do before going to sleep. If you already have a bedtime ritual, you should develop and follow a new one because the old one is associated with not sleeping.
3. Do not read, watch TV, or do anything else in bed besides sleep (and have sex). This is especially important if you associate doing these activities in bed with having trouble falling asleep.
4. If you do not fall asleep within about 10 minutes of getting in bed, you should get out of bed. (But, you should not watch the clock because doing so is likely to keep you awake.) Instead, you should go

into another room and do something relaxing. When you feel relaxed and sleepy, you should return to bed.
5. Again, if you do not fall asleep within approximately 10 minutes, you should get out of bed and relax in another room.
6. You should always go to sleep at the same time and get out of bed in the morning at the same time. This should be done even on weekends.

Incentives and Self-Rewards

Incentives and self-rewards represent other effective, self-management strategies. Incentives are the promise of rewards for engaging in desired behavior. Self-rewards are objects, activities, or self-statements that clients find enjoyable and that have a history of increasing their targeted behavior. The easiest form of self-reward to administer is self-praise, giving oneself a "pat on the back" for a job well done or for effort toward a goal. The following are some examples of how self-reward can be used. Samantha was a client who was having difficulty motivating herself to write a term paper. She used going to the movies on the subsequent Saturday night as an incentive for working diligently on the paper. As an intermediate reward, contingent on working hard on her project for at least 3 hours on a given day, she allowed herself to watch a half-hour TV show per night. In addition, she praised herself with statements such as "You're doing great!" "Keep up the good work!" "Nice section of the paper!" For self-rewards to be effective, individuals must consistently follow through with the planned rewards and withhold rewards for not engaging in the targeted behavior. (For a more detailed treatment of self-management training, see Kanfer & Gaelick, 1986).

Relaxation Strategies

Relaxation strategies can help deactivate problematic anxiety or anger responses. Some examples of these interventions include progressive muscle relaxation, meditation, and paced breathing. These strategies are described later in the chapter and in the next chapter.

Guided Imagery to Deactivate Maladaptive Responses

Guiding clients through imagery can serve many important therapeutic functions.[10] As mentioned previously, guided imagery can help therapists conduct fine-grained analyses of clients' problems, and imagery can help clients practice a solution to a problem. In addition, guided imagery can be highly effective at deactivating maladaptive cognitive, affective, motivational, and behavioral responses and at activating adaptive responses. This section discusses these guided imagery interventions. Specifically,

[10]For an excellent compendium of guided imagery techniques, see Lazarus (1977).

the section discusses interrupting unpleasant moods and decreasing anxiety. (Guided imagery also can help modify psychological structures, and interventions designed to accomplish this are discussed later).

Interrupting Unpleasant Moods

Imagery can interrupt unpleasant moods. Depressed clients, for instance, can be guided to vividly remember a pleasant and enjoyable experience from their past. Alternatively, therapists can guide these clients to anticipate a pleasant image of the future (Beck, Rush, et al., 1979; Lazarus, 1977).

Decreasing Anxiety

Beck et al. (1985) described a variety of imagery techniques that are helpful in alleviating anxiety. A few of these techniques are discussed here. *Time projection* can help clients realize that even if a negative event occurs, the importance of the event often fades over time (Beck et al., 1985; Lazarus, 1977). For instance, therapists can guide clients to imagine what life would be like 1 month, 3 months, 6 months, 1 year, and 3 years after a negative event.

Anxious clients can also benefit from *changing frightening images.* For example, Annya, whose husband traveled frequently for business, had spontaneous, anxiety-provoking images of her husband dying in a fiery airplane crash. In therapy, her therapist instructed her to intentionally imagine him arriving safely and without incident. As a result of changing this image, her anxiety decreased.

A third way that guided imagery can be used to reduce anxiety is by *exaggerating* naturally occurring images to help the client see how unlikely the events they fear are. Jerry, the graduate student with a public speaking phobia who was described earlier, benefited from imagery exercises. A few weeks before his presentation, he imagined that his audience would feel contempt for him. His therapist guided him through an exaggerated image of his audience's response. In the guided image, the audience jeered, threw tomatoes, forcibly removed him from the podium with a shepherd's hook, and demanded that he be expelled from the university. As a result of this exercise, Jerry realized that this image was laughably ridiculous. He realized that even if his speech went poorly, his peers and his professor were unlikely to condemn him.

Therapists can also teach anxious clients to vividly imagine a *safe place,* a real or imaginary place where they feel extremely safe and relaxed. Frequently individuals consider scenes that involve beaches, lakes, woods, mountains, or a favorite room in their home as safe places.

Activity Scheduling

Activity scheduling, as the name suggests, involves having the client plan in detail a variety of activities. Many studies have found activity scheduling to be an effective treatment component, especially for depressed subjects (e.g., Jacobson et al., 1996; Zeiss & Lewinsohn, 1979).

Depressed clients benefit from systematically scheduling activities. Therapists can provide clients with weekly calendar forms on which clients record planned activities. Calendars that are similar to week-at-a-glance calendars but provide hourly time slots beginning at 5:00 am and ending at 2:00 am can be extremely useful. This covers the time range during which most clients are awake. Initially, therapists should help depressed clients schedule several days of activities. For extremely depressed clients, therapists might need to be involved in helping plan clients' activities until their symptoms begin to lessen.

Scheduling activities can help a client deactivate a depressive mode (Beck, Rush, et al., 1979). First, scheduling activities allows clients to *challenge self-defeating beliefs* regarding their ability to derive pleasure from tasks or their ability to master tasks. Therefore, before engaging in a scheduled activity, clients often benefit from predicting how much pleasure they will derive from the activity. They rate the activity from 0 to 10, where 0 is *no pleasure at all*, 10 is the *most pleasure they have ever experienced*, and 5 is a *moderate amount of pleasure*. Immediately after they complete the task, they rerate and record their actual pleasure. Often, clients can see that they underestimated the degree they were able to enjoy activities. A similar procedure can help change clients' self-defeating beliefs about their ability to master tasks.

Second, scheduling activities on a calendar can help clients attempt tasks in a graded fashion based on *task difficulty*. Clients who feel extremely depressed or overwhelmed benefit from beginning with simple tasks, having successful experiences, and then working their way up to more difficult tasks. Depending on their level of dysfunction, tasks may begin with those related to simple hygiene or picking up an item at the local drug store. As clients have successes, they should increase the level of difficulty of the tasks they attempt.

Another advantage of activity scheduling is that for more difficult or complex tasks, clients can *plan steps toward task completion*. Often clients with moderate or severe depression (or anxiety) feel overwhelmed by tasks, but they feel less overwhelmed when the tasks are divided into manageable subtasks. Finally, scheduling activities on an activity calendar can *remind* clients of tasks to perform and *save them from having to make decisions* about what to do throughout the day. For a detailed demonstration of the use of activity scheduling with depressed clients, see chapter 8.

MODIFYING PSYCHOLOGICAL STRUCTURES

It is most therapists' hope that clients will achieve lasting, positive change in therapy. To accomplish this end, therapists must help clients modify psychological structures. According to cognitive theory and practical experience, the psychological structures that can be effectively modified include (a) cognitive schemas, (b) the template for determining whether a stimulus activates a mode (part of the orienting schema), (c) the conscious control system, and (d) behavioral strategies. Changing psychological structures in an adaptive direction results in decreasing the probability of future difficulties in the problem areas. This section discusses the following methods for changing psychological structures: (a) fostering an accepting attitude; (b) establishing life goals and life meaning; (c) cost-benefit analysis of a belief; (d) historical test of a core belief; (e) rewriting implicit rules; (f) guided imagery; (g) intentional exposure to cognitions, emotions, behaviors, or situations; (h) behavioral experiments; (i) mindfulness meditation; and (j) social skills training.

Fostering an Accepting Attitude

Many emotional problems (as well as geopolitical problems) appear to relate to the inability to accept, tolerate, or have compassion for oneself, one's feelings, one's behavior, other people, or the state of the world (Ellis & Dryden, 1987; Frankl, 1959; Linehan, 1993a; Rogers, 1961). A few clinical examples of this are warranted. When individuals are nonaccepting of their spouse by being critical, judgmental, or contemptuous, their attitude frequently worsens their marital problems (e.g., Beck, 1988; Gottman, 1994). A second example involves insomnia clients who fail to accept that they are not sleeping. Instead, they catastrophize and attempt to force themselves to sleep (with thoughts such as "Damn it, I must sleep! I'm GOING TO SLEEP!"). This paradoxically worsens their chances of falling asleep (Hauri & Linde, 1990; Lacks, 1987). Similarly, Beck, Rush, et al. (1979) discussed the important role of self-criticism in the development and maintenance of depression.

Conversely, having an accepting attitude appears to be conducive to mental health. Albert Ellis and colleagues (e.g., Ellis & Dryden, 1987) suggested that ideally rational-emotive therapy leads to a deep philosophical change characterized by clients "fully accepting themselves and tolerating unchangeable uncomfortable life conditions" (p. 18). Thus, when individuals who have typically been judgmental expand their capacity for acceptance, they have changed in an important way.

Therapists may foster accepting attitudes in clients in several ways. First, therapists work at having and conveying an unconditionally accepting attitude toward their clients (Ellis & Dryden, 1987; Linehan, 1993a; Rogers, 1961). Another way that therapists can foster acceptance is by modeling self-acceptance for their clients. Third, therapists can work with clients on using cognitive restructuring techniques to evaluate and modify judgmental, critical, demanding, and catastrophizing cognitions that contribute to nonacceptance of oneself, other people, or one's situation. These maladaptive cognitions often take the form of implicit rules such as "I should always be happy and upbeat" or "People should always treat me with respect."

Establishing Life Goals and Life Meaning[11]

Helping clients establish a sense of purpose or fulfillment in their lives—when previously one was lacking—represents an important change in psychological structures. Although cognitive therapy frequently involves helping clients find fulfillment and meaning, the cognitive therapy literature has generally omitted discussion of life meaning. This section attempts to integrate cognitive therapy with the work of psychologists who have explicitly addressed the issue of life meaning.

The Importance of Life Meaning

Victor Frankl was the founder of *logotherapy,* a school of therapy that focuses on people's search for meaning. Frankl (1959/1984) believed the search for meaning was the guiding drive in human beings and that a sense of meaninglessness was the cause of psychopathology. For example, Frankl (1959/1984) stated,

> Just consider the mass neurotic syndrome so pervasive in the young generation: there is ample empirical evidence that the three facets of this syndrome—depression, aggression, addiction—are due to what is called in logotherapy "the existential vacuum," a feeling of emptiness and meaninglessness. (p 143)

Almost 40 years later, depression, aggression, and addiction continue to be significant problems of our time. Whether or not clients state it explicitly, the distress that leads many to therapy relates to a sense of meaninglessness or lack of fulfillment.

Sources of Meaninglessness

Fabry (1998) suggested that *characteristics of contemporary Western society* contribute to a sense of meaninglessness for many people. Specifically, a sense of meaninglessness has become prevalent as a result of a rejection of traditional values and a deficiency in people's sense of responsibility.

Frankl (1959, p. XVI) suggested that certain *life philosophies* contribute to a crisis in meaning. Examples of such philosophies include: (a) *nihilism,* the belief that life has no meaning, (b) *hedonism,* the belief that people's own pleasure is the only worthwhile pursuit, (c) *pan-determinism,* the belief that individuals have no control of their lives as a result of various forces such as their genetic endowment, unconscious drives, early childhood events, and so on, and (d) *reductionism,* the belief that everything, including people, is reducible to the underlying biological processes and mechanisms.

Another source of meaninglessness involves *loss*—losing things that previously supplied meaning (Fabry, 1988). For example, midlife crises

---

[11] Wong and Fry (1998) edited an excellent book that focused on recent developments in the theory and research on human meaning.

tend to occur when people have reached their career goals or their children have "left the nest." Other losses that can contribute to a sense of meaninglessness include divorce, retirement, graduation from school (e.g., loss of lifestyle and regular contact with friends), being diagnosed with a serious illness, or losing a loved one. (Loss and grief are discussed at length in chap. 8.)

Another common obstacle to deriving a sense of meaning from life and one that also contributes to much human misery is excessive self-focused attention.

Sources of Meaning

Yalom (1980) observed that the potential sources of meaning in people's lives depend on where they are in the *life cycle.* Children rarely ponder, "What's the meaning of life?" or "What is the meaning of *my* life." In general, meaningful activities for them are clearly defined: developing trusting relationships, gaining a sense of mastery and power, and acquiring skills. For young adults, their meaning is also clearly defined: establishing a stable identity, coupling, and finding rewarding and fulfilling work. When young adults are struggling with meaning, they are likely to be having difficulty in one or more of these areas. In middle age, meaning typically comes from what Erikson (1950) called generativity—"the concern in establishing and guiding the next generation" (p. 267). In old age, according to Erikson (1950), individuals who have successfully navigated through earlier developmental tasks may derive meaning from a sense of "ego integration." Among other things this is "an acceptance of one's one and only life cycle as something that had to be and that, by necessity, permitted of no substitutions" (p. 268).

According to Frankl (1959/1984), people can discover meaning in life in three different ways: (a) by engaging in fulfilling *work*—one's job, creative pursuits, or a cause, (b) by being in a *loving relationship,* and (c) by the attitude they take toward *unavoidable suffering.*

Work. Work, broadly defined, is most likely to provide individuals with a sense of purpose if it has the following characteristics. First, people are more likely to derive a sense of meaning from their work if they *chose it* as opposed to it being imposed on them. Second, individuals are most likely to find their work fulfilling when it is *congruent with who they are*—their values, conscience, and sense of responsibility (Frankl, 1959/1984). Thus, various political, social, or religious/spiritual causes can be the basis of people's fulfilling life work. Third, deriving a sense of meaning from one's work is enhanced when individuals believe they are making a *creative and unique contribution.* Regarding creativity, Yalom (1980) wrote, "To create something new, something that rings with novelty or beauty and harmony is a powerful antidote to a sense of meaninglessness" (p. 435). People's contributions are unique if what they accomplish would have been done differently if someone else had done it or if it required specialized skills or talents.

Fourth, a sense of fulfillment and meaning often comes from work that is *challenging but not out of reach* and that requires focused attention (Csikszentmihalyi, 1990). Fifth, and perhaps the most important factor that contributes to a sense of purpose in one's work is *self-transcendence or altruism* (Frankl, 1959/1984). People who dedicate themselves to a cause that transcends themselves leave a legacy to the world that death cannot quickly erase. In the words of Yalom (1980), "leaving the world a better place to live in, serving others, participation in charity (the greatest virtue of all)—these activities are right and good and have provided life meaning for many humans" (p. 431). It should be noted that although self-transcendence involves unselfish care for the welfare of others or a cause, self-transcendence is not synonymous with martyrdom. Rather, individuals who engage in self-transcendent pursuits generally derive pleasure and satisfaction from these activities and do not engage in these pursuits at excessive cost to themselves.

Loving Relationships. Loving relationships also can provide individuals with a sense of meaning and purpose. Like fulfilling work, loving and being loved by another typically involves (a) *choice*—choosing to be in the relationship, (b) congruence with the person's sense of *self*—being consistent with his or her values, goals, and sense of responsibility, (c) *self-transcendence*— giving unselfishly to the partner, and (d) *unique contributions*—being difficult to replace.

Another source of meaning for many people relates to the previous two sources of meaning. Those who derive meaning from *religion* or *spirituality* often consider it a loving relationship (loving and being loved by God) and a life's work (serving God and being a good person; see Wong, 1998c). Each religion defines how to live what it deems to be a good and meaningful life. In addition, religions provide what they consider to be ultimate goals for individuals, such as going to heaven or transcending the pain of the earth (e.g., reaching Nirvana).

Unavoidable Suffering. Frankl (1959/1984), a survivor of the Nazi concentration camps, suggested that people can experience meaning when they suffer with dignity in the face of unavoidable pain. Frankl provided an example of a young man who found meaning in his misfortune, becoming a quadriplegic in an accident. The man decided to pursue clinical psychology because he believed that "my handicap will only enhance my ability to help others. I know that without the suffering, the growth that I have achieved would have been impossible" (as quoted in Frankl, 1959/1984, p. 148). On the other hand, Frankl (1959/1984) suggested that when a painful situation is avoidable, "the meaningful thing to do is to remove its cause, for unnecessary suffering is masochistic rather than heroic" (p. 148).

Wong (1998a) identified some additional sources of meaning. He factor analyzed subjects' conceptions and beliefs regarding what it is to live a meaningful life. Three of the factors that emerged were Positive Relationships, Self-Transcendence, and Religion. However, several additional factors emerged. These were Achievement, Self-Acceptance, Fairness (i.e., living in a supportive, empowering, and nondiscriminative community), Self-Realization, and Meaning and Purpose.

Cognitive Therapy Can Foster a Sense of Meaning

When a client's major problem is a lack of purpose or meaning, cognitive therapists can intervene in a variety of helpful ways. The first way is by helping clients understand the importance of having an overriding meaning and purpose (Yalom, 1980). Therapists can convey this directly, and finding meaning can be discussed explicitly with clients. In addition, therapists can help if clients' problems appear to stem from their pursuit of life goals that appear to be unfulfilling (e.g., hedonism, wealth). For such clients, therapists can educate them about pursuits that are more likely to provide them with a sense of meaning (Wong, 1998a).

Another major way cognitive therapy can help clients find meaning is by exploring the emotional obstacles that get in the way for the client. What is preventing the client from being in loving relationships, being involved in one's community or causes, or getting satisfaction from his or her job? Solving the problems that interfere with deriving a sense of fulfillment in these areas often gives clients a sense of meaning. Life philosophies—such as nihilism, pan-determinism, hedonism, and reductionism—can be obstacles to finding meaning. At times, guided discovery can help change a life philosophy that is contributing to a sense of purposelessness. However, frequently, it is more beneficial for clients to take a "leap of faith" that there is meaning, or at least withhold judgment about meaning. Simultaneously, they should engage in behavioral experiments in which they participate in some activities that have high probabilities of providing a sense of meaning. The activities should be congruent with their values, make a unique contribution, or transcend themselves. After engaging in a potentially fulfilling activity for a reasonable length of time, people often find that they feel fulfilled and that what they are doing is meaningful. Often the larger question about the meaning of life becomes unimportant to them (Yalom, 1980).

Often clients do not know what they could do that would give them a sense of purpose. Through guided discovery and self-exploration assignments, clients can discover potential sources of meaning that fit their personality, talents, and values.

To find hints for sources of meaning, clients can engage in the following thought exercises: recall past meaningful experiences including peak experiences, examine their values and explore their dreams to discover unconscious hopes and wishes, use fantasy to reveal what they consider meaningful, and consider what characteristics or pursuits they admire most in people whom they view as role models (Fabry, 1988).

Wong (1998b) suggested that clients benefit from being asked a series of "magical thinking" questions. These questions are:

> If you were free to do whatever you want and money is not an issue, what would you like to do on a daily basis right now,
>
> If God would grant you any three wishes, what would be your top three wishes, and
>
> If you were able to decide your future, what would be an ideal life situation for you 3 or 5 years down the road? (p. 419)

Fabry (1988) provided an extensive list of questions that help readers clarify their values, talents, and potential self-transcendent activities that might be fulfilling (pp. 67–78). Some questions that can be particularly helpful for clients who are searching for meaning include: "Tell me something that you enjoy and do well," "Tell me about the time when you felt most alive or best about yourself," "If you could imagine being on your death bed years from now and looking back over your life, what would you feel best about in terms of how you spent these years of your life?"

Regarding unavoidable suffering, Fabry (1988) suggested a variety of questions that can help people accept the negative situations that they experienced, including

> "What have I learned from this?"
>
> "Has it given me new tasks and challenges?"
>
> "Has it made me a stronger, more receptive person?"
>
> "Can I use this experience to help others in similar situations?"
>
> "Can the way I endure my situation serve as an example to others?"
>
> "Does this experience make me appreciate things I have taken for granted?"
>
> "What choices do I still have?"

Finally, clients can complete meaning questionnaires, such as the Personal Meaning Profile (Wong, 1998a). Therapists can use information from questionnaires to identify the depth and sources of meaning in clients' lives. Questionnaires can also help therapists determine the degree to which clients are leading a balanced life and living according to their values.

An example of a cognitive therapy client for whom finding a life purpose was important to overcoming his emotional difficulties was Bobby. Bobby was a middle-aged, university professor, who presented for chronic depression. He indicated that when he was a graduate student in biology in the 1960's, he was politically active. Bobby had high hopes of helping society become more humane, just, "in touch with what's important," and environmentally responsible. However, in the 1970s and 1980s, he became disillusioned and stopped participating in political activities. He also began to feel powerless and began wondering about his worth as a person and the value of his life. His first of several major depressive episodes occurred in the early 1970s, and although his depressive episodes partially remitted, he never experienced a full recovery. Bobby's doubts about his meaning in life lingered for the next 25 years. During that time, he went through the motions in his career and received tenure but failed to advance further despite his obvious talent.

In therapy, through guided discovery, Bobby decided to once again work toward making the world a better place. Here is an excerpt from his journal that summarized his new perspective:

> Even if I can't make a difference, I can fight the good fight! Now, society needs people to act more than ever because there is so much apathy. My efforts *will* make a difference, although it will probably be a small difference. But, who knows, I might influence students who influence others, and it could have a positive cascading effect. At the very least, I can feel good that I'm living by my morals and doing what I believe in.

As a result of this new perspective, Bobby and some of his graduate students got a small grant to work with the local zoo on strategies for saving a nearly extinct species of rainforest bird. After making the decision to get involved in making positive changes in the world, his depression went into full remission for the first time in 25 years.

Cost-Benefit Analysis of Beliefs

As mentioned earlier, considering the advantages and disadvantages of an automatic thought can be helpful for letting go of an unhealthy thought or image. Performing a cost-benefit analysis can also be a helpful step toward changing more enduring and pervasive cognitions (Beck, Freeman, et al., 1990; Freeman & Reinecke, 1993). Regarding beliefs, it is helpful for clients to consider the positive and negative impact the belief has on major life domains—sense of self, mental health, relationships, career, leisure, and physical health. During this process, the therapist ensures that the advantages for beliefs are not distorted. When clients consider the advantages and disadvantages with respect to life domains, they often see that their belief is self-defeating. Clients also are encouraged to select a self-enhancing, nondistorted new belief to replace their old belief. When selecting a new belief, it is helpful to consider the effects of the new belief on each major life domain. The recognition that the old belief was self-defeating and the new one is self-enhancing is an important first step toward changing one's perspective. (For an example of a cost-benefit analysis of a depressogenic belief, see chap. 8.)

Historical Test for Modifying a Core Belief

The Historical Test (McKay & Fanning, 1991) can help change a core belief as a result of the two main procedures that comprise the test. First, clients challenge the evidence that they have used to support their dysfunctional core belief. Second, they review historical evidence that contradicts their targeted core belief. (The Appendix presents a blank Historical Test.)

Figure 5.2 represents a completed Historical Test for Peggy, a 34-year-old woman diagnosed with borderline personality disorder. At the top of the test, clients write the targeted self-defeating core belief. The core belief that Peggy addressed in this test was "I'm disgusting."

In the left-hand column, clients list the "evidence" they have used to support the core belief plus rational challenges to this "evidence." In the right-hand column, clients record any other evidence against the core belief. The test asks clients to record this information for the following age ranges: 0–3, 4–6, 7–10, 11–15, 16–20 years old. Considering these age ranges serves a useful function. It aids in the client's recall of important childhood memories and issues. This is beneficial since early events are extremely important in the development of core beliefs.

McKay and Fanning (1991) suggested several questions that clients can use to challenge the "evidence" they have used to support their core beliefs about themselves. These questions include:

Was this normal behavior for that age level?

Did I have a choice or was my behavior determined by other people or situations?

Was my behavior adaptive? Did it help me cope with difficult circumstances? Was it how I survived?

Is there another explanation for this event besides my core belief?

How might the behavior or event be seen as a positive?"

As Fig. 5.2 shows, Peggy, with the help of her therapist, generated compelling challenges for refuting her self-defeating core belief. Her challenges allowed her to begin viewing her promiscuous behavior as a mistake that was understandable given the sexual abuse she had experienced and also understandable given how she viewed herself at that time. After several months of thinking about the content of the test, Peggy began to experience a lasting change in the way she viewed herself.

Rewriting Implicit Rules

Often strong dysfunctional beliefs take the form of implicit rules about how to behave, think, feel, relate to others, and so on (Beck, Freeman et al., 1990; J. Beck, 1995). Implicit rules often provide useful guidelines for living. However, they warrant attention in therapy if they frequently lead to

HISTORICAL TEST FOR MODIFYING A CORE BELIEF

Self-Defeating Core Belief: **I'm disgusting.**

"Evidence" For the Core Belief Plus Challenges	Any Other Evidence Against the Core Belief
0-3 years old (I was raped by my cousin.) BUT this doesn't make me disgusting. I was an innocent; what he did was disgusting.	I was an infant & young child. Young children are not disgusting. They are innocent and vulnerable and deserve protection.
4-6 years old (My parents treated me with contempt; they were always annoyed and impatient and didn't want to be bothered with me.) BUT they had their own serious problems; the way they treated me was a reflection of them and not something about me; they treated Sue and Dave [siblings] no differently.	There was nothing disgusting about my appearance--I was a normal looking kid. As a person, there was nothing disgusting about me either--I was abused and shell-shocked. That's sad and maddening, but NOT DISGUSTING.
7-10 years old	I tried to be generous, kind and liked; I had a lot of sympathy for other people who were mistreated, like kids who were bullied.
11-15 years old & 16-20 years old (I let boys have sex with me.) BUT this was a mistake and one that's common for girls who are molested and unloved; I just wanted to be loved and noticed and those are needs that everybody has; I eventually learned that being promiscuous just made me feel worse, or disgusting and unlovable so I stopped.	I continued being sensitive and kind to the underdog.

FIG. 5.2. Example of a completed Historical Test for modifying a core belief. Adapted with permission from McKay & Fanning (1991). *Prisoners of Belief.* New Harbinger Publications, Oakland, CA 94605, www.newharbinger.com

emotional disturbances (e.g., pervasive guilt, anger, or self-hatred) or functional impairment (e.g., debilitating perfectionism, interpersonal difficulties).

If a client has a dysfunctional implicit rule, the first step to changing it is to make the problematic rule explicit. (Chapter 4 describes helping clients become aware of their dysfunctional implicit rules.) The next step is to change the implicit rule to one that is self-enhancing. For example, Ralph had the following rule "I should always be nice to other people." This rule frequently resulted in his feeling guilty or inadequate, or it resulted in his allowing people to take advantage of him. Ralph examined this rule and the effects it had on his emotional well being and relationships. As a result, he decided to change the rule to "I'll strive to be nice to people. However, I will take my own needs into account too and, when appropriate, put myself first."

Guided Imagery for Modifying Psychological Structures

As mentioned previously, guided imagery can deactivate maladaptive cognitive, affective, motivational, and behavioral responses and activate adaptive ones. In addition, guided imagery can modify psychological structures. Specifically, guided imagery can desensitize clients to situations that elicit their maladaptive responses and can modify core beliefs.

Desensitizing Clients to Situations They Find Upsetting

Beck et al. (1985) observed that "anxiety may sometimes be eliminated or reduced with successive deliberate repetitions of a fantasy even though its content remains unchanged" (p. 216). Systematic desensitization and flooding in imagination are two well-established exposure-based treatments of phobias that use guided imagery (see Foa & Steketee, 1987; Wolpe, 1982). Additional information about exposure-based treatments is described below and in chapters 6 and 7.

Modifying Core Beliefs

This section describes two ways that therapists can use guided imagery to modify core beliefs. First, they can use guided imagery to modify powerful core beliefs that were established during early childhood (Beck, Freeman, et al., 1990; McGinn & Young, 1996; Young, 1990). Second, therapists can use guided imagery to modify beliefs with clients whose symptoms have remitted.

Using imagery to modify core beliefs established early in childhood is demonstrated here with the case of Benjamin. He was the client, introduced in chapter 1, who had major depression and social phobia as well as several problematic personality features (i.e., paranoid, obsessive-compulsive, and avoidant).

Guided imagery helped in modifying some of Benjamin's core beliefs. What follows is how Benjamin's therapist, Gloria, worked with him on one particular, representative scene. In the scene, his stepfather was beginning to ferociously attack and berate "Child Benjamin" as the result of his making a minor mistake. In the image, the therapist instructed "Adult Benjamin" to intervene, and she guided him in doing so. Adult Benjamin talked back to his stepfather forcefully, took Child Benjamin to a safe place, and talked Child Benjamin through the situation. Adult Benjamin conveyed a variety of messages to Child Benjamin to help him realize that although he made a mistake, he was OK. He stated to Child Benjamin, "Mistakes are OK; everyone makes mistakes; you are a good kid; your stepfather was acting in a very mean and unfair way; he acted the way he did because of his own problems and not anything negative about you." He also conveyed to Child Benjamin that he, Adult Benjamin, would always be there for him. During these imagery exercises, the therapist frequently asked Child Benjamin what was going through his mind, what he was feeling, and what he needed to hear from Adult Benjamin. In sessions, this type of imagery exercise was repeated many times. Subsequently, Benjamin reported feeling "safer than I've ever felt before knowing that I can take care of and comfort myself." Benjamin frequently came back to the image of himself providing comfort, reassurance, and kind words to his Child self.

A second way that therapists can use guided imagery to modify core beliefs relates to clients whose symptoms have remitted. Modifying beliefs is usually most successful when therapists help clients activate the relevant beliefs. As a result, if a client's symptoms have remitted, it is often necessary to "artificially activate the belief system by invoking imagery of situations that typically create negative emotional responses" (Sacco & Beck, 1995, p. 339).

Intentional Exposure to Avoided Emotions, Cognitions, and Situations

Just as rumination contributes to psychopathology, its opposite—excessively or persistently avoiding emotions, cognitions, behaviors, or situations—also appears to contribute to emotional problems (Salkovskis, 1985; Salkovskis & Campbell, 1994; Salkovskis, Clark, & Gelder, 1996; see also chap. 2, this volume). Avoidance contributes to the maintenance of many anxiety-related disorders, including posttraumatic stress disorder, panic disorder, phobias, obsessive-compulsive disorder, and avoidant personality disorder.

Clients who excessively avoid emotions, cognitions, behaviors, or situations frequently benefit from intentional and prolonged exposure to the avoided stimuli. For example, in panic disorder, an important component of therapy is exposure to physical panic sensations (also known as a panic induction). These are benign physical sensations that clients misinterpret as signifying a mental or physical catastrophe. In therapy for phobias, clients are exposed to the triggering place, object, or situation. Exposure for obsessive-compulsive disorder clients is to the stimuli that trigger their obsessions, and exposure is paired with prevention of compulsions.

Besides the well-developed, exposure-based treatment approaches for anxiety disorders (described extensively in chaps. 6 and 7), research suggests that *journaling*—a form of cognitive and emotional exposure—can result in significant health and mental health benefits (e.g., Booth, Petrie, & Pennebaker, 1997; Lepore, 1997; Pennebaker, Colder, & Sharp, 1990; Spera, Buhrfeind, & Pennebaker, 1994). For journaling to be effective, individuals must repeatedly write about the details of a traumatic event and their most distressing and personal thoughts and feelings about the event. Individuals must also use self-referential language (i.e., "I," "my," and "me"; Pennebaker, 1997).

Two mechanisms may be responsible for the beneficial effects of exposure. First, exposure may help clients disconfirm their distorted expectations. In anxiety disorders, clients overestimate the probability and severity of negative consequences that would result from contact with feared internal or external circumstances. In addition, they underestimate their coping resources. Second, exposure may also work at a more basic level. Through Pavlovian conditioning, exposure may desensitize individuals to the feared stimuli.

Designing Behavioral Experiments

Beck, Freeman, et al. (1990) discussed the importance of behavioral experiments in modifying maladaptive core beliefs. They wrote:

> Since the beliefs are so entrenched, they do not yield to the kind of everyday disconfirmations that generally lead to modification or elimination of less rigid beliefs. Repeated, systematic disconfirmations through devising and carrying out "behavioral experiments" can eventually erode these dysfunctional beliefs and lay the groundwork for more adaptive attitudes. (p. 60)

An example of using behavioral experiments follows. Sharon, a client with paranoid personality disorder, was afraid that if she let down her guard, she would be hurt by other people. As a result, she was constantly vigilant and never disclosed personal information to others. After working on trust in the therapeutic relationship, Sharon and her therapist selected a person whom Sharon knew and who seemed most likely to act in a trustworthy fashion. In addition, Sharon and her therapist chose a relatively minor matter that Sharon could disclose to this person. Both the therapist and Sharon made predictions about the outcome. The therapist predicted that the person would keep Sharon's confidence if Sharon made it clear to her that she wanted this information to stay between the two of them. Sharon predicted that she would "get burned." Fortunately, the person she chose proved her trustworthiness to Sharon.

After having positive results with this experiment, Sharon gradually shared more personal information with the selected person. She also shared information with two other people whom she had reason to believe would be trustworthy and loyal. Over time, Sharon developed a friendship for the first time in her life and allowed herself to be more trusting of select people.

As can be seen in Sharon's case, it often helps to perform mini-experiments in a graded fashion. In contrast, beginning with an experiment in which Sharon was required to disclose a great deal of personal information would have been too threatening to her and too great of a risk.

A helpful form of behavioral experiment involves clients acting "as if" they possessed certain characteristics or skills (Beck et al., 1985). For example, socially anxious clients can act as if they feel confident in a social situation. Similarly, they can act as if they are having a good time at an event, which increases the likelihood that they will have a good time. Clients with difficulties with motivation can act as if they are motivated to perform a task, which can help them "just do it." Following an "as if" experiment, clients can evaluate the effects of their behavior on the situation and their internal experience of it.

Mindfulness Meditation

Mindfulness meditation consists of skills gleaned from ancient Eastern traditions (Linehan, 1993a). In brief, mindfulness is learning to control one's attention. When people are in a state of mindfulness, they are alert and fully in the present moment, as opposed to worrying, regretting, brooding, or going through life in "autopilot" (Epstein, 1995; Kabat-Zinn, 1994). Mindfulness involves nonjudgmental observation of experiences and can help people achieve a sense of inner stillness. In addition, important goals for mindfulness meditation are to be compassionate and to have a sense of connectedness to the self, other people, and the world. Unlike the refocusing approaches, mindfulness meditation is a skill that requires discipline and commitment. However, it can provide pervasive and long-term benefits for mental health rather than simply coping with a particular distressing situation.[12]

In addition, many cognitive and behavioral skills share important characteristics with mindfulness or are forms of mindfulness. For example, the process of cognitive restructuring requires people to become objective observers of themselves, other people, and the situations in which they find themselves. Progressive muscle relaxation and paced breathing involve focusing attention on a single feeling or process. Interestingly, the process of narrowing one's attentional focus itself often results in deep relaxation. Exposure to unpleasant cognitions or emotions involves focusing on previously avoided internal experiences. Finally, fostering an accepting attitude is common to cognitive therapy and mindfulness meditation.

[12]Coping strategies that alleviate distress for the short term can be useful, as well.

Benefits of Mindfulness

At the present time, limited empirical research exists on mindfulness practice in the treatment of psychopathology. However, the research that exists suggests several client populations that may benefit from practicing mindfulness. For example, in a study with chronic pain patients (Kabat-Zinn, Lipworth, & Burney, 1985), mindfulness training resulted in significant *decreases in pain* and other indices of psychopathology. The training also increased subjects' functioning as compared to a traditional pain management program. The benefits were maintained at an 18-month follow-up. Patients having generalized anxiety disorder or panic disorder who were taught mindfulness skills experienced significant *decreases in anxiety, frequency of panic attacks, and depressive symptoms* (Kabat-Zinn, Massion, & Kristeller, Peterson, 1992). These benefits were maintained at a 3-year follow-up (Miller, Fletcher, & Kabat-Zinn, 1995).

Mindfulness practice is also included as part of some cognitive-behavioral treatment approaches. For example, in dialectical behavior therapy for clients with *borderline personality disorder,* Linehan (1993a, 1993b) considered mindfulness skills to be the foundation for all other skills—which include interpersonal effectiveness skills, emotional regulation skills, and distress tolerance skills. Teasdale and colleagues (Teasdale, Segal, & Williams, 1995) postulated that mindfulness practice is likely to reduce relapse rates in depressed clients successfully treated with cognitive therapy. They based this conclusion on several considerations. First, they suggested that a probable contributor to relapses is that clients whose symptoms have abated do not have opportunities to practice cognitive therapy skills. To practice cognitive restructuring, for example, clients must first have distressing thoughts. Such thoughts are infrequent when clients are not experiencing symptoms. In contrast, mindfulness meditation skills can be practiced on an ongoing basis, independent of symptoms. In addition, if depressive symptoms begin to return, clients who practice mindfulness are likely to become aware of these responses quickly and take corrective action—instead of avoiding early signs of maladaptive responses. This is because mindfulness meditation consists of nonjudgmentally focusing on whatever thoughts or emotions that arise, whether they are pleasant, unpleasant, or neutral. Finally, mindfulness practice facilitates "being in the moment" as opposed to ruminating about the past, worrying about the future, or (negatively) judging one's experience. Therefore, regular practice of mindfulness can help ward off depression.

Mindfulness practice is likely to convey a variety of other benefits as well. Those who practice mindfulness often indicate that mindfulness helps them *experience life more fully* (Tart, 1994). For example, it helps them fully experience their senses. The expression "stopping and smelling the roses" is an apt description of what someone who is practicing mindfulness might do.

Mindfulness practice can help *increase tolerance of distress and the ability to delay gratification* (e.g., Kabat-Zinn, 1990, 1994; Tart, 1994). People who meditate often experience impatience, boredom, or physical pain at some time during long meditations. Staying with the meditation for longer and longer periods despite these unpleasant feelings helps individuals develop tolerance for the feelings. During mindfulness practice, when these unpleasant feelings appear, individuals attempt to gently refocus their attention onto their breathing or whatever their focus is. Alternatively, individuals often benefit from mindfully attending to the unpleasant feelings, staying with the feelings with an accepting attitude.

Mindfulness practice can also help people *work through unpleasant feelings* (e.g., Kabat-Zinn, 1990, 1994; Tart, 1994). Mindfulness practice encourages people to work on becoming more objective, which in turn can provide them with further clarity. Individuals can use mindfulness to *expose themselves to intensely painful cognitions or emotions.* In such cases, individuals focus on the painful inner experience and stay with the experience, without judging, and without being swept away with it. In short, they do not respond automatically or maladaptively. When individuals' attention wanders from the painful internal stimulus, such as when they try to escape the pain by thinking of something else, they gently bring their attention back. Accepting, staying with, and fully experiencing unpleasant cognitions or emotions often helps to dissipate the unpleasant emotions and reduce the frequency or intensity of intrusive cognitions.

In contrast, by trying not to experience unpleasant cognitions or emotions, people often increase their distress. Attempts to suppress thoughts increase their frequency and intensity (Salkovskis, 1985; Salkovskis & Campbell, 1994). Similarly, trying not to experience unpleasant emotions frequently results in secondary emotions that compound unpleasant feelings (Ellis & Dryden, 1987). For example, people often feel angry with themselves for feeling depressed, anxious about being angry, depressed about being depressed, and so on. These secondary feelings are unnecessary and disappear with mindful acceptance of the initial feeling. When individuals feel sad, instead of thinking, "I can't stand this," they can accept the feeling, feel it fully, and then let it go by deploying their attention elsewhere.

In daily life, mindfulness practice potentially could help *improve interpersonal relationships* (Kabat-Zinn, 1990). Mindfulness encourages individuals to be as fully present as possible with other people. It also helps them see an interconnectedness among people and between people and the world at large and helps them to be nonjudgmental and compassionate. When individuals can hold these perspectives, their relationships are likely to benefit.

Teaching Clients to Become Mindful

To learn about an empirically based, mindfulness training program used at the Stress Reduction Clinic at the University of Massachusetts Medical

Center, refer to Kabat-Zinn (1990), which provides a detailed description of the approach. The program consists of eight weekly 2-hour sessions, at which two therapists meet with a group of clients (up to 30 participants). In addition, clients are required to practice on their own for at least 45 minutes per day. The practice consists of a variety of mindfulness meditations (e.g., sitting meditation, walking meditation, body scan meditation, hatha yoga).

Clients who are unable or unwilling to commit to such a rigorous meditation program can still benefit from mindfulness meditation. However, a key to benefiting is practicing daily. Practicing a few minutes several times per day can be helpful, especially if individuals attempt to remember to be mindful during times of stress. At such times, the ability to accept the situation and be in the moment can help them gain perspective and reduce their stress.

While practicing mindfulness, individuals attempt to focus on one thing such as the sensations in their stomach as they inhale and exhale. Breathing is one of the most commonly used foci of mindfulness meditation. However, nearly anything can be the focus of practice because ultimately the goal of mindfulness practice is to be mindful of as much of experience as possible. Other potential foci of practice include how the individual's legs feel while walking slowly in a corridor or the taste and texture of food while eating slowly. Eventually, a useful focus of practice is the individual's stream of cognitions. Observing one's thoughts without judgment and without being "overtaken" by them can provide new insight and clarity that help interrupt responses that previously had been automatic and problematic.

While practicing mindfulness, people's minds inevitably wander. The task of mindfulness is to bring the individual's attention back gently and nonjudgmentally—again and again. Bringing back one's attention nonjudgmentally can be of much greater value to the individual than being able to stay focused for a long stretch of time. The process of nonjudgmentally refocusing teaches the person self-compassion and patience. Whatever clients choose to focus on, it generally is helpful to stick to that focus throughout that practice session, as opposed to intentionally switching the focus during the session.

As with other useful skills for living, for therapists to be effective in teaching clients mindfulness meditations, it generally is important for them to have experience with the practice themselves. If therapists practice mindfulness themselves, they represent *role models* for their clients, and they learn first hand the struggles with and benefits from mindfulness practice. Through self-disclosure of the benefits they have personally received from mindfulness practice over many months or years, despite the difficulties along the way, therapists can help clients develop motivation to practice. In addition, therapists can frame their own difficulties in their mindfulness meditation—such as boredom, impatience, frustration, and distractibility—in a positive light. For example, if these difficulties have helped develop their patience and self-compassion, then sharing these insights with clients may prove motivating.

Also, therapists can reinforce clients' practice of mindfulness with praise and regular review. Therapists can discuss and work through difficulties clients are having in their practice, and they can provide encouragement and instruction. For example, clients' practice of mindfulness can benefit from instructions such as:

Therapist: If your mind wanders 10,000 times during a practice session, simply bring it back 10,000 times. Bring your mind back patiently and gently and without judgment. Try to become a nonjudgmental observer. If you observe yourself judging, try not to judge the judging. While being mindful, one should not reject anything or strive for anything. The mind can be like your field of vision while lying on your back in an open field on a summer day. Birds, insects, and airplanes fly in and out of the field of vision but you hold on to nothing. The key to being enriched by mindfulness is beginning practice and practicing as often as possible—even for just a few minutes at a time.

Finally, therapists can recommend guidebooks or tapes that can facilitate clients' mindfulness practice, such as Kabat-Zinn's guidebook.

Social Skills Training

Clients may have difficulty with social situations because they lack necessary social skills (e.g., Beck, Freeman, et al., 1990). These clients can benefit from social skills training. The training consists of educating clients about their skills deficits, modeling the appropriate skills, and using role plays and role reversals with detailed feedback to help clients practice the skills. On the other hand, clients may have difficulties in social situations because of a combination of skills deficits and mood symptoms interfering with the skills they have. This is often apparent with clients who have social phobia, depression, avoidant personality disorder, or dependant personality disorders. These clients can benefit from both skills training and skills for managing their moods (described previously).

6

Panic Disorder (PD) With Agoraphobia

1. Cognitive Model of a Panic Attack
2. Assessment and Conceptualization of PD
   a. Case Conceptualization Worksheet for PD
   b. Assessing the Risk of Fainting
   c. Questionnaires
   d. Consultation With Physicians Prior to Beginning Treatment
   e. Behavioral Assessment Test (BAT)
   f. Integrating Information Into a Case Conceptualization Summary Form
   g. Examples of Case Conceptualizations
      i. Case 6.A (Greg): PD With Agoraphobia
      ii. Case 6.B (Jimmy): PD Without Agoraphobia
      iii. Case 6.C (Jillian): PD With Agoraphobia
3. Cognitive Therapy of PD
   a. Presentation of a Case Conceptualization Illustration to a Panic Client
   b. Overview of Treatment Components
   c. Panic Induction Session(s)
      i. Benefits of Panic Inductions
      ii. Introducing Clients to Panic Inductions
      iii. Methods for Inducing Panic
      iv. Coping Skills Introduced During Panic-Induction Session
         (1) Paced Breathing
         (2) Cognitive Restructuring
         (3) Refocusing Attention
         (4) Coping Cards
   d. Interventions for Clients Who Fear Fainting
   e. Relaxation Training
   f. Eliminating Subtle Safety-Seeking Behavior
      i. Discontinuing High-Potency Benzodiazapines
   g. Preparing for Termination for Panic Clients Without Agoraphobia
   h. Treating Agoraphobic Avoidance: Exposure Therapy

- i. Preparing Clients for Exposure Therapy
  - (1) Providing a Rationale for Exposure Therapy
  - (2) Clients Benefit From Knowing What to Expect During Exposure Therapy
- ii. Graded Exposure
  - (1) Imaginal Flooding as Preparation for In Vivo Graded Exposure
  - (2) In Vivo Exposure Sessions
  - (3) Other Considerations for Exposure Therapy
- i. Clients With Core Beliefs, Issues, and Strategies That Predispose Them to Future Panic

4. Summary of Cognitive Therapy of PD: Integration and Sequencing of Treatment Components

Panic disorder (PD) is one of the most prevalent of the anxiety disorders. According to the National Institute of Mental Health, the lifetime prevalence of PD is 5.6% and the 1-year prevalence is between 2% and 4.2% (as quoted in Michelson, Marchione, Greenwald, Testa, & Marchione, 1996). Thus, in any given year in the United States, between 5 and 10 million people suffer from PD. Consequences of PD often include (a) depression; (b) other anxiety disorders, especially agoraphobia; (c) marital dysfunction; (d) abuse of alcohol, recreational drugs, or prescription medication; (e) peptic ulcers; (f) hypertension; (g) headaches; (h) unemployment; and (i) overuse of medical care systems (Markowitz, Weissman, & Quellette, 1989). PD represents approximately 60% of the anxiety disorders treated by health and mental health professionals (Michelson et al., 1996).

A *panic attack* is characterized by intense anxiety consisting of at least 4 autonomic and cognitive symptoms (from a list of 13 symptoms) that reach the height of intensity within 10 minutes of onset. The *DSM–IV* (APA, 1994) distinguishes panic attacks from *limited-symptom attacks*. Limited-symptom attacks include all the criteria of panic attacks but have fewer than four symptoms. Panic attacks can also be distinguished from *high anxiety*. High anxiety has similar symptoms to panic attacks but takes longer than 10 minutes to reach the height of intensity.

PD is characterized by recurrent, unexpected panic attacks. In addition, at least one attack is followed by at least one month of: (a) persistent concern about having additional attacks, (b) worry about the consequences or implications of the attacks, or (c) significant changes in behavior related to panic attacks (APA, 1994).

Agoraphobia often co-occurs with PD. However, some individuals have one of these disorders without the other. *Agoraphobia* is characterized by "anxiety about being in places or situations from which escape might be difficult or embarrassing or in which help may not be available in the event of having a spontaneous or situationally-predisposed Panic Attack or panic-like symptoms" (*DSM–IV*, APA, 1994, p. 396). Common agoraphobic situations include being alone, being out of the home, standing in a line, being in crowds, or traveling. People with agoraphobia often find situations more anxiety provoking when they are not accompanied by a "safe" person who can help in the event of a catastrophe.

COGNITIVE MODEL OF A PANIC ATTACK

The cognitive model of PD is based on the work of Aaron T. Beck and his colleagues (e.g., Beck & Clark, 1997; Beck et al., 1992; Brown, Beck, Newman, Beck, & Tran, 1997; Clark, 1986; Clark et al., 1994; Freeman & Simon, 1989; Sokol et al., 1989). Figure 6.1 illustrates the model with the case of Greg, a college student who developed PD during his first year away from home (described in detail in a later section as Case 6.A). The cognitive model is the foundation on which therapists develop individualized case conceptualizations for PD clients.

As shown in the diagram, panic attacks are characterized by vicious cycles. Panic attacks often begin with a *triggering stimulus.* For Greg, some of the triggering stimuli were internal events, such as anticipating being away from his mother and feeling angry. Other triggers were external to him and included being away from his apartment, driving, and ingesting caffeine. In the particular example illustrated in Fig. 6.1, the triggering stimulus for Greg was arguing with his mother.

The triggering stimulus activates an *orienting schema,* which functions as a gatekeeper to the panic (danger) mode. When the orienting schema is activated, it fully activates the already partially active (i.e., primed) panic mode. It fully activates all the systems of the mode (i.e., cognitive, affective, physiological, motivational, and behavioral).

An important occurrence in panic is that the client becomes *aware of the benign physical sensations of anxiety.* Greg's physical sensations consisted of chest pain, palpitations, sweating, tingling in his extremities, and hyperventilation (*physiological system*). Hyperventilation is particularly important because it often exacerbates other anxiety symptoms (Barlow, 1988).

Individuals who are panicking *catastrophically misinterpret* their physical sensations of arousal. Greg thought, "I'm having a heart attack." This thought fed back and caused more intense physical symptoms and sensations. This in turn further activated his catastrophic belief that he was having a heart attack. His tendency to misinterpret benign physical sensations related to his *core beliefs.* These included, "I am vulnerable to medical calamity, especially a heart attack," and "An accident could happen at any time." (To simplify Fig. 6.1, core beliefs were omitted.) Greg's core beliefs were shaped by his learning history, which is described in depth later in the chapter. In addition, people who panic become *hypervigilant to physical sensations* resulting in greater awareness of their symptoms, which they interpret as further evidence that the feared catastrophe will occur.

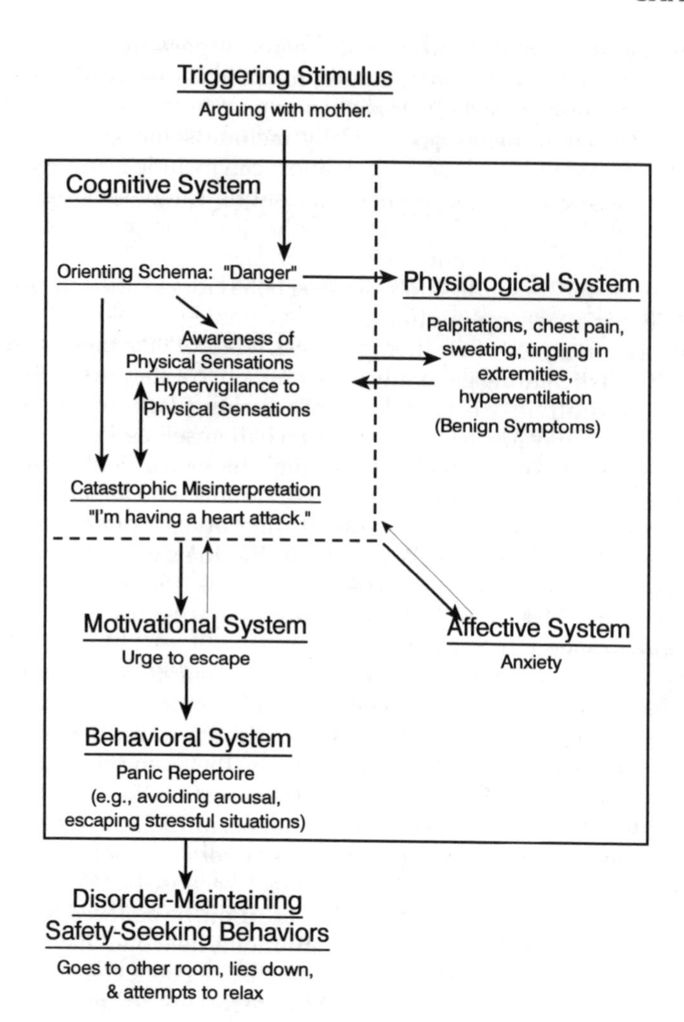

FIG. 6.1. Cognitive model of a panic attack.

As a result of catastrophically interpreting sensations, the other modal systems are activated. Individuals become aware of anxiety (*affective system*). In addition, their *motivational* and *behavioral systems* are activated. People suffering from PD generally feel inhibited from engaging in behaviors or being in situations that they associate with danger. Similarly, when panic sufferers find themselves in "dangerous" situations, they have urges to escape (*motivational system*). Their motivation often results in corresponding behavioral system activation. In the behavioral system, behavioral strategies from the individual's panic repertoire and procedural knowledge are activated. These, in turn, result in actual overt behavior. Individuals often engage in *disorder-maintaining safety-seeking behaviors* during panic attacks. These behaviors typically include some kind of escape or avoidance. Avoidance and escape behaviors can include frank agoraphobic avoidance, taking benzodiazapines, and subtle safety-seeking behaviors (Salkovskis et al., 1996). Safety-seeking behaviors tend to provide immediate anxiety relief but maintain the disorder.[13]

Some examples of subtle safety-seeking behaviors include the following. During a panic attack, individuals who have panic-provoking expectations of having a heart attack often attempt to rest, relax, or take their pulse. Those who are afraid of fainting generally sit or hold on to a stationary object. Individuals who are afraid of a mental collapse during attacks may do any of the following. They may touch the ground, pinch themselves, look for signs that their perception is "not crazy" by scanning the visual field, or attempt to suppress disturbing cognitions. Those individuals who are afraid of losing control and embarrassing themselves during attacks often isolate themselves from others. During panic attacks, individuals with any catastrophic cognitions may look for an escape route or ask for help. Greg's disorder-maintaining behaviors included frank agoraphobia and a variety of subtle safety-seeking behaviors.

An important mechanism by which disorder-maintaining safety-seeking behaviors maintain PD is by preventing disconfirmation of catastrophic cognitions. These behaviors appear to contribute to a phenomenon that panic clients commonly experience. Namely, they can have hundreds or thousands of panic attacks without ever learning that the catastrophic consequences that they expect to occur will not occur (Salkovskis et al., 1996). Greg experienced hundreds of panic attacks over a 6-month period. However, he continued to fear having a heart attack because he always lay down, rested, and attempted to calm himself. In addition, he believed that if he had not consistently avoided agoraphobic situations, he would have become so anxious that he would have had a heart attack. Greg believed that his behavioral strategies saved him from having a heart attack rather than believing that he was at minimal risk of having a heart attack.

ASSESSMENT AND CONCEPTUALIZATION OF PD

Besides the assessment procedures outlined in chapter 4, therapists should include specialized procedures in the assessment and case conceptualization of PD. This section describes the following facets of panic assessment: (a) using the Case Conceptualization Worksheet for PD to obtain a detailed understanding of the various elements of the cognitive model as they relate to a particular panic attack plus to track progress in therapy, (b) assess-

[13]For some individuals with panic, during some panic attacks, their conscious control system enables them to act against their maladaptive motivational responses.

ing the risk of fainting, (c) administering panic and agoraphobia questionnaires, (d) consulting with physicians prior to treatment, (e) using the Behavioral Assessment Test if the client is agoraphobic, and (f) integrating the information obtained from various sources in the Case Conceptualization Summary Form. This section also describes three clients with PD to illustrate the relationship between assessment and cognitive case conceptualization.

Case Conceptualization Worksheet for PD

Once the therapist diagnoses a client with PD, a fine-grained assessment of the client's panic attacks should be conducted. The therapist can often begin this during the intake interview. The Case Conceptualization Worksheet for PD (see the Appendix) can guide the therapist's assessment of the responses that comprise a panic attack. Specifically, the Case Conceptualization Worksheet prompts therapists for internal or external triggering stimuli, physical symptoms and sensations, catastrophic misinterpretations of physical sensations, and disorder-maintaining safety-seeking behaviors. Examples of completed worksheets are provided later in the chapter.

To facilitate assessment of catastrophic cognitions, Box 6.1 provides a list of common catastrophic thoughts and images that are central to panic attacks. To effectively assess for *disorder-maintaining safety-seeking behaviors* for the Case Conceptualization Worksheet, the therapist should use guided discovery. The following transcript provides an example of how a cognitive therapist might use guided discovery to learn about disorder-maintaining behaviors that a client engages in.

- Having a heart attack
- Having a stroke or embolism
- Suffocating
- Dying
- Going crazy
- Losing behavioral or emotional control
- Losing bowel or bladder control

Box 6.1. Common catastrophic thoughts or images that are central to panic attacks.

Therapist: Approximately how many panic attacks have you had?

Client: I don't know.

Therapist: You've had panic attacks for about 6 months, right?

Client: Right.

Therapist: On average, you've indicated that you had a few per day. What would you say the average was over the 6 months?

Client: I'd say I averaged about three per day.

Therapist: OK. There are about 180 days in 6 months times three per day. That would be about 540. Right?

Client: Right.

Therapist: During how many of those did you feel chest pressure and believe you were going to have a heart attack?

Client: Just about all of them.

Therapist: In other words, you had over 500 panic attacks with chest pressure and you never had a heart attack? How do you explain that?

Client: I've been very lucky, I guess.

Therapist: Was there anything you did to protect yourself from having a heart attack?

Client: I believe so. I always sit down or lie down and am very still until the feelings pass.

Therapist: That's what I call a disorder-maintaining, safety-seeking behavior. These behaviors have maintained your belief that you would have a heart attack in those situations. They've prevented you from seeing the truth that you wouldn't have a heart attack anyway. Do you see what I mean?

Client: Yes, that I never get to see that I wouldn't have a heart attack if I acted "business as usual."

Therapist: Right! Are there any other things you do to prevent a heart attack during a panic attack?

Client: I don't think there are other things I do during a panic attack. But, I eat a well-balanced diet and take vitamin E tablets each day to try to keep my heart healthy.

Box 6.2 lists questions that can help the therapist uncover disorder-maintaining, safety-seeking behaviors during guided discovery.

Besides helping therapists conduct fine-grained analyses of panic attacks, the Case Conceptualization Worksheet also can help *monitor ongoing progress* during therapy. Therapists should teach clients to use the worksheet for this purpose. Diligent use of the worksheet helps therapists and clients track the details of each panic attack. Also, the worksheet can indicate the frequency of attacks because therapists can instruct clients to record each attack and the date for each attack. Another advantage of the worksheet is that clients can and should use it immediately after experiencing panic symptoms. Therefore, it prevents memory problems from interfering with data collection.

Agoraphobia

Which situations or places do you find most anxiety-provoking?
  What is most anxiety-provoking about these situations?
What situations or places do you avoid because you are afraid that
  you will develop symptoms and won't be able to escape or get
  help?
Do you rely on someone with whom you are close to travel with you
  or be with you at home? Who?
    Do you ever travel alone?

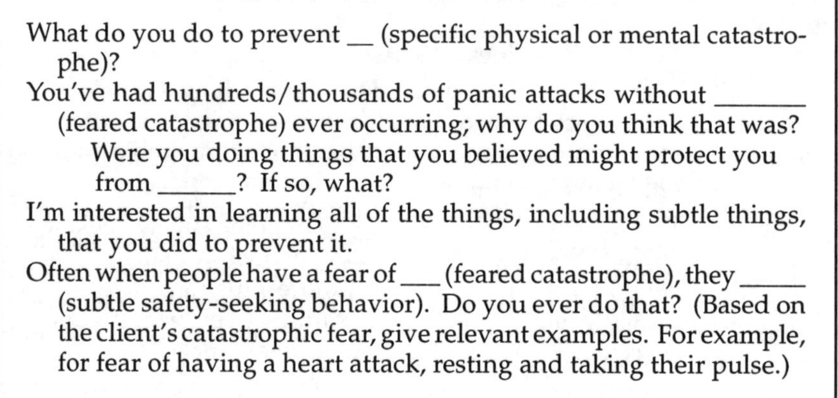

Subtle Safety-Seeking Behaviors

What do you do to prevent __ (specific physical or mental catastrophe)?
You've had hundreds/thousands of panic attacks without ______ (feared catastrophe) ever occurring; why do you think that was?
    Were you doing things that you believed might protect you from ______? If so, what?
I'm interested in learning all of the things, including subtle things, that you did to prevent it.
Often when people have a fear of ___ (feared catastrophe), they _____ (subtle safety-seeking behavior). Do you ever do that? (Based on the client's catastrophic fear, give relevant examples. For example, for fear of having a heart attack, resting and taking their pulse.)

Box 6.2. Questions for eliciting disorder-maintaining, safety-seeking behaviors.

Assessing the Risk of Fainting

Another important assessment issue for panic clients relates to their risk of fainting. (Therapists can often assess this during the intake interview.) Although many panic clients feel lightheaded or dizzy during an attack, the majority are at minimal risk of fainting. For most people, it is nearly impossible to faint when anxious. This is because when people experience anxiety, their blood pressure typically increases. In contrast, fainting occurs when cerebral blood pressure drops.

On the other hand, a subset of clients, *vasovagal responders,* can faint during an attack. When vasovagal responders become anxious—or interestingly when they see blood, injury, or invasive medical procedures—they experience a drop in blood pressure that can result in weakness or fainting.[14] (The prefix "vaso" means vascular and refers to blood vessels that relax when the vagus nerve fires—thus, "vagal.")

To determine whether clients are vasovagal responders, therapists should assess panic clients for blood-injury-injection phobias because people who are vasovagal responders often are phobic of these stimuli. They often have a history of either fainting or becoming extremely weak when they come in contact with the stimuli. Vasovagal responders also frequently have a history of fainting in panic-related situations, even when blood, injury, or injections are not involved. Therefore, therapists should assess any episodes of fainting, including a detailed inquiry of antecedents. Besides the vasovagal response, other factors that could be responsible for fainting include extreme heat, illness, or mood-altering substances. (Treatment approaches for vasovagal responders are detailed later in the chapter.)

Questionnaires

Once therapists have established that clients meet diagnostic criteria for PD, clinicians may administer one or more panic or agoraphobia questionnaires to provide them with clinically useful information.

The following panic and agoraphobia questionnaires have shown adequate reliability and validity and are clinically useful in assessing and tracking panic disorder clients' progress. Therapists can ask panic clients to complete these questionnaires between the intake and the first therapy session. Doing so provides the therapist with as much relevant information as possible prior to beginning treatment.

Panic Questionnaires:

Body Sensations Questionnaire (Chambless, Caputo, Bright, & Gallagher, 1984)

Panic Attack Cognitions Questionnaire (Clum, Broyles, Borden, & Watkins, 1990)

Panic Attack Symptoms Questionnaire (Clum, Broyles, Borden, & Watkins, 1990)

Agoraphobic Questionnaires:

The Agoraphobic Subscale of the Fear Questionnaire (Marks & Mathews, 1979)

Mobility Inventory for Agoraphobia (Chambless, Caputo, Jasin, Gracely, & Williams, 1985)

Agoraphobic Cognitions Questionnaire (Chambless, Caputo, Bright, & Gallagher, 1984)

---

[14]Beck et al. (1985) suggested that having a vagal response when seeing blood or injury may be adaptive in certain circumstances. Specifically, he suggested that if individuals are injured and bleeding, they are less likely to bleed to death if they faint. The reason for this is that as a result of fainting, individuals become inactive and their blood is directed away from their extremities and toward their body core.

Consultation With Physicians Prior to Beginning Treatment

Before beginning therapy proper, clients who meet diagnostic criteria for PD should get a complete physical examination. This allows the therapist to rule out the possibility that the client's panic attacks are the direct physiological effect of a medical condition. Most panic clients will have already had at least one recent physical exam. These clients will not need to have another. However, if a client has not had a thorough exam since the onset or exacerbation of PD, the therapist should urge the client to have one as soon as possible. Some of the more common medical problems that contribute to panic-like symptoms include: hypothyroidism, hypoglycemia, congestive heart failure, cardiac arrhythmias, mitral-valve prolapse, vestibular disease, pheochromocytoma, complex partial seizures, intracranial neoplasm, caffeinism, excessive use of bronchodilators, substance abuse, and substance withdrawal (APA, 1994). (Psychoactive substances—including caffeine, tobacco, alcohol, recreational drugs, and prescription drugs—also may contribute to PD. These disorders are covered by the Structured Clinical Interview for the *DSM–IV*, which is recommended for use during the intake evaluation.) Greg (Case 6.A), prior to presenting for cognitive therapy, had numerous medical workups including frequent visits to the local emergency room. These workups were negative except for a benign case of mitral-valve prolapse. Therefore, additional medical examinations were unnecessary and were discouraged by the therapist.

During the initial assessment, therapists should ask their clients for permission to contact clients' primary care physician and/or relevant specialists, such as cardiologists or neurologists. When a therapist consults with a physician about the panic client, the therapist should ask the results of the physical examination. The therapist should also inquire about possible explanations for the physical symptoms that the client misinterprets catastrophically. Such explanations can provide an understanding of the client's symptoms and can set the stage for cognitive restructuring of the catastrophic cognitions that maintain panic. In addition, the therapist should ask about whether panic-inductions through hyperventilation or vigorous exercise (described later) would be medically safe for the client. Heart conditions, pregnancy, and old age can be contraindications for panic inductions through hyperventilation or vigorous exercise. Finally, if the physician is prescribing high-potency benzodiazapines (i.e., Xanax, Ativan) for the client, the therapist should discuss possible changes in the medication.

Behavioral Assessment Test (BAT)

The BAT can be particularly helpful in elucidating elements of the cognitive model for agoraphobic clients. During the BAT, therapists instruct agoraphobic clients to expose themselves to the most anxiety-provoking situation that they can tolerate and stay as long as possible in the agoraphobic situation. For example, therapists may ask clients to drive as far as they can away from their home on a prearranged route. Clients then should record their level of anxiety (0–10), their cognitions and their disorder-maintaining safety-seeking behaviors (e.g., searching for escape routes, gripping the wheel tightly to prevent losing control). Whenever possible, agoraphobic clients should perform the BAT alone, without their therapists or other "safe" people present. Safe people typically decrease clients' anxiety and therefore confound the results of the test. Moreover, when exposure to actual phobic stimuli is not possible or practical (e.g., airplane trip), exposure in imagination is frequently helpful. Over the course of therapy, therapists can repeat the BAT to track clients' progress. A major benefit of the BAT is that it helps clients access even subtle factors that elicit and maintain their anxiety. Clients might have forgotten these factors if they had attempted to recall the information even minutes after the event.

Integrating Information Into a Case Conceptualization Summary Form

Information from the pretreatment questionnaires, intake evaluation, and the methods described previously should be integrated and recorded on a Case Conceptualization Summary Form. For each case presented in the next section, a summary form is illustrated.

Examples of Case Conceptualizations

Complete case conceptualizations of three individuals with PD are included in this section. For each client, a brief synopsis is given, followed by a Case Conceptualization Worksheet (completed by the therapist early in treatment), a Case Conceptualization Summary Form, and a Case Conceptualization Illustration, which represents a typical panic attack for the client. (To simplify the figures, the Case Conceptualization Illustrations shown for these clients do not include interventions.)

Case 6.A (Greg): PD With Agoraphobia

Greg was a 19-year-old undergraduate whose first panic attack occurred during his first semester of college during final exams. At that time, he had been under a great deal of stress, was tired, and was consuming more caffeine than usual. During panic attacks, he had a variety of physical symptoms and sensations including palpitations, chest pain, sweating, tingling in his extremities, and hyperventilation. In response to these symptoms, he had the catastrophic thought that he was going to have a heart attack. Greg made frequent visits to the emergency room, his internist, and a cardiologist, in response to his fear that he was having heart attacks. All these exams were negative for heart problems, although he did have mitral-valve prolapse.

Greg's core beliefs appear to have contributed to his misinterpretation of his benign physical sensations. He held the beliefs, "I am vulnerable to medical calamity, especially a heart attack," and "An accident could happen at any time." These beliefs appeared to be products of his learning history. Several childhood occurrences seemed to predispose him to expecting health-related catastrophes. First, when Greg was a young child, his parents were extremely concerned with health and safety. For example, they frequently read to him newspaper articles of accidents and rare diseases striking children. When he played vigorously, his mother frequently warned, "Children can have heart attacks too." Second, his beloved grandmother died suddenly of a heart attack when Greg was 7 years old. Third, his best friend died of colon cancer, which initially physical exams did not detect. Finally, another friend in high school died in a car crash.

As a result of his panic attacks, he engaged in agoraphobic avoidance as well as subtle safety-seeking behaviors such as staying still and trying to calm himself. Also, Greg's mother came in from out of town to live with him and help him through his problems. She became his "safe person." His agoraphobia and subtle safety-seeking behaviors appear to have both escalated and maintained the disorder. He became extremely agoraphobic and left the apartment only with his mother and only to see doctors.

Another apparent contributor to Greg's panic with agoraphobia was his dependency on his parents, which long predated the onset of his PD. He felt extreme ambivalence about leaving his parents to go to college and becoming more independent. On the one hand, he wanted a normal college experience, including independence and friends. In addition, he wanted to escape from his parents whom he resented and considered to be overbearing. On the other hand, he was afraid to be on his own and was afraid of what separating from his parents would do to them. At some level, he seemed to realize how much his parents needed him to depend on them. Greg's disorder permitted him to delay separation from his parents while simultaneously being conscious of the desire for independence (see Figs. 6.1, 6.2, and 6.3).

PANIC DISORDER CONCEPTUALIZATION WORKSHEET

Client's Name: Greg

PANIC SCENARIOS

TRIGGERING STIMULI	BENIGN PHYSICAL SENSATIONS	CATASTROPHIC MISINTERPRETATION OF SENSATIONS	SUBTLE OR GROSS SAFETY-SEEKING BEHAVIOR
External: Conflict with his mother, caffeine, physical exertion, being outside of his apartment. (Each causes increase in heart rate.)	Awareness of chest sensations, especially pain or palpitations; sweating; hyperventilation; tingling in his extremities.	I'm going to have a heart attack and die.	Sleeps much of the day to prevent exertion; if he begins to experience panic sensations, he lies down, rests and attempts to relax; frequently stays in his bedroom trying to stay as still and calm as possible to prevent himself from straining his heart.
Being away from his apartment (e.g., driving).		I'm going to have a heart attack and won't be able to get help in time.	Only leaves apartment with his mother (& this is only to go to doctor appointments) Scans street for pay phones.
Internal: Anticipating being away from his mother or going out of the apartment; anticipating being anxious which "will strain my heart."			

continued on next page

AVOIDED SITUATIONS OR INTERNAL STATES

1. Going out of the house
2. Being alone
3. Caffeine
4. Physical exertion
5. Arguing with his mother
6. Thinking about upsetting things

OTHER PROBLEMATIC SCENARIOS

TRIGGERING STIMULI	COGNITIONS	EMOTIONS	BEHAVIORS
Mother is irritable and complains that Greg's problems represent a hardship for her.	I can't stand her; I hate having to need her so much; I wish I had a normal life.	Anger Sadness	Goes to bed.

FIG. 6.2.(*cont'd*) Case Conceptualization Worksheet (Case 6.A, Greg).

CASE CONCEPTUALIZATION SUMMARY FORM

Client's Name: Greg

Identifying Information: 19-year-old undergraduate who is on a leave of absence from his studies; lives with his mother in an apartment. Currently, he never leaves his apartment without his mother, does not let her leave his sight and only leaves the apartment for doctors' visits. He has mitral-valve prolapse. He was referred by his primary care physician for panic disorder.

Presenting Problem: Panic attacks with agoraphobia.

Precipitant(s): First panic attack occurred during finals week when he was consuming more caffeine, sleeping less, and eating more erratically than usual.

Exhaustive List of Problems, Issues, and Therapy-Relevant Behaviors:

1. Panic attacks. 2. Extreme agoraphobia. 3. Dependence on mother. 4. Ambivalence toward mother--depends on her & resents her.	5. Chronic feelings of sadness & inadequacy. 6. Hypersomnia.

Diagnoses (Axis I): Panic Disorder with Agoraphobia; Major Depressive Disorder, Single Episode, Moderate

Personality Characteristics: Dependent Features.

Relevant Beliefs:

1. **I'm vulnerable to medical calamity, especially a heart attack.** 2. I'm generally helpless to prevent a heart attack; however, I might be OK if I'm always on guard, avoid overexerting myself, avoid going places where I can't get help, and have Mom with me all the time.	3. An accident can happen at any time. 4. If I sleep, I'm not exerting myself and putting myself at risk. 5. My life is miserable and sleep is a way to not have to think about it.

Origins of Core Beliefs:

(1) Parents directly and indirectly conveyed their extreme concern about his health and safety.
(2) One friend died of cancer after being misdiagnosed.
(3) Another friend was killed in a car crash.
(4) Grandmother died of heart attack.

continued on next page

WORKING MODEL

VICIOUS CYCLES / MAINTAINING FACTORS:
Subtle and gross avoidance of anxiety symptoms (especially rapid heart rate) and agoraphobic situations prevent disconfirmation of catastrophic belief that he would *die of a heart attack* and prevent habituation to anxiety-provoking cues; avoidance and escape are reinforced by anxiety reduction.

TREATMENT

Goals:
1. Decrease the frequency and intensity of panic attacks, preferably eliminate them.
2. Habituation to agoraphobic situations; decrease gross avoidance and subtle safety-seeking behaviors.
3. Increase independence from parents.

Possible Obstacles to Treatment: Feelings of dependency might make giving up symptoms frightening; parents may attempt to sabotage treatment.

Plan:
1. Exposure to physical exertion while not engaging in safety-seeking behaviors; cognitive restructuring, progressive muscle relaxation, paced breathing, & refocusing attention; graded exposure to agoraphobic situations.
2. Address issues of separation from mother & independence.

FIG. 6.3. (*cont'd*) Case Conceptualization Summary Form (Case 6.A, Greg).

Case 6.B (Jimmy): PD Without Agoraphobia

Jimmy was a 47-year-old, unhappily married, childless lawyer who presented approximately 3 years after the onset of PD. The onset of his symptoms had no clear precipitants. Although he was near a big work deadline during his first panic attack, he had many other equally stressful times without becoming symptomatic. In his panic attacks, he experienced feelings of unreality and dizziness that he catastrophically misinterpreted as signifying that he would lose control and "go crazy." These catastrophic cognitions amplified his anxiety. His major coping strategies were to consume alcohol or have sex. He used both strategies to reduce anticipatory anxiety and to reduce his anxiety once a panic attack had begun.

Alcohol and sex were strategies he used since he was a teenager for coping with anxiety. However, once he began having panic attacks, these behaviors became excessive and contributed to his difficulties. He began abusing alcohol frequently, which was interfering with his work and contributed to marital discord. In addition, being hung over increased the frequency of his panic attacks. Regarding using sex as an anxyolitic, he masturbated several times per day. For large blocks of times each week, he browsed the Internet for sex sites. He also frequented adult bookstores where he had sexual encounters with other customers. These maladaptive sexual behaviors contributed to his marital problems.

Jimmy's expectation that he would go crazy while experiencing anxiety symptoms seemed to be the result of his history. Specifically, his maternal grandmother had been institutionalized for much of her life for what appeared to be schizophrenia. This had been a secret that he discovered a few years before the onset of his PD. His mother had generalized anxiety and was dependent on Xanax. Because of his family history, he feared that he would become overwhelmed and incapacitated by anxiety (see Figs. 6.4, 6.5, and 6.6 for more information).

PANIC DISORDER CONCEPTUALIZATION WORKSHEET

Client's Name: Jimmy

PANIC SCENARIOS

TRIGGERING STIMULI	BENIGN PHYSICAL SYMPTOMS & SENSATIONS	CATASTROPHIC MISINTERPRETATIONS	DISORDER-MAINTAINING BEHAVIORS
External: Being at work, arguing with wife. **Internal:** Anticipating going to work; anticipating being anxious; imagining going crazy; anger.	Lightheadedness, dizziness, feelings of unreality, nausea.	I'm going to lose control and go crazy.	Drinks alcohol, engages in masturbation, browses the Internet for sex sites, or goes to an adult bookstore.

continued on next page

AVOIDED SITUATIONS OR INTERNAL STATES

1. Anxiety symptoms.
2. Being home with his wife.

OTHER PROBLEMATIC SCENARIOS

TRIGGERING STIMULI	COGNITIONS	EMOTIONS	BEHAVIORS
Wife makes purchases that he thinks are unnecessary, and he becomes anxious about its effect on their financial situation.	F_ _king B_ _ch! Not only shouldn't she spend so much money, but she shouldn't do things that make me anxious. Does she want to send me over the edge!	Anger.	Goes to bar to vent to buddies.

FIG. 6.4. (*cont'd*) Case Conceptualization Worksheet (Case 6.B, Jimmy).

CASE CONCEPTUALIZATION SUMMARY FORM

Client's Name: Jimmy

Identifying Information: 47-year-old, married, white, male lawyer.

Presenting Problem: Panic attacks.

Precipitant(s): No clear precipitants.

Exhaustive List of Problems, Issues, and Therapy-Relevant Behaviors:

1. Panic attacks. 2. Alcohol abuse to cope with anxiety. 3. Sexually addictive behavior.	4. Recent unsatisfactory work evaluation. 5. Marital discord.

Diagnoses (Axis I): Panic Disorder Without Agoraphobia; Alcohol Abuse; Sexual Disorder (Not Otherwise Specified)

Personality Characteristics: Avoidant of anxiety and upsetting issues.

Relevant Beliefs:

1. **I might have a nervous breakdown and become totally insane.** 2. If I feel lightheaded, dizzy, or like things aren't real, I'm on the verge of going crazy.	3. I can't deal with stress; if I'm stressed, I'll go nuts. 4. Sex and drinking can help me calm down enough so I won't go over the edge.

Origins of Central Core Beliefs: Grandmother had schizophrenia and was in mental hospital for much of her life. His mother had generalized anxiety and was dependent on Xanax.

continued on next page

WORKING MODEL

VICIOUS CYCLES / MAINTAINING FACTORS:
Drinking and sex decrease his anxiety in the short-term--as a direct physiological effect of these activities plus distraction from catastrophic misinterpretation of symptoms and hypervigilance. As a result, he never has the opportunity to disconfirm his belief that he will go crazy if he lets himself become extremely anxious. Similarly, avoidance of anxiety-provoking situations prevents disconfirmation of catastrophic belief and prevents habituation to these situations. These strategies are reinforced by anxiety reduction. Maladaptive strategies ==> alienating wife ==> increasing anxiety ==> increasing use of maladaptive strategies.

TREATMENT:

Goals:
1. Decrease the frequency and intensity of panic attacks, preferably eliminate them.
2. Decrease subtle and gross avoidance, including alcohol abuse and addictive sexual behavior.

Possible Obstacles to Treatment: His long history of avoiding upsetting situations, feelings, and issues puts him at risk for poor adherence to treatment and premature drop out.

Plan:
1. Exposure to anxiety while not engaging in disorder-maintaining, safety-seeking behaviors (i.e., alcohol abuse and visiting adult bookstore); cognitive restructuring, progressive muscle relaxation, paced breathing, & refocusing attention.
2. If sex, alcohol, and marital problems do not resolve once panic is treated, address these directly.

FIG. 6.5. (*cont'd*) Case Conceptualization Summary Form (Case 6.B, Jimmy).

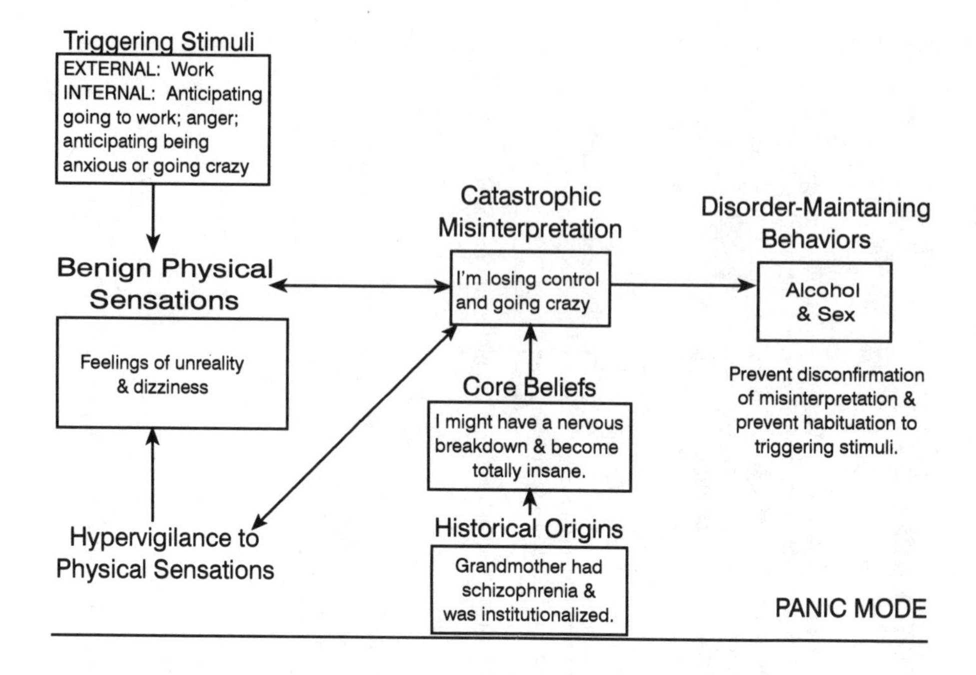

FIG. 6.6. Case Conceptualization Illustration (Case 6.B, Jimmy).

Case 6.C (Jillian): PD With Agoraphobia

Jillian was a 26-year-old, never-married, postal worker who lived with her fiance. Her PD with agoraphobia began 2 years before seeking cognitive therapy. The physical symptoms and sensations that she experienced during attacks included weakness (in which she often fell to her knees), dizziness, lightheadedness, rapid heart rate, nausea, cold sweats, and tingling sensations in extremities. As a result of these symptoms, she had the catastrophic cognitions that she would faint and humiliate herself. Some of her panic attacks were externally triggered by the sight of blood or getting injections. Other attacks were triggered by the anticipation of being anxious. She had unsuccessful therapy with interpersonal and psychodynamic therapists. At the time she began cognitive therapy, she was taking Xanax as needed, totaling approximately 4 mg per day.

Jillian's first spontaneous panic attack occurred a few days after she had fainted while having blood drawn during a medical exam. During the first attack, she was in a crowded shopping mall at Christmas time and suddenly thought, "What if I faint here too?" As soon as she had this thought, she reportedly had a surge of anxiety and sat down on the nearest bench.

PANIC DISORDER CONCEPTUALIZATION WORKSHEET

Client's Name: Jillian

PANIC SCENARIOS

TRIGGERING STIMULI	BENIGN PHYSICAL SYMPTOMS & SENSATIONS	CATASTROPHIC MISINTERPRETATIONS	DISORDER-MAINTAINING BEHAVIORS
External: Sight of blood or injury; being in crowds. **Internal:** Anticipating getting anxious or being in crowds.	Feeling weak, lightheaded, cold sweats, nausea, rapid heart rate, tingling in extremities.	I'm going to lose control; I'm going to faint and humiliate myself.	Takes Xanax. When possible, lies down; otherwise, locks legs and holds on to person or stationary objects.

AVOIDED SITUATIONS OR INTERNAL STATES

1. Watching TV or movies that are likely to have violence.
2. Being in crowds (e.g., shopping)

OTHER PROBLEMATIC SCENARIOS

TRIGGERING STIMULI	COGNITIONS	EMOTIONS	BEHAVIORS
None noted.			

FIG. 6.7. Case Conceptualization Worksheet (Case 6.C, Jillian).

CASE CONCEPTUALIZATION SUMMARY FORM

Client's Name: Jillian

Identifying Information: 26-year-old, postal worker, lives with fiance; vasovagal responder; emotionally healthy; two-year history of panic disorder.

Presenting Problem: Panic attacks, fear of fainting.

Precipitant(s): A few days prior to her first attack (2 yrs ago), she had fainted while giving blood.

Exhaustive List of Problems, Issues, and Therapy-Relevant Behaviors:

1. Panic attacks. 2. Fear of fainting and making a fool of herself. 3. Avoids crowds, seeing movies/TV with potential violence. 4. Takes Xanax as soon as she begins to feel anxious or dizzy. 5. Dependent on Xanax.	

Diagnoses (Axis I): Panic Disorder with Agoraphobia; Specific Blood-Injury-Injection Phobia; Sedative Dependence

Personality Characteristics: Well-adjusted; generally finds life to be fulfilling; flexible coping with most life problems; fulfilling relationships.

Relevant Beliefs:

1. I might faint if I see blood. 2. I might faint if I get into a crowd. 3. If I faint, I'll make a fool of myself.	

Origins of Core Beliefs: History of fainting when exposed to sight of blood, needles and when in crowds.

continued on next page

WORKING MODEL

VICIOUS CYCLES / MAINTAINING FACTORS:
To prevent fainting, she avoids crowds and experiences in which she may be exposed to blood or injury (e.g., TV and movies with violent themes), takes Xanax when feels anxious, or lies down. These prevent possible disconfirmation of her catastrophic expectations and are reinforced by anxiety reduction.

TREATMENT:

Goals:
1. Decrease the frequency and intensity of panic attacks, preferably eliminate them.
2. Learn skills for decreasing her chances of fainting.
3. Habituation to agoraphobic situations; decrease subtle and gross avoidance.

Possible Obstacles to Treatment: Dependence on Xanax.

Plan:
1. Panic induction while not engaging in disorder-maintaining safety-seeking behaviors (i.e., lying down).
2. Coping strategies (cognitive restructuring, progressive muscle relaxation, paced breathing, & refocusing attention).
3. To decrease the likelihood of fainting, client will learn applied muscle tension skills that she will practice in blood-phobia situation.
4. Work with primary care physician to discontinue Xanax.
5. Exposure to feared situations,

FIG. 6.8. (*cont'd*) Case Conceptualization Summary Form (Case 6.C, Jillian).

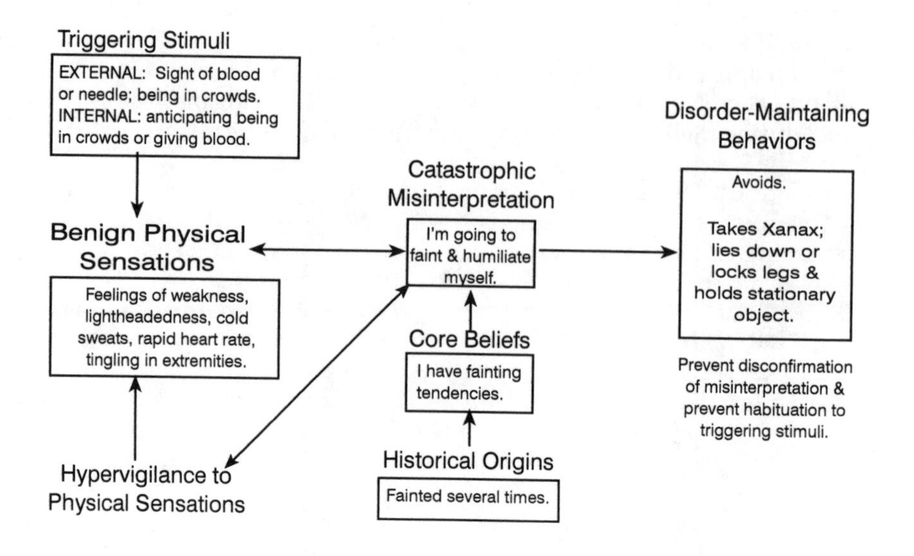

FIG. 6.9. Case Conceptualization Illustration (Case 6.C, Jillian).

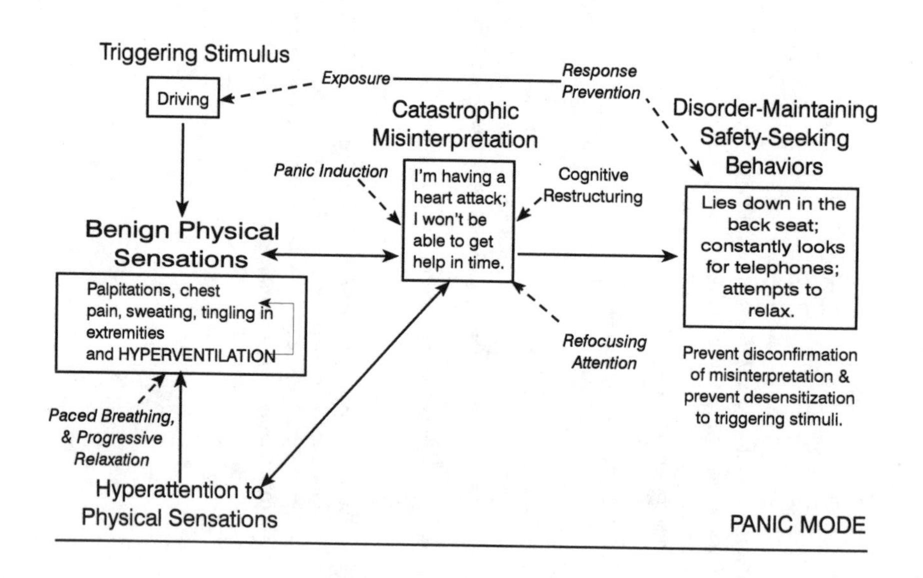

FIG. 6.10. Presenting the Case Conceptualization Illustration to a panic client.

After resting for about 20 minutes, a friend—with whom she had been shopping—escorted her to her car and drove her home.

Jillian apparently was a vasovagal responder. She had fainted on several other occasions. Many of these involved either giving blood or getting shots during medical consultations or seeing injury. She also fainted once when she was ill on a hot day.

As a result of her fear of fainting, Jillian engaged in a variety of disorder-maintaining safety-seeking behaviors. She avoided being in crowds and seeing violent TV shows and movies. When she began to feel anxious or anticipated being in anxiety-provoking situations, she took Xanax. In addition, when she was feeling faint and the situation permitted, she lay down. Otherwise, she straightened her legs in a locked position and attempted to hold on to a person or stationary object.

Other than her anxiety problems and her dependence on Xanax, Jillian appeared to be an emotionally healthy person. For example, she generally was happy, had close and fulfilling relationships with people, including her fiance, and performed well at work (see Figs. 6.7, 6.8, and 6.9 for more information).

COGNITIVE THERAPY OF PD

Beck and colleagues developed a treatment package for PD that is highly effective (Arntz & van den Hout, 1996; Beck et al., 1992; Brown et al., 1997; Clark et al., 1994; Magraf & Schneider, 1991; Öst & Westling, 1995). Approximately 85% of patients in the outcome studies cited above were panic-free at termination. 80% maintained their panic-free status at 1-year follow-ups. The treatment package intervenes at each point in the cognitive model. Before discussing treatment components, this section describes how the therapist can present the Case Conceptualization Illustration to a panic client.

Presentation of a Case Conceptualization Illustration to a Panic Client

Early in treatment, the therapist presents the panic client with a Case Conceptualization Illustration. The illustration graphically depicts the client's idiosyncratic experiences within the cognitive model of PD. Presented here is an excerpt from a session in which Greg's therapist showed him an individualized Case Conceptualization Illustration. As she was drawing the model, she explained it to Greg in the following way (see Fig. 6.10).

Therapist: If it's all right with you, I'd like to illustrate for you a framework for understanding panic attacks and how treatment fits into the framework.

Greg: I'd really like to hear this.

Therapist: Great! To begin with there often is a triggering stimulus. There are many different types of triggering stimuli. For example, they could be external situations, such as leaving your apartment, driving, or arguing with your mom. Or, they can be internal events. For example, a triggering stimulus can be a scary thought, like anticipating going to class. Another internal triggering stimulus is your heart racing due to walking up the flight of stairs to your apartment. Do you prefer which one I illustrate?

Greg: How about driving?

Therapist: Fine. In response to the triggering stimulus, driving, you experience benign physical sensations of anxiety. For you, these often include palpitations, chest pain, tingling in your arms and legs, and hyperventilation. Next, and this is crucial, you catastrophically misinterpret these sensations. Specifically, you think, "I'm going to have a heart attack" and "I won't be able to get help." These are terrifying thoughts. As a result of catastrophically misinterpreting your symptoms of anxiety, your anxiety symptoms intensify. That is, catastrophic thoughts feed back to increase your benign physical sensations. You can see how these reverberate up and back resulting in more and more anxiety. The catastrophic thoughts also result in your becoming hyperattentive to what is going on in your body. A natural response to thinking you're having a heart attack is to pay careful attention. However, by doing so, you increase your anxiety even more. When you tune into symptoms because you're afraid of dying, it feels like strong evidence that you are right—that you are having a heart attack. As you can see, this is a vicious cycle (points in circling motion). I should also tell you a little more about hyperventilation. Hyperventilation is a very important symptom because it typically intensifies the other anxiety symptoms. Greg, does this sound like what happens to you so far?

Greg: Exactly.

Therapist: Another important part of this is what you do about your anxiety. These are disorder-maintaining safety-seeking behaviors. So, for example, you sometimes lie down in the back seat of the car to prevent yourself from getting too overwhelmed, which you fear will result in a heart attack. This behavior prevents you from learning that even if you're overwhelmed and having intense symptoms, you won't have a heart attack.

It also interferes with a natural process of your desensitizing to scary situations. The process of desensitization occurs throughout the animal kingdom even in primitive species like fish. Therefore, it can occur without higher level thinking. When animals are repeatedly exposed to a triggering situation and nothing bad happens, their fear eventually disappears. Can you see how safety-seeking behaviors maintain your panic disorder?

Greg: Yes. It makes sense.

Therapist: It is very important that we find all of your disorder-maintaining behaviors so that you can gradually give them up. Disorder-maintaining behaviors include major avoidance, like staying in your apartment most of the time. But, it can also be a subtle behavior like trying to calm yourself when you're anxious because of your catastrophic expectations. Are you aware of any other things you do to prevent yourself from having a heart attack during panic attacks?

Greg: I try to avoid fighting with Mom. If we start to fight, I go in the other room and lie down. Or, I tell her, she's got to stop, or it will kill me. Also, I take my pulse a lot.

Therapist: Yes. Are there things that you do when you're driving to try to make sure you'd get help if you had a heart attack?

Greg: I only drive with mother, and I'm constantly looking for telephones in case of emergency.

Therapist: Any other disorder-maintaining safety-seeking behaviors?

Greg: That's all I can think of right now.

Therapist: OK. Let me point out one last thing. When a person panics, all of his or her systems are activated as if there were actual danger. Thoughts, emotions, physical responses, motivation, and behavior all are crying out "Danger!" As a result, it is helpful to think of the response as a panic mode. Does that sound like what you experience?

Greg: Exactly.

Therapist: Anything missing from this illustration?

Greg: No. It looks quite complete.

Therapist: Good. Now, let me show you what we can do to help you overcome your panic. I am going to suggest several things. None of these by itself is usually enough to stop panic attacks. However, as a package, they are extremely effective in helping people become panic free. In outcome studies, 85% of people who got this treatment were panic free at the end of treatment. Moreover, these effects are quite durable. There have been a few long-term studies, not many because it is hard to keep track of people. But, the studies I've seen have tracked clients for 1 year. 80% of clients continued to be panic free at 1 year. In psychotherapy outcome studies, this is quite remarkable.

Greg: Great!

Therapist: So, let's look at what we can do. First, we need to address the catastrophic misinterpretations. You've said, when you are not in the middle of panic attacks, you're able to believe that you probably aren't going to have a heart attack. Therefore, what we need to do is find a way to help you remember and believe a realistic perspective during an attack. I'll show you ways to do that.

Second, we can interrupt the overbreathing with paced breathing techniques. Third, to decrease your benign symptoms of anxiety, I can teach you to deeply relax your muscles. As you learn to decrease your overall level of anxiety, it will help you decrease the frequency, intensity, and duration of panic attacks. Fourth, to disrupt your hyperattention to physical sensations, I will show you some strategies for refocusing your attention. Finally, as you are mastering these skills and having control over your panic attacks, we will work on decreasing your use of disorder-maintaining safety-seeking behaviors. This may include repeated, systematic exposure to feared situations that you will have control over. Any comments or questions about any of this?

Greg: No, it sounds very good. I'm glad I'm finally seeing someone who understands what I'm going through!

Overview of Treatment Components

Figure 6.11 overlays the cognitive model of PD with interventions that target each element of the model. The client's **catastrophic misinterpretations** of panic symptoms are altered through *panic inductions, cognitive restructuring,* and *refocusing attention.* **Hypervigilance to internal events** is decreased through *refocusing attention.* **Benign physical sensations,** including **hyperventilation,** are reduced through *paced breathing* and *progressive relaxation training.* **Disorder-maintaining behaviors** are eliminated through *exposure to triggers* (physical sensations, situations or places) with *response prevention.* Each of these interventions is described in the subsequent sections.

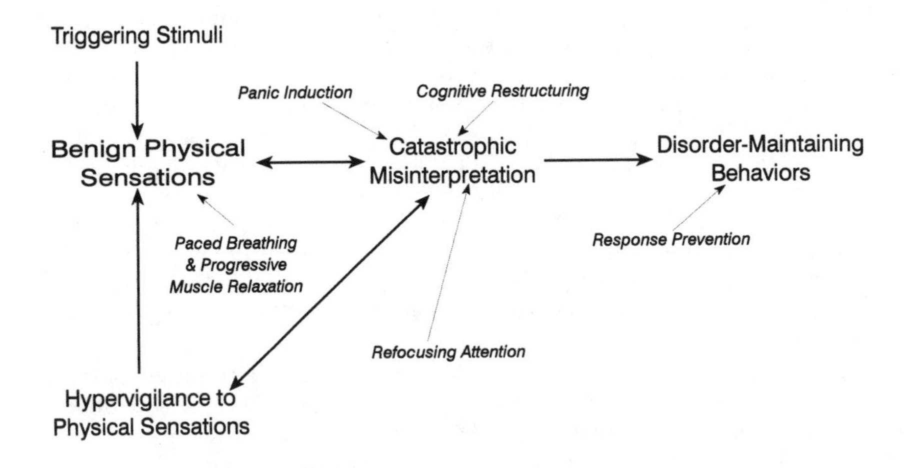

FIG. 6.11. Panic model overlaid with interventions.

Panic Induction Session(s)

An important treatment component with PD clients is intentionally and repeatedly inducing panic attacks during sessions. In brief, panic inductions involve using various manipulations to replicate symptoms of panic attacks and to directly test the client's catastrophic belief. This section describes (a) the benefits of panic inductions, (b) an approach for introducing clients to panic inductions, (c) methods for inducing panic, and (d) coping skills introduced during panic-induction sessions.

Benefits of Panic Inductions

The benefits of panic induction are many. The most important benefit is that it helps clients *directly test their catastrophic beliefs about attacks and begin to realize these are unfounded.* Clients expect a catastrophe if they experience particular types of pronounced symptoms. During panic inductions, therapists attempt to induce extreme symptoms to help clients realize that their fear is unfounded. Consider for example clients who are afraid that having a rapid heart rate will cause them to have a heart attack. Therapists can induce panic by having them do strenuous calisthenics beyond the point at which clients feel they must stop. This shows them that experiencing a very rapid heart rate does not result in a heart attack.

To have a direct test of the catastrophic beliefs, the therapist encourages the client to resist engaging in disorder-maintaining behaviors during the induction. For example, Greg (Case 6.A) was encouraged to not lie down when panic was induced in the session. Jimmy (Case 6.B) obviously did not have his typical pathological coping strategies—alcohol and addictive sexual behavior—available to him during in-session inductions. Jillian (Case 6.C) was asked to resist lying down, locking her legs, or holding on to stationary objects. Another way panic inductions can help disconfirm catastrophic beliefs is that clients generally realize, "If my therapist intentionally brought on an attack, she must be sure that I'm not going to have a heart attack."

A second benefit of clients experiencing panic symptoms during sessions is that it allows clients, in a controlled environment, to *practice coping strategies while experiencing panic symptoms.* In contrast, if clients learn coping techniques while they are not experiencing panic symptoms, they are less likely to generalize the skills to naturally occurring attacks.

Third, inductions can sometimes help clients decatastrophize their beliefs by providing them with *benign explanations* for their panic symptoms. For example, when panic is induced by hyperventilation, clients may conclude, "Since hyperventilating brought on panic feelings during this session, maybe I'm overbreathing before real attacks too."

A fourth benefit is that panic inductions help clients *desensitize to sensations that they fear.* In PD, anxiety is both a response and a triggering stimulus. Repeated exposure can help clients view anxiety as less frightening (i.e., make it less likely to trigger a more intense anxiety response). Consequently, therapists should strive to produce as many of the client's naturally occurring panic symptoms as possible. To accomplish this, the therapist often must use several different induction methods with a particular client.

Fifth, by inducing panic symptoms in session, the therapist *demonstrates that panic attacks are controllable.* The fact that therapists can intentionally cause clients to have panic attacks demonstrates for clients that therapists have control over the attacks. As a result, clients often conclude, "Eventually I may be able to get control of turning on and turning off these attacks." Moreover, in the vast majority of cases—within 5 or 10 minutes following the panic induction—the therapist can help clients dramatically diminish their physiological arousal. This further demonstrates for clients that their panic is controllable.

A final benefit of using panic inductions is that clients often *gain confidence in their therapists.* For example, many clients conclude, "My therapist understands my panic attacks so well that she can bring them on and help me stop them."

Introducing Clients to Panic Inductions

To induce panic, the therapist first explains the procedure to the client. The therapist focuses on maintaining rapport while at the same time increasing anxiety that will facilitate the induction. For example, the therapist might introduce the procedure in the following manner:

Therapist: Today, I'd like to do a diagnostic experiment to see what panic is like for you. I've checked with Dr. X [the client's internist or cardiologist for whom the client signed a release of information], and she indicated that what I have in mind is safe for you. To begin with, please fill out this symptom questionnaire[15] for what a typical panic attack is like for you. [The client completes the checklist.] Next, I'm going to ask you if you're willing to do something that will be extremely unpleasant. But, it is also extremely important in learning to overcome your panic. I'd like you to ______ (panic-induction procedure based on the client's idiosyncratic symptoms) to see if we can bring on a panic attack. I hate to ask you to do this. However, it's extremely important to your treatment, and I'll do it with you. Are you willing to do this?

Client: You're going to make me have a panic attack?!

Therapist: I won't make you do anything you're not ready to do. However, having panic symptoms in here is extremely important to your learning to master these attacks. Studies show that panic inductions are a crucial part of successful therapy. 85% of clients who participate in this treatment are panic-free at the end of therapy.

Client: I'll do anything to get rid of this problem, and I'll just have to trust you.

Therapist: Good. One last thing before we get started. When you feel like you can't go on any further, please let me know. However, it's extremely important that you try to go at least a little beyond that point. OK?

Client: OK.

Methods for Inducing Panic

Therapists should select methods for inducing panic based on the case conceptualization, including the client's idiosyncratic physical sensations, catastrophic cognitions, and, when necessary, panic triggers. Cognitive-behavioral researchers and theorists have suggested several ways that therapists can induce panic attacks in their clients (e.g., Barlow & Cerny, 1988; Brown et al., 1997).

[15]The client completes the Panic Attack Symptoms Questionnaire (Clum et al., 1990). This is a scale that contains 36 items reflecting symptoms frequently experienced during a panic attack. The questionnaire shows adequate psychometric properties and was shown to successfully differentiate a group of anxiety-disordered individuals with panic attacks from anxiety-disordered clients without panic attacks.

Before discussing panic induction methods, a note about determining the similarity between induced symptoms and actual attacks is warranted. Because inductions should generate symptoms that clients experience as being similar to an actual panic attack, therapists should ask clients to rate the similarity of induced attacks to naturally occurring attacks, from 0, *not at all similar,* to 10, *exactly the same.* If the similarity is less than 5 out of 10, the therapist should attempt a different approach to inducing panic.

Most clients benefit from panic inductions through hyperventilation. This procedure often results in clients experiencing a variety of panic symptoms. Hyperventilation inductions are especially useful for clients who, during attacks, are aware of changes in their breathing or experience lightheadedness, dizziness, or tingling sensations in their extremities. During inductions, therapists encourage clients to breathe deeply through their mouths for 2 minutes. Therapists demonstrate the desired breathing rate, approximately one breath per 2 seconds, as well as the depth of breathing. For clients who fear having heart attacks, physical exertion (e.g., jumping jacks) elicits a rapid heart rate and is recommended. For clients who experience chest pain or pressure during panic attacks, they can press in on their chest with folded arms to induce panic. For those who have panic attacks triggered by changes in temperature or who experience sweating, hot flashes, or chills during attacks, inductions can consist of exposure to noticeable temperature changes, such as entering a room with a blasting space heater. Exposure to bright lights, fluorescent lights or the sight of parallel lines can be used to induce panic for clients whose attacks are triggered by visual distortions and feelings of unreality. Clients who experience difficulty breathing during attacks and are afraid of suffocating benefit from breathing through a coffee straw, which restricts their air intake.

Whatever the method of induction, therapists should urge clients to continue with the induction for at least a few seconds beyond the point at which they believe they must stop. When clients go beyond this point, they learn that even when they are having extremely intense symptoms, their catastrophic beliefs do not come true. To maintain rapport, therapists should encourage and praise their efforts with comments such as "You're doing great ... just a little bit longer."

For Greg (Case 6.A), the two types of panic inductions that were most helpful were physical exertion and hyperventilation. The hyperventilation induction was useful for exposing him to many panic symptoms, including tingling in his extremities and increased heart rate. However, he experienced panic inductions through hyperventilation as being rather dissimilar to real attacks. For example, he felt extremely lightheaded during these induction, whereas he usually did not feel lightheaded during actual attacks. In addition, hyperventilation inductions did not activate his catastrophic belief that he was having a heart attack. On the other hand, panic inductions through physical exertion did trigger his catastrophic belief that he was having a panic attack. During the latter type of induction, his symptom profile was similar to an actual attack, and he was moderately afraid of having a heart attack. Therefore, repeatedly using the physical exertion approach helped him realize that his catastrophic belief was unfounded.

Jimmy (Case 6.B) feared losing control and going crazy as a result of feelings of unreality and dizziness. Based on his individualized case conceptualization, Jimmy's therapist believed he had a particularly low threshold for dealing with distress. As a result, she modified the panic induction procedure. She started with hyperventilation. However, she started slowly with him and gave him a great deal of control over the procedure. They jointly decided that he would begin by hyperventilating for just 10 seconds. Gradually, over two sessions, they increased the duration of his hyperventilating to 2 minutes. In addition, he eventually agreed to keep hyperventilating for a few seconds beyond the point at which he felt he needed to stop. Although Jimmy felt lightheaded while hyperventilating, he reported that during a natural attack, his dizziness and feelings of unreality were qualitatively different from what he experienced while hyperventilating.

Therefore, his therapist worked with him on a second method for inducing panic, which involved him spinning around in a swivel chair. During this second type of induction, Jimmy and his therapist also started slowly and gradually increased his level of challenge. At first, he was allowed to spin himself in the chair and the induction lasted for just a few seconds. Over time, the inductions lasted for a much longer duration and the therapist took over control of the spinning.

After many such panic inductions, Jimmy agreed to step up the intensity of inductions and push himself "to the limit." His therapist spun him around quickly for a full 5 minutes. Jimmy reportedly had a panic attack during this procedure. However, after a few minutes of guided coping, he returned to his baseline anxiety level. This helped increase his confidence level, resulting in his willingness to repeat the procedure several times. A few sessions later, with his permission, Jimmy's therapist added extremely anxiety-provoking imagery to the induction. She had him imagine "going totally crazy" and being locked up in a mental institution for life. Jimmy learned that despite some of the most intense panic attacks he ever experienced, he did not go crazy. This he found extremely helpful in disconfirming his catastrophic expectations.

For Jillian (Case 6.C), the most effective method for inducing panic symptoms was hyperventilation. She experienced lightheadedness and dizziness and most of the other symptoms she experienced during attacks, including a fear of fainting. She described the symptoms she experienced during these inductions as being extremely similar to actual attacks.

If attempts to induce panic by replicating key somatic sensations fail, therapists can use panic-relevant imagery to facilitate the induction (Barlow & Cerny, 1988). Specifically, while therapists are attempting to induce symptoms, they can instruct clients to (a) imagine being in a situation in which they have frequently experienced severe attacks, (b) imagine having the physical sensations that they usually have during attacks, and (c) imagine having their catastrophic fears come true, such as having a heart attack or going crazy.

In subsequent sessions, therapists should repeat panic inductions as much as needed. Repeated experience with panic inductions is important to disconfirm catastrophic misinterpretations of sensations, desensitize to panic triggers, and practice coping.

Also, for these reasons, therapists should encourage clients to do panic inductions as self-help assignments between sessions. By suggesting that clients induce panic by themselves, therapists are indirectly making the point that clients' physical sensations during a panic attack are benign. Moreover, those clients who are ready to induce panic on their own get a head start on practicing their coping skills in the face of physical symptoms. However, when suggesting that clients attempt panic inductions on their own, it usually is beneficial for therapists to inform clients that doing so may be quite difficult for them. They should also acknowledge that, at this point, clients may choose not to try an induction on their own and that is all right. (Initially, giving them permission to not do an induction on their own prevents clients from feeling like they failed or that they disappointed the therapist. Similarly, it prevents them from thinking that their therapist did not understand how unpleasant and frightening panic is for them.)

Coping Skills Introduced During Panic-Induction Session

A benefit of panic inductions is that they permit clients to learn coping skills in the face of actual symptoms. During the first session in which the therapist uses a panic induction, he or she introduces clients to several coping skills. The therapist introduces paced breathing, cognitive restructuring, refocusing attention, and the coping card, in the order listed.

Paced Breathing. When people are extremely anxious, their breathing often becomes erratic. This can contribute to their anxiety. Often during panic attacks, people breathe more rapidly than usual. As a result, when individuals are experiencing panic, the ratio of oxygen to carbon dioxide is too high (i.e., they get too much oxygen). This can contribute to their feeling lightheaded and having other anxiety symptoms. Other clients unintentionally hold their breath several times per minute while they are anxious. This also can disturb their oxyen/carbon-dioxide balance, which can contribute to symptoms.

As a result of these breathing problems, it is generally helpful for clients to learn to pace their breathing at somewhere between 8 and 12 breaths per minute. Furthermore, it helps to provide them with an audiotape that paces 8 breaths per minute on one side and 12 breaths per minute on the other. On the tape, the speaker repeats "in, out, in, out .... " at the appropriate rate.

Usually, therapists first introduce clients to paced breathing immediately after the first panic induction. Paced breathing helps them decrease anxiety and get a sense that their panic is manageable. Therapists play either the 8- or 12-breaths-per-minute pace based on how rapidly clients are breathing. If clients are breathing extremely rapidly, it is advisable to use the 12-breath pace because 8 breaths per minute is likely to be too slow. Otherwise, the slower pace is preferable.

After clients have calmed down following the paced breathing exercise, they are given the tape to take home with instructions such as the following:

> It is important to practice paced breathing a couple times per day for 5 to 10 minutes per time. After listening to and pacing to both sides of the tape for a few minutes, pick the side that is more comfortable for you. One side has 8 breaths per minute and the other has 12 breaths per minute. When you practice, start the tape, and pace with it for several seconds. Stop the tape for a minute or two and try to maintain the pace. Restart the tape to make sure you are on track. This will help you internalize the pace.
>
> It is important to pace your breathing many times per day to keep your overall level of anxiety lower and to help internalize the slow-breathing rate. Many people find that using a watch that has an hourly chime feature helps them remember to practice. When the chime sounds each hour, you can spend a minute focusing on your breathing. Do you have a watch you could use for this or could you borrow one for a couple weeks?
>
> Also, it can be very helpful to use transitions in your day as reminders to pace your breathing. For example, you can use switching activities, such as getting up from your desk, as a reminder to focus on your breathing. Similarly, you can use hanging up the phone or walking somewhere as reminders. Could you incorporate these kinds of reminders in your schedule? Let's explore how you could do this.

Cognitive Restructuring. The single most important panic-coping skill that clients can develop is to decatastrophize their beliefs regarding their benign physical sensations. After introducing clients to paced breathing, therapists help clients begin to decatastrophize key panic beliefs by helping them discover benign explanations for their physical symptoms. For example, Greg's (Case 6.A) therapist suggested that the pain in his chest during panic attacks could be due to tense intercostal muscles and that a rapid heart rate is a normal part of anxiety. To decatastrophize Jimmy's (Case 6.B) belief that dizziness and feelings of unreality were a sign of going crazy, the therapist presented him with a copy of the diagnostic criteria of panic attacks (which Jimmy fully met). She also provided him with a list of psychosis questions from the Structured Clinical Interview for the *DSM–IV* (none of which Jimmy met). Examples of questions for assessing psychosis that can help clients realize that they are not "crazy" include the following:

While awake, did you ever hear things that other people couldn't hear, such as the voices of people whispering or talking?

While awake, did you ever have visions or see things that other people couldn't see?

Did you ever receive special messages from the TV, radio, or newspaper, or from the way things were arranged around you?

Did you ever feel that someone or something outside yourself was controlling your thoughts or actions against your will?

Did you ever feel that certain thoughts that were not your own were put into your head or taken out of your head?

Did you ever feel as if your thoughts were being broadcast out loud so that other people could actually hear what you were thinking?

Did you ever believe you had magical or otherwise extraordinary powers?

Jimmy found seeing the diagnostic criteria for panic attacks and psychosis to be very helpful and reviewed the information often. Also, it helped him disconfirm his catastrophic beliefs to repeat panic inductions during which the therapist pushed him to the limit. The panic induction also can provide benign explanations for key sensations. For example, if a panic induction through hyperventilation results in symptoms that are at least moderately similar to a naturalistic attack, the therapist can guide the client to the conclusion that overbreathing probably plays a role in bringing on panic symptoms.

Refocusing Attention. As illustrated in the panic model in Fig. 6.1, clients with panic focus their attention on catastrophic cognitions and on physical sensations of panic. Focusing on the catastrophic cognitions fuels their panic attack. Alternatively, if panic clients can refocus their attention elsewhere, they can interrupt the panic cycle.

Barlow and Cerny (1988) suggested that the purpose of refocusing is to interrupt catastrophic cognitions but not to distract from internal sensations. They believe that distraction from physical sensations prevents adequate exposure.[16] They provided the following refocusing procedure:

> instruct the client purposefully to direct attention away from catastrophic thoughts and images and toward the details of the tasks in which he/she is engaged ... the purpose [of refocusing] is to recognize the anxiety symptoms, but not ruminate about them .... Encourage the client to recognize the bodily changes (e.g., increased heart rate) but not to linger on the catastrophic thoughts associated with the elevated heart rate. (p. 142)

---

[16]This conclusion is consistent with findings of a study in which OCD subjects' attention was manipulated during exposure therapy (Grayson, Foa, & Steketee, 1982).

For example, after his therapist provided him with refocusing instructions, Greg attempted the procedure in various situations. When Greg had a panic attack in class, he worked at keeping his attention off his catastrophic thoughts and on the lecture material. (After gaining some coping strategies, Greg had resumed attending some classes.) He also allowed himself to acknowledge his physical sensations but tried very hard not to dwell on them. Over time, his ability to refocus his attention in this helpful way improved dramatically.

During panic attacks, clients should attempt to focus on activities that they were already doing when the panic attack began. If a panic attack occurred during leisure time, they can engage in an activity that they find enjoyable or that otherwise has value for them (e.g., gardening, talking on the phone, chores). It is important for clients to try not to let their panic attacks prevent them from doing necessary or enjoyable activities. They should try not to let the panic attacks "get the best of them."

As a last resort, if clients' level of panic is extreme and they have a strong urge to engage in a disorder-maintaining behavior (e.g., going home, pulling off the road, taking Xanax, going to the ER), they can use distraction techniques that take their attention away from their physical sensations. However, when they do this, they should be aware that they are losing an opportunity for full exposure. To effectively take their attention off their physical sensations, they need to engage in a cognitive task that taxes their attentional resources.

For example, Greg was religious and derived comfort from reading scripture. He found attempting to recall recently learned verses or committing new verses to memory helped keep his mind off his physical symptoms. Jillian (Case 6.C) was a baseball fan. As a distraction task, she attempted to imagine in detail plays from various World Series games. Alternatively, she reviewed in her mind all the batting and fielding statistics of her favorite players for the last few years. Jimmy (Case 6.B) was an attorney. As a distraction task, he attempted to review in his mind the details of recent Supreme Court decisions. Another client was an old-movie buff. He attempted to recall in detail everything that happened and everything that was said during favorite scenes.

When neither the therapist nor the client has ideas for tailoring refocusing tasks to the client's life, some generic approaches can be useful. For example, a client can talk to a friend either without telling the friend that he is in the midst of a panic attack or, instead, telling the friend that he is having an attack but indicating that he wants to converse about other matters. Clients can serially subtract 7s from numbers beginning with 1000 or multiply together three or four digit numbers. Another generic refocusing technique is for clients to describe objects that are in front of them in minute detail, as if they were scientists from another planet.

Coping Cards. Clients often benefit from therapists' writing the decatastrophizing statements and coping strategies on a coping card. During panic attacks, clients' primal threat mode is intensely activated resulting in profound cognitive distortions. Among the distortions are clients' inability to remember mode-inconsistent, benign explanations for their panic attacks. As a result, coping cards are extremely helpful during panic attacks. They help remind clients of benign explanations for what is happening and remind them what they can do to help themselves. During the early weeks of therapy, clients benefit from always keeping the coping card with them. Box 6.3 shows a coping card that Greg and his therapist developed.

Interventions for Clients Who Fear Fainting

Many panic clients report feeling lightheaded or dizzy during attacks, and some of these clients fear fainting. When the vast majority of panic clients feel lightheaded or dizzy, they are at minimal risk of fainting. Their dizziness is generally the result of overbreathing and having too much oxygen, whereas fainting results from having too little oxygen to the brain. When asked, these clients typically report never having fainted during a panic attack. If they ever have fainted, it had to do with something else such as having the flu, being in hot climatic temperatures, or having a hypoglycemic episode. For clients without a history of fainting, it is often extremely reassuring for them to learn that it is nearly impossible for them to faint during their panic attacks. This information can then be recorded on their panic coping card to decatastrophize their cognitions about fainting.

On the other hand, a subset of panic clients—vasovagal responders—is at risk for fainting. These clients benefit from an additional coping technique called *applied muscle tension* (Öst, Fellenius, & Sterner, 1991). Applied muscle tension involves individuals vigorously tensing their arm, chest, and leg muscles simultaneously until they feel warmth rise in their face. This is a signal that they are experiencing a slight increase in blood pressure in their head, which decreases the probability that they will faint. During a session, therapists should give clients instructions for applied muscle tension and an opportunity to practice until they feel warmth rise in their faces.

As self-help assignments between sessions, clients with blood-injury-injection phobia or who have a history of fainting when anxious should practice applied muscle tension daily for several weeks. Practice consists of doing 5 repetitions of simultaneously tensing their arms, chest, and legs for 10–20 seconds and then interrupting with rest periods of 20–30 seconds. In addition, when learning to decrease the probability of fainting, clients should monitor antecedents to lightheadedness or dizziness. To do this, they can ask themselves the questions presented in Box 6.4.

Finally, after a few weeks of practice, clients should begin gradually exposing themselves to phobic objects or situations while practicing applied tension. For example, Jillian (Case 6.C) practiced applied tension daily for

1. I thought I was going to have a heart attack but my thoughts were distorted. MY CHEST PRESSURE AND TINGLING SENSATIONS ARE THE RESULT OF OVERBREATHING, TENSE CHEST MUSCLES, & SCARY THOUGHTS.
2. By breathing normally, I can make the symptoms lessen. I have control over my symptoms since changing my breathing can make the symptoms better. [USE PACED BREATHING TAPE.]
3. These symptoms can't be dangerous if I can bring them on and lessen them just by my breathing.
4. I AM NOT HAVING A HEART ATTACK. The pain in my chest is probably due to tight chest muscles. **MY HEART IS HEALTHY.** I've had several complete heart exams including sophisticated tests by experts. I was misinterpreting my chest pain as being serious. Plus, I REALLY GOT MY HEART RATE UP IN INDUCTIONS & HAD NO PROBLEMS.
5. I've had over 500 panic attacks. If panic attacks were really heart attacks, I would be dead by now. Since I'm alive and well & my tests are normal, my heart is fine.
6. A much more reasonable explanation of my symptoms is that I'M HAVING A PANIC ATTACK, NOTHING WORSE. All of the symptoms I am experiencing are mentioned in lists of panic symptoms that my therapist showed me.
7. Focusing on negative thoughts makes my anxiety worse. REFOCUSING on what I'm doing can reduce my symptoms. DON'T LET THIS PANIC GET THE BETTER OF ME & STOP ME FROM HAVING A NORMAL LIFE!
8. Think of this PANIC ATTACK AS AN OPPORTUNITY TO GET OVER MY PANIC. It's an opportunity to practice coping skills & to see that nothing terrible will happen. Invite the panic and see what happens (it might actually make it better). Allow myself to focus on the physical symptoms but try not to allow myself to think scary thoughts.
9. By stepping outside of the panic and observing, it will help make the panic go away. WATCH THE SYMPTOMS as they change. How intense is the anxiety at the moment?
10. LAST RESORT. Distract myself with something that takes extreme concentration. Such as: talk to Holly on the phone—tell her that I'm having a panic attack but that I want to talk about something else to distract me. Or work on memorizing a new verse of scripture.

Box 6.3. Panic coping card.

- In what situations do you feel even a little faint?
- What thoughts or images do you have prior to feeling even a little faint?
- What emotions do you feel prior to feeling even a little faint?
- What physical sensations do you have prior to feeling even a little faint?

Box 6.4. Questions that help identify antecedents to feeling faint.

2 weeks. Then, with her therapist's help, she constructed a hierarchy from least anxiety-provoking to most anxiety-provoking stimuli related to her blood-injection phobia. She practiced exposure to hierarchy situations between sessions. For each hierarchy item, she exposed herself to it while practicing applied tension. Usually, it took several trials of prolonged exposure and applied muscle tension practice for her to desensitize to the stimulus and gain confidence in her coping ability. After approximately 2 months, she could effectively cope with all of the items on her hierarchy. In addition, she consistently remembered to use applied tension whenever she felt the slightest bit faint. She also remembered to use applied tension whenever she came into contact with situations, cognitions, or feelings that had a high probability of eliciting a vasovagal response.

The first hierarchy item was viewing TV shows and movies in which violent acts were shown but without graphic detail. (Her fiance previewed, selected, and recorded relevant shows for her.) To maximize the efficiency of practice, she repeatedly viewed a particular part of a relevant scene until she gained mastery over it. The next item was exposing herself to TV shows and movies that did show "blood and guts." After mastering these shows, she arranged to visit her family doctor's office where she spent blocks of time viewing phobic stimuli (i.e., hypodermic needles and vials of blood). The next hierarchy item was allowing herself to come up close to and view dead animals that were on the side of the road. (She lived in a location in which it was easy for her to find fresh carrion several times per week.) Next, she watched educational television shows that graphically depicted entire surgical operations. Finally, she "graduated" by donating blood at a blood drive.

Relaxation Training

Progressive muscle relaxation (Jacobson, 1938) is a procedure consisting of systematically tensing and then completely relaxing each of 12 muscle groups. Extensive research has demonstrated that this approach is effective for decreasing muscle tension and overall arousal (for a review, see Hillenberg & Collins, 1982). Concerning PD, the goals of relaxation training are twofold: (a) to decrease the frequency of panic attacks by reducing resting baseline autonomic activity throughout the day, and (b) to help clients decrease the intensity and duration of panic attacks once they have begun.

Prior to beginning relaxation training, therapists should assess clients for relaxation-induced anxiety or relaxation-induced panic. A small minority of clients experience high anxiety or even panic when they attempt to relax (Barlow & Cerny, 1988).[17] Therapists can ask clients, "Do you have any concerns or fears about learning to relax in the way I described?" Clients who experience relaxation-induced anxiety can still derive great benefit from relaxation training. However, therapists should modify the training to accommodate these clients' anxiety. For example, these clients often benefit from being given as much control as possible while learning to relax. Therapists can give them permission to keep their eyes open during the procedure and invite them to stop the procedure at any time. In addition, it is sometimes necessary to begin exposing them to brief relaxation inductions, sometimes for just 15 or 30 seconds, and gradually increase the time for relaxing.

The first progressive muscle relaxation induction typically is done with panic clients in session. In addition, clients often benefit from having an audiotape of the procedure to take home to guide their practice. (For a copy of a progressive muscle relaxation script from which therapists can make relaxation tapes, see Barlow & Cerny, 1988.)

For the first 2 weeks of relaxation practice, clients ideally should practice relaxation twice daily. In addition, they should monitor their practice on a monitoring form. On this form, clients record the date and time of their practice, their anxiety and muscle tension before and after practicing, and any comments they have about the practice (e.g., difficulties they experienced or insights they gained about obtaining deeper relaxation during the practice). (The Appendix provides a blank copy of a progressive muscle relaxation monitoring form.) After the first week or two of consistent daily practice, clients typically benefit from alternating between practices with and practices without the tape.

Once clients can consistently achieve a state of deep relaxation using the 12-muscle-group approach, therapists teach them a variety of methods for making relaxation more "portable." That is, clients learn to use relaxation in settings and situations in which they need it most. First, therapists help clients decrease the amount of time they spend doing the relaxation procedure. Therapists provide clients with ways to combine muscle groups to reduce time. Box 6.5 describes how clients may combine muscle groups. Clients benefit from using the eight muscle groups relaxation until they can consistently achieve deep relaxation. (Often clients can achieve this in a week or two). Then, clients should reduce the muscle groups even further, to four groups.

---

[17]Anecdotally, relaxation-induced anxiety of ten seems to be related to either being sexually molested as a child or having an implicit rule that demands that one should never relax or recreate.

EIGHT MUSCLE GROUPS

1. Both arms
2. Both lower legs
3. Abdomen
4. Chest (by deep breath)
5. Shoulders
6. Back of neck
7. Eyes
8. Forehead

Followed by deepening exercise and then pairing breathing with the word "relax."

FOUR MUSCLE GROUPS

1. Both arms
2. Chest
3. Neck
4. Face

Followed by deepening exercise and then pairing breathing with the word "relax."

Box 6.5. Combining muscle groups to reduce relaxation time over the course of treatment.

A second way that therapists help make relaxation more portable is that they instruct clients to work on gradually generalizing their practice to naturalistic conditions. These include sitting up, having their eyes open, practicing in a variety of locations, and tensing their muscles in ways that are not noticeable to others. Generalization practice helps enable clients to get relaxed many times per day, which helps them keep their overall muscle tension and anxiety low.

Finally, to facilitate clients' learning to relax rapidly, therapists should use *cued relaxation.* Cued relaxation is a classical conditioning procedure that involves having clients pair feelings of deep relaxation with a cue (i.e., conditioned stimulus). In the progressive muscle relaxation protocol, toward the end, clients focus their attention on their breathing. The audiotape instructs them to say to themselves "in" each time they inhale, and "relax" each time they exhale. On the relaxation audiotape, 1 or 2 minutes can be allotted for the pairing of these words with the breathing cycle. After practicing the entire progressive relaxation protocol 20 or 30 times over the course of several weeks, the association between feeling deeply relaxed and the cues should be firmly established. At this point, but not before, clients can use the cues tied to breathing several times per day to keep their overall level of tension and anxiety relatively low.

Eliminating Subtle Safety-Seeking Behavior

For clients to overcome their PD, they must eliminate their subtle safety-seeking behaviors (as well as their frank agoraphobic behavior, covered in a later section). As previously discussed, panic inductions help clients begin to eliminate many of these behaviors. However, other safety-seeking behaviors cannot be addressed during office visits. For example, when Greg was driving with his mother to therapy appointments, he constantly scanned for places that might have telephones in case he had a heart attack. After reiterating the importance of eliminating these safety-seeking behaviors, Greg's therapist encouraged him to resist these kinds of behaviors. Greg wrote on his Case Conceptualization Worksheet when he resisted the urge to engage in safety-seeking behaviors. He also added conclusions from these behavioral experiments to his coping cards so he could access them during a panic attack. Over a couple months of therapy, Greg had effectively eliminated these behaviors.

A final note about safety-seeking behaviors merits comment. The safety behaviors many clients use are potentially helpful coping strategies such as attempting to relax, refocus their attention, or slow their breathing. Unfortunately, panic clients use these potentially helpful strategies detrimentally. Typically, when clients use these techniques, they do so to prevent (medical or mental) catastrophes or "unbearable" panic attacks and not simply to decrease unpleasant sensations. Thus, clients' maladaptive mindsets when engaging in these behaviors help maintain their catastrophic beliefs. Other reasons why clients derive less than satisfactory results from potentially helpful strategies include: prematurely discontinuing them, not using a combination of strategies, or not using strategies optimally, such as attempting to refocus their attention on TV instead of on something that requires greater levels of attention.

Discontinuing High-Potency Benzodiazapines

Many panic clients present at psychological outpatient clinics dependent on high-potency benzodiazapines, such as Xanax and Ativan. Use of benzodiazapines represents another important disorder-maintaining safety-seeking behavior that should be eliminated in cognitive therapy. Although benzodiazapines are effective at reducing panic symptoms, they can strongly maintain PD. This can result both from their direct physiological effects as well as beliefs that clients develop from taking these drugs.

Xanax and Ativan have short half-lives. That is, they are quickly absorbed, utilized, and eliminated from the body. As a result, they provide quick relief from panic symptoms. However, their ability to rapidly reduce anxiety (short half-life) is the same property that makes them highly addictive. Clients come to rely on these medications because the medications are highly reinforcing. They provide quick and easy relief. Individuals begin to believe that they cannot cope without these drugs.

Furthermore, efforts to wean themselves off the drug are punished by withdrawal symptoms. Unfortunately, the withdrawal symptoms typically mimic anxiety symptoms. The withdrawal symptoms can include: autonomic hyperactivity, increased hand tremor, insomnia, nausea or vomiting, psychomotor agitation, and anxiety (APA, 1994). (Rapid discontinuation can also result in seizures.) Clients taking high-potency benzodiazapines frequently develop withdrawal symptoms *between their scheduled doses* and therefore feel a strong urge to take the medication ahead of schedule. This makes discontinuing the medication even more difficult. When clients attempt to decrease the medication, their anxiety gets markedly worse. Besides withdrawal symptoms, individuals often need more medication to derive the same anxiolytic effect, that is, they develop tolerance. Furthermore, as the dose of medication increases, attempts to discontinue its use result in more pronounced withdrawal symptoms.

Another problem with using high-potency benzodiazapines, especially on an as-needed basis, is that it interferes with effective cognitive therapy (e.g., Sanderson & Wetzler, 1993; van Balkom, de Beurs, Koele, & Lange, 1996). Probably several factors account for this. First, when clients are using these drugs, their motivation for using coping strategies may diminish since they have a pharmacological method for deriving quick relief. Second, high-potency benzodiazapines decrease clients' opportunities for practicing coping skills in the presence of a fully activated anxiety response. Finally, using these medications may decrease clients' confidence in their ability to cope because they can attribute management of symptoms to the medication instead of their own coping efforts.

As a result of the serious problems with taking high-potency benzodiazapines, a major target of cognitive therapy for PD is helping clients discontinue these drugs. Clients benefit from beginning to discontinue high-potency benzodiazapines early in the therapeutic process. The process of tapering benzodiazapines should be done under the supervision of the client's physician to ensure client safety. In addition, the therapist and physician should consult about the tapering process. (Physicians generally seem to be quite receptive to consulting about the tapering process. This is especially the case when they learn that their clients are learning effective coping strategies for dealing with panic.)

In order for clients to succeed at discontinuing benzodiazapines, they usually must believe they have effective means for coping with panic that can replace the drugs. Thus, they usually must first experience a sense of mastery from coping strategies as well as decreased frequency and intensity of panic attacks prior to being willing to start tapering benzodiazapines. Therefore, it often makes sense to begin tapering benzodiazapines a session or two after the session in which therapists induce panic and teach coping strategies (i.e., decatastrophizing, paced breathing, refocusing attention).

Discontinuing benzodiazapines often consists of switching clients from high-potency benzodiazapines such as Xanax and Ativan to low-potency benzodiazapines such as Klonopin and a slow taper. For example, the dosage of the agent can be reduced by 10% or so every 3 days. In addition, it often is beneficial for clients to take benzodiazapines on a fixed schedule as opposed to an as needed basis (Maxmen & Ward, 1995). When clients take benzodiazapines on an as needed basis, it can powerfully condition them to feel and believe they are reliant on the medication. In contrast, when benzodiazapines are taken on a fixed schedule, clients are not immediately and powerfully reinforced for taking the medication to escape from anxiety. When they are on a fixed schedule and anxiety surfaces, they become motivated to engage in coping behaviors that they learn have a positive effect.

Preparing for Termination for Panic Clients Without Agoraphobia

As with most other therapeutic interventions, clients benefit from having a plan that will prepare and enable them to continue their therapeutic work on their own after termination. For panic, it is especially important for clients to continue to practice the coping skills that they learned during therapy and to induce panic. Therapists encourage clients to periodically induce panic so that they will have regular practice with coping skills. A way to approach this topic with clients is illustrated here.

Therapist: I much prefer clients to have an occasional panic attack once they stop therapy. The reason for this is that it helps you practice coping skills. Furthermore, if you do not have a panic attack in 6 months and then you eventually have one, you might think "This is terrible. I have panic disorder again. I'm back to where I was a year ago. I'm a basket case." Whereas, if you have a panic attack every month or two, you can see that it's not terrible and you can effectively deal with it.

Client: I see what you mean.

Therapist: Therefore, clients benefit from doing panic inductions every few weeks. Would you be willing to do that?

Client: Yes. I won't like it. But I know it's important, so I'll do it.

Therapist: How will you remember to do it?

Client: I'll write it in my day planner for every 3 weeks.

Therapist: Great!

Treating Agoraphobic Avoidance: Exposure Therapy

Extensive research has demonstrated that exposure to agoraphobic stimuli is highly effective in the treatment of agoraphobia (e.g., Bouchard et al., 1996; Michelson et al., 1996; Michelson, Mavissakalian, & Marchione, 1985; Rijken, Kraaimaat, deRuiter, & Garssen, 1992; Sharp & Power, 1996; van den Hout, Arntz, & Hoekstra, 1994; Williams & Falbo, 1996). This section suggests guidelines for conducting exposure therapy and illustrates their use with case examples.

Cognitive-behavioral theory suggests three mechanisms that are likely to be responsible for the effectiveness of exposure therapy for agoraphobia. The first is *disconfirming catastrophic cognitions.* By exposing themselves to feared situations without experiencing a catastrophe, clients learn that their fears are unfounded. Second, repeated exposure leads to *habituation.* Habituation is a decrease, and ultimately a disappearance of, physiological responding as a result of repetitive presentations of a stimulus that is not noxious (Kandel & Schwartz, 1985). Foa and Steketee (1987) suggested that "habituation in the fear context provides the information that physiological responses associated with fear decrease despite the presence of the feared cue. This new information about the absence of arousal weakens the response-stimulus associations in the fear structure" (p. 84).

Thus, each time an individual's anxiety diminishes while confronting an agoraphobic situation, the situation becomes a less powerful trigger of the fear response in the future. Third, clients develop *self-efficacy* for coping with the situation. They gain confidence in their ability to confront the triggering situation.

Preparing Clients for Exposure Therapy

If clients know what to expect during exposure therapy, they are more likely to feel in control and their anxiety is likely to be more manageable. This facilitates the exposure process. Therapists should prepare clients by giving them a rationale for the procedure and educating them about what to expect during exposure.

Providing a Rationale for Exposure Therapy. Therapists should remind clients of the cognitive model of PD and emphasize the ways that avoidance behavior maintains anxiety. Therapists can use the Case Conceptualization Illustration to show clients that facing agoraphobic situations is important in overcoming agoraphobia.

Some agoraphobic clients doubt that exposure to phobic stimuli can help them. Although they occasionally had exposure to phobic situations, they subsequently remained equally afraid of these situations. Guided discovery may help these clients realize that the manner in which they were exposed to feared situations was counterproductive. Some combination of the following typically occurred that prevented agoraphobic clients from benefitting from their own exposure experiences. First, they generally did not repeatedly expose themselves to the phobic stimuli. Second, they did not remain in the phobic situation long enough for habituation to occur. Third, they waited too long between exposure attempts. Fourth, they engaged in disorder-maintaining safety-seeking behaviors that prevented disconfirmation of their catastrophic beliefs. Finally, their exposure experiences occurred before they had developed mastery over their panic attacks and before they had a repertoire of coping strategies.

Here is a transcript demonstrating how therapists might address clients' doubts about exposure exercises.

Client:	I've been in these situations before but, if anything, they made me more afraid of the situations.
Therapist:	Let's explore this. Tell me about the situations in which you exposed yourself to the agoraphobic situations.
Client:	OK. [The client describes a few times separated by many months in which he had brief exposures to agoraphobic places but escaped quickly.]
Therapist:	Let's consider an analogy. Suppose a person was afraid of dogs and had an experience once every 3 months or so in which an unleashed dog unexpectedly came up to him. However, he escaped the situation each time as soon as possible. Would he overcome his fear of dogs?
Client:	No.
Therapist:	What would it probably take for him to get over his fear of dogs?
Client:	He'd have to have control over when and where and which dogs he had contact with .... Plus, he'd have to have experiences with dogs more often.
Therapist:	Exactly! What about the length of time he was exposed to dogs?
Client:	It would have to be longer .... And, of course, it better not be a vicious dog!
Therapist:	Yes. Are there parallels with your fear of driving and the reasons your fear has not abated despite some occasions of exposure?
Client:	I see what you mean. I haven't had enough exposure—not enough different times and I escaped too quickly—so I never learned I could handle it.

Clients Benefit From Knowing What to Expect During Exposure Therapy. Therapists should educate clients about the reactions they possibly could experience during exposure sessions. Clients are likely to experience some panic-like symptoms. However, these symptoms are often much less pronounced than they were prior to successfully learning relevant coping skills. This is especially the case when clients' panic attacks have stopped. It is possible, though unlikely, that during exposure clients might become so anxious that they vomit or cry. Vasovagal responders have a small chance of fainting when exposing themselves to phobic stimuli. However, fainting is unlikely if clients practice applied muscle tension procedures (described earlier). If any of these extreme reactions occur, they are likely to disappear after a few exposure sessions.

Clients also benefit from knowing more about the places or situations to which they will expose themselves. For example, if they are working on driving, it is often helpful for them to look at a map of unfamiliar places to which they plan to drive. Also, they may initially drive with someone else on a chosen route before trying it alone. Therapists should also inform clients that, like most human activities, they are likely to have "ups" and "downs." Some exposure sessions even to the same stimulus may be more difficult some days than others. However, over time, with repeated, prolonged, and frequent practices, their anxiety is likely to diminish markedly.

Graded Exposure

In most outcome studies, subjects were presented with agoraphobic stimuli in a graded fashion. Agoraphobic subjects began with situations or places that they expected would elicit very low levels of anxiety and gradually worked up to stimuli that were extremely anxiety provoking (e.g., Michelson et al., 1985; Michelson et al., 1996; van den Hout et al., 1994).

To prepare for graded exposure, clients and therapists work together to construct exposure hierarchies. Each hierarchy should consist of approximately 10 situations or places that elicit a broad range of anxiety levels. For each hierarchy item, clients assign an expected level of anxiety from 0 to 100, where 0 equals *no anxiety at all,* 50 equals *moderate anxiety,* and 100 equals *the most anxiety they have ever experienced.* Hierarchy items should be obtained from the intake evaluation, agoraphobia questionnaires, and ongoing discussions with the client. Box 6.6 illustrates an exposure hierarchy for Jillian (Case 6.C) for her fear of being in crowds. As the reader can see, hierarchy items can represent several different situations or places and can vary on other dimensions such as time of day.

Therapists should be aware of the underlying dimensions that play important roles in eliciting the client's anxiety when exposed to an agoraphobic situation. Considering the underlying dimensions allows inclusion of a complete range of situations for each important fear dimension. For example, Greg's perception of threat related to the degree of difficulty he would have getting medical attention in the event that he

100	Traveling in a subway car during rush hour when it is extremely crowded and not enough room to sit down
95	Shopping mall right before Christmas
90	Sporting event in crowded stadium
80	Extremely crowded restaurant
70	Downtown at 5:30 p.m. on weekday when crowds are rushing home
60	Crowded shopping mall during typical weekend
50	Church service
35	Downtown at 2:30 p.m. on weekday
30	Shopping mall at nonbusy time during weekday

Box 6.6. Example of an exposure hierarchy (Case 6.C, Jillian).

would have a heart attack. He and his therapist identified several specific subdimensions that they used when constructing his driving hierarchy. Greg and his therapist identified the following subdimensions: (a) his mother was driving him versus he was driving his mother versus he was driving alone, (b) amount of traffic, (c) highway versus city driving, and (d) distance from the hospital.

Table 6.1 shows a matrix that helped in developing the initial driving hierarchy. The columns represented whether his mother was driving him (Mom & Greg), he was driving his mother (Greg & Mom), or he was driving alone (Alone). The rows represented two embedded dimensions—whether he was driving in the city or highway and the amount of traffic.

Box 6.7 shows Greg's driving hierarchy. All of the driving situations represented in Greg's initial hierarchy occurred very near his home. The city driving was within a five-block radius of his apartment. The highway ramp was two blocks from his home and driving occurred over the length of one exit. The reason for not varying the distance from his apartment was that Greg's anxiety, related to driving, quickly reached a ceiling. Driving more than a few blocks away from his apartment led to Subjective Units of Distress Scale (SUDS) levels of 100. After he had mastered the situations in this hierarchy, however, a new hierarchy was constructed and included distance from apartment as a dimension.

Often, developing separate hierarchies for different underlying dimensions or themes of the phobia is beneficial. This increases the likelihood that the client will attempt a complete range of situations relating to important fear dimensions. For example, Greg developed another hierarchy for going to class and sitting in class. As mentioned earlier in the chapter, Jillian developed a hierarchy related to her blood-injection phobia.

TABLE 6.1

Driving Hierarchy Matrix

	Mom & Greg	*Greg & Mom*	*Alone*
City Driving			
No traffic	50	65	85
Moderate traffic	65	70	90
Heavy traffic	60	75	95
Rush hour	80	90	100
Highway Driving			
No traffic	70	80	100
Moderate traffic	80	90	100
Heavy traffic	90	100	100
Rush hour	100	100	100

100 Greg driving, mother present, highway, heavy traffic
100 Mother driving, highway, rush hour
95 Greg alone, city, heavy traffic
90 Greg driving, mother present, city, rush hour
85 Greg driving alone, city, no traffic
80 Mother driving, highway, moderate traffic
75 Greg driving, mother present, city, heavy traffic
70 Mother driving, highway, no traffic
65 Greg driving, mother present, city, no traffic
60 Mother driving, city, moderate traffic
50 Mother driving, city, no traffic

Box 6.7. Driving hierarchy for Greg.

After beginning to construct the exposure hierarchy, as a self-help assignment, clients should reflect on their hierarchy and consider modifications. They may think of new situations that would be useful to include in the hierarchy. In addition, they may decide to adjust their ratings of how much anxiety they anticipate having in some exposure situations and may alter the ordering of items.

Imaginal Flooding as Preparation for In Vivo Graded Exposure. Several studies have compared the effects of *in vivo*[18] to imaginal flooding for agoraphobic subjects (Chambless, Foa, Groves, & Goldstein, 1982; Emmelkamp & Wessels, 1975; Mathews, Johnston, Lancashire, Munby, Shaw, & Gelder, 1976; Stern & Marks, 1973). (As compared to graded exposure, flooding begins exposure with a highly anxiety-provoking stimulus, and exposure continues until the stimulus no longer elicits anxiety.) The results of these studies were mixed. Some found that flooding *in vivo* was superior to flooding in imagination (Emmelkamp & Wessels, 1975; Stern & Marks, 1973), whereas, others found no significant differences between these treatments (Chambless et al., 1982; Mathews et al., 1976).

When comparing flooding in imagination to systematic desensitization, which is graded exposure in imagination paired with relaxation, flooding is usually superior (e.g., Gelder et al., 1973; Marks, Boulougouris, & Marset, 1971). Foa and Steketee (1987) suggested that the inferior results for systematic desensitization were likely the result of insufficiently high levels of arousal in this procedure.

As a result of these findings, in preparation for graded *in vivo* exposure, clients should be flooded in imagination. Although exposure in imagination has not been found to be more effective than exposure *in vivo*, many clients benefit from practicing hierarchy items in imagination as preparation for *in vivo* practice (Barlow & Cerny, 1988).

When therapists direct clients in exposure in imagination, they should initially instruct clients to close their eyes and relax. Then, therapists instruct them to imagine vividly a particular situation that is toward the top of their exposure hierarchy. When imagining the situation, therapists should instruct clients to also imagine experiencing anxiety symptoms. Periodically, therapists should remind clients to focus attention on anxiety and maintain the visualization.

Throughout the imagery procedure, therapists have their clients rate their anxiety on a SUDS, from 0 to 10, every 2 minutes. Frequently, during practice in imagination, clients' SUDS rating drops precipitously—often within a few minutes the SUDS level drops to 0. After the SUDS rating is 0 out of 10, clients should continue to imagine being in the feared place or situation for an additional several minutes. This allows clients to begin to associate the stimulus with not being anxious.

Even if a client's SUDS rating does not drop quickly, exposure in imagination should continue until anxiety decreases noticeably. Unfortunately, at times, practical considerations interfere with these recommendations. Consider, for example, during a 1-hour therapy session, a client's SUDS score remains high and unchanged for most of the session. After 40 or 50 minutes, the therapist should probably guide the client in the use of coping strategies such as paced breathing, cognitive restructuring, and cued relaxation. These procedures help clients end the exposure session without

---

[18]*In vivo* exposure refers to exposure to actual agoraphobic stimuli.

heightening their sensitivity to the triggering stimulus. In subsequent sessions, the client can initially be exposed in imagination to items that are lower on the hierarchy. Alternatively, longer sessions can be scheduled to ensure clients have sufficient time for within session habituation to occur. Therapists should encourage clients to practice imaginal exposure between sessions, using items to which they have habituated in session.

In Vivo Exposure Sessions. Whenever possible, during exposure to a particular hierarchy item, clients should adhere to the following procedures. They should stay in the phobic situation for a prolonged period of time until they no longer feel uncomfortable. In most outcome studies, the duration of exposure to an agoraphobic situation was 60 or 90 minutes (Bouchard et al., 1996; Michelson et al., 1985; Michelson et al., 1996). Even when clients quickly experience marked reductions in anxiety, they should remain in the situation for 60 to 90 minutes. This helps establish nonfearful associations with the place or situation and helps build their confidence. Second, clients should resist urges to engage in safety-seeking behaviors. Third, clients can use panic coping strategies (i.e., cognitive restructuring, paced breathing, refocusing attention, and cued relaxation during exposure).

Early in exposure therapy or during early exposure sessions to a particular hierarchy item, clients' high level of anxiety may warrant temporary modifications of this approach. If therapists insist on the approach described in the previous paragraph without modification, they increase the risk that clients will fail to adhere to self-exposure assignments or will drop out of treatment prematurely. Therefore, therapists and clients should collaboratively agree on appropriate, temporary modifications. For example, clients may occasionally distract themselves from physical sensations. Although this strategy may dilute the effects of exposure, it probably is more advantageous than the client's escaping the situation altogether. Another temporary modification is that, as a last resort, clients can truncate an exposure session, take a short break, and return to the situation to complete exposure. Ideally, when they return, they should remain in the agoraphobic situation until they experience a marked decrease in anxiety. Over time, these modifications should be phased out.

Other Considerations for Exposure Therapy. Therapists should consider several other issues when designing and implementing exposure therapy. These include (a) the use of cognitive restructuring, (b) the number of repetitions of an exposure situation, (c) the frequency of self-exposure practice, (d) the number of treatment sessions devoted to exposure, and (e) relapse prevention.

Agoraphobic clients benefit from *cognitive restructuring* consisting of either of the following two foci. The first focus is on panic-related cognitions. Clients who retain some fear of a medical or mental catastrophe should review the coping cards they developed for panic attacks.

The second focus of cognitive restructuring relates to the fear of not being able to get help or of being embarrassed if they experience intense anxiety symptoms. The Dysfunctional Thought Record and the Thought Evaluation Worksheet—described in chapter 5—are excellent tools for generating rational, nonanxiety-provoking responses to these agoraphobic cognitions. For example, Jillian (Case 6.C) had the agoraphobic thought, "People will think I'm a fool if I faint when I'm in the mall." She found it helpful when completing the Thought Evaluation Worksheet about this to (a) identify cognitive distortions (i.e., fortune-telling, mind-reading), (b) consider the evidence (i.e., "In the past, when I fainted, people were kind and appeared to be nonjudgmental"), and (c) consider the worst case scenario (i.e., "People think I'm a fool, but I'm unlikely to see these people again; I'll live through it; a month later, it will have been an unimportant event in my life").

The *number of repetitions to exposure situations* should depend on the number of repetitions necessary to achieve minimal distress. Once clients achieve minimal distress, they should expose themselves to the hierarchy item several additional times to increase their sense of mastery and develop relaxed associations with the place or situation.

Regarding the *frequency of self-exposure practice,* whenever possible, clients should engage in at least three self-exposure sessions per week. Engaging in frequent self-exposure practice is likely to decrease the overall duration of treatment.

The *number of therapy sessions devoted to exposure* should depend on the individual client's response to treatment. In most outcome studies, 7 to 14 sessions were devoted to exposure to agoraphobic places and situations (Bouchard et al., 1996; Michelson et al., 1985; Michelson et al., 1996; Rijken et al., 1992; van den Hout et al., 1994; Williams & Falbo, 1996).

To *prevent relapses,* during treatment, clients should strive to overlearn adaptive responses. Specifically, during exposure practices, they should stay in the agoraphobic situations beyond the point at which they first feel comfortable. They should repeat exposure to situations beyond the practice at which it no longer elicits anxiety. Also, clients should include items at the top of their exposure hierarchies that go beyond what they would normally encounter in their lives.

In addition, to decrease the likelihood of relapsing, therapists should instruct clients about what to do following terminating from therapy. For example, former clients periodically should expose themselves to situations or places that previously elicited anxiety and with which they do not have regular contact in their daily lives. In addition, if fear or avoidance begins to reemerge, clients should begin cognitive restructuring and exposure work immediately to prevent a full-blown episode from occurring, or they should return to therapy.

Clients With Core Beliefs, Issues, and Strategies That Predispose Them to Future Panic

After the first five or six therapy sessions, panic clients will have learned a variety of coping strategies. Moreover, by this time, clients are likely to have dramatically reduced the frequency and intensity of panic attacks. However, many clients will continue to have problematic core beliefs, issues, and behavioral strategies. These either continue to impair their functioning, result in subjective distress, predispose them to future emotional problems, or place them at risk for relapsing after termination.

Specifically, clients with PD frequently have one or more of the following unresolved issues or problems: (a) unresolved grief; (b) conflicts about dependence versus independence; (c) extreme drive to accomplish goals, be productive, or be perfect; (d) exaggerated demand that they be in complete control of themselves and their environment; (e) avoidance of unpleasant emotions; or (f) hypervalent schemas relating to helplessness, vulnerability to harm, or medical catastrophe. To protect clients from relapses or further distress, therapy should address these other important issues after clients have begun to master their panic attacks. In Greg's (Case 6.A) therapy, after he mastered coping techniques, was no longer having panic attacks, and was substantially less agoraphobic, he and his therapist addressed core issues. For him, these included dependence versus independence. Therapy also focused on his core beliefs about health and safety, namely: "I'm vulnerable to medical calamity" and "An accident could happen at any time." For Jimmy (Case 6.B), excessive alcohol use, destructive sexual behavior, and marital problems were addressed directly in therapy. Jillian (Case 6.C) was free of long-term psychopathology. Therefore, she and her therapist terminated treatment once she had mastered her panic with agoraphobia and blood-injection phobia.

SUMMARY OF COGNITIVE THERAPY OF PD: INTEGRATION AND SEQUENCING OF TREATMENT COMPONENTS

This section describes in detail the integration and sequencing of the various treatment components for PD. According to the general format of cognitive therapy sessions, at the beginning of each session, therapists review the previous week. For panic clients, the review includes the frequency, intensity, symptoms, and circumstances of panic attacks. The review also includes clients' use of coping strategies and their disorder-maintaining behaviors (including use of benzodiazapines), as well as any significant events of the week. In addition, therapists and clients jointly bridge from the previous session. They review self-help work that clients have done since the last session and select the focus of the current session. At the end of the session, they agree on self-help assignments for clients to attempt before the next session.

The first session or two of cognitive therapy for PD is usually devoted to assessment. Following assessment, a session is usually dedicated to educating clients about PD. To accomplish this, therapists introduce clients to an *individualized case conceptualization*, which is based on the cognitive model of panic and a comprehensive assessment. Also, therapists teach clients to use Case Conceptualization Worksheets for monitoring their panic responses and give clients cognitive therapy literature on PD and its treatment.

During the next session, often the third or fourth session and after getting medical clearance, the therapist performs the first *panic induction*. Before the induction, clients complete a symptom questionnaire for a typical panic attack. Next, the panic induction is attempted. Ideally, during the induction, clients experience symptoms similar to naturalistically occurring attacks. Therapists assess clients' cognitions to determine whether they experienced catastrophic cognitions during the induction. The physical symptoms clients have during an induced attack should resemble those that occur in naturally occurring attacks to a moderate or pronounced degree. However, clients frequently do not catastrophically misinterpret these symptoms as a result of the context in which the symptoms occur.

Immediately after the panic induction, therapists can help clients decrease their physiological arousal through *paced breathing*. Although clients' level of arousal usually would return quickly to their baseline even without intervention,[19] intervening with clients after an induction helps them believe that their symptoms are controllable. Moreover, the presence of panic symptoms provides an opportunity to teach clients coping strategies that are extremely helpful during naturalistic attacks. Within 3 to 5 minutes of pacing their breathing with an audiotape that paces at a rate of 8 or 12 breaths per minute, clients are typically feeling significantly less anxious.

During the panic induction session, therapists also introduce clients to *refocusing attention* and *cognitive restructuring*. In this session, cognitive restructuring consists of therapists' using Socratic questioning to help the client see that their catastrophic beliefs are irrational. In addition, cognitive restructuring focuses on providing clients with compelling, noncatastrophic explanations for the physical sensations that they experience during panic attacks. The therapist and the client then develop a *coping card* to remind the client of coping strategies and statements for decatastrophizing beliefs. Therapists suggest that clients always keep the coping card with them, so that if they have a panic attack, they will have ready access to the information. This is especially helpful, because during an attack, individuals generally have great difficulty remembering benign explanations for symptoms and useful coping strategies. Refocusing is most helpful when attention is directed to ongoing activities and physical sensations and away from catastrophic cognitions. (Distraction away from physical sen-

---

[19]This is probably because during an induction the panic symptoms occur in a safe environment and therefore are usually not magnified by clients' catastrophically misinterpreting the symptoms.

sations helps the client feel better in the short-run but appears to dilute the effects of exposure.) As self-help assignments, clients benefit from practicing paced breathing with an audiotape that the therapist provides for them. In addition, they benefit from frequently reviewing their coping card and the Case Conceptualization Illustration. Clients also are encouraged to look for subtle safety-seeking behaviors that maintain their catastrophic beliefs.

Therapists should also encourage clients to attempt panic inductions at home. Those clients who are ready to induce panic on their own get a head start on practicing their coping skills in the face of physical symptoms.

In a subsequent session, often the fourth or fifth, therapists introduce clients to *progressive muscle relaxation* and provide them with an audiotape with which to practice at home. As self-help work, clients continue practicing coping strategies, including progressive muscle relaxation and cognitive restructuring, and are encouraged to induce panic. Over time, clients generally gain the courage to attempt panic inductions at home. Therapists also encourage them to engage in behavioral experiments in which they resist some disorder-maintaining behaviors to test their panic-related catastrophic beliefs. In addition, as soon as clients are beginning to feel mastery over panic attacks and have less frequent and less intense anxiety, they should begin to taper off their benzodiazapines. Clients should only do this under a physician's supervision, and the process can usually begin after the fourth or fifth session.

Once clients' panic attacks have become markedly less frequent, if they remain agoraphobic, therapists should address their *agoraphobia* directly. To expedite treatment of agoraphobia, it is often helpful for clients to practice *flooding in imagination.* This procedure consists of imagining a highly anxiety-provoking agoraphobic situation until it no longer elicits anxiety. This prepares clients for graded *in vivo exposure. In vivo* exposure consists of clients repeatedly and frequently exposing themselves to agoraphobic situations for a prolonged period of time until habituation occurs. Then, they proceed to a slightly more anxiety-provoking item on their exposure hierarchy.

Finally, cognitive therapy addresses *core beliefs, issues, or strategies* that predispose clients to relapsing or contribute to other problems. As mentioned above, Greg's (Case 6.A) struggle over the issue of dependence versus independence interfered with overcoming his agoraphobia. Once he worked through the beliefs and associated anxiety, guilt, and anger over this issue, he progressed quickly through therapy for his agoraphobia, and he became symptom-free. Although Jimmy (Case 6.B) was able to master his panic attacks, he continued to have problems with alcohol, inappropriate sexual behavior, and marital problems. As a result, these became foci of later treatment. In addition, he began attending Alcoholics Anonymous meetings, which also aided in his improvement.

As with most other therapeutic interventions, clients benefit from having a plan that enables them to continue their therapeutic work on their own after termination. With panic, it is especially important for clients to continue to practice the coping skills that they learned during therapy and induce panic. Therapists encourage clients to periodically induce panic so that they will have regular practice with coping skills. Regarding agoraphobia, clients should periodically expose themselves to situations or places that previously elicited anxiety and with which they do not have regular contact in their daily life. In addition, if fear or avoidance begins to reemerge, clients should begin cognitive restructuring and exposure work immediately to prevent a full-blown episode from occurring, or they should return to therapy.

7

Obsessive-Compulsive Disorder (OCD)

1. Introduction
2. Cognitive Model of OCD
   a. Types of Pathological Interpretations in OCD
      i. Overestimating the Probability and Negativity of Events
      ii. Exaggerating or Distorting Perceptions of Responsibility
      iii. Viewing Themselves as Seriously Defective
      iv. Expecting Debilitating Distress
      v. Expecting That They Need to Be in Perfect Control
   b. Psychosocial Vulnerabilities to OCD
3. Assessment and Conceptualization of OCD
   a. Questionnaires
   b. Case Conceptualization Worksheet for OCD
   c. Downward Arrows Technique
   d. Examples of Case Conceptualizations
      i. Case 7.A (Elise): OCD Washer
      ii. Case 7.B (Carlos): OCD Checker
      iii. Case 7.C (Frances): OCD With Overt and Covert Compulsions
4. Cognitive Therapy of OCD
   a. Presentation of the Case Conceptualization Illustration to Clients
   b. Engagement in Cognitive Therapy
   c. Increasing Clients' Awareness of OCD Processes
   d. Cognitive Restructuring With OCD Clients
      i. Restructuring Overestimations of the Probability and Negativity of Events
      ii. Restructuring Exaggerated or Distorted Perceptions of Responsibility
      iii. Restructuring Likelihood TAF
      iv. Restructuring Moral TAF
      v. Restructuring Beliefs About Foreseeability
      vi. Restructuring Views of Self as Seriously Defective
      vii. Restructuring Expectations of Debilitating Distress
      viii. Restructuring the "Need" to be in Perfect Control

INTRODUCTION

According to the *DSM–IV* (APA, 1994), obsessive-compulsive disorder (OCD) is characterized by "recurrent obsessions or compulsions that are severe enough to be time consuming (they take more than 1 hour per day) or cause marked distress or significant impairment" (p. 417). At some time during the disorder, the person realizes that these symptoms are excessive or unreasonable. ***Obsessions*** are recurrent and persistent cognitions that the person experiences as intrusive and inappropriate and that cause significant distress. The person attempts to ignore or suppress the cognitions or to neutralize them with other thoughts or actions. The obsessions of individuals suffering from OCD often involve one of the following themes.

First, a subcategory of individuals with OCD fear that they will become *contaminated,* resulting in their own or other people's illness or death. Examples of common "contaminants" include: dirt, germs, cancer, HIV, bodily fluids, bodily wastes, asbestos, chemicals, radiation, and sticky substances.

A second OCD theme relates to *making mistakes.* Many OCD clients fear that they will make mistakes that will result in catastrophes. For example, some believe that they might forget to turn off an appliance leading to a house fire. Others worry that they will make a mistake at work (e.g., typing a single, wrong character on the computer screen) that could result in bankrupting the company. Still others worry that they will throw away something that may be important later.

Third, many individuals suffering from OCD believe that they are at risk for *losing control of their behavior.* Some believe that their loss of control will result in serious harm to themselves or others. For instance, they may worry that they will put poison in food, strangle a child, push a stranger in front of a car, or run over a pedestrian. Others with OCD worry that they will lose control of their behavior in a socially inappropriate manner. For example, they may fear that they will not be able to stop themselves from swearing, being rude, picking their noses, or disrobing in public. Still others are concerned that they will lose control of their behavior in a sinful way. They may be afraid that they will be blasphemous or make sexual advances outside their marital relationship.

A fourth OCD theme relates to clients' belief that they *must be perfect*. They may fear one of several catastrophic consequences will result from being imperfect. For example, they may believe that if they do something imperfectly, they will not be able to proceed to other things (e.g., "I can't take on any new life commitments—like going back to school or starting a new relationship—until my house is perfectly organized"). Alternatively, they may believe that imperfection will lead to social humiliation or rejection.

A fifth theme has to do with *superstitious beliefs*. "Step on a crack and you'll break your mother's back" is a game for many children. However, for some individuals with OCD, this type of intrusive thought can lead to great distress and corresponding compulsions.[20]

Compulsions are repetitive overt or covert behaviors. (The *DSM–IV* refers to the latter as "mental acts." Reasons for using different terminology are discussed later.) Compulsions are done in response to obsessions to prevent a dreaded consequence (content of the obsession) or to diminish anxiety. Clients engage in these overt or covert behaviors to excess or do them stereotypically. Common examples of *overt compulsions* include:

(a) *cleaning* or *washing*, such as hand washing, showering, or cleaning oneself repeatedly;

(b) *checking for safety or to prevent damage to one's home or car*, such as repeatedly checking to see that appliances or faucets are turned off or that doors are locked;

(c) *checking for mistakes;*

(d) *hoarding* by excessively collecting mail, trash, or objects;

(e) *asking for reassurance* from others to share responsibility in case of a catastrophe;

(f) *superstitious overt behaviors* such as avoiding cracks in the pavement; and

(g) *arranging or organizing objects in perfect symmetry.*

---

[20]Superstitious behavior of this kind can be thought of as existing on a continuum. At one extreme are people with delusions, who believe the superstition despite much evidence to the contrary and in opposition to what almost everyone else in their culture believes. Not quite as extreme but close to the delusional pole of the continuum are many individuals with OCD. At some time during their disorder, they realize that their beliefs are unreasonable. In the middle are people, for example, who not only "knock on wood" but feel somewhat uncomfortable taking for granted some good fortune without protecting themselves in this magical manner. At the other pole of the superstition continuum are people who do not believe in superstitions at all.

Before describing common examples of covert compulsions, a note about terminology is warranted. I use the term covert compulsion instead of mental act. Covert compulsion emphasizes the functional equivalence of this cognitive process with an overt compulsion. Both covert compulsions and obsessions are cognitive processes. What differentiates them is that covert compulsions are intentional and reduce anxiety, whereas obsessions are unintentional intrusive cognitions and cause anxiety.

Examples of covert compulsions include: (a) *counting* to a certain number, (b) *praying*[21] or *intentionally thinking "magical" words,* (c) *repeating* in one's mind every word others say, and (d) *neutralizing* by attempting to undo a catastrophic mental image. For example, a parent may try to imagine that her child looks safe and healthy in response to an image of the child being mutilated.

COGNITIVE MODEL OF OCD

Salkovskis (1989) succinctly summarized the cognitive model of OCD. He stated "obsessions are intrusive cognitions, the occurrence and content of which patients interpret as an indication that they might be responsible for harm to themselves or others, unless they take action to prevent it" (p. 678).

Figure 7.1 represents the cognitive model of OCD. Obsessions and compulsions often begin with a *triggering stimulus.* The triggering stimulus activates an *orienting schema,* which functions as a gatekeeper to the OCD (danger) mode. When the orienting schema is activated, it fully activates the already partially active (i.e., primed) OCD mode. It fully activates all the systems of the mode (i.e., cognitive, affective, physiological, motivational, and behavioral).

When the mode is activated, the individual experiences an *intrusive, unpleasant cognition.* Intrusive, unpleasant cognitions are themselves normal and nearly universal. (However, for individuals who do not suffer from OCD, intrusive unpleasant cognitions are not associated with an activated orienting schema.) Individuals with OCD *pathologically interpret the significance* of the content or occurrence of these intrusive cognitions (e.g., when departing from their homes, many OCD checkers think, "I may have left the toaster plugged in," which they interpret as meaning there is a good chance that their houses will burn down).[22] These individuals interpret intrusive cognitions as very important, personally significant, revealing, cat-

[21]Of course, for many people, prayer, and more generally spiritual belief and practice, contribute to their overall emotional well being. However, clients with OCD can pray compulsively to prevent the catastrophe that they are anticipating or to decrease anxiety. When treating such clients, therapists should strive to respect clients' religious beliefs while simultaneously helping them overcome their pathology. Consulting or collaborating with clergy often helps this process.

[22]The cognitive models of PD and OCD are similar in that they both involve misinterpretation of internal stimuli. In panic, the stimuli are benign physical sensations, whereas in OCD, the stimuli are intrusive cognitions.

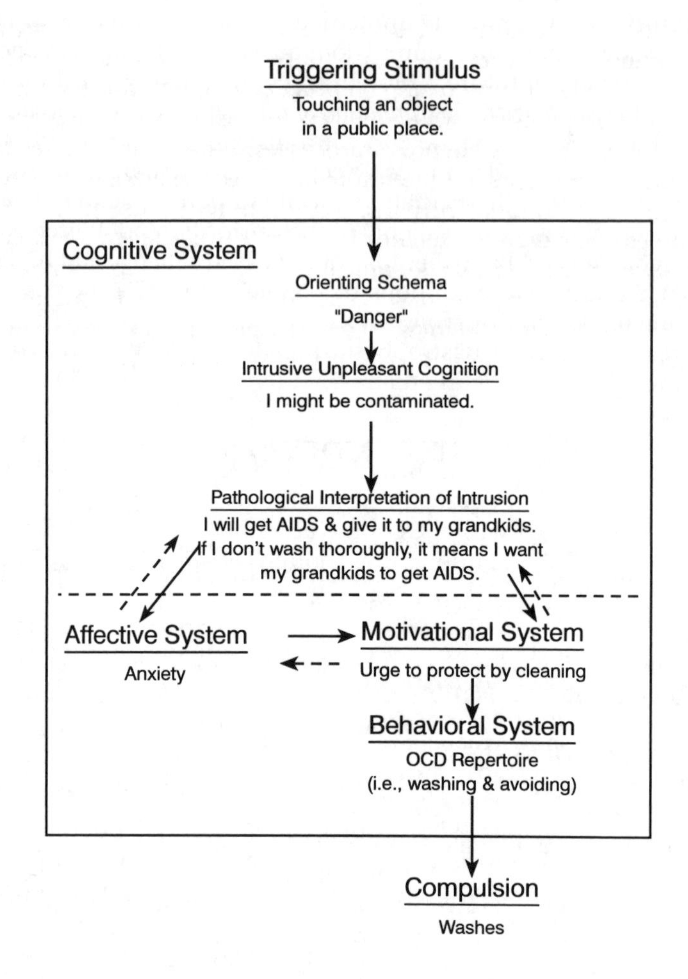

FIG. 7.1. Cognitive model of OCD.

astrophic, and their responsibility (Rachman, 1997). As a result, they experience marked *anxiety* (*affective system*).

As part of the OCD individual's modal response, and in response to the anxiety and the content of the obsession, their *motivational and behavioral systems* become activated. Individuals with OCD engage in *compulsions*—overt or covert behaviors designed to (a) prevent the catastrophic content of the obsession from occurring, (b) decrease their responsibility should a catastrophe occur, or (c) decrease anxiety.

Compulsions often provide immediate—although often short-lived—*anxiety reduction.* Therefore, compulsions are *negatively reinforced* and more likely to occur in the future.[23] Moreover, compulsions *prevent the disconfirmation of the pathological interpretation of intrusive cognitions.* In addition, by prematurely decreasing anxiety, compulsions *prevent desensitization* to triggering situations and to intrusive cognitions. Finally, because compulsions require plans for immediate, critically important action, they make intrusive cognitions more salient, higher priority, and therefore more likely to recur. It is probably because of increased salience and higher priority that the intrusive cognitions of people with OCD increase in frequency, intensity, and duration.

As a result of feared catastrophes associated with intrusive cognitions and as a result of anticipating distress, individuals with OCD frequently attempt to *avoid triggering stimuli.* Like in phobias, avoidance in OCD helps maintain the disorder. Avoidance prevents individuals from having experiences that could help disconfirm their pathological interpretation of intrusive cognitions and desensitize individuals to the triggering stimuli. Similarly, individuals with OCD may attempt to *suppress their intrusive cognitions.* Attempts at suppressing thoughts usually increase their frequency and intensity.

Much research supports the cognitive model of OCD. The evidence regarding the importance of pathologically misinterpreting intrusive cognitions is discussed later. However, before that discussion, evidence for the other parts of the model are cited briefly.

First, research shows that a large percentage of the nonclinical population regularly has negative intrusive cognitions. Many of the intrusive cognitions are unpleasant (Edwards & Dickerson, 1987; Gibbs, 1996; Salkovskis & Harrison, 1984). Moreover, in normal populations, the themes of unpleasant intrusive cognitions are similar to OCD themes. For example, Edwards and Dickerson (1987) found that in a nonclinical sample, a large proportion endorsed having frequent intrusive cognitions about violence, harm to self or others, or being physically ill or diseased. Second, thought suppression experiments have found the following: when nonclinical subjects are instructed to suppress their thoughts, their rates of intrusive cognitions and their levels of distress increase (Salkovskis & Campbell, 1994; Trinder & Salkovskis, 1994). Third, laboratory studies of OCD have consistently found that exposure to OCD-triggering stimuli results in increased physiological indices of arousal that subjects perceive as unpleasant (Boulougouris, Rabavilas, & Stefanis, 1977; Grayson et al., 1982; Grayson, Nutter, & Mavissakalian, 1980; Kozak, Foa, & Steketee, 1988; Lelliott, Noshirvani, Marks, &

---

[23]Although in the vernacular, people are often labeled "compulsive" gamblers, overspenders, or overeaters, these impulse disorders do not meet *DSM* criteria for compulsions because each is done to obtain *positive* reinforcement or pleasure—not simply to escape distress.

Monteiro, 1987). Fourth, most laboratory studies have found that when subjects with OCD perform compulsions, physiological indices of their arousal decrease (Hodgson & Rachman, 1977; Hornsveld, Kraaimaat, & van Dam-Baggen, 1979; Roper & Rachman, 1976; Roper, Rachman, & Hodgson, 1973).

Types of Pathological Interpretations in OCD

People who do not suffer from OCD appear to experience intrusive cognitions with content similar to that of people suffering from OCD. However, a crucial way that individuals with OCD seem to differ from the general population is how they interpret these intrusive cognitions. In OCD, pathological interpretations of intrusive cognitions usually take one of the following forms:

overestimating the probability and negativity of events ("X [negative event] is likely and will be catastrophic"),

exaggerating or distorting perceptions of responsibility ("This thought means I will be responsible for X [catastrophic event]"),

viewing themselves as seriously defective ("Because I'm thinking this way, I am a bad person"),

expecting debilitating distress ("If I keep having this thought and the level of anxiety, I'll go crazy"), and

expecting that they need to be in perfect control ("I will be rejected/humiliated if I am imperfect"; "I am not in adequate control of myself").

Each of these cognitive distortions is discussed next.

Overestimating the Probability and Negativity of Events. People with OCD, as well as people with anxiety disorders in general, tend to interpret intrusive cognitions as signifying that negative events are likely and will be catastrophic (e.g., Beck et al., 1985; Rachman, 1997; Salkovskis, 1989, 1996; van Oppen & Arntz, 1993). These tendencies provide the substrate for obsessions in vulnerable individuals. In other words, habitually expecting catastrophes is necessary but not sufficient for experiencing OCD. (Individuals with OCD must also feel responsible for anticipated catastrophes and believe they must act or think in a way to prevent them.)

Exaggerating or Distorting Perceptions of Responsibility. Salkvoskis (1985) made the observation that a distorted perception of responsibility was an essential feature of OCD. OCD clients exhibit a variety of distortions related to responsibility. First, individuals with OCD overestimate their responsible for negative events. For example, they often believe that if they have any influence over an outcome, it means that they are completely responsible for the outcome (Salkovskis, 1996).

Many OCD clients also believe that they are responsible for potentially catastrophic future events simply because they had cognitions about the event. This blurring of thought and action has been referred to as *Thought-Action Fusion* (TAF; see Rachman, 1993). One type of TAF is referred to as *Likelihood TAF*. This is the belief that having a thought about a negative event may actually increase the probability that the negative event will occur. For example, individuals with Likelihood TAF who have the thought that they will be poisoned by food believe that their thought makes it probable. Freeston and Ladouceur (1993) found that 88% of OCD subjects sampled endorsed the belief "Thinking about it [a negative event] increases the chances that it will happen."

A second type of TAF is *Moral TAF*, the belief that having a thought about doing harm is morally equivalent to engaging in the harmful behavior (Rachman, 1997). Individuals with OCD also may have a related belief. They may believe not engaging in a compulsion in response to an obsession is equivalent to wanting the harm involved in the obsession to happen (Salkovskis, 1996).

Another way that people with OCD distort their perceptions of responsibility relates to the issue of *foreseeability* (Salkovskis, 1996). OCD sufferers often believe that they would be responsible for a potential catastrophe if it was foreseeable and they either failed to foresee it or failed to try to prevent it. This is the case even if the potential catastrophe is highly unlikely. OCD clients often consider it their responsibility to *try to foresee* any conceivable catastrophe because foresight can lead to action that may prevent catastrophic events. Thus, they often believe that they have a *duty to foresee* and a *duty if they* foresee. As a result, they spend enormous amounts of time thinking about any possible catastrophe and then performing overt or covert actions to prevent them. Needless to say, individuals with these sorts of cognitions and strategies typically become overwhelmed with the impossibility of their mission. They cannot possibly try to prevent all foreseeable catastrophes. In addition, large social and personal barriers to attempting to do so exist. For example, individuals with OCD are often extremely ashamed of engaging in behaviors that they realize others view as bizarre or ludicrous.

Some individuals with OCD develop a convoluted solution to this dilemma. Because they cannot act to prevent all possible catastrophes, they can at least *try to worry about them*. They believe that their worry can magically prevent the catastrophe or decrease their responsibility if a catastrophe were to occur. This type of compulsion can be considered the compulsive counterpart to TAF. Having the "right" emotion (i.e., worry) prevents a catastrophe or is the moral equivalent to taking an overt preventive action.

Salkovskis (1996) suggested several other types of responsibility beliefs among OCD sufferers. For example, individuals with OCD believe that (a) failing to prevent (or failing to try to prevent) harm to self or others is the same as having caused the harm in the first place and (b) responsibility is not reduced by other factors such as something being improbable.

Two interesting findings from research that manipulated responsibility are worth mentioning briefly. Ladouceur, Rhéaume, and Aublet (1997) gave nonclinical subjects one of four sets of information. The information manipulated their perceptions of responsibility for an event as well as how negative the potential outcome of a mistake would be. Subjects who were led to believe that they could be highly responsible for a mistake that could have extremely negative consequences responded in ways that resembled OCD checkers. Conversely, Lopatka and Rachman (1995) found that with OCD checkers, experimental manipulations that decreased their perceptions of responsibility resulted in decreases in their discomfort and urges to check.

Viewing Themselves as Seriously Defective. Rachman (1997) observed that individuals suffering from OCD often pathologically interpret their intrusive cognitions in a manner that supports negative core beliefs about themselves, such as "I am an evil person," "I am dangerous," "I am unreliable," "I may become totally uncontrollable," "I am weird," or "I am going insane." Freeston and Ladouceur (1993) found empirical support for this suggestion. A large proportion of their sample of OCD subjects interpreted their intrusive cognitions as evidence for an enduring and highly negative view of themselves. For example, 72% believed, "Having this thought means that I am not like other people." 64% endorsed, "Thinking about it means that I am going crazy." 48% believed, "Having this type of thought means that I will lose control and become violent." 48% believed, "Thinking about it means that I will never get better." 40% believed, "Thinking about it means that I am a bad person."

Expecting Debilitating Distress. Freeston and Ladouceur (1993) found that a large proportion of their OCD sample believed that their intrusive cognitions signified that they would experience unacceptable or debilitating distress. These thoughts and the percentage of subjects endorsing them follow: "If I think about it, I will become very anxious" (92%), "If I start to think about it, I will be unable to stop" (68%), "If I think about it now, I will be unable to do things that I have to do" (52%), and "If I think about it while I am doing something, it completely ruins whatever it is I am doing" (40%). Related cognitions not assessed in Freeston and Ladouceur (1993) but that individuals with OCD seem to experience frequently include: "I can't stand having these thoughts and feeling like this," "I'm powerless to change this," "It's not worth suffering like this," and "Even though it [obsession] is ridiculous, if I just do it, I'll feel better."

Expecting That They Need to Be in Perfect Control. Studies have found that compared to nonclinical subjects, OCD subjects are more perfectionistic (e.g., Frost & Steketee, 1997). For example, an OCD client had the intrusive cognition, "My books aren't perfectly lined up." He interpreted this as meaning "I can't get on with my life if they aren't right." Others with OCD expect to be punished, humiliated, or rejected if they are imperfect. Still others expect long-term ill health or personal or financial catastrophe will occur as a result of being imperfect.

Individuals with OCD frequently believe that their intrusive cognitions signify that they will lose control over their thoughts or behavior. In addition, they often believe that they should have perfect control over their thoughts (Salkovskis, 1996). As a result, they typically interpret their inability to control their intrusive cognitions as evidence that they are weak, morally depraved, dangerous, or might lose control of their behavior.

Psychosocial Vulnerabilities to OCD

Rachman (1997) postulated that people who go on to develop OCD learn early in life that all of their value-laden cognitions are significant. They also typically strive for moral perfection and engage in cognitive distortions, especially relating to responsibility. He cited evidence that other psychosocial vulnerabilities include major life stressors, anxiety, and depression.

ASSESSMENT AND CONCEPTUALIZATION OF OCD

To obtain information necessary for an effective case conceptualization, therapists benefit from using a variety of pretreatment questionnaires, the Structured Clinical Interview for the *DSM–IV,* skillful questioning, and behavioral observations. Besides the general information obtained during assessment, once a diagnosis of OCD is made, the therapist should perform a careful functional analysis of the client's problematic responses. This should include the various triggering stimuli, intrusive unpleasant cognitions, pathological interpretations of the intrusive cognitions, and compulsions or avoidance behaviors. Other sources of information about OCD clients can come from OCD questionnaires, the Case Conceptualization Worksheet (which guides therapists' questions and records clients' answers), and the downward arrows technique.

Questionnaires

OCD-specific questionnaires can help quantify the severity of OCD and assess a range of obsessions and compulsions that might be missed in a clinical interview. Another advantage of using questionnaires is that they enable the therapist and the client to track progress over the course of therapy.

Some questionnaires that can be particularly useful in assessing and treating clients with OCD are the Yale-Brown Obsessive Compulsive Scale (Goodman et al., 1989), the Maudsley Obsessive Compulsive Inventory (Hodgson & Rachman, 1977), the Responsibility Questionnaire (Rhéaume,

Ladouceur, Freeston, & Letarte, 1994, 1995), and the Frost Multidimensional Perfectionism Scale (Frost, Marten, Lahart, & Rosenblate, 1990).

Case Conceptualization Worksheet for OCD

Once the therapist diagnoses a client with OCD, the therapist should conduct a fine-grained assessment of the client's obsessions and compulsions. The therapist can often begin this during the intake interview. The Case Conceptualization Worksheet for OCD (see the Appendix) can guide the therapist's assessment of an OCD client's problematic responses. Specifically, the Case Conceptualization Worksheet prompts therapists for intrusive cognitions, pathological interpretation of intrusive cognitions, and overt or covert compulsions or avoidance. (In addition, clients can use the Case Conceptualization Worksheet as a format for self-monitoring.)

Downward Arrows Technique

To uncover the significance or meanings that clients attach to intrusive cognitions, the downward arrows technique (described in chapter 4) can be most helpful. Figure 7.2 presents an example that demonstrates the use of downward arrows for uncovering the meanings a client gives to an intrusive cognition. For Frances (Case 7.C), a triggering situation was the combination of both seeing an object owned by a loved one and considering discarding the object. This was the case even if the object had no practical or sentimental value. When thinking about throwing away an old hairbrush of her daughter's, Frances had the following intrusive thought: "Even thinking about throwing out her brush means I don't care about her." As a result of this kind of thinking, Frances hoarded her loved ones' possessions—which represented one of her compulsions.

Frances' therapist began with the intrusive thought just mentioned. For each cognition Frances supplied, her therapist asked her, "If ______ were true, what would that mean about you as a person or about the things that are most important to you?" or "If ______ were true, what would be the worst or most upsetting part for you?" Figure 7.2 illustrates Frances' responses.

Thus, the reader can see from the example of Frances, the downward arrows technique makes it possible for the therapist to probe about the underlying meanings of intrusive thoughts.

Examples of Case Conceptualizations

This section includes completed case conceptualizations of individuals with OCD. For each client, a brief synopsis, a Case Conceptualization Worksheet for OCD (filled out by the therapist early in treatment), and a Case Conceptualization Illustration is presented. Elise (Case 7.A) was an

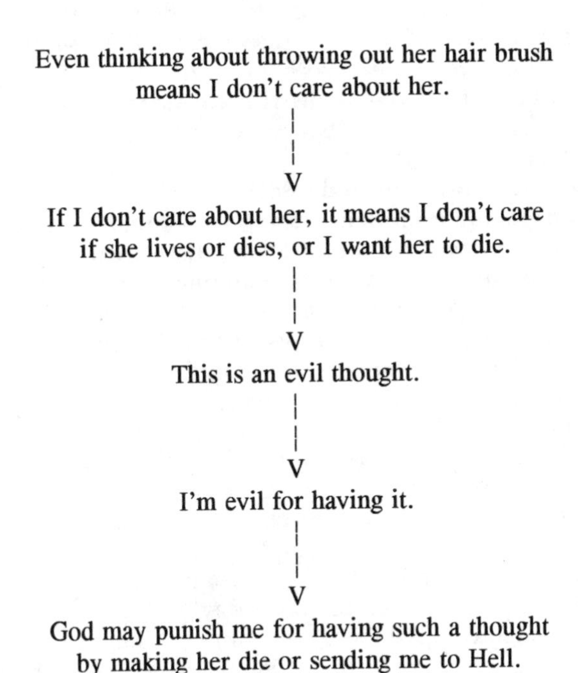

FIG. 7.2. An example of the downward arrows technique.

OCD "washer," Carlos (7.B) was an OCD "checker," and Frances (Case 7.C) had both overt and covert compulsions. In the subsequent section that discusses treatment, these three cases are referred to more fully to show how conceptualizations help guide treatment.

Case 7.A (Elise): OCD Washer. Elise was a 52-year-old, divorced secretary who lived alone and had been suffering from OCD for the 10 years preceding her presentation for therapy. Her psychological symptoms began after her husband left her for his secretary. Immediately upon learning about her husband's infidelity, Elise had a major depressive episode. Over the following year, OCD symptoms gradually began. Prior to that time, Elise reportedly had never experienced OCD. However, she had experienced two other major depressive episodes, one following the breakup of a relationship in college and another after the death of her father.

Elise's major obsession related to becoming HIV-positive and then infecting her grandchildren. For Elise, triggering stimuli, which elicited obsessions and compulsions, included objects that other people may have touched. She found it particularly difficult to touch public toilets, grocery carts, door knobs, elevator buttons, and money. She reported that these objects were particularly difficult because many other people may have touched them. When confronted with these stimuli, Elise's intrusive cognition was "What if it's contaminated?" She interpreted this thought to mean that by touching these objects, she had a good chance of becoming infected with HIV.

As a result of her anxiety related to HIV infection, Elise engaged in a variety of disorder-maintaining behaviors. She avoided touching objects that others were likely to have touched. She wore white gloves whenever possible so that she could detect possible contaminants. Elise also washed her hands frequently and quickly because she wanted to remove the contaminants but was afraid of getting chapped hands. Chapped hands, she reasoned, could result in open sores, which would make her more vulnerable to contamination. Therefore, her washing ritual consisted of washing quickly and then using large amounts of hand cream to prevent chapping. At work, Elise curtailed her washing ritual. There, she used antibacterial towelettes every 15 minutes or so. However, during her lunch, she went to her car, cleaned her hands, and then rubbed in hand cream for approximately 20 minutes. Because she was afraid that if she sat on a public toilet she would become contaminated, Elise avoided using the restroom and avoided drinking fluids during the work day.

Although Elise developed OCD soon after her husband left her, OCD did not appear to prevent her from dealing with this event. During the first 18 months after her husband's departure, she experienced a full range of feelings, including rage and intense sadness. She thought a great deal about her husband during that period, hated him, and longed for him. However, gradually, her focus on him diminished. On the other hand, her mood never completely recovered. In the years after her divorce, she continued to be moderately depressed. Although she invested emotionally in her children and grandchildren, she did not develop other relationships or activities. This appeared largely the result of time and energy constraints due to her emotional problems.

Elise attributed her core belief "I must be perfect in everything I do or else something terrible will happen" to childhood events. Specifically, she attributed the belief to how she dealt with being molested by a neighbor. The neighbor molested her from the time that she was 6 years old until she was 9 years old (see Figs. 7.3, 7.4, & 7.5).

OBSESSIVE-COMPULSIVE DISORDER CONCEPTUALIZATION WORKSHEET

Client's Name: Elise

OCD SCENARIOS

TRIGGERING STIMULI	INTRUSIVE COGNITIONS	PATHOLOGICAL INTERPRETATION OF INTRUSIONS	OVERT OR COVERT COMPULSIONS
Touching anything in public places, especially objects that are likely to be touched by many people.	I might touch deadly germs.	There's a decent chance that I will get AIDS and spread it to my grandkids.	
		If I wash without using cream, my hands might bleed and make me more likely to get AIDS.	Washes hands quickly, uses hand cream.
		If I don't wash extremely thoroughly and avoid touching contamination, it means I want my grandkids to get AIDS.	Uses white gloves when she needs to touch objects that may have been touched by the public (e.g., mail box, door); thoroughly checks object for contaminants.

continued on next page

AVOIDED SITUATIONS OR INTERNAL STATES

1. Public places, especially public restrooms. Does not drink anything at work to prevent herself from having to use the bathroom.
2. Touching objects with her hands, especially objects that may have been touched by many people.
3. Uses gloves to avoid touching objects directly.

OTHER PROBLEMATIC SCENARIOS

TRIGGERING STIMULI	COGNITIONS	EMOTIONS	BEHAVIORS
Grandchildren visiting.	I might contaminate them. I'm weird and shouldn't be like this. I should enjoy their visit. I'm making everyone miserable. I have an awful life.	Anxious Angry Sad	Mopes. Tells family she is exhausted and needs to sleep.

FIG. 7.3. (*cont'd*) Case Conceptualization Worksheet (Case 7.A, Elise).

CASE CONCEPTUALIZATION SUMMARY FORM

Client's Name: Elise

Identifying Information: 62-year-old, divorced secretary; obsessions and compulsions that consume on average 2 hrs/day, 10 year history.

Presenting Problem: Worry about becoming infected with HIV, depression.
Precipitant(s): Husband left her for his secretary.

Exhaustive List of Problems, Issues, and Therapy-Relevant Behaviors:

1. Intrusive cognitions and pathological interpretations of these cognitions.
2. Compulsions--excessive washing, avoids touching objects, especially in public places.
3. Depressed mood, low energy, insomnia.
4. No social network.
5. Does not enjoy family visits because she is afraid of contaminating family.

Diagnosis (Axis I): OCD; Major Depressive Disorder, Recurrent, Severe

Personality Characteristics: Perfectionism

Relevant Beliefs:

1. I must be perfect in everything I do or something terrible will happen.
2. I will get AIDS and spread it to my grandkids.
3. If I don't wash thoroughly and avoid touching contamination, it means I want my grandkids to get AIDS.
4. Cleanliness is next to Godliness.
5. If things are not perfectly clean, people could get sick.

Origins of Key Core Beliefs: Was sexually molested beginning when she was 6-years-old by a teenage neighbor. As a result of this event, she developed the belief, *I must be in perfect control of everything or something terrible will happen.*

continued on next page

WORKING MODEL

VICIOUS CYCLES / MAINTAINING FACTORS:
Her obsessions involve becoming HIV positive and infecting her grandchildren. As a result, she engages in compulsive washing and avoids touching objects in public. These behaviors reduce her anxiety in the short run but prevent disconfirmation of her belief that she will become contaminated and prevent her from desensitizing to feared objects.

TREATMENT:

Goals:
1. Decrease frequency, intensity, & duration of obsessions and compulsions; decrease avoidance of "contaminants."
2. Decrease overall anxiety.
3. Improve mood.

Possible Obstacles to Treatment: Depression

Plan:
1. Refer to psychiatrist to evaluate for selective-serotonin-reuptake inhibitors.
2. Cognitive restructuring--e.g., the probability that catastrophic expectations regarding contamination will come true.
3. Exposure to "contaminants" while engaging in response prevention--not washing or using hand cream.
4. Cognitive restructuring of depressive automatic thoughts and beliefs.

FIG. 7.4. *(cont'd)* Case Conceptualization Summary Form (Case 7.A, Elise).

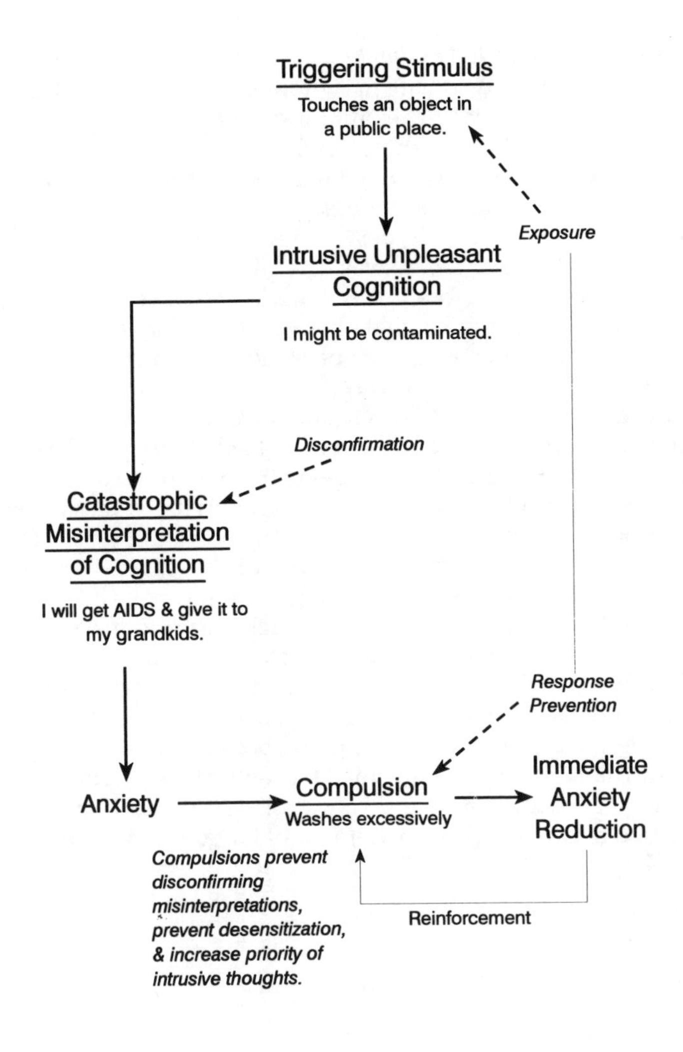

FIG. 7.5. Case Conceptualization Illustration (Case 7.A, Elise).

Case 7.B (Carlos): OCD Checker. Carlos was a 40-year-old, married, account clerk who lived with his wife and two young children. Obsessions and compulsions became debilitating approximately 3 months prior to seeking therapy during a highly stressful time at work. One day, he was rushing to work and was preoccupied with an assignment. He failed to see a jogger and almost hit her. He thought, "I could have killed her." From that point on, Carlos became hypervigilant to potential driving dangers. Approximately 3 weeks later, he was driving home from work and went over a bump. Moments before this, "something looked weird" in his peripheral vision. He thought he might have hit someone. As a result, he circled back. However, when he circled back, he also thought he might have hit something. Over the next several months, driving became progressively more difficult and time consuming for Carlos.

When driving, the stimuli that were most likely to trigger Carlos' obsessions and compulsions included changes in the color or texture of the pavement, bumps, intersections, crosswalks, heavy traffic, many pedestrians, and poor visibility. He misinterpreted the intrusive cognition "something is wrong" as meaning that the probability that he hit someone was high. In response to his anxiety-provoking thought that he may have hit someone, he frequently looked in his rearview mirror, circled back to make sure he did not hit someone, and carefully watched pedestrians to make sure that he could account for each one. Carlos also avoided driving whenever possible and attempted to keep driving excursions as brief as possible.

Some childhood events seemed to predispose Carlos to the expectation that he could make a tragic driving mistake. Both of his parents were excessively concerned with health and safety issues. In addition, his mother never learned to drive because of her fear of having an accident (see Figs. 7.6, 7.7, & 7.8).

OBSESSIVE-COMPULSIVE DISORDER CONCEPTUALIZATION WORKSHEET

Client's Name: Carlos

OCD SCENARIOS

TRIGGERING STIMULI	INTRUSIVE COGNITIONS	PATHOLOGICAL INTERPRETATIONS OF INTRUSIONS	OVERT OR COVERT COMPULSIONS, OR AVOIDANCE
Going over a bump in the road; changes in pavement color or texture; heavy traffic; pedestrians; crosswalks.	Something's wrong.	I might have hit someone. I must anticipate and prevent any car accident; I have to be sure where every car and pedestrian is. Thinking that I may have hit someone makes it more likely to be true. I have to be sure I didn't hit someone. Any possibility that I will cause a crash means I need to worry about it because I will be responsible.	Circles back to make sure no one was hit and to account for all pedestrians. Repeatedly checks the rearview mirror.

continued on next page

AVOIDED SITUATIONS OR INTERNAL STATES

1. Drives only when necessary.
2. Especially avoids driving (a) when the roads are crowded, (b) in places with intersections or crosswalks, and (c) at times when there is glare.

OTHER PROBLEMATIC SCENARIOS

TRIGGERING STIMULI	COGNITIONS	EMOTIONS	BEHAVIORS
None noted during intake evaluation.			

FIG. 7.6. (*cont'd*) Case Conceptualization Worksheet (Case 7.B, Carlos).

CASE CONCEPTUALIZATION SUMMARY FORM

Client's Name: Carlos

Identifying Information: 40-year-old, married, male account clerk; lives with wife and two children; happily married.

Presenting Problem: Obsessions and compulsions.
Precipitant(s): Nearly hit a jogger during a stressful time at work.

Exhaustive List of Problems, Issues, and Therapy-Relevant Behaviors:

1. Obsessions & compulsions. 2. Depression, anhedonia, insomnia, decreased appetite. 3. Hypervigilance to danger and harm. 4. Fear of going crazy.	

Diagnoses (Axis I): OCD; Major Depressive Disorder.

Personality Characteristics: Perfectionism and scrupulousness.

Relevant Beliefs:

1. **I might make a mistake that could kill someone.** 2. I should be able to anticipate and prevent any car accident. 3. Thinking that I may have hit someone makes it more likely to be true. 4. I have to be sure I didn't hit someone.	5. Any possibility that I would cause a crash means I need to worry about it because I would be responsible. 6. I must be perfect and have perfect foresight.

Origins of Key Core Beliefs: Parents were extremely concerned with health and safety issues. As a result of fear, his mother never learned to drive. These issues apparently predisposed him to believing that he could make a fatal driving mistake.

continued on next page

WORKING MODEL

VICIOUS CYCLES / MAINTAINING FACTORS:
Obsessions relate to causing a car accident. As a result of his obsessions, he avoids driving or engages in checking compulsions (e.g., circled back); these decrease anxiety but prevent disconfirmation of this catastrophic belief and prevent desensitization to driving situations.

TREATMENT:

Goals:

1. Decrease the frequency, intensity, and duration of obsessions and compulsions, decrease avoidance.
2. Improve mood.

Possible Obstacles to Treatment: None noted.

Plan:

1. Cognitive restructuring of Thought-Action Fusion as well as beliefs that one should foresee every possible hazard and that Foreseeability = Responsibility.
2. Exposure to driving with response prevention consisting of not circling back and not looking in the rear view mirror unless backing up or changing lanes.

FIG. 7.7. (*cont'd*) Case Conceptualization Summary Form (Case 7.B, Carlos).

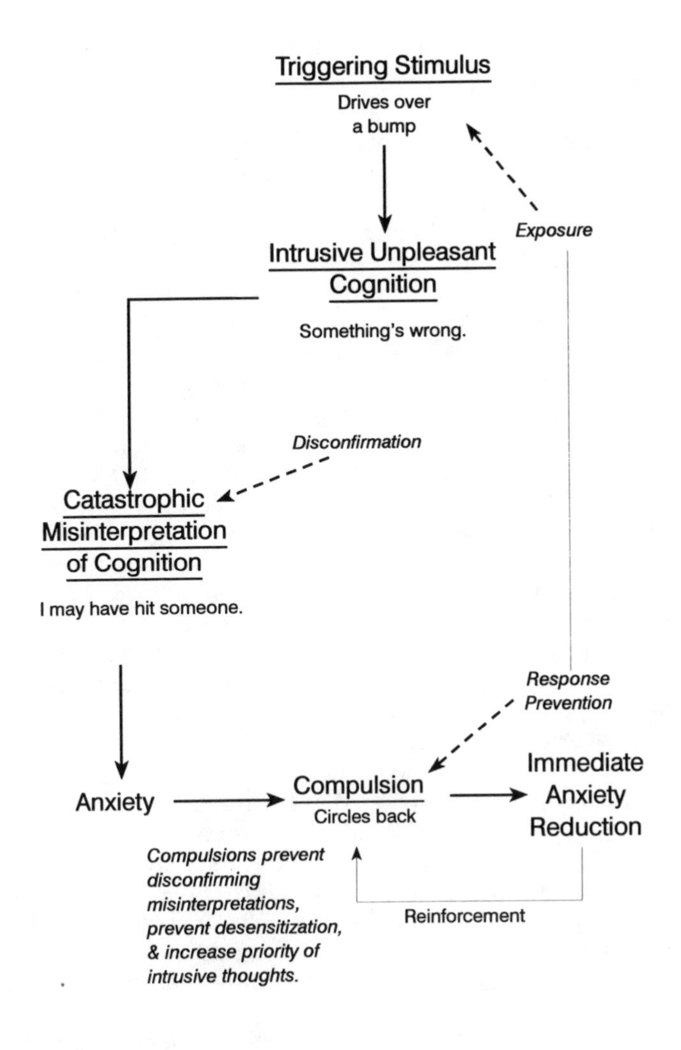

FIG. 7.8. Case Conceptualization Illustration (Case 7.B, Carlos).

Case 7.C (Frances): OCD With Overt and Covert Compulsions. Frances was a 37-year-old, married lawyer who lived with her husband and 4-year-old daughter. She reluctantly sought treatment at her husband's urging. Although they were happily married and he was generally supportive, he was becoming tired of her chronic distress and lack of time resulting from her psychological problems. She initially went to her family doctor who prescribed Anafranil for her. Although her mood improved from severely depressed to moderately depressed, her obsessions and compulsions remained largely unchanged. As a result, she sought cognitive therapy.

Since early childhood, Frances engaged in a variety of OCD behaviors. The underlying OCD theme for her related to her core belief that she would suddenly lose a loved one or something precious to her, like her vision. Within this broad domain, Frances exhibited five patterns of obsessions and compulsions. The first was triggered by seeing or thinking about a useless object that a loved one owned or even touched on a single occasion. She then had the intrusive thought, "If I throw this away, I don't care about her." She interpreted this catastrophically. Specifically, she thought, "It means, I don't care if she lives or died, I'm evil, and God will damn me." As a result, she hoarded useless items that had no sentimental value.

Frances' second OCD pattern involved seeing something beautiful, which was a triggering situation for her. If she saw something beautiful, she often had the intrusive thought, "I didn't appreciate this as much as I should have." She interpreted this to mean that God might blind her for being unappreciative. In response, she covertly repeated the Lord's Prayer until she felt she had done so with sufficient sincerity.

Frances' third pattern was triggered by learning of a news story in which someone was tortured or brutally killed. In response, she had the image of this happening to her daughter. Frances interpreted the occurrence of that image as increasing the probability that it could happen. Her covert compulsion consisted of attempting to undo the image by vividly imagining her daughter being unhurt and happy. In addition, Frances attempted to vividly create the image that she—and not her daughter—was the victim of torture or a grisly murder.

Fourth, she repeatedly had the intrusive thought that she forgot to lock an outside door or secure the windows. She interpreted this to mean that an intruder would come in and hurt her family or burglarize them. Triggers for this were going to bed at night and leaving the house. In these circumstances, she checked the locks and windows numerous times.

Fifth, Frances had obsessions that she left on an appliance and had a vivid image of the house burning down. As a result, she unplugged all her appliances and repeatedly checked all her appliances, her stove, and her furnace every time she left her home.

Frances' fear of losing someone she loved appeared to result from the sudden death of her mother when Frances was 7 years old (see Figs. 7.9, 7.10, & 7.11).

OBSESSIVE-COMPULSIVE DISORDER CONCEPTUALIZATION WORKSHEET

Client's Name: Frances

OCD SCENARIOS

TRIGGERING STIMULI	INTRUSIVE COGNITIONS	PATHOLOGICAL INTERPRETATIONS OF INTRUSIONS	OVERT OR COVERT COMPULSIONS
Seeing an object that a loved one had contact with -- for example, her daughter's old, no longer used comb that is missing teeth -- and considering throwing it away.	If I throw this away, it means I don't care about her.	If I don't care about her, it means I don't care if she lives or dies, or I want her to die; this is an evil thought; I'm evil for having it. God may punish me for having such a thought by making her die and sending me to Hell. If she dies for some other reason, I will think she died because of my wanting her to die and feel overwhelmingly guilty the rest of my life. If I have these [intrusive] thoughts about my daughter, I will become so depressed and guilty that I'll be institutionalized for the rest of my life.	Saves item that loved one touched (even just once) or commented on.
Seeing something beautiful.	I didn't appreciate it the way I should have.	I will go blind if I take my eyes for granted by not praying.	Repeats the Lord's Prayer in her head until it feels sincere.

continued on next page

ADDITIONAL OCD SCENARIOS

TRIGGERING STIMULI	INTRUSIVE COGNITIONS	PATHOLOGICAL INTERPRETATIONS OF INTRUSIONS	OVERT OR COVERT COMPULSIONS
Leaving house; going to sleep.	Maybe I didn't lock the door or check appliances enough.	Something terrible will happen (e.g., fire, burglary), and my family will be hurt.	Checks locks, stove, etc. numerous times before leaving the house and at bed time.
Seeing or reading about a terrible killing or torture.	Imagines this happening to her daughter.	This could really happen to her. Seeing this in my mind could make it happen.	Attempts to vividly imagine her daughter is unhurt and happy; in addition, attempts to vividly imagine it happens to herself instead.

AVOIDED SITUATIONS OR INTERNAL STATES

1. Looking at beautiful things.
2. Watching TV news or movies with murder, molestation, torture, etc.

OTHER PROBLEMATIC SCENARIOS

TRIGGERING STIMULI	COGNITIONS	EMOTIONS	BEHAVIORS
None noted.			

FIG. 7.9. (*cont'd*) Case Conceptualization Worksheet (Case 7.C, Frances).

CASE CONCEPTUALIZATION SUMMARY FORM

Client's Name: Frances

Identifying Information: 37-year-old, married, female lawyer.

Presenting Problem: Obsessions and compulsions, high anxiety, OCD consumes her free time.
Precipitant(s): None noted.

Exhaustive List of Problems, Issues, and Therapy-Relevant Behaviors:

1. Obsessions and compulsions related to losing a loved one or something precious to her. 2. Demanding job. 3. Her child has serious behavior problems.	

Diagnoses (Axis I): OCD; Major Depressive Disorder, Recurrent, Mild

Personality Characteristics:

Relevant Beliefs:

1. **I will suddenly lose a loved one or something precious to me.** 2. Thinking bad thoughts can make them come true. 3. If something bad happens to someone I love, I'll believe it's because of my thinking. Therefore, I'll become so guilty that I'll go crazy and be institutionalized for the rest of my life.	4. I am evil and will be Damned. 5. God may punish me if I take Him for granted.

Origins of Key Core Beliefs: Her mother died when she was 4-years-old; for many years, Frances blamed herself for her mother's death because she had angry thoughts toward her when she became sick and was first admitted to the hospital.

continued on next page

WORKING MODEL

VICIOUS CYCLES / MAINTAINING FACTORS:
Pathologically misinterprets unpleasant intrusive cognitions, results in extreme anxiety. Compulsions decrease anxiety and therefore are reinforced. The compulsions and avoidance prevent disconfirmation of pathological interpretations. The anxiety reduction also prevents habituation to triggering stimuli and intrusive cognitions.

TREATMENT:

Goals:
1. Decrease frequency, intensity, and duration of obsessions and compulsions.
2. Improve mood.

Possible Obstacles to Treatment: Pervasiveness of obsessions and compulsions.

Plan:
1. Cognitive restructuring of the following beliefs: Moral Thought-Action Fusion, Expectations of Debilitating Distress, Need to Have Perfect Control, View of Self as Defective.
2. Exposure to all triggers (e.g., leaving home, seeing beautiful things) with response prevention (not checking appliances, not compulsively praying, not checking locks, discarding useless objects touched by loved ones); procedures for exposure with response prevention of covert compulsions.

FIG. 7.10. (*cont'd*) Case Conceptualization Summary Form (Case 7.C, Frances).

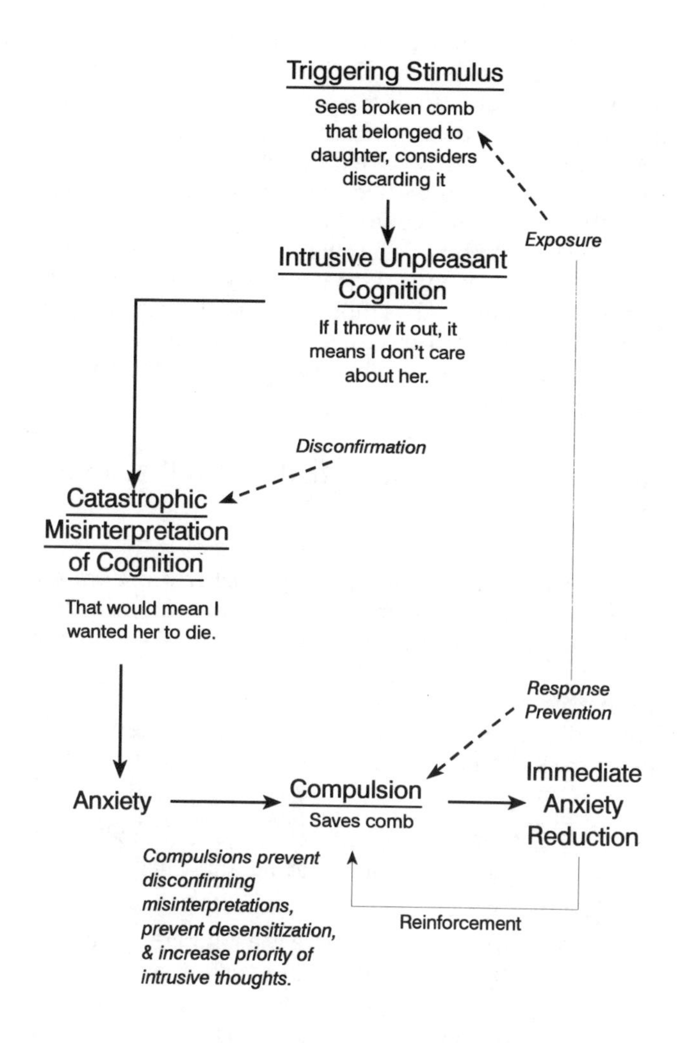

FIG. 7.11. Case Conceptualization Illustration (Case 7.C, Frances).

COGNITIVE THERAPY OF OCD

An extensive literature has demonstrated that exposure with response prevention is effective for individuals with OCD (e.g., Foa & Goldstein, 1978; Kasvikis & Marks, 1988; Marks, Hodgson, & Rachman, 1975; O'Sullivan, Noshirvani, Marks, Monteiro, & Lelliott, 1991). As the name suggests, exposure with response prevention consists of clients being exposed to

OCD-triggering stimuli and being prevented or preventing themselves from engaging in compulsions. Until recently, exposure with response prevention was considered to be the psychological treatment of choice for OCD. However, results of recent outcome studies have suggested that cognitive therapy is as effective as exposure with response prevention and shows trends for being more effective (Emmelkamp & Beens, 1991; van Oppen et al., 1995; see Abramowitz, 1997, for a quantitative review).

Cognitive therapy targets OCD clients' pathological interpretations of intrusive cognitions. An important component of cognitive therapy is carefully selecting behavioral or thought experiments that test pathological misinterpretations of intrusive cognitions. When an experiment is designed in this manner, it represents a highly-targeted form of exposure with response prevention.

Presentation of the Case Conceptualization Illustration to Clients

As the first step in cognitive restructuring, the therapist presents the OCD client with a Case Conceptualization Illustration. The illustration graphically depicts the client's idiosyncratic experiences with the cognitive model of OCD.

Here is an excerpt from a session in which Elise's therapist presented her with an individualized Case Conceptualization Illustration (see Fig. 7.5). As he discussed an element of the conceptualization or an intervention, he drew it for her.

Therapist: Elise, if it sounds all right to you, I'd like to illustrate for you a framework for understanding and treating your OCD.

Elise: Sounds good.

Therapist: Good. To begin with there is a triggering stimulus—this can be an object, a situation, or even a feeling. In your case, the triggering stimulus is an object that other people may have touched. What this triggers is an unpleasant, intrusive thought or image. For you the thought is, "I might be contaminated."

Intrusive, unpleasant thoughts are normal. Everyone has them. I once was visiting a different city and stayed in a dormitory in a room that was about 20 stories up. Much to my surprise, the window opened. For a moment, I had an image of leaping out of the window. I had no intention or desire to jump out of the window. I closed the window, jumped back, and laughed it off. The reason I was able to laugh it off was that I knew it's OK and normal to have thoughts like this. However, if I took the thought seriously, I might have set myself up for having problems. That's what happens to people with OCD. They take these thoughts very seriously. They catastrophically misinterpret intrusive thoughts.

When you have the intrusive thought, you think, "I'll get AIDS and give it to my grandkids." This interpretation causes you to be extremely anxious. Psychologists call these catastrophic misinterpretations of intrusive thoughts. To prevent the catastrophe and reduce anxiety, people with OCD attempt to do something. Sometimes they avoid the triggering situation. For example, you try not to touch objects in public, or you wear gloves. Other times, people with OCD do some behavioral compulsion, that is, a behavior designed to prevent a catastrophe. In your case, you wash your hands and use hand lotion. Or, people with OCD sometimes engage in "thinking compulsions." They try to think a thought or avoid thinking a thought to somehow prevent the catastrophe. So far, does this framework sound like what you experience?

Elise: Yes.

Therapist: Are there any parts that don't seem to fit?

Elise: No.

Therapist: Now, it was my understanding that you don't have "thinking compulsions." Is that right?

Elise: Yes, that's right.

Therapist: OK. Compulsions and avoidance are important in maintaining the whole problem in three ways. First, they immediately decrease anxiety. Because they decrease anxiety, they are reinforced or strengthened. They make you feel better, so you're more likely to do them in the future so that's how the compulsions are maintained. Second, compulsions prevent natural processes of getting over a fear from happening. Let me give you an analogy. Say a person is afraid of dogs and every time he sees a dog, he crosses the street. What happens to his fear of dogs over time?

Elise: It stays the same.

Therapist: Right. Why is that?

Elise: He never has good experiences with dogs.

Therapist: Yes. And, he doesn't even have neutral experiences, in which he doesn't get bitten or growled at. He never learns that his fear is unfounded and that there are a lot of friendly dogs. In OCD, avoidance and compulsions also prevent people from learning that their fear is unfounded. In your case, you never learn that you won't contract HIV from touching objects in public places.

Another important way that compulsions maintain OCD is that they prevent, what psychologists call, desensitization from occurring. Through repeated exposure, people can be conditioned to no longer respond to a triggering stimulus. The same process occurs throughout the animal kingdom, including primitive animals like fish. Therefore, desensitization can occur without higher reasoning. In OCD, avoidance and compulsions decrease anxiety artificially. Therefore, they prevent complete exposure to the triggering stimulus. This in turn prevents desensitization. Another thing that compulsions and avoidance do is that they make the intrusive thoughts more likely to forcefully come to mind. If I'm washing my hands to prevent my grandkids from getting AIDS, it makes the thought "I might be contaminated" seem more true. Does this drawing make sense and fit?

Elise: Yes.

Therapist: Good. Let's talk about what we need to do to overcome this then. Any ideas based on the drawing?

Elise: Well, the compulsions seem like they are important to the whole thing. But, I'm not ready to stop doing them.

Therapist: You're right; compulsions are very important. Eventually, when you're ready to, when you expose yourself to the triggering situations without washing, your anxiety will probably go up at first. But then, it will come down. This will allow your natural process of habituation to the situation to occur. More important, you'll see that what you're afraid of won't happen. Facing fear is essential to overcoming it. But, we can take it slowly. Plus, before we work on the compulsions, it will help a lot to discuss your interpretations of these intrusions. Does that seem like an acceptable place to start?

Besides the information discussed already, therapists should provide clients with relevant explanations or demonstrations. For example, OCD clients often benefit from seeing an extensive list of intrusive cognitions experienced in normal populations and the prevalence of such thoughts (e.g., Freeston et al., 1996). For clients who engage in thought suppression, the therapist should educate them on the negative effects of thought suppression on thought frequency and discomfort level. Often, it is helpful to demonstrate how thought suppression with a benign image—such as an image of a purple elephant—increases the frequency and intensity of the suppressed thoughts. Therapists can point out to clients that to not think about something, one has to think about it. As the reader can see later, thought suppression experiments also can help clients modify beliefs relating to Moral TAF and to the "need" to be in perfect control of their thoughts.

Finally, clients may benefit from thought sampling from which they learn that they experience an enormous stream of intrusive cognitions—some pleasant, some unpleasant, and others neutral. Thought sampling can consist of writing down every thought one has during a 1-hour time block, for example, while sitting in a crowded public place. (Being among people is likely to elicit a wide variety of cognitions.) This helps normalize the occurrence of intrusive unpleasant cognitions and decrease the shame clients often feel about the problem.

Engagement in Cognitive Therapy

For clients who initially have trouble accepting the cognitive model for OCD, the therapist's first task is to attempt to engage them in therapy. While engaging OCD clients, therapists express empathy for the pain that the clients are feeling given the frightening nature of the clients' cognitions. In addition, therapists show their understanding that given clients' beliefs and level of distress, it is perfectly reasonable that they act to prevent the catastrophe they expect. Next, the discussion focuses on helping clients realize that there is another possible reason for their distressing intrusive cognitions. That other possibility is simply that the clients are worried about and believe that they are at high risk for a catastrophic occurrence (Salkovskis, 1996).

The transcript that follows illustrates how a therapist might attempt to engage an OCD client who initially does not accept the cognitive model. The excerpt is from a therapy session illustrating the process of engaging Carlos (Case 7.B) who did not initially accept the case conceptualization, which his therapist presented to him.

Therapist: Let's summarize our differing positions now, if you don't mind.

Carlos: Fine.

Therapist: I think we understand each other's position, but let's be sure. You believe that you have a good chance of hitting someone while you're driving. As a result, you believe it is essential that you (1) anticipate any possible accident, (2) check exhaustively, and (3) worry about it.

Carlos: Yes. That's it in a nutshell.

Therapist: OK. Now, would you mind summarizing what I believe about your situation?

Carlos: That my problem is not that I'm at a high risk for causing a terrible accident, but my problem is that I'm consumed with worry about it.

Therapist: Exactly right! This might sound like a silly question, but if my position is right, would you want to know?

Carlos: Of course!

Therapist: Why?

Carlos: Because, it would mean that I'm a nervous wreck for nothing.

Therapist: All right. Then, examining the evidence for both of our positions more fully seems crucially significant for your life. Do you agree that it would be a good idea for us to look at this together?

Carlos: Yes.

Increasing Clients' Awareness of OCD Processes

Increasing clients' awareness of OCD processes helps them become more objective about their intrusive cognitions, pathological interpretations of intrusive cognitions, and their—sometimes subtle—avoidance or compulsive behaviors. They can begin to consider these processes as clinical phenomena to study as opposed to reality. In addition, clients can begin to recognize the themes that underlie multiple triggering stimuli and OCD responses. Finally, increasing awareness helps clients and therapists find cognitions that are useful targets for cognitive restructuring.

For clients to become more cognizant of OCD processes, therapists should teach them to objectively recognize and record each of these elements on the Case Conceptualization Worksheet for OCD. Therapists should encourage clients to use these extensively. In addition, therapists can teach clients to use the downward arrows technique to identify their interpretations of their intrusive cognitions.

Cognitive Restructuring With OCD Clients

Initially, therapists use guided discovery to help clients restructure their pathological cognitions with the explicit suggestion that clients would benefit from attempting to internalize the questioning process. Over the course of therapy, the client learns the process of cognitive restructuring.

The approach advocated in this book relies heavily on the work of two research groups, Freeston et al. (1996) and van Oppen and Arntz (1993). Both groups have empirically demonstrated effective cognitive therapy for OCD. The goal of cognitive restructuring is not to decrease the unpleasant intrusive cognitions. Rather, the goals are to dismiss intrusive cognitions as passing thoughts, decrease pathological interpretations of intrusive cognitions, and decrease efforts to engage in compulsions or avoidance. However, a probable and welcome outcome of accomplishing these therapy goals is a decrease in the frequency and intensity of intrusive cognitions.

The Dysfunctional Thought Record (DTR) and the Thought Evaluation Worksheet (TEW) described earlier can be extremely helpful in teaching clients to restructure their own cognitions. In addition, because the OCD themes are usually repetitive, clients benefit from reviewing their completed forms frequently. This can be especially helpful when clients are likely to encounter or intentionally expose themselves to OCD-triggering situations or when they are considering avoiding a trigger. The forms can help clients maintain their resolve to expose themselves to triggers and to prevent themselves from engaging in compulsive behaviors. It is often helpful for clients to carry these forms with them. Clients can use the forms to prime themselves with OCD-inconsistent interpretations that help them with exposure with response prevention. However, it is important to take care that clients do not begin to use cognitive restructuring techniques as a form of neutralizing that would maintain their problem. This issue is addressed later in the chapter.

Another general approach when working with OCD clients is to repeatedly ask them to *use accurate language* when referring to their symptoms. For example, OCD clients often state that they *have to* engage in their compulsions. Early in therapy, Frances frequently stated that she could not resist saying the Lord's Prayer when she saw something beautiful. Carlos often suggested that when he was driving, he "*had* to circle back to make sure I didn't hit someone." More accurate language for Carlos' experience was a statement to the effect "It *felt strongly* like I couldn't resist circling back because of my OCD. Actually, it was that I was *not willing to resist.*" For clients who insist that they could not resist a compulsion, guided discovery often helps them see otherwise. For instance, therapists could ask clients questions such as "Could you resist for $10 million?" or "If your child's life depended on _________ (resisting the compulsion), would you resist?"

Restructuring Overestimations of the Probability and Negativity of Events. To demonstrate the process of guided discovery to restructure overestimations of the probability of negative events, an extensive therapy transcript from Elise's therapy follows. Her therapist helped her realize that a series of exceedingly improbable events would have to occur before the catastrophe she feared could occur. Moreover, after combining these probabilities, the chance that the catastrophe would occur was astronomically small.

Therapist: What's the evidence that if you don't avoid touching things like door knobs and if you don't wash extensively, you will contract and spread AIDS to your grandkids?

Elise: The evidence is that I've been washing all these years and none of us have AIDS.

Therapist: How solid do you think this evidence is?

Elise: Very.

Therapist: I've got to be honest with you, Elise. I don't think it is very strong at all. Let me give you an analogy and see what you think of it. Suppose a 99-year-old man died, and his son was asked the secret of his father's longevity. His son said, "He lasted so long because he smoked, drank, gambled, cursed, chased women, and was nasty every day of his life." And, the son said this in seriousness. What would you think of his explanation?

Elise: Well, we don't know how long he would have lived if he had been a decent guy instead and had a cleaner life, and he probably would have lived just as long.

Therapist: Exactly! Do you see any parallels between this story and your explanation for why you and your grandkids haven't developed AIDS?

Elise: Rationally, I see what you're getting at. Since I've never tried it the other way, I don't know whether we would have gotten AIDS. OK, but I'm not willing to take risks with my grandkids.

Therapist: I don't blame you. I wouldn't take unnecessary risks with my loved ones either. But, if you don't mind, let's go back to the issue about the quality of the evidence. How good was the evidence you suggested about why you and your grandkids didn't get AIDS?

Elise: Not good. We don't know what would have happened the other way.

Therapist: What's an alternative possibility rather than you and your family will get AIDS from touching door knobs and the like?

Elise: ... That we won't. I guess.

Therapist: Can you think of evidence that supports this other possibility?

Elise: No. I started washing like this about 10 years ago when my first granddaughter was born and before then the epidemic wasn't nearly as bad.

Therapist: OK. Then, we'll have to look for evidence beyond your personal experience. Have you ever heard from a reliable medical source or a reliable news program, newspaper, or whatever that cases of AIDS develop as a result of touching objects in the way you are describing?

Elise: No. But, they can't account for every case of AIDS either. I've thought about this a lot. What if someone had a little cut on their finger and a drop of blood got on the knob and I had a little cut on my finger. Stranger things have happened. Can you guarantee me that it is impossible for someone to develop it that way?

Therapist: No, I can't ... but let's try to see if we can come up with some sense of how likely something like this would be. OK?

Elise: Yes.

Therapist: In the last 10 years, have you ever seen blood on a door knob?

Elise: I'm pretty sure I did once.

Therapist: OK, let's say you did once. During the last 10 years, how carefully have you inspected door knobs you've been in contact with?

Elise: Extremely so. I use a handkerchief every time I touch a door knob and inspect it for signs of blood or bodily fluids.

Therapist: So, if there were blood or bodily fluids on a door knob you would have seen it?

Elise: I think so.

Therapist: OK. The one time you saw it, how much blood was on the door and was it wet or dry?

Elise: Just a drop, and it was dried.

The therapist elicited a variety of other estimates from the client to calculate the probability that on a given occasion, she would become infected (see Table 7.1 for these probabilities). The session continued.

Therapist: Let's go over these estimates again. Do you see any that you think are off base? Or, do you think we forgot anything when making these calculations?

Elise: No. They all look like reasonable ballpark estimations.

Therapist: OK. Let's plug them into the calculator ... OK. The probability of there being an undried drop of HIV-positive blood on a door knob that your touch on a day when you have an open cut on the palmar surface of your hand and the drop of fluid touches the exact spot of your sore and you would become infected is 1 in 1.39 quintillion! Let me write this out long hand for you.

Then questioning proceeded to evaluate the probability that even if Elise were to become HIV positive that she would pass it on to her grandchildren through casual contact. The results were an astronomically small number. The final calculation was multiplying the two astronomically small numbers together resulting in an even much smaller number.

Elise: That actually makes me feel much less scared.

Therapist: That's great to hear! Plus, what do you think an expert on AIDS would say about getting AIDS in this way?

Elise:	That it couldn't happen.
Therapist:	Uh huh ... What are the advantages of worrying about this and acting on this worry?
Elise:	I guess given the tiny odds, there's none. But, I doubt I'll be able to just turn off the worry.
Therapist:	Probably not, but knowing that infection this way is essentially impossible and there are no advantages is a big step in the right direction! What are the disadvantages of worrying about this?
Elise:	It's hurting my health, my relationships with my family, I have no fun anymore, and it eats up my time. Even though I can think this way now, why does it still feel like I can get AIDS this way?

TABLE 7.1

Probability of Elise Becoming Infected From a Door Knob

The following numbers constitute the estimated probability that on a given occasion, the client would touch a door knob that had a drop of undried, HIV-infected blood when she had an open wound on the palmar surface of her hand, and her cut touched the exact spot where the undried blood was located, and she would become infected:

Number of blood spots on door knobs in 10 years or 3650 days:
1/3650

Probability that a drop of blood would be infected with HIV:
1/300 (i.e., guess about proportion of U.S. population that is HIV-positive)

Proportion of time that a drop of smeared blood would be wet and therefore potentially infectious during the time that the client might be in contact with the knob:
30 seconds before drying/54,000 seconds (i.e., 15 waking hours per day)

Number of days per year the client had an open cut on the palmar surface of her hands and fingers:
2/365

Probability that a drop of blood on a door knob would touch the exact spot of an open wound on his hand:
1/50

Probability that if an infected, wet drop of blood touched an open wound, the person would become infected:
1/10

1/3650 × 1/300 × 30/54,000 × 2/365 × 1/50 × 1/10

TOTAL PROBABILITY: 1 in 1,390,000,000,000,000

Therapist: You've been thinking this way for a long time. Therefore, it may take awhile and take effort on your part for this new rational belief to "sink in." This is a cognitive distortion that cognitive therapists call emotional reasoning, believing something because it *feels* true even though all the evidence points the other way. When you feel this way, it's important to remind yourself that it is this kind of distortion. Or, you can just tell yourself, "That's my OCD talking."

Restructuring Exaggerated or Distorted Perceptions of Responsibility. An approach that is helpful for many OCD clients who overestimate their responsibility for catastrophe is to construct a *pie chart of responsibility* (Ladouceur, Leger, & Rhéaume, 1995; Salkovskis, 1996; van Oppen & Arntz, 1993). To use this pie chart, the therapist asks the client to list all of the factors that may have played a role in the anticipated catastrophe, besides the client's own possible role. Next, the therapist instructs the client to (a) consider each factor separately, (b) estimate the percentage of responsibility that factor would have in the catastrophic outcome, and (c) draw a corresponding piece of pie that is proportional to its percentage of responsibility. After including all of the factors, clients should consider their own role. By the time they draw a pie piece corresponding to their own role, typically little pie is remaining. This process illustrates for clients that they probably would have little responsibility should the catastrophe occur.

Restructuring Likelihood TAF. Carlos (Case 7.B) exhibited Likelihood TAF. He believed that his thought—that he may have hit someone with his car—increased the likelihood of the event actually happening. In sessions, Carlos and his therapist conducted a series of thought experiments. For example, an experiment involved Carlos holding a hammer over his therapist's thumb as he thought repeatedly and emphatically, "I'm going to smash her thumb as hard as I can." Carlos expressed great reluctance to do this experiment but eventually agreed to do it. This experiment—and ones like it—helped Carlos begin to learn that an intrusive thought was different from an intention. Also, he learned that thinking a thought was different from acting on it.

Carlos and his therapist also generated thought experiments that Carlos performed as self-help assignments between sessions (following Freeston et al., 1996). Each experiment involved Carlos' thinking about an event that would happen within 24 hours. Each evening, he thought about the particular event for 15 minutes during which he tried as hard as he could to make it come true.

During the first week, Carlos bought a statewide lottery ticket and imagined winning with the ticket that he purchased. For the next assignment, the thought experiment involved imagining a negative event, although one that did not involve people being harmed. The event was that a vacant house in his neighborhood burned down on the next day when no one was nearby. During the following week, Carlos' thought experiment was to imagine that his new clock radio caught on fire on the following day when no one was home. Next, Carlos' task was to imagine that he caused a minor car accident with no injuries. After several more weekly thought experiments, Carlos was to imagine that he caused a major car accident on the following day. In the image, his entire family (who were his passengers) as well as a car full of people in the other vehicle died. Carlos successfully accomplished all but the last experiment on successive weeks. Although he avoided the final task for 2 weeks, once he accomplished it, his Likelihood TAF was largely resolved.

Restructuring Moral TAF. Moral TAF is the belief that having a thought about engaging in a personally unacceptable behavior is the moral equivalent of engaging in the overt behavior. Frances (Case 7.C) exhibited a variant of this belief: "If I throw this (object of my child's) away, it means I don't care about her (i.e., her daughter). If I don't care about her, then I must want her to die. This is an evil thought. I'm evil for having it."[24]

Frances' therapist encouraged her to survey other people whom she trusted and who were likely to be frank with her about what types of unpleasant thoughts pop into their minds. She learned that unpleasant intrusive cognitions—including ones in which loved ones get hurt—were common.

Frances' therapist also asked her to consider a definition of morality that emphasizes the difference between thought and action. The definition was borrowed from Freeston et al. (1996). Specifically, they defined morality as *"actively choosing to act or not act on a number of different possibilities according to values and principles" (p. 439).* In addition, Frances' therapist elaborated on the belief that morality has to do with intentions, plans, and actual behavior, and is unrelated to intrusive thoughts. Frances found

---

[24]Prior to addressing Frances' Moral TAF, the therapist used guided discovery to help Frances address the thought, "Throwing this away means I don't care about her." Frances was able to recognize that this type of thinking was "emotional reasoning" or "magical thinking." She also was able to generate evidence against the belief that throwing away objects with which her daughter had contact meant that she did not care about her. Specifically, she recognized that there was a great deal of evidence that she cared for her daughter, as illustrated by other thoughts that she had such as: "I try to make her happy," "I'm nice to her," "I feel loving feelings for her much of the time," "I'm proud of her," "There's no one more important to me than her," and "I would not hesitate to give my life for her."

When her therapist asked about evidence that she did not love her daughter, Frances indicated that sometimes she got very angry with her. However, with prompting, Frances was able to realize that almost universally parents of teenagers get very angry with them at times. Moreover, parents of children with behavior problems like her daughter's at times get frustrated or angry with their children. She was able to see an alternative and benign explanation for throwing away these objects—namely, to prevent the accumulation of too many possessions. In addition, she focused on the fact that most other people do not save all of the trivial objects that their significant others come in contact with and this does not mean that they do not love their significant others.

these definitions were particularly helpful, as do many OCD individuals who have vivid ego-dystonic images of harming their loved ones.

Frances also benefited from making unsuccessful efforts to control nonthreatening cognitions, such as trying to suppress the thought or image of a purple elephant. This helped her recognize that regardless of content, efforts to suppress thoughts usually fail or even increase intrusive cognitions. Her therapist suggested that it is generally even more difficult to suppress thoughts that involve issues relating to what is most important to us. Specifically, it is most difficult to suppress thoughts related to the health and well-being of ourselves or others.

Also, Frances found it helpful to learn that intrusive thoughts are analogous to naturalistic problem solving (Salkovskis, personal communication, November 16, 1998). In problem solving, the brainstorming phase involves generating as many solutions to a problem as possible, including outlandish ones. This process facilitates the creative process by preventing premature censoring. Intrusive cognitions can be thought of as generating possible solutions in brainstorming. Intrusive cognitions of all kinds, even violent thoughts, sometimes can provide people with potentially useful plans. Salkovskis (personal communication, November 16, 1998) gave an example of an extreme situation, namely that someone is on an airplane that is being highjacked. In that situation, the thought of hitting someone—the highjacker—over the head with a fire ax might be one of many options worth considering.

Finally, since many of Frances' obsessions and compulsions related to religious themes, her therapist discussed these with her at length. He was very careful to respect her beliefs while also asking her to reevaluate them. He asked if she would like to have her clergyperson involved in these sessions. She decided that that was not necessary. Here is an excerpt from a therapy session.

Therapist: As you know, I'm not a clergyman and therefore I'd like you to use your own discretion about what I'm saying. If you ever feel uncomfortable about this, please let me know. Furthermore, don't hesitate to disagree with anything I'm saying. OK?

Frances: OK.

Therapist: Most people who believe in God believe God is good. Do you believe that?

Frances: Yes.

Therapist: Do you think that God treats people fairly?

Frances: Yes.

Therapist: It wouldn't be fair to punish people for being born with two eyes. Right?

Frances: Right.

Therapist: Why?

Frances: Because they were born that way; it's human nature.

Therapist: We've discussed how intrusive thoughts are normal. You said that you believe that.

Frances: Yes.

Therapist: And that it's normal to have a whole range of intrusive thoughts—pleasant thoughts, neutral thoughts, and unpleasant thoughts. Research supports that people in general have each of these categories of thoughts. And, you found that your friends had this range, too.

Frances: Yes . . . I see where you're going with this. It wouldn't be fair to punish people for human nature.

Therapist: Who created humans to have intrusive thoughts?

Frances: God did. OK. So, since God is good, He wouldn't punish me for having intrusive thoughts. Yes, but maybe He has given people a test to overcome these bad thoughts.

Therapist: Perhaps, but what happened when you sincerely tried to overcome the thoughts of purple elephants?

Frances: I thought of them.

Therapist: That happens with nearly everyone who tries that experiment. Wouldn't it be a pretty unfair test if everyone who sincerely tried to be good ended up failing?

Frances: Yes, it would be unfair.

Therapist: Back to your friends. Do you consider them to be good, bad, or middle-of-the-road people?

Frances: I think they're all really good people. That was an important consideration when I chose them as friends.

Therapist: I know it's impossible to know, and if you'd rather not speculate I understand. But, what's your guess about whether they will go to heaven or hell?

Frances: It's impossible to know, but they're really good people, and I can't imagine them going anywhere but heaven.

Therapist: Even though they sometimes had "bad thoughts"?

Frances: Yes. Their hearts are good.

Therapist: Do you see the double standard here?

Frances: What you're saying makes sense. I'll think about it some more.

Therapist: Good.

Over the next couple weeks, Frances' fear of damnation began to diminish. She reportedly began focusing more on scriptures relating to forgiveness and acceptance than on damnation.

Restructuring Beliefs About Foreseeability. Carlos (Case 7.B) experienced cognitive distortions related to the connection between foreseeability and responsibility. His beliefs included "I should be able to anticipate and prevent any car accident" and "I have to be sure where every car and pedestrian is." In cognitive restructuring these beliefs, the therapist first had Carlos consider the advantages and disadvantages of this perspective. The disadvantages were numerous and strong. The beliefs contributed to his experiencing high anxiety, hypervigilance to potential danger and possible catastrophes, and diminished pleasure in life because he felt compelled to be preoccupied with danger. The only advantages were that the beliefs could possibly prevent a catastrophe, and "it is the right thing to do."

The therapist frequently asked Carlos to consider "How would a particular respected but *reasonably* cautious friend (Marty) think about this situation?" This helped Carlos realize that—although a reasonable driving strategy is to attempt to anticipate and prevent obvious mishaps—it is pathological to exhaustively search for anything that might go wrong. For example, it makes sense for car owners to follow their owner's manual every 3 to 6 months to see if their brakes are responding properly and have a mechanic inspect them once per year or so. However, it is highly excessive to test one's brakes every day. Also, the therapist and Carlos discussed the concept of "acceptable risks." Carlos recognized that Marty was not hypervigilant but functioned well in the world. From this observation, Carlos concluded that Marty either implicitly or explicitly accepted normal risks associated with living in the world.

Also, OCD individuals often benefit from a discussion of other people's responsibility for their own behavior. For example, although it makes sense for motorists to take some precautions when passing bicyclists, bicyclists are responsible for their own behavior. They are responsible for following the rules of the road, not darting in front of cars, only riding when visibility is good, and keeping their bikes in good repair. Similarly, pedestrians are responsible for staying out of the road except when crossing and only crossing when it is safe to do so. Finally, Carlos' therapist guided him in making a pie chart of responsibility. This helped him see that he would have very little responsibility if a cyclist unexpectedly darted in front of his car.

Restructuring Views of Self as Seriously Defective. OCD clients' negative core beliefs about themselves often change as a result of restructuring other OCD-related distortions. For example, Frances stopped believing she was evil after cognitive restructuring her Moral TAF beliefs. However, if cognitive restructuring of OCD-related beliefs does not modify clients' negative core beliefs about themselves, more direct approaches to changing dysfunctional beliefs are necessary.

Restructuring Expectations of Debilitating Distress. Frances (Case 7.C) held the belief that because of her intrusive cognitions, if one of her family members died, she would experience overwhelming anxiety and guilt that would ruin her life. What follows is a sample of Frances' expectations about how the death of a loved one would affect her, which she described toward the beginning of treatment.

> If someone I love dies, I will think he or she died because that's what I wanted. Therefore, I'll feel overwhelmingly guilty and depressed and won't be able to function. Therefore, I'll be institutionalized for the rest of my life, and die alone.

The therapist guided Frances through a retrospective analysis of when she had felt most guilty and most anxious in the past. Frances reported that she felt most guilty when her grandmother who raised her died. (This was due to Moral TAF.) In fact, she could not imagine feeling more guilty. For approximately 15 months after her grandmother's death, she felt extreme guilt, anxiety, and depression. During those 15 months, Frances' performance reviews at work dropped from Excellent to Average or Above Average. However, she retained her job, and her subsequent performance reviews were again excellent. (She needed some cognitive restructuring to help her accept a less than perfect work performance during times of great emotional pain, such as those 15 months.) But, most important, she remained "sane" and her husband stayed with her throughout that time and was supportive. She realized that her husband was devoted to her and appreciated the support she had provided for him during past difficulties he experienced.

Frances and her therapist performed panic inductions through hyperventilation (described in chap. 5), which were particularly helpful in restructuring her catastrophic cognitions. Panic inductions showed her that high anxiety was reversible and did not lead to a catastrophe. In addition, inductions facilitated her learning useful coping strategies, like paced breathing and refocusing attention to manage her symptoms.

Restructuring the "Need" to Be in Perfect Control. To help OCD clients restructure the demand they often place on themselves to be in perfect control, it is often helpful to conduct thought suppression experiments. These experiments help clients realize that attempting to have perfect control of their thoughts paradoxically decreases their control. They begin to realize that humans simply are not "built" to have perfect control of their thoughts. As a result, clients can begin to give up unreasonable expectations for control. In addition, individuals with OCD often do not expect other people to have perfect control of their thoughts and behavior. Once clients see their double standard, they can begin to have more reasonable expectations regarding their ability to control their thoughts. Finally, clients can consider the advantages and disadvantages of demanding that they are in perfect control.

Final Considerations in Cognitive Restructuring with OCD Clients. When teaching OCD clients how to cognitively restructure their pathological beliefs, there is the danger that they will begin using these techniques as a form of compulsion. Specifically, OCD clients can begin to use the techniques to excess, stereotypically, or as ways to neutralize or suppress intrusive cognitions. Therapists should be vigilant for clients misusing the cognitive restructuring process in these ways. For example, OCD clients who believe they must do Dysfunctional Thought Records or Thought Evaluation Worksheets, or risk debilitating distress, should resist the urge to use these tools. As mentioned earlier, these clients may also benefit from panic inductions that show them that despite extreme anxiety, they retain their sanity. Once they realize that they are not at risk for decompensation, they may resume using Dysfunctional Thought Records and Thought Evaluation Worksheets. Therapists should educate clients that it is possible to misuse cognitive restructuring so that they can be cognizant of this possibility.

Similarly, OCD clients often *seek reassurance* from their therapists to lessen their responsibility in case of a catastrophe. Their reasoning for this often takes the following form: "If my therapist knows about this and tells me not to worry and that nothing bad will happen, if something bad does happen, she will be partially responsible." As any therapist who has reassured an OCD client knows, reassurance does not work. OCD clients are only temporarily reassured. More important, providing reassurance interferes with improvement. Reassurance prevents clients from having opportunities to disconfirm their catastrophic expectations and to desensitize to triggering stimuli. It is therefore important to educate clients about how reassurance seeking fits into their case conceptualization. In addition, the therapist and the client should come to an understanding about reassurance. The therapist will not provide reassurance, and the client will attempt to resist seeking reassurance from the therapist or anyone else.

Cognitively Guided Exposure With Response Prevention for Overt Compulsions

Exposure with response prevention appears to disconfirm automatically some distorted interpretations of intrusive cognitions. However, the cognitive model suggests that clients benefit from attempting to carefully target exposure with response prevention to disconfirm crucial pathological interpretations (see Freeston et al., 1996; Salkovskis, 1996; van Oppen & Arntz, 1993). Of course, the ability to target crucial pathological interpretations depends on careful assessment and case conceptualization.

Van Oppen and Arntz (1993) described the treatment of a man who was obsessed about making a mistake when depositing his paycheck. He feared writing the wrong account number, resulting in the bank putting the money into another patron's account. He also feared that he would be unable to get his money back, lose his home, and would therefore lead a life of poverty. The authors suggested that exposure consisted of the client's performing mini-experiments. These were designed to test the client's beliefs about the consequences of writing down the wrong account number on a deposit slip. One experiment was to attempt to deposit a small sum of money using the wrong account number. This enabled the client to see whether the bank would put the money in another person's account and, if it did, whether the client could get his money back. A second experiment was to attempt to deposit a large sum of money into his account using his wife's account number instead of his own. This enabled him to see whether the bank would detect the "error" and give him an opportunity to correct it. In addition, the client could have anonymously telephoned a bank executive, explained he had OCD, discussed his concerns, and asked how the bank would handle such a situation.

Procedures for Cognitively Guided Exposure With Response Prevention. During sessions, clients and therapists carefully plan experiments to test key pathological beliefs. As described in the sections on cognitive restructuring, many behavior and thought experiments can be effectively conducted in sessions. In addition, sometimes clients benefit from getting some practice with exposure in the therapist's presence. Consider for example a client who checked newspapers because he was afraid that an important paper may have gotten stuck between the newspaper pages. Initially, when he began working on this problem, it helped him to bring a stack of newspapers to sessions. With his therapist's encouragement, the client gave her newspapers without checking them.

However, clients often can and should carry out much of the work on their own in naturalistic settings. There are several potential benefits of having OCD clients highly involved in designing exposure experiments and performing them in naturalistic settings. These include increasing clients' sense of responsibility for their treatment, teaching clients to be their own therapists, increasing generalization of therapy gains to naturalistic settings, and maximizing cost-effectiveness.

Outcome studies that examined the effects of including family members in exposure therapy have been equivocal (e.g., Emmelkamp, van Linden van den Heuvell, Ruphan, & Sanderman, 1989). Therefore, deciding whether to include one or more family members should be based on (a) the clients' preferences, (b) the family members' willingness to participate, and (c) clinical judgment about whether a particular family member is more likely to be helpful or detrimental in the therapy process. For example, if family members are highly critical, their involvement is likely to be detrimental. On the other hand, family members who are interested in helping, are patient, and are not overbearing can often be of great assistance to the OCD client.

Another important treatment decision is whether clients should be exposed to low or high level anxiety-provoking stimuli first. Outcome studies (e.g., Hodgson, Rachman, & Marks, 1972) have found that graded exposure works as well as flooding (i.e., exposure to a highly anxiety-provoking stimulus first). The advantage of the gradual approach is that it is often more easily tolerated by the client. However, because there are no differences in efficacy, clients and therapists can decide jointly where to start.

Other important decisions concern the duration of exposure with response prevention sessions or homework assignments and the number of sessions. Exposure with response prevention should last until the client has experienced a substantial diminution of anxiety within the session (Steketee & Foa, 1985). If a client exposes himself or herself to a stimulus for a short time and stops exposure when the anxiety is high, the client may further sensitize him- or herself to the stimulus. Typically, exposure with response prevention lasts between 45 minutes and 2 hours. The number of exposure sessions depends on the individual client's response. However, most successful outcome studies used between 15 and 20 sessions over 4 to 16 weeks (e.g., Steketee & Shapiro, 1993). Finally, as compared to exposure in imagination, exposure *in vivo* tends to be somewhat more effective in treating OCD clients. However, the addition of imaginal flooding to *in vivo* exposure often improves treatment outcome, especially when clients' obsessions concern highly unlikely feared catastrophes (Foa, Steketee, & Milby, 1980).

Facilitating Exposure With Response Prevention in Resistant Clients Who Have Distorted Perceptions of Responsibility. Some OCD clients resist exposure and response prevention because of excessive perceptions of responsibility. For these clients, therapists can use temporary measures to reduce their clients' discomfort and urges to check. For example, therapists can *temporarily* share clients' responsibility by accompanying them or allowing family members to accompany them during exposure sessions. Therapists can also temporarily provide them with reassurance.[25] For example, therapists might state, "This is really very safe. I leave my house every morning without unplugging appliances or checking the stove. But when you leave without checking and unplugging, if anything should happen, I'll be responsible." After clients become engaged in the process and their fears begin to lessen, efforts to reduce their perceptions of responsibility should be gradually faded out. Ultimately, clients should engage in exposure with response prevention unaccompanied by others, plan the exposure with response prevention alone without telling anyone, and not receive any reassurance.

Specific Examples of Exposure With Overt Response Prevention. The examples that follow illustrate procedures that were used with the OCD clients introduced earlier in the chapter. Procedures were selected

[25]Lopatka and Rachman (1995) demonstrated that making statements that reduced OCD subjects' perceptions of responsibility to naturalistic triggering stimuli in the subjects' own homes reduced their discomfort and urges to engage in compulsions.

based on individualized case conceptualizations. There may be some parts of the treatment package that are similar for most OCD clients. However, therapists must tailor other aspects of the treatment to individual clients based on the unique characteristics highlighted in their case conceptualizations. In addition, the conceptualizations help the therapist select which interventions are potentially the most useful.

Elise (Case 7.A) began graded exposure to "contaminated" objects by going to public places that had low levels of people traffic. For example, she went to a small specialized library in a nearby college during spring vacation. She began by touching objects that only a few people would touch, such as walls. In addition, initially, she was permitted to test the surface for undried bodily fluids with white gloves. Her Subjective Units of Distress Scale (SUDS) ratings decreased with repeated and prolonged exposure. As her ratings dropped, she exposed herself to stimuli that were more anxiety provoking until she reached the top of her distress hierarchy. The top of her distress hierarchy consisted of doing the following. She intentionally made paper cuts on each finger of her hand. Then, she went to a heavily trafficked place, such a football stadium during a big game. Without testing the surfaces for undried bodily fluids, she went into a bathroom stall and rubbed her hands all over the stall, toilet handle, and the toilet seat. Response prevention consisted of not washing for 2 hours after exposure.

Carlos (Case 7.B) began prolonged exposure to driving situations that caused him the least degree of distress. Specifically, he began driving during periods of light traffic when visibility was good. He drove on roads that were recently resurfaced. In addition, he initially drove on streets that did not have crosswalks or blind intersections. As his SUDS scores dropped, he progressed to slightly more anxiety-provoking driving situations, and so on, until he mastered driving in situations that initially caused him the greatest distress, namely on roads with bumpy, patchy pavement, during rush hour, on streets with crosswalks and closely spaced intersections. Response prevention consisted of not looking in the rearview mirror except when backing up and not circling back to see if he hit something.

With respect to Frances' (Case 7.C) compulsive checking before leaving her home, an exposure hierarchy was constructed (see Fig. 7.12). From least to most anxiety-provoking, the levels of stimuli on her hierarchy included:

low-voltage appliances, such as her clock radio,

intermediate-voltage appliances with no heating coils,

high voltage appliances with no heating coils, such as a window unit air conditioner,

appliances with heating coils, such as her toaster and coffee maker, and

stove, furnace, and hot water heater.

Exposure with response prevention began by Frances' departing from her home without checking or unplugging the appliances that were least distress-eliciting. When she mastered the lower-level items and habituated to them, she moved up the hierarchy to appliances that initially caused her greater levels of distress.

In addition, after Frances had progressed several steps up the hierarchy, additional exposure tasks consisted of departing from the house after intentionally leaving on low-risk appliances (see Fig. 7.12). After about 3 weeks of daily exposure, she felt markedly less anxious about leaving the house without checking low-risk appliances. Frances believed that the probability of fire was lower, and she found it much easier to resist checking.

Exposure With Response Prevention of Covert Compulsions

Covert compulsions consist of intentionally calling forth thoughts or images to prevent catastrophe or decrease distress. Until Salkovskis and Westbrook (1989) developed a highly effective modification to exposure with response prevention, covert compulsions appeared to be particularly resistant to treatment.

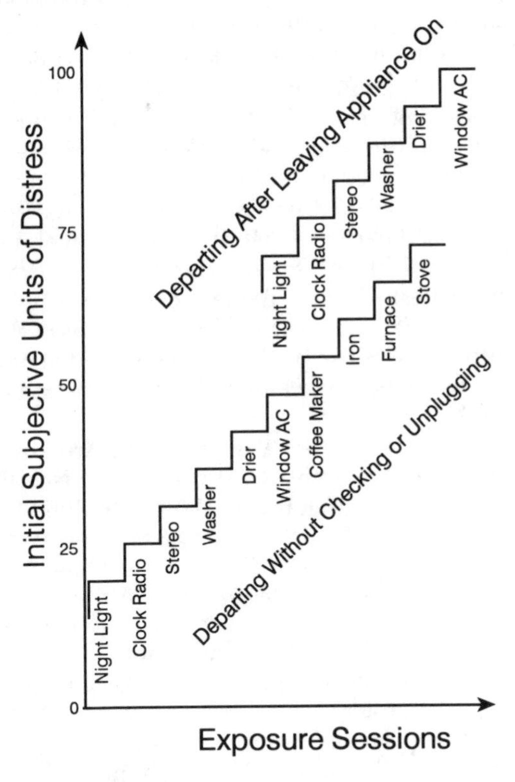

FIG. 7.12. Exposure hierarchy for Frances.

Salkovskis and Westbrook designed their procedure based on their observations of the factors that make covert compulsions extremely resistant to treatment. Namely, individuals can perform covert compulsions extremely quickly, with little effort, and "unhindered by physical and social constraints usually present with overt compulsive behaviors" (p. 152). Therefore, the researchers designed an exposure procedure that minimizes the time available for OCD clients to engage in covert rituals. In addition, their procedure hastens clients' habituation to triggering stimuli by exposing them to stimuli that are maximally predictable. Habituation appears to occur more rapidly to a constant stimulus than to one that has highly variable properties (see Watts, 1979).

Specifically, Salkovskis and Westbrook's approach consists of exposing clients to one of their obsessions recorded in the client's own voice on a continuous tape loop (i.e., the outgoing message tape for answering machines). The continuous tape loop continuously repeats a recorded message at a fixed interval. Most commercially available tape loops repeat at 20-second, 30-second, 1-minute, or 2-minute intervals. Therefore, clients are repeatedly exposed to the same exact stimulus in rapid succession. This procedure gives them little time between presentations to engage in covert compulsions. Exposure to the obsession itself is another way that this procedure makes the presented stimulus more predictable. (The researchers suggested that exposure to a triggering stimulus is more likely to elicit variable cognitions.) For Frances (Case 7.C), the recorded stimuli included her various intrusive cognitions, such as "I will go blind" and "My daughter will be killed."

When clients are having difficulty resisting covert compulsions, tape loops can be altered to help interrupt the compulsions. For example, the shortest possible tape loop, such as one lasting only 20 seconds, can be used. Such a short tape loop often leaves insufficient time between presentations of the stimulus to engage in the covert compulsion. Another variation to the exposure procedure is simultaneously exposing a client to two different obsessions each associated with a different covert compulsion, one in each ear (using stereo recording).

Before exposure sessions, therapists educate clients about the difference between intrusive thoughts and covert compulsions, namely that intrusive cognitions are unintentional and distress-provoking, whereas compulsions are intentional and distress-decreasing. Clients are instructed that during exposure sessions, they should resist engaging in covert compulsions. If they have difficulty resisting, and alterations in the tape do not help, the therapist can teach them to use distraction or thought stopping (see Kirk, 1983). To be effective, distraction should consist of a clearly defined task such as counting backwards or engaging in a card-sorting task (e.g., Salkovskis, Westbrook, Davis, Jeavons, & Glenhill, 1997). Clients should only use distraction and thought stopping when other approaches to preventing covert compulsions fail. They should also use them as sparingly as possible. This is because these procedures may in some circumstances interfere with habituation to triggering stimuli (Grayson et al., 1982). Nonetheless, their use is clearly preferable to failing to prevent compulsions. As clients make progress resisting their compulsions, distraction and thought stopping should be faded out.

Facilitating Generalization in the Treatment of Covert Compulsions. Once clients have been treated successfully with exposure with response prevention—that is, when exposure to triggering stimuli results in little anxiety and clients can resist compulsions—they are ready for a variety of procedures that will help them generalize their practice to more naturalistic conditions. First, tape loops of other obsessions should be used. Frances, for example, was exposed to and mastered each variation on the theme involving her loved ones' being hurt or killed. Subsequently, she was exposed to her pathological interpretations of the intrusive cognitions, such as "I don't care about my daughter," "I will go to hell," and "I will be institutionalized for the rest of my life and lose everything that is important to me."

Second, to help clients generalize treatment gains to naturalistic conditions, stimuli should be presented less predictably than in the initial exposure sessions. One way to do this is for the therapist to stop the tape loop after each presentation of the obsession. The duration of the pause should vary in order for them to be unpredictable to the client. Also, to make the stimuli less predictable, a regular audiotape can be used in which the client vocalizes a series of different obsessions. Thus, in contrast to the tape loop procedure in which the client is repeatedly exposed to the same stimulus, during the generalization procedure, clients can be exposed to several different obsessions. The tape can be rewound as many times as necessary to desensitize the client to the various obsessions.

A third important method for helping clients generalize treatment gains is to expose them to external triggering stimuli as opposed to obsessions. Because external triggering stimuli are more distal to the compulsions than are the obsessions, external triggering stimuli can result in great variability in intrusive thoughts.

For Frances, external triggers included reading and seeing tragic or catastrophic news stories or movies. Exposure to these triggers was included in her generalization training. In self-exposure sessions, she constructed tape loops by reading the most upsetting sentence or two of news stories into a tape recorder. Then, she listened to the tape loop until her SUDS rating dropped to near 0. After mastering a taped stimulus in session, she took it home and practiced twice per day until her SUDS rating was near 0. Subsequently, she made stimulus tapes of other gruesome news stories and habituated to these. After mastering these, she exposed herself to tape loops in which she substituted the name of a loved one for the victim of the crime or accident. After completing this series of flooding exercises, she watched 1 hour of local news per day. As a result of this approach, violent news stories caused her only mild levels of distress.

A fourth way that therapists can facilitate generalization is for them to have their clients practice in naturalistic environments where there are triggering stimuli for the client. For example, Salkovskis (personal communication, November 16, 1998) described the use of this procedure with a client who had an intrusive thought that if she went to the butcher shop, she would grab the butcher's knife and kill him. Salkovskis (after being certain that these thoughts were ego-dystonic!) had the client go to the butcher shop while listening with headphones to a tape loop of herself saying, "I'm going to kill the butcher." (The client and butcher survived the ordeal!)

A final important way that therapists can help clients generalize practice to naturalistic conditions is through mood inductions. For most OCD clients a depressed or anxious mood increases the frequency, intensity, or duration of their obsessions or compulsions. Therefore, clients benefit from being exposed to triggering stimuli after they or their therapists induce a relevant mood. Mood inductions can be achieved by using imagery of sad or anxiety-provoking events or situations.

SUMMARY

According to the cognitive model of OCD, a crucial factor that differentiates people with OCD from the general population is their misinterpretation of intrusive cognitions. People who do not have OCD typically are able to dismiss unpleasant intrusive cognitions simply as annoyances. In contrast, individuals with OCD pathologically interpret intrusive cognitions as being highly important, personally significant, catastrophic, and their responsibility. As a result they feel distress, which they attempt to decrease by some corrective action or mental act—that is, by engaging in a compulsion.

Therapists base individual case conceptualizations on an integration of the cognitive model and individual clients' experiences of OCD, which therapists obtain through careful assessment. When assessing OCD clients, a careful functional analysis is performed of the various internal and external triggering stimuli, with corresponding intrusive unpleasant cognitions, pathological interpretations of these intrusive cognitions, and overt and covert compulsions. Sources for this information can come from OCD questionnaires, the downward arrows technique, Case Conceptualization Worksheets, and interviewing.

Treatment consists of cognitive restructuring of clients' misinterpretations of intrusive cognitions as well as exposure to triggering stimuli with response prevention, that is, preventing their compulsions. The goal of cognitive restructuring is to decrease OCD-causing pathological interpretations of intrusive cognitions and dismiss intrusive cognitions as simply passing thoughts. For each type of pathological interpretation of intrusive cognitions described, a variety of effective approaches for cognitive restructuring was presented. A few examples are mentioned here.

One client (Elise) feared contracting AIDS from touching objects in public places and transmitting the virus to her grandchildren. Her therapist used guided discovery that helped her see that a series of extremely improbable events would have to occur before the catastrophe could ever occur. Moreover, after combining these probabilities, the chance that the catastrophe would occur was astronomically small.

With respect to excessive or unreasonable perceptions of responsibility, clients often benefit from constructing a pie chart of responsibility. In addition, the text described an OCD client (Carlos) who experienced Likelihood Thought-Action Fusion (TAF). He benefitted from thought experiments that demonstrated to him that having a thought about a negative event did not make the event occur. Frances, who experienced Moral TAF was (a) guided through thought suppression experiments that demonstrated that attempts to suppress thoughts are counterproductive, (b) encouraged to survey respected others about their intrusive cognitions that helped her see that people whom she considered moral had negative intrusive thoughts, and (c) encouraged to examine her religious views that contributed to her Moral TAF.

This same client feared that her intrusive cognitions would result in debilitating depression and guilt that would ruin her life forever. As part of cognitive restructuring, her therapist guided her through a retrospective analysis of past times when she had felt most guilty and depressed. The client learned that she could get through highly difficult times without losing the things that were most important to her. For other clients whose pathological beliefs relate to experiencing debilitating anxiety, a panic induction through hyperventilation can be particularly helpful in restructuring their catastrophic cognitions.

Next, the chapter guided the reader in the effective use of exposure with response prevention. This treatment procedure typically consists of clients being systematically exposed to triggering stimuli, usually in a graded manner, and then being prevented from engaging in their compulsions. Cognitive theorists presume that the mechanisms by which exposure with response prevention reduce obsessive-compulsive symptoms are both disconfirmation of pathological interpretations of intrusive cognitions and habituation to anxiety-provoking stimuli. According to the cognitive model, the most efficient way to use exposure with response prevention is to carefully target crucial pathological interpretations in order to expedite disconfirmation of these beliefs.

Finally, treatment of clients with covert compulsions was addressed. An effective procedure for these clients was presented that involves modification of exposure with response prevention. Using a continuous tape loop, clients are exposed to the obsessions associated with covert compulsions. The tape loop continuously repeats the obsession with little time between presentations. This minimizes the time available for clients to engage in covert rituals. In addition, the procedure hastens clients' habituation to the obsession because it is presented in a maximally predictable way. Procedures for helping clients generalize their treatment gains were described.

8

Chronic or Recurrent Major Depressive Disorder

1. Cognitive Model of Depression
   a. Chronic or Recurrent Depression
   b. Cognitive Correlates and Possible Cognitive Vulnerabilities to Depression
      i. Perfectionism
      ii. Hopelessness
      iii. Sociotropy and Autonomy
2. Assessment and Conceptualization of Depression
   a. Interview
      i. Suicidality
      ii. Negative Life Events That Precipitate Depression
         (1) Grief
      iii. Behavioral Observations
   b. Case Conceptualization Worksheet for Depression
   c. Questionnaires
      i. Beck Depression Inventory–II
      ii. Hopelessness Scale
      iii. Dysfunctional Attitude Scale
      iv. Attributional Styles Questionnaire
      v. Beck Self-Concept Test
      vi. Sociotropy-Autonomy Scale
      vii. Multidimensional Perfectionism Scale
      viii. Assertion Inventory
   d. Activity Calendar
3. Examples of Case Conceptualizations
   a. Case 8.A (Abby): Inactive, on Disability, Sociotropic Orientation, Episode Triggered by Loss of Marriage
   b. Case 8.B (Benjamin): Perfectionistic, Self-Critical, Hypervigilant to Interpersonal Threat
   c. Case 8.C (Catherine): Extreme Standards for Achievement Contributing to Exhaustion Resulting in Shift to Depressed Mode

d. Case 8.D (Mary): Guilt, Self-Hatred, and Alcohol Dependence, Precipitated by Son's Accidental Death That Resulted From Her Mistake
4. Cognitive Therapy of Depression
   a. Presentation of a Case Conceptualization Illustration to a Depressed Client
   b. Case 8.A (Abby): Inactive, on Disability, Sociotropic Orientation, Episode Triggered by Loss of Marriage
      i. Activity Scheduling
         (1) Increasing Pleasure
         (2) Increasing a Sense of Mastery
      ii. Core Belief Work
   c. Case 8.B (Benjamin): Perfectionistic, Self-Critical, Hypervigilant to Interpersonal Threat
      i. Addressing Possible Obstacles to Treatment
      ii. Treating Insomnia
      iii. Core Belief Modification
         (1) Restructuring "I'm Afraid That If I Relax My Guard in One Area, I Will Make Huge Errors All the Time"
         (2) Restructuring "If a Job's Worth Doing, It's Worth Giving It My All"
         (3) Restructuring "If I Don't Do a Job Well, I'm Lazy and No Good"
         (4) Restructuring "If I Find That I Can Relax My Standards, It Means I've Wasted Years of My Life Being Worried, Not Having Fun, and Alienating Other People, and It Means I'm Stupid"
      iv. Expressing Emotion Exercises
      v. Behavioral Experiments
   d. Case 8.C (Catherine): Extreme Standards for Achievement Contribute to Exhaustion, Resulting in Shifts to Depression
      i. Cost-Benefit Analysis
      ii. Thought Evaluation Worksheet
      iii. Activity Scheduling to Achieve Balance
   e. Case 8.D (Mary): Guilt, Self-Hatred, and Alcohol Dependence, Precipitated by Son's Accidental Death That Resulted From Her Mistake
      i. Finding Life Meaning
      ii. Grief Work
5. Summary

Major depressive disorder represents a mental health epidemic. The lifetime prevalence of major depressive disorder is between 8.7% and 21.3% for women and between 3.6% and 12.7% for men (Kaelber, Moul, & Farmer,

1995). According to the *DSM–IV* (APA, 1994), up to 15% of people with severe major depressive disorder die of suicide. Depression in individuals over 55-years-old is associated with a fourfold increase in mortality of all kinds as compared to similar aged, nondepressed individuals. Major depressive disorder also is associated with increased rates of absenteeism, failed marriages, increased medical utilization, and disability (Kaelber et al., 1995). In 1990, the total estimated cost of depression was $43.7 billion per year: $12.1 billion from lost productivity, $11.7 billion from days of lost work, $8.3 billion from hospitalizations, $7.5 billion from lost lifetime earnings from suicide, $2.9 billion from outpatient care, and $1.2 billion from medication (Greenberg, Stiglin, Finklestein, & Berndt, 1993).

Depression appears to be a progressive disorder. With each episode of depression, the risk of having a subsequent episode is greatly increased. For example, approximately 50% to 60% of individuals who have one episode of major depression go on to have a second (APA, 1994, pp. 341–342). Individuals who have two episodes have a 70% chance of having a third, and those who have three episodes have a 90% chance of having a fourth. In addition, life stressors are more likely to trigger the first and second episodes of depression than later episodes.

Risk factors for major depression include (a) female gender; (b) prior depression; (c) being divorced, separated, or widowed; (d) being abused; (e) adverse major life events (e.g., job loss); (f) psychiatric disorders (e.g., anxiety disorders, substance misuse disorders, psychosis); (g) poor general health; and (h) low socioeconomic status (SES, see Kaelber et al., 1995). Factors that are likely to maintain depression include social skills deficits (see Lewinsohn & Gotlib, 1995) as well as deficits in the ability to maintain rewarding intimate relationships (Klerman et al., 1984). Moreover, several cognitive factors appear to render individuals vulnerable to depression or maintain depression in affected individuals (discussed later).

According to the *DSM–IV* (APA, 1994), a major depressive episode is characterized by at least 2 weeks in which the individual experiences a depressed mood and/or diminished interest or pleasure in almost all activities most of the day nearly every day. Besides having a depressed mood and/or diminished interest, the individual must have at least 5 out of a list of 9 other depressive symptoms during the episode. The other symptoms are (a) significant changes in weight or appetite; (b) frequent insomnia or hypersomnia; (c) psychomotor agitation or retardation; (d) fatigue or loss of energy; (e) feelings of worthlessness or excessive or inappropriate guilt; (f) diminished ability to think, concentrate, or make decisions; and (g) recurrent thoughts of death or suicide. The symptoms must cause clinically significant distress or impairment in functioning. In addition, the individual must never have experienced a manic episode, a mixed (depressed and manic) episode, or a hypomanic episode. The symptoms are not due to the direct physiological effects of a substance or a general medical condition and are not better accounted for by normal bereavement. Finally, a major depressive disorder consists of the presence of a major depressive episode that is not better accounted for by a psychotic disorder. (When psychotic symptoms are present only during a depressed episode, the episode is coded as a major depressive episode with psychotic features).

COGNITIVE MODEL OF DEPRESSION

Figure 8.1 illustrates the cognitive model of depression with Sammy, a college student who had recurrent major depression. A *triggering stimulus* activates an *orienting schema,* which functions as a gatekeeper to the depression mode. When the orienting schema is activated, it fully activates the already partially active (i.e., primed) depression mode. It fully activates all the systems of the mode (i.e., cognitive, affective, physiological, motivational, and behavioral).

For Sammy, a triggering stimulus was being at a party and standing by himself. In response to the triggering situation, Sammy became aware of negative automatic thoughts (cognitive system), an intensification of feelings of sadness (affective system), feeling "deflated" (motivational system), and an urge to leave the situation (motivational and behavioral systems). In this situation, the triggering stimulus was external to him. Alternatively, triggering stimuli may be internal to the individual. Internal triggering stimuli can take one of several forms, including (a) having a spontaneous depressogenic thought or image, (b) having physical sensations such as pain, or (c) having other emotions such as anger or anxiety. Any of these can trigger depressive cognitions.

In depression, the cognitive content frequently is self-defeating and distorted. For example, while standing by himself at a party, Sammy experienced the following *automatic thoughts*: "I'm going to have a terrible time here," "I probably won't talk to a single person," "I'm ugly and have nothing to say," and "People will see I am depressed." In this situation, Sammy engaged in the following types of categories of distortions: "mind-reading," "fortune telling," "all-or-none thinking," and "over-generalizing" (see Burns, 1989).

Beck, Rush, et al. (1979) suggested that the *core beliefs* activated during depression fall into three broad domains, which they referred to as the *cognitive triad.* The depressive cognitive triad consists of a negative view of the self, the world, and the future. Depressed individuals typically view *themselves* as defective, inadequate, incapable, diseased, deprived, undesirable, and worthless. Regarding their view of the *world,* people suffering from depression believe that the world—especially their social world—makes excessive and overwhelming demands on them, treats them harshly, or presents insurmountable obstacles to life goals. Finally, when depressed individuals consider their *future,* it is often through the "negative filter" of hopelessness. They expect unending hardship, frustration, and deprivation. Sammy's core beliefs were, "I'm a loser" (self-related belief), "People

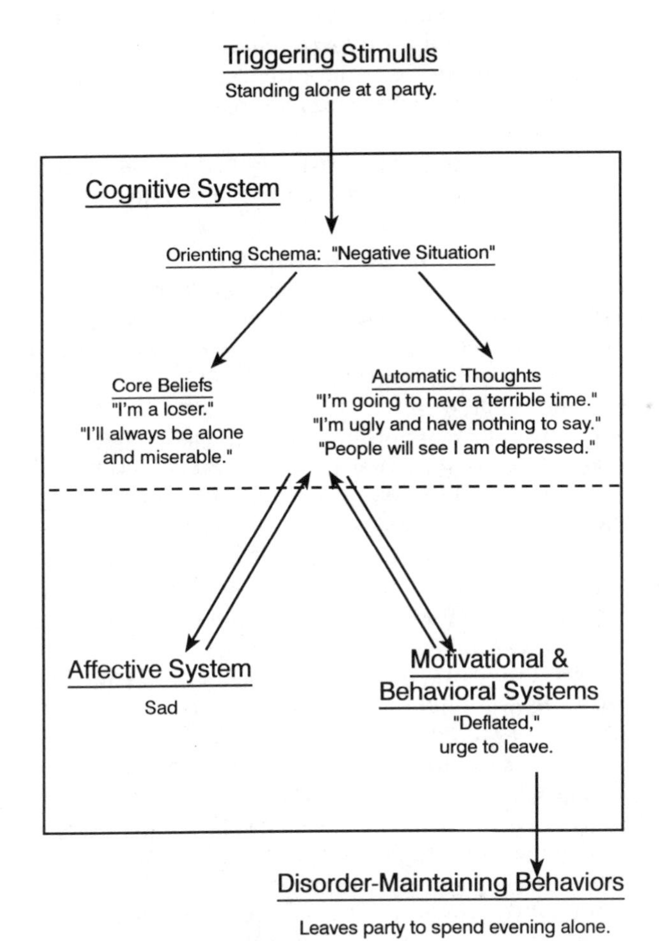

FIG. 8.1. Cognitive model of depression.

are too superficial to give a depressed guy a chance" (world-related belief), and "I'll be alone and miserable for my entire life" (future-related belief).

Weishaar (1996) elaborated on the cognitive processes that are operative when a depressive mode is hypervalent. For depressed individuals,

> thinking becomes more rigid and biased, judgments become absolute, and the individual's core beliefs about the self, one's personal world, and the future become fixed. Errors in logic, called cognitive distortions, negatively skew perceptions and inferences, and lead to faulty conclusions. (p. 226)

Much evidence supports the presence of self-defeating cognitive content and processes in depression (for a review, see Sacco & Beck, 1995).

Besides activated cognitive and affective systems, the depressive mode involves the *motivational and behavioral systems.* Regarding the motivational system, when individuals are depressed, they typically experience little energy, have urges to sleep, urges to avoid people, and feel inhibited to engage in activity. Thus, their difficulty with motivation frequently results in *disorder-maintaining behaviors.*

Disorder-maintaining behaviors seem to fall into three categories: (a) failing to engage in potentially reinforcing activities, (b) socially alienating behaviors, and (c) covert disorder-maintaining behaviors. First, depressed individuals engage in low rates of activities that potentially are pleasurable or can elicit feelings of self-efficacy. That is, they fail to engage in potentially reinforcing activities. In contrast, they engage in high rates of activities that are aversive (e.g., Lewinsohn, Sullivan, & Grosscup, 1980; Libet & Lewinsohn, 1973). Depressed individuals often become extremely inactive. Extreme inactivity prevents depressed people from disconfirming depressogenic cognitions, such as "I can't do anything right" or "Nothing is fun anymore." In addition, being inactive often provides opportunities for depressed individuals to engage in rumination, which tends to maintain depression (e.g., Nolen-Hoeksema & Morrow, 1991, 1993; Nolen-Hoeksema et al., 1993; Nolen-Hoekseman et al., 1994). When individuals are alone and inactive, they have excessive amounts of time to dwell on their problems, criticize themselves and others, and generate pessimistic expectations for the future.

The second type of disorder-maintaining behavior involves acting in socially alienating ways. Some common examples include complaining, expressing pessimism, exhibiting hostility, looking depressed, not exhibiting interest in others, clinging to others, and so on. These behaviors lead to adverse changes in their social environment (e.g., hostility or rejection) that maintain their depression. (The bidirectional nature of these interactions is known as reciprocal determinism.)

In addition to the overt types of disorder-maintaining behaviors, depressed individuals also often engage in covert disorder-maintaining behaviors. For example, depressed individuals might *intentionally* think negatively. This can be the result of beliefs such as "If I expect the worst, I won't be as disappointed when it occurs." This type of thinking strengthens depressive beliefs.

As illustrated in Fig. 8.1, because of Sammy's internal experience, he left the party soon after he arrived and went back to his dorm room. For the rest of the evening, he watched TV and focused on his problems. These behaviors prevented Sammy from disconfirming his negative automatic thoughts. They also prevented him from attaining positive reinforcement that could have generated a sense of mastery or pleasure thereby interrupting his depressed mood.

Chronic or Recurrent Depression

In chronic depression, individuals generally have easily or chronically activated depressive cognitive schemas. The direction of causation—whether the activated schemas contribute to depression or the depression contributes to keeping these schemas activated—is unclear. However, the relationship is likely to be bidirectional. Why do some individuals have chronically activated depressive schemas? Perhaps, individuals with this problem had early, severe, repetitive, or uncontrollable negative events. They may also have a biological vulnerability to rigid schemas.

The problems experienced by individuals with chronic depression share important characteristics with the problems experienced by personality-disordered individuals. Individuals with chronic depression often exhibit pathological patterns of cognition, affect, and behavior that are pervasive across life domains, inflexible, and persistent. As the reader can see in the cases presented in this chapter, many clients with chronic or recurrent major depressive disorder also have comorbid personality disorders.

In recurrent depression, an individual is likely to have a depressogenic cognitive schema (vulnerability) triggered by a life event that is congruent with the schema. For example, individuals who highly value relationships may be vulnerable to depression after the loss of a significant relationship.[26]

Cognitive Correlates and Possible Cognitive Vulnerabilities to Depression

Perfectionism, hopelessness, sociotropy, and autonomy have been studied extensively with respect to their association with current and future depression and dysphoria. This section briefly summarizes the findings of these studies.

Perfectionism

Both cross-sectional and prospective studies consistently have found that dimensions of perfectionism were related to depression (Blatt, Quinlan, Pilkonis, & Shea, 1995; Hewitt & Flett, 1990, 1991a, 1991b, 1993; Hewitt, Flett, & Ediger, 1996; Hewitt, Mittelstaedt, & Flett, 1990; Saddler & Sacks, 1993). For example, as compared to nondepressed controls, depressed patients were significantly higher in self-oriented and socially-prescribed perfectionism[27] (Hewitt & Flett, 1991a). Self-oriented

[26]Although many individuals with recurrent depressive episodes are likely to be vulnerable to becoming depressed, some are likely to have recurrent episodes as a result of recurrent extreme negative life events that would contribute to symptomatology in all but the most resilient people.

[27]In a factor analysis, Hewitt and Flett (1991b) found the following perfectionism factors: *self-oriented perfection*, which they defined as a need for one's own perfection; *other-oriented perfectionism*, the need for others to be perfect; and *socially prescribed perfectionism*, the belief that others expect perfection from oneself.

perfectionism interacted with achievement stress to influence subsequent depression scores (Hewitt & Flett, 1993; Hewitt et al., 1996), and socially prescribed perfection interacted with interpersonal stress to affect subsequent depression (Hewitt & Flett, 1993). Finally, in a large outcome study that compared the effects of various types of treatments for depression (i.e., cognitive-behavioral, interpersonal, imipramine, and placebo), perfectionism scores on the Dysfunctional Attitude Scale predicted outcome of each type of treatment (Blatt et al., 1995).

Hopelessness

Studies have found that hopelessness is significantly correlated with concurrent depression (e.g., Abramson, Garber, Edwards, & Seligman, 1978; Beck, Riskind, Brown, & Steer, 1988) and predicts subsequent depression (McCranie, & Riley, 1992; Rholes, Riskind, & Neville, 1985). In addition, changes in hopelessness early in cognitive therapy predict changes in depression at the end of therapy (Hollon et al., 1992).[28]

Sociotropy and Autonomy

Sociotropic individuals highly value close interpersonal relationships, being loved and accepted, and having positive social interactions. In contrast, people with an *autonomous* personality orientation highly value independence, achievement, mobility, freedom of choice, and solitude (Clark & Beck, 1991; Clark, Ross, Beck, & Steer, 1995; Clark & Steer, 1996; Clark, Steer, Haslam, Beck, & Brown, 1997). Sociotropy and autonomy are independent factors. Thus, individuals can exhibit strong tendencies for one of these characteristics and low tendencies for the other, strong tendencies for both characteristics, or weak tendencies for both.

In general, studies have found, in both depressed and college samples, that sociotropy was related to depression. They also found that sociotropy interacted with interpersonal stress to influence subsequent depression (e.g., Alford & Gerrity, 1995; Allen, de L Horne, & Trinder, 1996; Clark, Beck, & Brown, 1992; Moore & Blackburn, 1994). However, these same studies failed to find a relationship between autonomy and depression. Some theorists have suggested that the failure to find relationships between autonomy and depression reflect psychometric limitations of the

[28]Abramson and colleagues (e.g., Abramson, Alloy, & Metalsky, 1995; Abramson, Metalsky, & Alloy, 1989) theorized that what they refer to as hopelessness depression (HD) represents an important subtype of depression. According to the theory, HD is the result of an interaction between particular types of causal attributions and stressors. Specifically, people who are prone to hopelessness depression attribute negative events, which they consider to be important, to global and stable causes. In addition, they may infer negative characteristics about themselves in response to the negative event. The theory also predicts that individuals who experience HD have different symptoms than clients with other types of depression (for a review of HD, see Abramson, Alloy & Metalsky, 1995). The model for depression presented in this chapter does not include HD because, to date, the verdict is still out about the usefulness of this categorization.

Sociotropy-Autonomy Scale. Others have suggested that the autonomy construct itself is problematic (for a review see Clark & Steer, 1996). Some prospective studies with remitted depressive patients have found autonomy to interact with autonomous events to affect subsequent depression (e.g., Hammen, Ellicott, Gitlin, & Jamison, 1989). In addition, a subfactor of autonomy, Solitude, was found to interact with autonomous events to influence subsequent depression (Clark & Oates, 1995).

ASSESSMENT AND CONCEPTUALIZATION OF DEPRESSION

Besides the general information obtained during assessment, once therapists make a diagnosis of major depressive disorder, they should probe further for specific information about their clients' depression. When assessing depressed clients, therapists should perform a careful functional analysis. This should include the various triggering stimuli, automatic thoughts, underlying beliefs, emotions, and behaviors. Sources of information about depressed clients can come from the interview, the Case Conceptualization Worksheet (which guides therapists' questions), and depression questionnaires.

Interview

Some comments about interviewing depressed clients are warranted. Specifically, therapists should assess for suicidality and negative events that may have precipitated the depressive episode. In addition, therapists should carefully observe clients' behavior.

Suicidality

Therapists should carefully assess depressed clients for suicidality. A useful tool in assessing suicide risk is the Scale for Suicidal Ideation (SSI; Beck, Kovacs, & Weissman, 1979). The SSI is a structured interview consisting of 19 items on a 3-point scale.[29] The SSI assesses a broad range of factors that have been found to be predictive of suicide attempts. For example, it assesses the strength of respondents' wishes to live or die, the reasons for wanting to commit suicide, attitudes toward suicide, plans, intentions, availability of suicide methods, sense of control over suicidal thoughts and impulses, frequency of suicidal thoughts, whether the respondent had ever attempted suicide in the past, and so on.[30]

[29]The researchers subsequently developed a questionnaire version.

[30]Once therapists determine the level of risk, they must triage the client to the most appropriate level of care (i.e., outpatient, intensive outpatient, partial hospitalization, inpatient), contract for safety, and provide emergency plans. For a review of effective approaches for managing suicidality, see Beck, Rush, et al., 1979; Freeman & White, 1989; Freeman & Reinecke, 1993; Rush & Beck, 1988).

Negative Life Events That Precipitate Depression

During the interview process, therapists should assess the significant negative life events that may have occurred in the months preceding the onset or the exacerbation of depressive symptoms. Chapter 4 described procedures for assessing negative life events that precipitate psychological problems. These procedures are not reiterated here. However, the discussion of grief as a negative life event that can precipitate psychological problems is discussed here. This is because depression is often precipitated by significant losses.

Grief.[31] Therapists should ask clients about major recent losses. Although many clients spontaneously describe important losses, others fail to do so.

To help the reader know what to look for when assessing for grief, this section begins by describing abnormal grief reactions. Klerman et al. (1984) suggested that therapists should assess seven areas associated with abnormal grief. These are (a) multiple losses, (b) inadequate grief in the bereavement period (that is, being unaware of sorrow and longing), (c) avoidance behavior related to the death (such as, avoidance of the funeral or the grave site), (d) appearance of symptoms around significant dates related to the life and loss of the deceased, (e) fear of the illness or injury that caused the death, (f) preservation of the environment as it was when the loved one died, and (g) absence of family or other social supports during the bereavement period. In addition, a client may have an intense grief reaction to a recent loss of an individual who was insignificant in the client's life. In such cases, it is important for the therapist to search for unresolved grief over an earlier significant loss.

Bowlby (1980) suggested there are two main variants of abnormal grieving: (a) chronic mourning characterized by intense grieving that persists beyond a year of the loss, and (b) prolonged absence of conscious grieving. In the latter variant, the bereaved are often

> tense and often short-tempered. No references to the loss are volunteered, reminders are avoided and well-wishers allowed neither to sympathize nor to refer to the event. Physical symptoms may supervene: headaches, palpitations, aches and pains. Insomnia is common, dreams unpleasant. (p. 153)

To decrease the probability of overlooking the latter variant of abnormal grieving, therapists should review all of the people who played significant roles in the client's life. Which of these people are no longer in the client's life? Did the client ever feel sorrow over and miss the lost person(s)? Does the client have unresolved feelings toward the lost person(s), such as guilt, anger, shame, and anxiety?

---

[31]Refer to Bowlby (1980) for an excellent treatment of the characteristics of normal and abnormal variants of grief and to Klerman et al. (1984) for effective methods for treating bereaved, depressed clients.

Bowlby (1980) observed two other pathological variants of mourning—"mislocation" of the dead person and euphoria. Mislocation refers to the sense that the deceased resides in a location that is inappropriate—such as in an animal, in another person, or in an inanimate object. In contrast, in normal grief, the bereaved often locates the deceased in an appropriate place such as the grave or in his or her favorite chair. In euphoric responses, the bereaved either fails to accept that the loss occurred or acknowledges that the death occurred and further claims that the death is greatly advantageous to the bereaved.

Therapists should assess a variety of issues related to the loss. Specifically, the therapist should ask about: (a) the nature of the client's relationship with the deceased; (b) the circumstances of the death, such as how did it happen, who was there, and when and where did it occur; (c) the meaning of the loss to the client, including the consequences for the client's life; (d) possible connections between the loss and the client's presenting problems; and (e) the client's thoughts and feelings about the loss.

Regarding feelings about the lost person; therapists should be alert to several specific reactions. Therapists can consider the following questions.

Is the client angry with the deceased for not being more careful or for abandoning him or her?

Is the client angry with himself or herself or others for not preventing the death?

Is the client afraid that the same fate will come to him or her or a loved one?

Does the client feel guilty about the circumstances of the death or how he or she treated the deceased while still alive?

Does the client feel ashamed (e.g., if the deceased died of suicide)?

Behavioral Observations

Depressed clients' behavior during sessions often provides useful information. For example, therapists' observations of clients' behavior can help identify symptoms that facilitate diagnosis (such as psychomotor retardation or slow speech). In addition, clients' behaviors during interviews can provide therapists with clues about social skills deficits, which, by alienating others, may contribute to the maintenance of their depression. (These are types of disorder-maintaining behaviors.) Common social-skills deficits that depressed individuals exhibit include making negative statements about the self, the world, or the future; flat affect; expression of hostility; insensitivity to social cues; failure to exhibit interest in other people; and lack of smiling.

Besides observing clients' spontaneous behavior in sessions, it can be helpful to observe them during role plays of problematic social situations. Role plays can center on any number of interpersonal interactions including interactions involving the clients' partners/spouses, supervisors, friends, and strangers. During role plays, therapists should elucidate the cognitions and emotions that clients are experiencing. In addition, it is often useful for therapists to ask clients whether the problems they are having in social interactions predated the depression. This helps determine whether the skills deficits are (mood) state dependent or state independent.

Case Conceptualization Worksheet for Depression

Once therapists diagnose clients with depression, they should conduct fine-grained assessments of the clients' problems. The therapist can often begin this during the intake interview. The Case Conceptualization Worksheet for Depression can guide the therapist's assessment of a depressed client's problematic responses (for a blank copy of the Case Conceptualization Worksheet for Depression, see the Appendix). Specifically, the Case Conceptualization Worksheet prompts therapists for triggering stimuli, cognitions, emotions, and responses (both adaptive and disorder-maintaining). (In addition, clients can use the Case Conceptualization Worksheet as a format for self-monitoring. Examples of worksheets completed by therapists are provided later in the chapter.)

Questionnaires

This section briefly describes several psychometrically sound questionnaires helpful in assessing depression. The questionnaires can provide information regarding how clients compare with normative samples, can be used to track clients' progress over the course of therapy, and can help identify cognitions, affects, and behaviors to target in therapy. Therapists can choose from the following questionnaires.

Beck Depression Inventory–II

The Beck Depression Inventory–II (BDI–II; Beck, Steer, Ball, & Ranieri, 1996) is a 21-item scale that asks the respondent about depressive symptoms, which occurred during the last 2 weeks. For example, the scale inquires about vegetative symptoms of depression, as well as guilt, hopelessness, failure, and suicidal ideation. Each item ranges from 0 to 3. Besides providing an overall score that helps determine a client's level of depression, the BDI–II also helps therapists identify particular symptoms that they can target in therapy. Questions #2 (the hopelessness item) and #9 (the suicide item) are particularly helpful at assessing suicide risk.

Hopelessness Scale

The Hopelessness Scale (HS; Beck, Lester, & Trexler, 1974) is a 20-item, true–false self-report instrument that assesses hopelessness and pessimism. It appears to be a highly sensitive indicator of suicide risk (see Beck, Brown, Berchick, Stewart, & Steer, 1990).

Dysfunctional Attitude Scale

The Dysfunctional Attitude Scale (DAS; Weissman & Beck, 1978) was designed to measure depressogenic core beliefs. Clients rate how much they agree with each of 100 statements on a scale from 1 *totally disagree* to 7 *totally agree.*

Attributional Styles Questionnaire

In the Attributional Styles Questionnaire (ASQ; Seligman, Abramson, Semmel, & von Baeyer, 1979), clients are presented with 12 hypothetical situations (6 positive and 6 negative). They are asked to determine what they consider is the cause of the hypothetical events. They rate each event on its level of internality (internally vs. externally caused), stability over time (temporary vs. enduring), and globality (specific vs. pervasive regarding life areas).

Beck Self-Concept Test

The Beck Self-Concept Test (BST; Beck, Steer, Epstein, & Brown, 1990) has clients rate themselves on 25 personal characteristics. A total score reflects clients' overall self-concept. Responses to the individual characteristics provide useful clinical information relating to core beliefs about the self.

Sociotropy-Autonomy Scale

The Sociotropy-Autonomy Scale (SAS; Beck, Epstein, Harrison, & Emery, 1983) is a 60-item questionnaire that provides sociotropy and autonomy scores. Respondents rate how much of the time they believe each statement on a 5-point scale ranging from 0 (0%) to 4 (100%).

Multidimensional Perfectionism Scale

The Multidimensional Perfectionism Scale (MPS; Hewitt & Flett, 1991b) consists of 45 items that measure clients' self-oriented, other-oriented, and socially prescribed perfectionistic beliefs.

Assertion Inventory

Assertion Inventory (AI; Gambrill & Richey, 1975) is a 40-item instrument that measures discomfort with assertion, response probability of engaging in assertive behavior, and identification of situations where assertion is problematic.

Activity Calendar

The assessment of depressed clients is often aided by having clients record all of their activities on a calendar for a week. For example, therapists might ask clients to record activities between the intake evaluation and the first therapy session. Completed activity calendars can help determine the amount of potentially rewarding versus punishing activities in which the clients engage. In addition, completing an activity calendar early in therapy establishes a baseline activity level for the sake of future comparison.

Abby (Case 8.A) completed an activity calendar between the intake evaluation and the first therapy session. This assessment exercise helped her therapist realize the extent of Abby's inactivity. Abby spent most of her time napping or watching TV. Another case in which using an activity calendar was helpful in conceptualizing the client's problems was Catherine (Case 8.C) She was a young professor who oscillated between highly productive times when she felt very positive about herself and times when she felt exhausted and depressed. Catherine presented during a nondepressed time with the hope of preventing future depressive episodes. It became clear from her daily monitoring of activities that she was forcing herself to work nearly every waking moment. She took no breaks for relaxing, exercising, or socializing, and she worked late and slept little.

EXAMPLES OF CASE CONCEPTUALIZATIONS

This section includes complete case conceptualizations of four individuals with chronic or recurrent major depressive disorder. For each client, a brief synopsis is given, followed by a Case Conceptualization Worksheet (completed by the therapist early in treatment), a Case Conceptualization Summary Form, and a Case Conceptualization Illustration that represents a depressive scenario for the client.

Case 8.A (Abby): Inactive, on Disability, Sociotropic Orientation, Episode Triggered by Loss of Marriage

Abby was a 25-year-old, divorced woman who lived alone and was on disability for major depressive disorder during the 3 years prior to seeking cognitive therapy. She had been in therapy prior to presenting for cognitive therapy. However, when her former therapist was leaving to take a maternity leave, she transferred Abby to a cognitive therapist. At the time she began cognitive therapy, her depression had remained severe. Prior to her disability, Abby was a custodial worker and worked with a supervisor with whom she had much conflict.

The event that appeared to precipitate Abby's depressive episode was that her husband asked her for a divorce. Her first and only other episode of depression occurred when she was 20 and her boyfriend left her for another woman.

Abby's symptoms of depression included depressed mood, anhedonia, low energy, sleep disturbance (including frequent awakenings, early morning awakenings, and sleeping on and off throughout the day), psychomotor retardation, self-criticism, and difficulty concentrating. In addition, Abby had suicidal ideation with vague thoughts of "taking pills," although she did not intend to hurt herself because she was afraid to die.

Abby spent her days sleeping and watching TV. These behaviors seemed to maintain her depression in two ways. First, they provided her with little opportunity for improving her self-esteem or gaining satisfaction. This was especially the case in the life area that was central to how she felt about herself and her life—relationships with men. Second, watching TV and sleeping all day provided her with much time for ruminating about her situation.

Abby's depressive cognitions were mostly internally triggered. She had unlimited time to think about her situation and spent much of the time ruminating about herself and her future. With respect to external triggers, some TV shows and commercials elicited her sadness and loneliness. For example, seeing a happy couple or seeing an attractive young woman on TV elicited sad and lonely feelings.

Abby's core beliefs that were hypervalent during the depressive episode included "I'll always be alone," "I'm overweight and not cute," "Life has no meaning if I don't have a husband," "I failed as a wife," and "I am a failure as a woman." (These beliefs were often fully in her awareness. The core beliefs also contributed to automatic thoughts including "I hate my life," "I can't enjoy anything unless I have a man in my life," "If I never have a man again, I may as well be dead," "There's no point in doing anything," "I don't like anything anymore," and "I can't even do the simplest things.")

Although the loss of her marriage was the most proximal factor that contributed to Abby's depressive episode, her highly sociotropic orientation appeared to make her extremely vulnerable to social loss. She appeared to develop her sociotropic orientation as a result of receiving little reinforcement for achievement and independence. Her parents were not interested in her performance. She was average in terms of academics, athletics, and other performance domains. On the other hand, she was well-liked by her peers and derived much satisfaction from close peer relationships. Over time, she invested most of her energy in peer relationships and later dating. In addition, her mother modeled passive and subservient behavior in her marriage to her father. Abby was the third of three children, and her older sister overprotected her "baby" sister (see Figs. 8.2, 8.3 & 8.4).

CASE CONCEPTUALIZATION WORKSHEET FOR DEPRESSION

Client's Name: Abby

TRIGGERING STIMULI	COGNITIONS (CORE BELIEFS CAPITALIZED)	EMOTIONS	BEHAVIOR (Disorder-Maintaining or Adaptive)
Free time (nearly all of her time).	I hate my life; IF I NEVER HAVE A MAN AGAIN, I MAY AS WELL BE DEAD. I'LL ALWAYS BE ALONE; I'm overweight and not cute; LIFE HAS NO MEANING IF I DON'T HAVE A HUSBAND; I failed as a wife; and I AM A FAILURE AS A WOMAN. There's no point in doing anything; doing things won't change my life, and I don't like anything anymore.	Sad and lonely	Sleeps and watches T.V. most of the time.
Sees a happy couple on a TV show.	That will never be me; I'LL ALWAYS BE ALONE.	Sad and lonely	

FIG. 8.2. Case Conceptualization Worksheet (Case 8.A, Abby).

CASE CONCEPTUALIZATION SUMMARY FORM

Client's Name: Abby

Identifying Information: 25-year-old, divorced woman, lives alone, was a custodial worker until disabled by major depressive disorder three years prior to seeking cognitive therapy.

Presenting Problem: Depression
Precipitant(s): Husband asked for a divorce.

Exhaustive List of Problems, Issues, and Therapy-Relevant Behaviors:

1. Depressed mood, hopelessness, anhedonia, inactivity, insomnia. 2. Passive suicidal ideation (no plans or intentions). 3. Isolation. 4. Disability.	

Diagnoses (Axis I): Major Depressive Disorder, Recurrent, Severe, Without Psychotic Features.
Personality Characteristics: Dependency.

Relevant Beliefs:

1. If I never have a man again, life has no meaning, and I may as well be dead. 2. I'll always be alone. 3. I'm overweight and unattractive. 4. A wife should never get angry at her husband.	5. I failed as a wife and therefore am a failure as a woman. 6. There's no point in doing anything. 7. I can't even do the simplest things.

Origins of Key Core Beliefs: Parents had little interest in her achievement; she was a mediocre student and did not excel in any extracurricular activities. She derived most of her satisfaction from friendships first and then boyfriends. Her mother was a homemaker and exhibited extreme dependency on her husband. Abby was the third of three children and had an older sister who was extremely protective of her. These childhood circumstances appear to have contributed to her sociotropic orientation that interacted with her loss of significant relationship (i.e., husband divorced her) contributing to her depression.

continued on next page

WORKING MODEL

VICIOUS CYCLES / MAINTAINING FACTORS:

Her belief that "a wife should never get angry at her husband," contributes to her blaming herself for her failed marriage. (She attempted to understand why the marriage failed but was unwilling to blame her husband.) Self-blame contributes to her depression and interferes with her seeking new relationships.

Staying in bed, watching TV, and social isolation provide little opportunity for her to improve her self-esteem or experience satisfaction. This is especially the case in the area of life that is most important to her—relationships. In addition, her inactivity provides her with unlimited opportunities for ruminating on her problems.

TREATMENT:

Goals:

1. Improve mood, hope, energy, etc. as measured by a decrease in Beck Depression Inventory scores to nondepressed range.
2. Resume normal life activities, especially returning to work and reconnecting with other people.

Possible Obstacles to Treatment: Feelings of hopelessness, lack of energy and motivation; disability status--improvement would require that she return to working with a supervisor with whom she had conflict.

Plan:

1. Scheduling activities that are potentially enjoyable or can provide a sense of mastery; subdividing activities into small manageable steps; mastery and pleasure ratings.
2. Cognitive restructuring of depressogenic automatic thoughts as well as relevant beliefs.
3. Problem solve regarding work situation.

FIG. 8.3. (*cont'd*) Case Conceptualization Summary Form (Case 8.A, Abby).

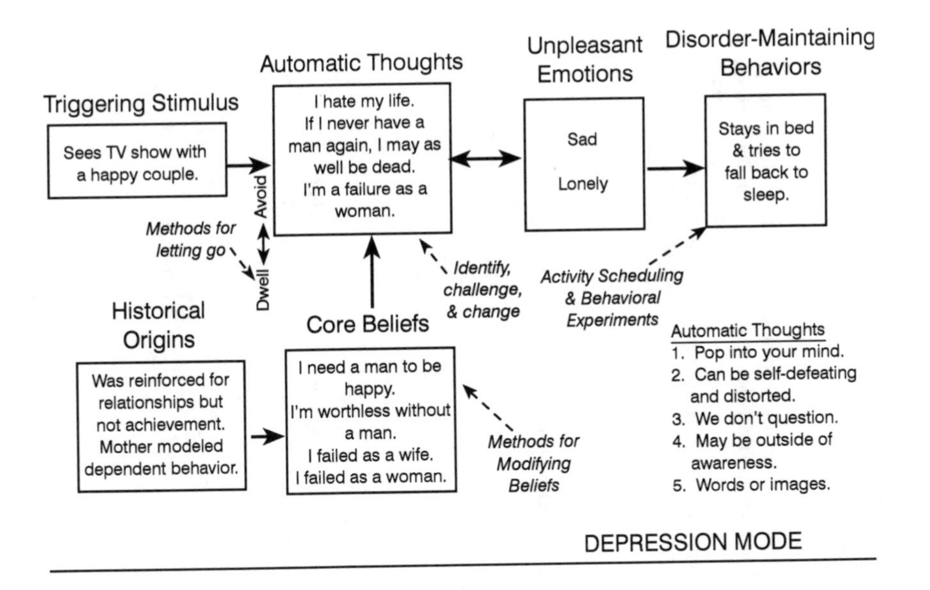

FIG. 8.4. Case Conceptualization Illustration (Case 8.A, Abby).

Case 8.B (Benjamin): Perfectionistic, Self-Critical, Hypervigilant to Interpersonal Threat

Benjamin was a 44-year-old, married, middle manager in state government who lived with his wife and two teenage children. (A description of this client and his case are presented in chapters 1 and 5, pp. 17–21 and 115–116; see also Figs. 8.5 and 8.6 in this chapter.)

CASE CONCEPTUALIZATION WORKSHEET FOR DEPRESSION

Client's Name: Benjamin

TRIGGERING STIMULI	COGNITIONS (CORE BELIEFS CAPITALIZED)	EMOTIONS	BEHAVIOR (Disorder-Maintaining or Adaptive)
External:			
Makes minor error at work.	How can I be so dumb!	Angry at Self	
	PEOPLE WILL REJECT ME; PEOPLE WILL BE CRUEL AND CRITICAL.	Anxious	Avoids boss and coworkers.
	I'M A FAILURE.	Sad and Angry at Self	Berates self for hours (e.g., I should pay more attention; I'm a lousy employee; I deserve to be fired).
	I have to criticize myself to prevent this from happening again.		
	I MUST BE PERFECT.	Anxious	Attempts to do everything perfectly.
His teenaged daughter lost a $20 bill, and he gets angry and yells at her.	I'm a terrible father; I'm a loose cannon.	Angry at Self	
	I'm going to screw her up.	Anxious	
	I'M BAD; I'M INADEQUATE.	Sad, Guilty, Angry at Self,	Isolates himself from his family; berates self and ruminates about what he did.
	I'M OUT OF CONTROL.	Anxious	
Internal:			
Thoughts and images of previous mistakes or times when he became angry, irritable, or impatient with family.	I'M A FAILURE; I'M OUT OF CONTROL;	Angry at Self and Guilty	
	LIFE WILL ALWAYS BE IMPOSSIBLE FOR ME; I'LL ALWAYS BE MISERABLE AND A HOPELESS FAILURE.	Sad	Broods.

FIG. 8.5. Case Conceptualization Worksheet (Case 8.B, Benjamin).

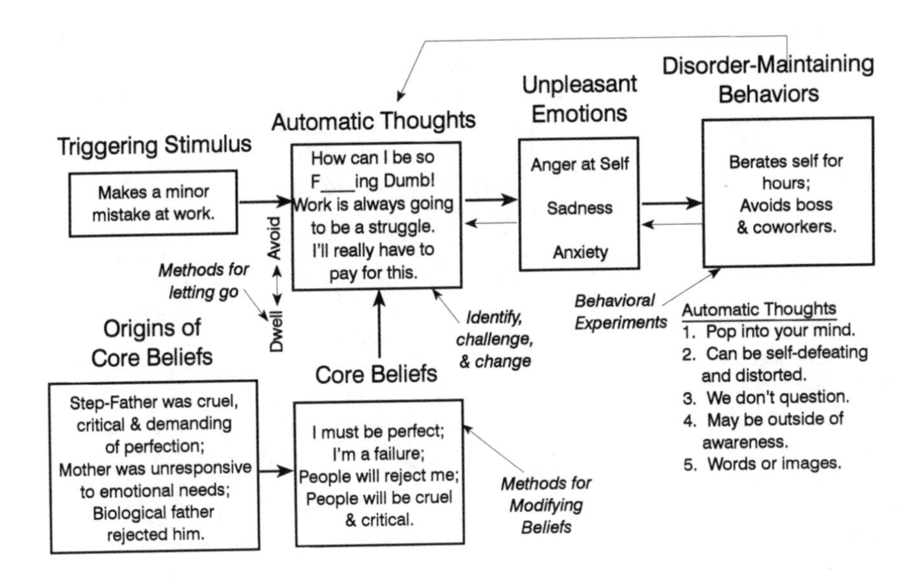

FIG. 8.6. Case Conceptualization Illustration (Case 8.B, Benjamin).

Case 8.C (Catherine): Extreme Standards for Achievement Contributing to Exhaustion Resulting in Shift to Depressed Mode

Catherine was a 35-year-old, never-married, professor of history at an Ivy League university. She was a highly promising, young academician who had produced two books in the first 2 years of her appointment at the university. Prominent historians in her area of expertise (i.e., history of science) regarded her second book as a significant contribution to the field. She was seeking treatment to learn ways to prevent future episodes of depression and was not depressed at the time she sought treatment.

Approximately once or twice per year, Catherine had major depressive episodes. What was remarkable about her condition was the suddenness of her changes from depressed to nondepressed states. She experienced a profound change in her mood, as well as how she viewed herself, the world, and the future. During depressive episodes, she suffered from depressed moods, feelings of incompetence, excessive guilt, extreme self-criticism, criticism of and competitiveness with others, and difficulty concentrating.

When she was in nondepressed modes, Catherine was energetic, driven in her work, highly productive, self-confident, accepting of some of her mistakes and shortcomings, kind toward others, and in need of less sleep than in her depressive phases. Despite her increases in energy and hypomanic "flavor" during her nondepressed mode, she never met criteria for a manic or hypomanic episode.

The following beliefs appear to have contributed to Catherine's depression and her driven approach to life and work: "I must be a superstar" and "I must be courageous and strong at all times." Moreover, she believed that "If I am not extremely productive, I'm weak, a disgrace, and a nothing."

The factors that appear to have triggered the phase shift from a nondepressed to a depressed mode included exhaustion due to overworking herself, others' criticism of her work, not accomplishing as much as she expected, not being involved in a romantic relationship, gaining even small amounts of weight, and changing her behavior due to anxiety. An example of changing her behavior due to anxiety had to do with flirting with men. Occasionally, as a result of feeling anxious about not being in a romantic relationship, she flirted with a man. She viewed this as a "weak" behavior—"Flirting is OK, but not to prevent anxiety."

Catherine attributed the development of these depressogenic beliefs to her father. He was a world-renowned mathematician and expected nothing less than a stellar performance at all times from his brightest child. He also stressed his view that because she was an African American, her performance had to be exceptional to remove any doubt about how she attained her status. Indeed, Catherine was at the top of her class throughout her entire schooling, and her teachers and professors recognized her as having extraordinary talents and promise. She had little experience being less than "the best" at her various pursuits.

Catherine's belief that she was not normal seemed to result from a variety of factors. First, she recognized that she was intellectually gifted. Second, she recognized that she was unusual in the intensity of her drive to accomplish and succeed and in her dramatic shifts in her mood and outlook on life. Finally, being an African American who had lived and attended school in predominantly white circles contributed to her sense of differentness (see Figs. 8.7, 8.8, & 8.9).

CASE CONCEPTUALIZATION WORKSHEET FOR DEPRESSION

Client's Name: Catherine

TRIGGERING STIMULI	COGNITIONS (CORE BELIEFS CAPITALIZED)	EMOTIONS	BEHAVIOR (Disorder-Maintaining or Adaptive)
External:			
Others' criticism of her work.	They don't know what they're talking about; how dare they find fault in my work!	Anger	Becomes distracted and unproductive because of self-doubts. Attempts to make up for lost time by not exercising & decreasing amount of time she sleeps.
	Maybe they're right; maybe I'm off track. I MUST BE A SUPERSTAR.	Anxiety	
Internal: Thinking about not being involved in a romantic relationship.	I'm never going to be like everybody else. I'M NOT NORMAL.	Anxiety	Goes out with someone she is not interested in, just to be dating; but then feels weak and disgraceful for doing so.
Exhaustion due to overworking herself. Not reaching self-imposed ambitious work goals. Gaining even small amounts of weight. Letting anxious feelings affect her behavior.	I MUST BE STRONG AND COURAGEOUS AT ALL TIMES OR ELSE I'M WEAK & A DISGRACE.	Anxiety	

FIG. 8.7. Case Conceptualization Worksheet (Case 8.C, Catherine).

CASE CONCEPTUALIZATION SUMMARY FORM

Client's Name: Catherine

Identifying Information: 35-year-old, never-married, professor of history at an Ivy League university. She was a highly-promising, young academician; once or twice per year, she had major depressive episodes—sudden, dramatic changes between depressed and nondepressed modes.

Presenting Problem: Episodic depression, though currently, she is not depressed.

Precipitant(s): not applicable.

Exhaustive List of Problems, Issues, and Therapy-Relevant Behaviors:

1. Depressive Episodes--including feelings of incompetence, excessive guilt, extreme self-criticism and criticism and competitiveness with others, and difficulty concentrating.
2. Hypersensitivity to criticism.
3. Workaholism.
4. Subthreshold eating problem; meticulous about not gaining weight, though she had an accurate body image and did not binge or purge.
5. Hypertension.

Diagnoses (Axis I): Major Depressive Disorder, Recurrent, In Full Remission

Personality Characteristics: Excessive standards for achievement.

Relevant Beliefs:

1. I must be a superstar.
2. I must be strong and courageous at all times or else I'm weak and a disgrace.
3. I must have an ideally thin and muscular body.
4. I must reach all of my daily goals with excellence.
5. I'm not normal.
6. It's not normal that I'm not married yet.

Origins of Key Core Beliefs:

Beliefs 1-3: Her father was a world-renowned mathematician who expected nothing less than a stellar performance at all times from his brightest child. Catherine was top of her class throughout her schooling, and her teachers and professors recognized her as having extraordinary talents. Therefore, learned to expect to be "the best."

Beliefs 5 & 6: Intellectually gifted; unusual in the intensity of her drive to accomplish and succeed, as well as in her dramatic shifts in her mood and outlook on life.

continued on next page

WORKING MODEL

VICIOUS CYCLES / MAINTAINING FACTORS:

Her belief that she "must be a superstar" and "must be strong and courageous at all times" results in her pushing herself to exhaustion. Exhaustion, in turn, contributes to decreases in productivity and depression. Depression strengthens her belief "I'm not normal."

Criticism from others or not reaching her own excessive expectations appear to interact with her belief that she must be a superstar. This interaction can result in activating her depressive mode.

TREATMENT:

Goals:

1. Decrease the frequency and intensity of depressive episodes.
2. Increase balance in lifestyle and self-care to prevent exhaustion.
3. Modify self-defeating automatic thoughts and beliefs.

Possible Obstacles to Treatment:

1. She may resist making changes in her lifestyle that would lead to more balance.
2. She may miss sessions or not complete self-help assignments, since they take time away from work.
3. She may consider that going to therapy represents being weak resulting in her attempting to terminate as quickly as possible.

Plan:

1. Conduct a cost-benefit analysis of "I must be a superstar."
2. Cognitive restructuring of relevant beliefs.
3. Activity scheduling to insure balanced activities and increase self-care behaviors.

FIG. 8.8. *(cont'd)* Case Conceptualization Summary Form (Case 8.C, Catherine).

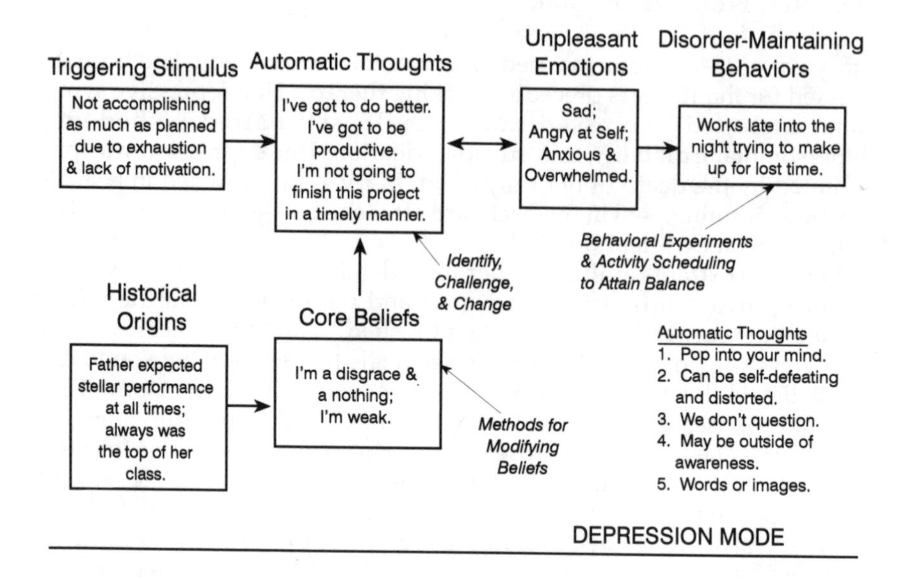

FIG. 8.9. Case Conceptualization Illustration (Case 8.C, Catherine).

Case 8.D (Mary): Guilt, Self-Hatred, and Alcohol Dependence, Precipitated by Son's Accidental Death That Resulted From Her Mistake

Mary was a 45-year-old, married, obese factory worker who had been depressed for the 15 years preceding seeking therapy. Her depressive symptoms included depressed mood, guilt, self-hatred, anhedonia, hypersomnia, irritability, and suicidal ideation. Her depression was precipitated by the death of her only child. Mary's son drowned in a small, plastic swimming pool in the backyard after she had gone inside for a few minutes to take a telephone call.

Mary felt extreme guilt about her son's death. She strongly believed the following that contributed to her guilt and depression: "I'm the lowest scum on the earth," "I deserve to be punished," and "I can't let myself be happy ever again." She also believed that she had wanted her son to die. She believed this for two reasons. First, her son had behavior problems, and in response, Mary frequently felt frustrated and angry with him. Second, Mary believed that her lapse in judgment, leaving him alone for a few minutes while he was in the pool, represented a wish that he die.

In response to her guilty and depressed feelings and her beliefs, Mary used several disorder-maintaining strategies. For example, she drank alcohol to excess. Alcohol use seemed to worsen her depression, often contributed to heated arguments with her husband, and caused her to have occasional blackouts. In addition, she had developed a significant tolerance to alcohol. Other disorder-maintaining behaviors for Mary included binge eating and isolating herself from others.

Mary decided to seek therapy for two reasons. First, her husband had recently become depressed for the first time. She assumed that his depression resulted not only from a recent job loss but also from having a chronically depressed and alcoholic wife. She loved him and decided that it was not fair to punish him by having so many problems. Second, Mary recently caused a car accident as a result of her drinking. She got a driving-under-the-influence (DUI) arrest, and she realized how close she was to killing other people. As a result, she decided to start going to Alcoholics Anonymous meetings as well as to begin therapy (see Figures 8.10, 8.11, & 8.12).

CASE CONCEPTUALIZATION WORKSHEET FOR DEPRESSION

Client's Name: Mary

TRIGGERING STIMULI	COGNITIONS (CORE BELIEFS CAPITALIZED)	EMOTIONS	BEHAVIOR (Disorder-Maintaining or Adaptive)
Internal: Thinking about her son's death. **External:** Having free time.	I'M THE LOWEST OF SCUM ON THE EARTH. I wanted Joshua to die. I DESERVE TO BE PUNISHED. Suicide would be letting me off the hook. I CAN'T LET MYSELF BE HAPPY AGAIN.	Self-hatred Sadness Guilt	Drinks alcohol or binges on sweets.

FIG. 8.10. Case Conceptualization Worksheet (Case 8, Mary).

CASE CONCEPTUALIZATION SUMMARY FORM

Client's Name: Mary

Identifying Information: 45-year-old, married, obese, factory worker who had been depressed for the 15 years preceding her seeking therapy.

Presenting Problem: Depression, self-hatred.
Precipitant(s): Her son drowned when she left him alone for a few minutes.

Exhaustive List of Problems, Issues, and Therapy-Relevant Behaviors:

1. Depression, self-hatred, profound guilt, anhedonia.	5. Social isolation.
2. Unresolved grief.	6. Husband is depressed.
3. Alcohol dependence.	
4. Over-eating and obesity.	

Diagnoses (Axis I): Major Depressive Disorder (Chronic); Alcohol Dependence; Binge Eating Disorder

Personality Characteristics:

Relevant Beliefs:

1. I'm the lowest of scum on the earth.	5. I can't let myself be happy again.
2. I wanted Joshua to die.	
3. I deserve to be punished.	
4. Suicide would be letting me off the hook.	

Origins of Key Core Beliefs:
Her son died while he was under her care.

continued on next page

WORKING MODEL

VICIOUS CYCLES / MAINTAINING FACTORS:
Her drinking and binge eating are driven by a desire both to momentarily escape extremely painful emotions and to punish herself in the long run. These strategies prevent her from working through the issues related to her son's death. In addition, isolation from friends and family prevents her from having social support that may provide a framework in which she could begin to forgive herself.

TREATMENT:
Goals:
Client's Goal: To act less depressed, in order not to depress her husband further.
Therapist's Unstated Goals for Client: To forgive herself; decrease guilt and self-hatred; improve mood; decrease binge eating.
Shared Goal: Decrease the frequency and extent of alcohol use.

Possible Obstacles to Treatment: Mary's beliefs that she deserves to be punished and should not allow herself to be happy.

Plan:
1. Outpatient detox program and AA meetings while concurrently having cognitive therapy.
2. Cognitive restructuring especially of the beliefs that she wanted her son to die, that she deserves to be punished, and that she cannot let herself be happy ever again.
3. Work on positive ways she can "atone" for her mistake (e.g., charity work involving children's causes).
4. Develop social support.
5. Address the triggering stimuli, cognitions, emotions, and consequences of alcohol use and binge eating.

FIG. 8.11. (*cont'd*) Case Conceptualization Summary Form (Case 8.D, Mary).

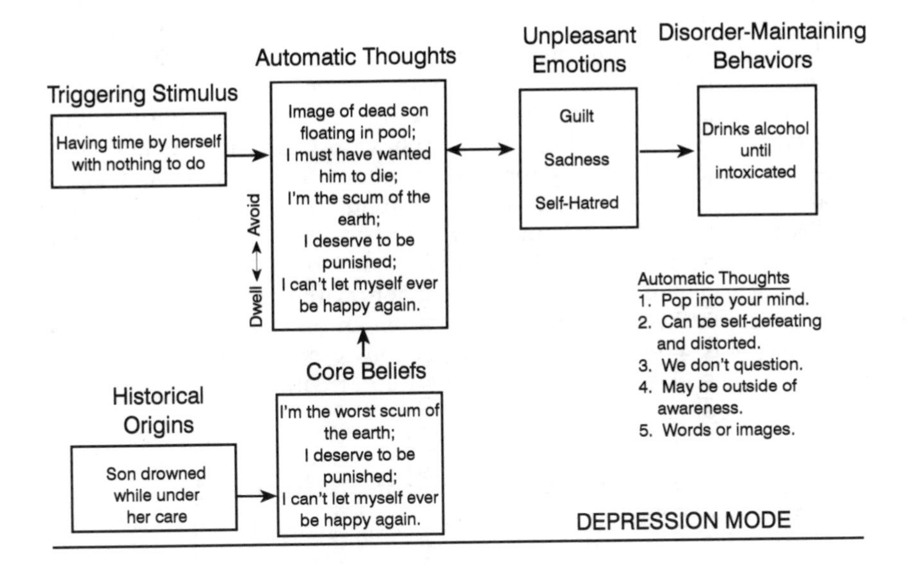

FIG. 8.12. Case Conceptualization Illustration (Case 8.D, Mary).

COGNITIVE THERAPY OF DEPRESSION

In the vast majority of studies, cognitive therapy of depression has been found to be at least as effective as other forms of treatment (for a meta-analysis, see Dobson, 1989). In addition, cognitive therapy shows promise of being superior to other forms of psychotherapy as well as antidepressant medication in preventing relapses (e.g., Evans et al., 1992; Hollon, Shelton, & Davis, 1993; Hollon, Shelton, & Loosen, 1991).

As suggested in the cognitive model of depression section, chronic and recurrent depressions share many characteristics with personality disorders. Therefore, clients with chronic or recurrent depression typically benefit from a combination of the treatment approaches outlined by Beck and colleagues for depression (Beck, Rush, et al., 1979) and personality disorders (i.e., Beck, Freeman, et al., 1990; Freeman & Leaf, 1989). Beck, Rush, et al. (1979) outlined effective methods for reducing the acute symptoms of depression. Although that text also suggested some approaches to altering "silent assumptions," Beck, Freeman, et al. (1990) built on the previous work.

In brief, cognitive therapy for chronic or recurrent depression should consist of the following sequence. First, therapists and clients collaborate to develop a useful case conceptualization that serves as a working model for therapy. Second, therapists guide clients to increase activities that have potential for giving them pleasure or a sense of mastery. Next, clients learn to become cognizant of self-defeating automatic thoughts. Fourth, therapists encourage clients to engage in behavioral experiments and cognitive-evaluation procedures for testing automatic thoughts and beliefs. Finally, therapists teach clients other techniques for modifying depressive modes or at least helping them find ways to decrease the frequency and intensity of mode activation (Beck, Rush, et al., 1979; Sacco & Beck, 1995).

This section begins with an example of how therapists can introduce a Case Conceptualization Illustration to their chronically or recurrently depressed clients. The remainder of the section describes the use of cognitive therapy procedures and is organized around treatment of the specific clients presented earlier.

Presentation of a Case Conceptualization Illustration to a Depressed Client

As the first step in cognitive restructuring, the therapist presents the depressed client with a Case Conceptualization Illustration. The illustration graphically depicts the client's idiosyncratic experiences within the cognitive model of depression. Here is an excerpt from a session in which Sammy's therapist presented him with an individualized Case Conceptualization Illustration. (Sammy is the undergraduate presented at the beginning of the chapter.) As Sammy's therapist explained an element of the conceptualization to him, she drew it (see Fig. 8.13).

Therapist: If it's all right with you, I believe it would be helpful for me to illustrate for you a framework for understanding and treating depression.

Sammy: OK.

Therapist: This framework is called the cognitive therapy approach to depression. To begin with, there may be a triggering stimulus, a situation or internal experience that triggers your response. Should we use the situation at the party you told me about earlier?

Sammy: OK.

Therapist: So, the triggering situation was being at a party and standing by yourself. In that situation, you experienced a change in your emotions. You started feeling more depressed, right?

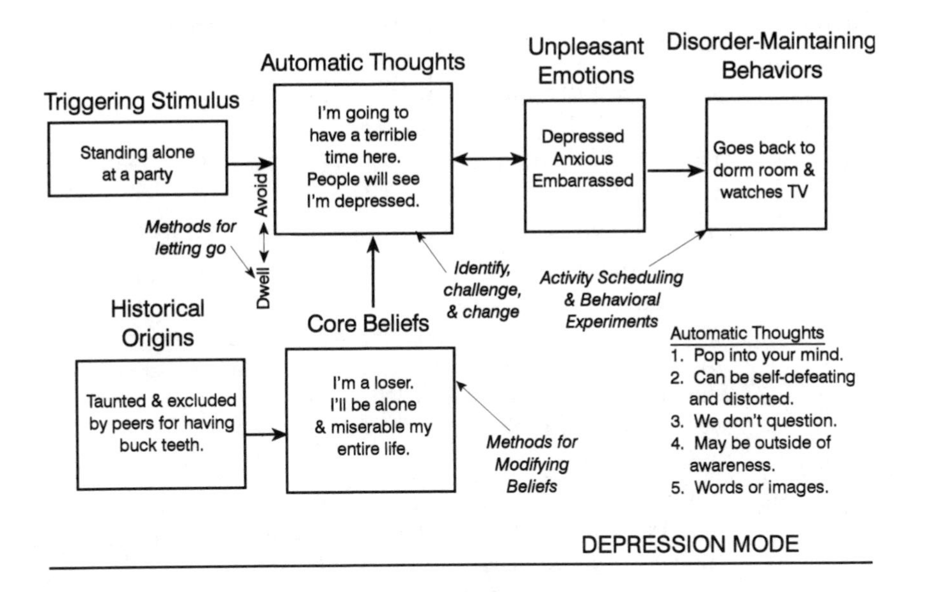

FIG. 8.13. Presenting the Case Conceptualization Illustration to a depressed client.

Sammy: Right.

Therapist: According to the cognitive therapy approach, a situation doesn't cause us to feel a particular way. It triggers it but doesn't cause it. What causes it is what's going through your mind in the situation. What we call automatic thoughts. At the party, what was going through your mind?

Sammy: I was thinking, "I'm going to have a terrible time here" and "I probably won't talk to a single person."

Therapist: Any other thoughts or images in that situation?

Sammy: Yes. "I'm ugly and have nothing to say" and "People will see I'm depressed."

Therapist: Sounds like you were experiencing a great deal of pain there.

Sammy: A whole lot.

Therapist: I'm wondering if you were having other emotions besides depression.

Sammy: Yes, I was feeling anxious.

Therapist: Um hum. Any shame?

Sammy: Yes, I was feeling really embarrassed.

Therapist: Yes ... So you were having these thoughts and feeling really upset. Did that affect your behavior?

Sammy: It did. I left the party soon after I got there.

Therapist: And then, what did you do?

Sammy: I went back to my dorm room and watched TV and felt sorry for myself.

Therapist: So would you say that this behavior made you feel worse?

Sammy: Much worse.

Therapist: This kind of behavior is really quite common for depressed people. And, as you just said, it often contributes to maintaining unpleasant feelings. Therefore, these can be called disorder-maintaining behaviors. What questions or comments do you have about this model, so far?

Sammy: None. It's quite clear.

Therapist: Let me tell you more about automatic thoughts, characteristics that I think are important. First, automatic thoughts, as their name suggests, are automatic as opposed to being effortful or intentional. They just pop into your mind. Second, automatic thoughts can be self-enhancing and rational or they can be self-defeating and distorted. Everyone has some self-defeating and distorted thoughts from time to time. But, when you're depressed, the frequency of them goes way up. In a little while, I'll show you a list of distortions that people often make.

Third, unfortunately, we tend to believe automatic thoughts are true without questioning them. If someone else says something, we may question it in our mind. However, when we have automatic thoughts, they're just kind of there, and we tend to accept them without really thinking about them.

Fourth, automatic thoughts can be fully in our awareness and long-lasting. Or, they might be only at the fringes of our awareness, or they may even be completely out of our awareness. That makes them particularly difficult. They're really important in causing our emotions and behavior. But, we may not even be aware we're having them. Even if we are aware, we may tend to not question them. Fortunately, there are ways to become aware of automatic thoughts and begin to evaluate them to see if they are appropriate and useful. To begin with, we need a signal that we are having an automatic thought. From this diagram, do you have any idea of possible signals.

Sammy: Not really.

Therapist: It's probably so obvious to you that you don't see. Changes in your emotions or behaviors can be a signal.

Sammy: Oh, right.

Therapist: When you suddenly have a change in either of these and you don't know why, you can ask yourself one of several questions. You can ask yourself, "What's going through my mind right now?" or "What does this situation mean to me?" or "What's the most upsetting part of this situation?" One of those questions almost always will help you find the automatic thought. Let me make one final point about automatic thoughts. Automatic thoughts can either be words, as the ones we identified for the party situation, or they can be mental pictures or images. Are you aware of having any mental pictures or images? For example, daydreams, fantasies, almost video clips in your head or a snapshot of a person's face.

Sammy: No, not really.

Therapist: Some people are more verbal and others are more visual. On the other hand, sometimes people tell me that they don't have mental images. However, they come back the following week and say, since they were aware that they might have a mental image, they noticed that they did have some. Any questions or comments about what we've discussed so far?

Sammy: No, it all makes good sense. It describes me to a "T."

Therapist: Good. Now, I've drawn this as if it's linear. Situations cause automatic thoughts, cause emotions, cause behaviors. In fact, it's not linear. When you become more depressed for example, you're more likely to have depressing thoughts; that is, the emotions contribute to the thoughts. When you engage in disorder-maintaining behaviors, it contributes to having depressing thoughts and feelings. All these factors probably interact.

In fact, when people become depressed, they often go into a depressed mode. All their systems are affected by depression, their thoughts, their emotions, their motivation, their eating and sleeping, and their behavior. But, I think it's clearer to draw it in this simplified way because it helps show the ways we can intervene on these components. I'll show you that in a few minutes.

So far, I've been talking mostly about cognitive content. However, the process of thinking is important, too. When people are depressed, they often (a) ruminate or dwell on upsetting things, (b) try to avoid thinking about upsetting things, or (c) do a little bit of both. Are you aware of doing either or both?

Sammy: Yes, I do both. I try to get my mind off of myself by watching TV, and I try not to think about how miserable I am. But, these depressing thoughts keep coming back and spinning around in my head.

Therapist: Yes. That's something we can talk more about later, too. Another thing that is important is that these automatic thoughts don't just come out of the blue. Not only are they triggered by situations but also they come from deeper beliefs. What cognitive therapists call core beliefs. These are long-standing, deeply held beliefs about ourselves, other people, the world, and the future. Do you have a sense for what core beliefs might have been triggered in the situation at the party?

Sammy: "I'm a loser" and "People are too superficial to give a depressed guy a chance."

Therapist: Was that last one associated with feeling angry?

Sammy: Yes, now that you mention it.

Therapist: Any other core beliefs, meanings about that situation?

Sammy: That "I'll be alone and miserable for my entire life."

Therapist: Those are intensely painful beliefs. Are there times when you feel like you're not a loser or even that you're a winner or that you might not be alone?

Sammy: Yes, when I'm not depressed, or when a girl seems interested in me. I feel pretty good about myself, then.

Therapist: That's good to hear because some people don't have balancing beliefs. Their beliefs are unconditional. Now, these core beliefs tend to come from somewhere, too. They often come from our personal history. Often these are things that happened in our childhood. Are you aware of things that happened in your past that may have contributed to the belief that you are a loser?

Sammy: I had buck teeth as a kid. And, the other kids were really cruel, taunted me, and excluded me.

Therapist: That's just the kind of thing I meant. Anything else?

Sammy: My sister used to tease me too.

If clients are candidates for medication, if they are at moderate or high risk for suicide or are functioning very poorly, therapists should consider antidepressant medication. In such cases, therapists can add the following to their presentation of the Case Conceptualization Illustration.

Therapist: One last thing, I'll add to the model. That is, almost all of what I've drawn occurs in a biological context. You can't have a thought, memory, emotion, or behavior without all kinds of biological things happening. The neurons or nerve cells in our brains fire as a result of electrical currents. They release neurotransmitters, which are chemicals. Our hormones also affect how we think and feel, and even our inborn temperament can affect how we think, feel, and behave.

Next, the therapist can show the client interventions and how they correspond to the illustration. Here is how Sammy's therapist introduced this topic.

Therapist: Now, let's talk about the kinds of things we can do to help you get out of this depressed mode. First, you can learn to identify your automatic thoughts and core beliefs. Once you identify them, we can start challenging and changing them. On the behavioral side, we can work on motivation and increasing activities that have potential for lifting your mood and giving you more confidence. This can help interrupt your rumination by increasing your activities and giving you less time to think. You need to think about this stuff but in a productive way. Rumination is like spinning your wheels. There are also things we may do to modify your core beliefs. There are many different interventions we can use, and we'll decide as we go. The things I've mentioned are likely to have a very positive effect on how you're doing. I suggest we start with these. How does this plan sound to you?

Sammy: It sounds very promising. How do we start?

Case 8.A (Abby): Inactive, on Disability, Sociotropic Orientation, Episode Triggered by Loss of Marriage

Activity Scheduling

Activity scheduling can help activate depressed clients by (a) increasing their participation in potentially rewarding activities, (b) decreasing their involvement in activities that they find aversive, and (c) increasing their sense of mastery. Lewinsohn et al. (1980) stated this succinctly. They suggested that the goal of activity scheduling "is to enhance the quantity and quality of the person's reinforcement related interactions" (p. 322).

Besides increasing the ratio of pleasant to unpleasant activities, activity scheduling has other benefits. Therapists can frame scheduled activities as behavioral experiments that test depressive beliefs. Specifically, activity scheduling can help clients disconfirm their beliefs that they are unable to derive enjoyment from activities or accomplish tasks. Activity scheduling also frequently helps clients interrupt their ruminations about their problems.

Abby's activity schedule that she completed during assessment indicated that she engaged in very few activities that could contribute to enjoyment or provide a sense of mastery. Moreover, she believed that she could neither derive pleasure from activities nor accomplish tasks (e.g., "I can't enjoy things unless I'm in a relationship with a man," "I can't do the simplest things," "There's no point in doing anything"). Therefore, the goals of the initial therapy sessions were to increase the ratio of pleasant to aversive activities and engage in activities that could elicit a sense of mastery to modify some cognitions that were maintaining her depression.

First, the therapist provided a rationale to Abby for increasing response-contingent positive reinforcement. Namely, depressed individuals often engage in low levels of potentially gratifying activities and increasing these activities has been shown empirically to decrease symptoms of depression.

When asked for feedback about this approach, Abby indicated that she understood it, and it made sense. Given that an issue for Abby was dependency, the therapist attempted to anticipate concerns she might have about the approach but was reluctant to admit. He indicated that some clients who hear about this approach believe it is too simplistic and does not address the substantive issues. He asked if this issue was of concern to her. Abby hesitantly admitted that she wondered if such an approach would help her with what she considered her major problems. That is, her feeling like a failure and not having a man. The therapist agreed that activity scheduling might not help with those problems directly. However, he suggested that after a few weeks of engaging in potentially reinforcing activities, her mood was likely to improve and her other depressive symptoms would lessen. A reduction in symptoms likely would enable her to begin addressing the other important issues in her life. Abby expressed a willingness to begin with this approach.

Increasing Pleasure. To increase pleasant activities, Abby's therapist suggested the self-help assignment outlined in Table 8.1. Abby was to generate a list of 25 activities she enjoyed doing or had enjoyed prior to her depression. The therapist provided her with a list of 320 potentially pleasant activities to provide ideas for her (MacPhillamy & Lewinsohn, 1975). In addition, he informed her that often when people are depressed they have difficulty remembering times when they were not depressed. Therefore, he suggested that it may be helpful for her to ask family and friends about what activities she enjoyed when she was not depressed.

Once Abby generated 25 activities that she enjoyed or had enjoyed prior to her depression, she followed instructions that her therapist gave her (adapted from Tobi, 1996). For each item, she determined whether (a) cost was prohibitive, (b) she had engaged in the activity since she had been depressed, and (c) she preferred to engage in the activity alone or with another person. Next, she circled the five activities that she enjoyed most that were within her budget. In addition, she agreed to do at least one of these per day. Abby also agreed to predict and record on an activity calendar how much pleasure she would derive from each activity and subsequently record her actual level of pleasure. Comparing and recording predicted versus actual pleasure ratings helped Abby disconfirm her beliefs about her ability to enjoy activities. Moreover, it helped her remember that she enjoyed activities. This was important for Abby because she—like most depressed people—had difficulty remembering positive experiences.

In the next session, Abby reported on her efforts to increase pleasant activities. The activities that she engaged in were going to a movie with her sister, listening to music and singing along, and riding her bike. She predicted that she would get 0 out of 10 enjoyment from each of these activities. In actuality, her rated level of enjoyment ranged from 2 out of 10 to 6 out of 10. Her therapist encouraged her to draw conclusions about her belief "If I

TABLE 8.1

Increasing Pleasant Activities

1. Please generate a list of 25 activities that you enjoy or that you enjoyed prior to your depression. To accomplish this you may brainstorm, look at a list of pleasant activities, or ask family or friends for help brainstorming.
2. Next to each activity for which cost may be prohibitive, place a "$."
3. Next to each activity that you would prefer to do alone, place an "A."
4. Next to each activity that you would prefer to do with another person, place a "P."
5. Next to each activity that you would prefer to do alone sometimes and with another person sometimes, place an "A&P."
6. Next to each activity that you have not done since becoming depressed, place a "ND."
7. Circle 5 activities that you enjoy the most and for which cost is not prohibitive.
8. Do at least one of these activities each day.
9. Before engaging in the activity, predict how much pleasure (P) you will derive from it. Rate these on a scale from 0 to 10, where 0 = *not at all*, 5 = *moderate enjoyment*, 10 = *enjoy a great deal*. Record these predictions in your therapy notebook or on an activity calendar.
10. Immediately after engaging in the activity, rate your actual level of pleasure (0 to 10).

don't have a man in my life, I can't enjoy anything." Abby concluded that this belief was not entirely true. She was able to derive some pleasure from activities although she was not in a relationship with a man. Abby's therapist asked that she record this conclusion in her therapy notebook.

When Abby's therapist encouraged her to express any concerns about this assignment, Abby admitted that these activities only lifted her mood for the time that she was engaging in them, that is, just for a few hours that week. Her therapist suggested that over several weeks, as she continued engaging in pleasant activities, the positive effect on her mood would likely be more enduring. In addition, they could work at scheduling her days so that much of her time was spent engaging in activities that were enjoyable or provided a sense of mastery.

Increasing a Sense of Mastery. Besides not engaging in activities that had the potential for being enjoyable, Abby also avoided tasks that required skill, concentration, or effort. For example, she had let her housework go. Her apartment had piles of dirty clothes and unopened junk mail. She had not dusted or vacuumed her apartment for several months. In addition, dirty dishes were piling up in her sink, and her kitchen and bathrooms were filthy. Cognitions that interfered with her motivation to keep up with housework and other maintenance tasks included "I can't even do the simplest things," "There's no point in doing anything," and "I can't get myself to do anything."

In order for Abby to feel that cleaning her apartment was manageable, her therapist helped her develop *graded tasks*. They divided tasks into manageable subtasks. They also planned finite time blocks for working on the tasks. Abby agreed to start cleaning a little bit every day and to gradually increase the amount of time she spent until the apartment was in order. In addition, she and her therapist planned specifically what she would work on cleaning each day. They agreed that each day during the first week, Abby would set a timer for 15 minutes and do housework for at least that long. She could choose to continue past 15 minutes but should not attempt to push herself too much—doing so might punish, rather than reinforce, her effort.

Rather than placing specific tasks in each slot on her activity calendar, Abby was encouraged to simply block out time for cleaning. The reason for this was that Abby would likely have felt discouraged if she did not complete a task written on the calendar. What was important at this stage of her treatment was that she was spending time doing something that could begin to increase her perceptions of self-efficacy. Therefore, she and her therapist listed the tasks that she needed to do and categorized them as "highly unpleasant," "moderately unpleasant," or "mildly/not unpleasant." Next, she selected tasks from the "mildly/not unpleasant" category that were most pressing and began with those. Before working on a task, she was to predict how much mastery she would feel from working on the task (from 0 to 10, with 0 representing *none*, 10 *extremely high*, and 5 *moderate*).

When she completed an item, if she had time remaining in her "cleaning" time block, she was to proceed to another high-priority item from that category. Abby's therapist also encouraged her to do at least one task per day that she could finish, such as taking out the garbage or doing one load of laundry. Finishing tasks could contribute to a sense of accomplishment.

Through imagery, Abby's therapist had her anticipate practical problems and the cognitions and emotions that might obstruct her progress. Abby quickly realized that she did not have the appropriate cleaning supplies. When asked what she could do about it, she replied that she could stop at the grocery store on the way home from the session. However, she expressed concern that she had so many different items she needed at the grocery store that it seemed daunting. The therapist reminded her that they were attempting to break down tasks into manageable subtasks. He asked her what she could do about feeling overwhelmed about going into the grocery store. Abby suggested that she could buy the cleaning supplies and just get a few other items that she needed. In addition, if she decided which items to purchase before she went into the store, the task would seem less daunting. The therapist asked that she write these items down on her notes from this therapy session. (It is often helpful to have extremely depressed or anxious clients write notes about sessions, to aid their memory.) Next, the therapist asked Abby to imagine beginning to do the first item on the list—taking out the garbage. Abby did not foresee any difficulties with this. However, when she imagined being faced with the prospect of doing the dishes, a variety of cognitions and emotions interfered with her motivation. As a result, Abby's therapist introduced a Motivation Worksheet (Fig. 8.14).

In the left-hand column of the worksheet, Abby's therapist recorded Demotivating Cognitions. In the right-hand column, Abby recorded Motivating Responses and Plans that she and her therapist generated. When therapists, as opposed to their clients, write the demotivating cognitions, it may help prevent further strengthening the client's self-defeating cognitions. On the other hand, having clients write the motivating responses and plans may help them commit to thinking adaptively and follow the motivation plans.

Abby agreed to read over this worksheet each day at the time slated to do housework. In the subsequent session, she reported that doing so enabled her to start working. In addition, once she started, she almost always worked during the allotted time and often worked beyond that time.

At the next session, Abby reportedly had followed her schedule and engaged in at least 15 minutes per day of work around the apartment. She felt slightly better but was having self-defeating cognitions that prevented her from feeling positive about her accomplishment. She thought, "What's the big deal—so I vacuumed the rug and did some dishes. Anybody can do that. In the past, I was able to clean the whole apartment all at once and in about 2 hours." Through guided discovery, Abby changed her perspective.

MOTIVATION WORKSHEET

Task: Doing housework.

When to Read Worksheet: Each day, at the time on calendar slated for cleaning.

DE-MOTIVATING THOUGHTS	MOTIVATING THOUGHTS & PLANS
I'm too tired.	*I'm tired, but I'm not too tired to start—do 15 minutes of work.*
I hate this.	*It probably won't be as bad as I think. I'll probably be glad that I did something when I'm through. Listen to some jazzy music while I clean to make it less of a chore.*
I'll never get this place in control.	*That's true if I never begin. If I do some work every day, eventually I will get it cleaned up. Even though it's a huge mess, it's just an apartment, it's not like it's a mansion with 40 rooms.*
What's the point, no one will see it if it's a pigsty.	*I see it, & it makes me feel depressed to live in a pigsty; so it does matter.*
Maybe I'll do some later; I'll take a nap (or watch TV or eat) now instead.	*I always say I'll do it later & hardly ever get back to it. I'll never get my life in control if I keep avoiding things I need to do. Do it now & get it over with!*
I can't even do the simplest things.	*I can load the dishwasher, & that's all I need to do right now.*

FIG. 8.14. Motivation Worksheet.

Therapist: Imagine a marathon runner gets mononucleosis and is in bed most of the time for several months. When she is ready to begin running again, how far and how fast is she likely to run as compared to before her illness?

Abby: Not very far or fast.

Therapist: The first week back, do you think that running a single mile slowly might be an accomplishment for her?

Abby: Yeah, probably.

Therapist: Suppose she thought, "What's wrong with me, running only a mile means I'm a failure; any 10-year-old can run one mile." How might that affect her training?

Abby: It might make her give up. It might make her work harder, but probably it would make her give up.

Therapist: What might be a more useful attitude for her?

Abby: I have no idea.

Therapist: If she runs a mile every day for 2 weeks, how will she feel physically compared to the first day?

Abby: Better, she'd start to be getting into better shape.

Therapist: So, what could she tell herself the first day she was running to have a productive attitude.

Abby: She could tell herself, "It's only the first day. If I run a mile for a week or two, I'll feel stronger and be able to do more. I've gotta give myself some time. Gradually, I can get back into top shape again."

Therapist: That seems like a very useful attitude. You should go into coaching!

Abby: (Chuckles)

Therapist: Do you see the parallels to your situation?

Abby: Yes, it's better to give myself time to gradually get back to myself.

Therapist: Yes. Do you think you could take that perspective?

Abby: Yes, I think so.

After another week of graded tasks, Abby felt somewhat more hopeful and more energetic. Regarding cleaning, she decided to increase time to 30 minutes per day. She also felt ready to do some high priority tasks from the "moderately unpleasant" category.

Abby decided that a priority would be getting her apartment a little cleaner each day. She decided that she would clean dishes as she used them and dispose of mail immediately when she received it. She did not count either task as part of her 30 minutes of cleaning. During the following week, she increased cleaning time to 45 minutes per day. At the end of the week, she had caught up with her housework. Abby felt some relief and hope resulting from the realization that she could accomplish this. She also was somewhat hopeful that she would be able to get her life in order.

Core Belief Work

Once Abby's mood and energy began to lift, she and her therapist began working on core beliefs. They agreed to begin working first on the belief,

"Life has no meaning if I don't have a husband." Abby had learned from activity scheduling that she could derive some pleasure from activities without a man. Thus, the rationale for working on this belief next was that it was a natural extension of the activity schedule.

Another rationale for working on this belief first rather than her other relevant beliefs—"I'll always be alone," "I'm overweight and unattractive," "I failed as a wife," and "I am a failure as a woman"—related to her motivation for making positive change. Abby's motivation for finding meaningful activities likely would be higher if she were neither in a committed relationship with a man nor searching for one. In contrast, if she were in a relationship with a man, she would likely feel like she had everything she wanted, and her motivation would decrease. In short, Abby would be at risk for repeating an old, maladaptive pattern in which she was living for a man, clinging to him, and afraid of losing him.

First, Abby completed a Thought Evaluation Worksheet. She was able to generate self-enhancing responses. Some responses she generated in the worksheet included "In the past 2 months, I have been able to enjoy activities alone and with girlfriends," "I know two divorced women who are not in committed relationships but appear to be happy and feel they have meaningful lives," and "I heard a famous, 100-year-old woman on the radio who had never been married but seemed to be very happy; she even said that she thought she had lived a long and happy life BECAUSE she never got involved with men." In addition, Abby realized a serious disadvantage of her belief that her life would be meaningless without a man. Namely, it placed her at risk of settling for a man who was not good for her. Despite her ability to generate self-enhancing responses, she continued to believe deeply the content of her self-defeating belief.

Abby's therapist also used *rational-emotional role plays* with Abby. This procedure seemed to help Abby believe her rational responses more deeply. However, Abby seemed to need to actually find other sources of meaning to change this core belief and more importantly to find fulfillment.

Abby's therapist educated her about the various ways people derive life meaning. He then encouraged her to explore activities that might provide her with a sense of meaning. Abby tried becoming involved in some charitable groups and attended several meetings for each charity to give each a fair chance. However, she did not find any of these activities particularly fulfilling.

Abby also began exploring crafts. She began an adult education pottery class and found that she really enjoyed pottery. She greatly enjoyed time on the pottery wheel that she described as "very peaceful and still." In addition, she enjoyed giving ceramic pieces away as gifts to family and friends who expressed great appreciation for these gifts. Subsequently, Abby began going to craft fairs and occasionally sold some pieces. She enjoyed going to the fairs, seeing other people's work, and talking to people who visited her booth. In short, pottery became a major focus of Abby's life. After 4½ months of therapy, her Beck Depression Inventory (BDI) scores dropped to the mildly depressed range.

As the next step, therapy focused on beliefs that were preventing Abby from being willing to meet men and begin dating again. Abby's therapist used several interventions to help her modify her beliefs *"I'm overweight and unattractive"* and *"I'll always be alone."* These included: (a) using Thought Evaluation Worksheets, (b) polling trusted female friends about her attractiveness, and (c) behavioral experiments (e.g., going on blind dates and to singles functions), which helped her realize that men were, in fact, interested in dating her.

Next, Abby and her therapist began to analyze her belief that *"a wife should never get angry at her husband."* Her therapist targeted this belief because it appeared to contribute to Abby's conclusion that she was a failure as a wife and woman. When asked where she learned this rule of wifely conduct, she indicated that her mother explicitly told her this throughout Abby's childhood. Abby's therapist suggested that for the rules that play a large role in an individual's life, it is important to objectively evaluate their effects. As a result of this process, the individual can decide whether to retain the rule, modify it, or discard it completely.

Abby's therapist used metaphors and Socratic Questioning to help Abby see that this rule was detrimental to both her mother and her lives. In addition, she learned the importance of experiencing emotions without inhibition. Specifically, emotions can provide important information about a situation or problem and can lead to adaptive behaviors for changing the situation. Similarly, Abby realized that if a friend's husband treated her friend as Abby's husband treated Abby, Abby would have been furious at the friend's husband. As a result of this discussion, Abby concluded that by not allowing herself to be angry with her husband, she let him get away with his objectionable behavior.

At this point, Abby admitted that she also believed that if a wife got angry with her husband, he might decide she was "more trouble than she is worth" and leave. She realized, though, that her husband left despite her never getting angry with him. Abby agreed to ask her female friends who seemed to be in stable marriages whether they ever got angry with their husbands. After a couple weeks of polling, she concluded that nearly all of them occasionally expressed anger toward their husbands. Several sessions later, Abby reported believing completely that it is OK for women to express anger at their husbands in an appropriate, nonhostile manner.

This work facilitated Abby's being able to feel anger toward her ex-husband for leaving her, mistreating her, and not meeting her needs. She stopped thinking of herself as a *"failure as a wife and as a woman."* Moreover, she realized that her husband bore a large part of the responsibility for the unsuccessful marriage. Subsequently, Abby was able to explore the events of her marriage in a balanced fashion. She was able to reflect on the things she did well and those she might change in future relationships.

At this point, Abby and her therapist began discussing Abby's displeasure with her work situation. As a result of problem solving, she decided to do the following: return to work and try to discuss with her supervisors ways that they could work more effectively together. In addition, Abby planned to take a 1-day workshop on "partnering with your supervisor." If her relationship with her supervisor did not improve within a month or 2, then she planned to look for a new job.

After 21 weekly therapy sessions, Abby had been asymptomatic for 2 months and was using cognitive therapy strategies effectively. She was greatly enjoying her avocation of pottery, and she had begun casual dating, which she enjoyed. Although she hoped to eventually get in a serious relationship with a man, she was not in a rush to do so and this felt good to her. By mutual agreement, sessions became less frequent. Sessions were first tapered to every other week. Then, she had "booster sessions"—first monthly, then quarterly, then biannually. During the 2 years following treatment, Abby exhibited many positive changes. First, she had not been depressed. Second, she felt more confident than ever before. Third, she had gotten involved with a man who treated her well and with whom she appeared to have an open and honest relationship. Finally, she appeared to strike a healthy balance between her love life and other interests.

Case 8.B (Benjamin): Perfectionistic, Self-Critical, Hypervigilant to Interpersonal Threat

Addressing Possible Obstacles to Treatment

In their first meetings together, Benjamin's therapist began addressing possible obstacles to therapy. She suggested to Benjamin that often when people have a core belief that others will be harshly critical, the belief is operative in the therapy context as well as in the clients' outside life. She gently explored whether Benjamin thought that he might worry about her being critical of him. Benjamin agreed that it was likely that his fear of criticism would occur with her.

The therapist suggested that if this happened, it could be quite beneficial because it would parallel what happened outside therapy. Thus, Benjamin would have an opportunity to check out his assumptions with his therapist. In addition, he and his therapist could better understand his cognitions and feelings through open discussions of these processes. Benjamin agreed to mention concerns of this nature when they arose. The therapist disclosed to Benjamin that she considered herself a nonjudgmental person and did not expect perfection from herself or from him. She also suggested that although he likely would benefit a great deal from doing self-help assignments, she did not want the assignments to be a source of worry and excessive time expenditure. Finally, she suggested that it might be useful for him to, without telling her, intentionally make occasional errors in the self-help assignments to test her response.

Treating Insomnia

After addressing potential obstacles to treatment, Benjamin and his therapist decided to work on his insomnia because it was a pressing issue. Therefore, a few early sessions focused on improving his sleep. His therapist worked with Benjamin on three procedures for improving sleep. These were stimulus control (described in chapter 5), sleep restriction,[32] and progressive muscle relaxation performed in the early morning when he was having difficulty sleeping (described in chapter 6). After a few weeks, Benjamin's sleep improved a great deal. He rarely woke up too early and felt considerably better rested during the day.

Core Belief Modification

Once Benjamin's sleep was no longer a pressing problem, the focus of therapy was on modifying a relevant core belief. The belief was that other people would punish, reject, condemn, or criticize him harshly if he made minor mistakes. The rationale for beginning with this belief was that it appeared to be important in contributing to his other problems and maintaining his depression.

Benjamin's therapist guided him through a retrospective review of what happened on the occasions when he made errors at work. In the 6 years that he had been at his job, to his knowledge, he had made only a handful of errors. In addition, all of his errors were minor. On two occasions, his supervisor noticed the errors and called them to his attention. However, these errors did not affect Benjamin's subsequent performance evaluations and pay raises. Nonetheless, he worried that if his supervisor had discovered his other errors, the supervisor would have reprimanded him. Through guided discovery, Benjamin realized that the errors that the supervisor had not noticed were no more serious than those he had detected.

Benjamin also believed that if he had made more serious mistakes, his supervisor and coworkers would have judged him harshly. As a result, Benjamin agreed to pay attention to errors that coworkers made to ascertain the consequences. (He generally was so worried and preoccupied with his own work that he did not notice the quality of his coworkers' performance.) After attending to coworkers' job performance for about a month, Benjamin learned that making errors was common. One employee made what Benjamin regarded as a fairly significant error with no resulting job loss, demotion, or public reprimand. Once the error was corrected, within a few days the employee and his supervisor were "business as usual."

[32]Sleep restriction consists of clients' dramatically reducing the amount of time in bed at night. Typically, in response to severe sleep deprivation that occurs with sleep restriction, the quality of sleep quickly improves. As a result of this, clients begin to associate the bed with sleep and relaxation as opposed to anxiety and alertness. Once clients are sleeping soundly for the length of time they are in bed, the amount of time in bed can be gradually increased (e.g., 15 minutes additional every few days). However, for each particular increase in the time in bed, if there is a drop in the quality of sleep (e.g., increased awakenings, feeling unrested in the morning), the sleep time should be cut back to the previous level.

Benjamin completed a Thought Evaluation Worksheet for a hypothetical mistake that was similar in magnitude to ones he had made in the past. The highly anxiety-provoking automatic thought that he addressed was "I'll be reprimanded by my boss and treated with contempt by my coworkers." Box 8.1 illustrates the rational responses that Benjamin and his therapist generated about this hypothetical situation.

Distortion: Fortune-Telling Error.
Evidence for A.T.: Boss has mentioned errors in the past; he has little time for me. (Reframe: he's got a lot on his mind.)
Evidence against A.T.: He's given me positive evaluations and fairly large raises. My boss's boss has been complimentary about my work.
Alternative explanation: Perhaps, he mentioned the errors just to call them to my attention so I could correct them, not to criticize me. It's inevitable that people will make mistakes once in awhile. A minor error once in awhile is unlikely to affect how my work is perceived.
What would I tell a friend in similar situation: It's easy to make this type of mistake. Try to let it go; it's no big deal.
Worst case scenario: I will get a reprimand. Probability: 5%; BUT I would live through it; over time, I would work hard and probably reestablish myself as a good employee.
Best case scenario: The boss and coworkers will think this was really no big deal at all and quickly forget it.
Most realistic scenario: Same as best case!
Advantages of A.T. in this situation: If I am reprimanded, I'll be more prepared; therefore, it will hurt less. BUT, it's extremely unlikely that I'll get reprimanded, so I'm upsetting myself for nothing. Even if I would get reprimanded, I don't need to add to it by putting myself down.
Disadvantages of A.T. in this situation: It makes me very upset. It makes me act in ways that call negative attention to me.
Constructive plan: Focus on my work; when my thoughts go to the mistake, remind myself of the worksheet responses, think about the project I'm working on, or think about something positive.

Box 8.1. Benjamin's Thought Evaluation Worksheet responses for "I'll be reprimanded by my boss and treated with contempt by my coworkers."

As a result of this therapeutic work, Benjamin concluded that making errors probably would not result in dire consequences. His anxiety decreased markedly when he thought of making a minor mistake. Despite this conclusion, he was not yet willing to decrease his perfectionism at work. He held several beliefs that prevented him from lessening his standards. First, he thought "If I relax my guard in one area, I will make huge errors all the time," "If a job's worth doing, it's worth doing well and giving it my all," "If I don't give 110%, I'm lazy and no good," and "If I find that I can relax my standards, it means I've wasted years of my life being worried, not having fun and alienating other people, and it means I'm stupid."

Restructuring "I'm Afraid That If I Relax My Guard in One Area, I Will Make Huge Errors All the Time." As a result of completing Thought Evaluation Worksheets, Benjamin realized that he lacked good evidence for this belief and that the thought was a cognitive distortion (i.e., all-or-nothing thinking). Furthermore, he realized that an alternative, realistic way of looking at this situation was the following: "Relaxing standards will be difficult for me; if anything, I will have a tendency to go back to perfectionism; there really is little danger that I will stop doing at least a good job in most things." This realization made him much less anxious about relaxing his standards.

Restructuring "If a Job's Worth Doing, It's Worth Giving It My All." Through guided discovery, Benjamin realized that some people who are good at what they do and successful do not try to do everything perfectly. He also realized that attempting to do everything perfectly caused him a great deal of stress and consumed a great deal of time. His therapist disclosed that she believed that for herself some jobs were worth doing with excellence, some were worth doing well, some were only worth doing in a mediocre fashion, and some were not worth doing at all. For example, she believed that the benefits of doing a mediocre job sweeping her garage—saving time and effort, far outweighed the costs of having an imperfectly swept garage. Similarly, she enjoyed gardening imperfectly.

Restructuring "If I Don't Do a Job Well, I'm Lazy and No Good." Through guided discovery, Benjamin realized that the distortions in his thinking about performance and self-worth came from internalizing messages from his abusive stepfather. As a result, he adamantly committed to trying to change these beliefs so that his stepfather would stop having power over him.

Restructuring "If I Find That I Can Relax My Standards, It Means I've Wasted Years of My Life Being Worried, Not Having Fun, and Alienating Other People, and It Means I'm Stupid." Again through guided discovery, Benjamin realized that if he could relax his standards, he would likely save many future years of pain for himself. He recognized that calling himself stupid was a distortion (i.e., labeling). To develop empathy for himself, Benjamin's therapist had him reconsider whether it was stupid to internalize this belief. Benjamin admitted that as a child it was adaptive for him to be exacting. Otherwise, his stepfather would have harshly criticized and punished him. When pressed, he admitted that it was indeed smart for him to act this way.

Expressing Emotion Exercises

Expressing emotion exercises were extremely helpful to Benjamin. They contributed to his becoming more compassionate toward himself, modifying his maladpative schemas (e.g., I'm lazy, stupid, and no good), and decreasing his perfectionistic standards. For example, Benjamin's therapist used guided imagery with him to work through representative childhood scenes that contributed to the development of Benjamin's maladaptive beliefs. Chapter 5 described in detail the imagery procedures Benjamin's therapist used to help him successfully modify core beliefs. In sessions, imagery exercises were repeated many times, and Benjamin reported feeling "safer than I've ever felt before knowing that I can take care of and comfort myself." As a result of these exercises, Benjamin frequently came back to images of himself providing comfort, reassurance, and kind words to himself.

Other expressing emotions exercises helped Benjamin gain clarity and self-compassion. Benjamin wrote letters to his deceased mother, his stepfather, and his biological father. He and his therapist used imagery and role playing to give Benjamin opportunities to vent feelings toward them, as well. Benjamin journaled in detail about traumatic childhood events and his most private and distressing automatic thoughts, core beliefs, and emotions associated with the events. In addition, he journaled about links between current upsetting events and childhood events with the associated cognitions and emotions. Benjamin reported that journaling conveyed a variety of benefits for him. It helped him become more objective about what happened to him, it increased forgiveness toward himself, and it helped him separate past traumatic events from current interpersonal events.

Behavioral Experiments

After Benjamin's belief that he must be perfect became weaker, he was willing to begin trying to lessen his standards slightly—first at home and later at work. However, he often had questions about what were reasonable performance standards. As a result, he decided to look toward two people as "gold standards" to get a sense for what might be reasonable performance standards. These individuals did a good job at their work but also seemed to have a balanced perspective. At home, he tried some behavioral experiments to see the effects of modifying his behavior. For example, on an occasion in which he lost his temper with his daughter, he did not retreat. He took a brief walk to cool down but then returned and apologized to her. Benjamin's daughter responded positively to this, and he felt good about how he had handled the situation. (His therapist prepared him for the possibility that he may not get positive results immediately and that he might have to try an experiment several times to give it a fair chance.)

Over several months, Benjamin became proficient at recognizing perfectionistic thinking and labeling it as such. He stopped working unnecessarily long hours and checking over his work multiple times. As a result of decreasing his perfectionism, he made some minor errors at work and saw that no catastrophic consequence occurred. In addition, he intentionally asked for a 2-day extension on a project rather than trying to stay up all night to finish. Previously, he would not have considered this kind of approach for fear of being harshly criticized. Over time, he began to relax his standards, he reported feeling less depressed, more connected with his family than ever before, and felt less anxious at work.

Case 8.C (Catherine): Extreme Standards for Achievement Contribute to Exhaustion, Resulting in Shifts to Depression

Catherine's (Case 8.C) therapist determined that Catherine did not have the possible obstacles to therapy that he initially considered when conceptualizing the case. Specifically, when asked, Catherine indicated that she did not believe that going to therapy was a sign of weakness. In addition, even when busy at work, she planned to make therapy sessions and self-help assignments priorities because she very much wanted to prevent future depressive episodes. Catherine impressed her therapist as being extremely motivated for therapy and quite insightful about her problems. However, at the time of the intake, these insights had not yet led to significant changes in Catherine's approach to life.

Cost-Benefit Analysis

An approach that was helpful for Catherine was a cost-benefit analysis of having the belief that she must be a superstar. Her therapist suggested that she do this in the following areas: sense of self, mental health, relationships, career, spirituality, leisure, and physical health. (Table 8.2 shows her completed cost-benefit analysis.) This approach helped her realize the costs of driving herself to an extreme degree and the benefits of balancing work with self-care and relationships. This realization, in turn, increased her willingness to begin altering her schedule. Table 8.2 illustrates the results of the cost-benefit analysis.

Thought Evaluation Worksheet

In addition, she learned to use Thought Evaluation Worksheets effectively. For example, she completed a worksheet in response to an evening in which she failed to accomplish as much as she had intended. Her most upsetting automatic thought in that situation was "I'm going to be a disgrace," which elicited strong feelings of anger toward herself and intense anxiety. Box 8.2 illustrates her rational responses.

Catherine reportedly benefited from the exercises, although the various conclusions she drew were ones she had considered prior to the exercises. She found that often having a written summary of these was quite compelling and helped her stop overworking.

TABLE 8.2

Cost-Benefit Analysis of Catherine's Belief, "I Must Be a Superstar"

Life Area	*Advantages*	*Disadvantages*
Sense of self	I feel good about myself when I'm being productive and creative.	I feel badly about myself when I'm not productive. Overall, I don't like the rollercoaster of moods. It makes me feel like I'm not normal.
Mental health	None.	Makes me feel "not normal," weak, and disgraceful.
Relationships	None.	Not enough time for friends & love relationships; makes me competitive & no fun to be around → feeling "not normal."
Career	Probably increases my productivity in the short run.	Burns me out. Probably contributes to the cycle of high productivity, exhaustion, and low productivity.
Spirituality	None.	I forget about everything but work; when I'm depressed, I feel spiritually bankrupt.
Leisure	None.	No time for it.
Physical health	None.	May contribute to my hypertension; often don't make time for exercise & to eat properly.

Activity Scheduling to Achieve Balance

Catherine also benefited from activity scheduling. The purpose of activity scheduling for her—in contrast to many individuals with depression who need to increase activities—was to help get her life in balance and prevent exhaustion. This is because her conceptualization suggested that exhaustion and working to the exclusion of taking care of her various needs triggered the switch to her depressed mode. Her new schedule consisted of 10 hours of work per day, Monday through Saturday. This was a dramatic reduction in work hours for her. In addition, she scheduled time for reading the newspaper, relaxing, exercising, and getting together with friends.

Catherine found that attempting to follow a more balanced schedule elicited self-defeating, anxiety-provoking cognitions such as "I must get work done; I've got to make up for lost time; I'm inefficient, so I need to

Distortion: Fortune-telling labeling, mental filter.
Evidence for A.T.: None.
Evidence against A.T.: I rarely miss a deadline; I still have time to meet this one.
Alternative explanation: Missing a deadline does not mean I'm a disgrace; it's quite common for people to ask for extensions on manuscript deadlines; my worth need not depend on productivity; this is an old belief based on my childhood; it's not based in the reality of the situation.
What would I tell a friend in similar situation: Same as alternative explanation.
Worst case scenario: I don't finish the manuscript on time. Probability: 15%; I would live, even if it did happen; it wouldn't hurt my career in any appreciable way; being a few months late on a single deadline wouldn't even affect my chances of getting a book contract with this press again.
Best case scenario: I finish on time; but better yet, regardless of whether I finish on time and am super productive, I begin to like myself and think I'm worthwhile independent of productivity and meeting deadlines.
Most realistic scenario: I finish on time but still define my worth to a large extent on my productivity. However, over many months, I will gradually begin to decouple my worth from my productivity.
Advantages of A.T. in this situation: Makes me work harder, BUT it's often not very productive work.
Disadvantages of A.T. in this situation: Tires me out, makes me feel bad about myself.
Constructive plan: Accept less productive times as natural ebb and flow of human performance; they are unavoidable. Cut down work time by 10–20% (rather than try to increase it to make up for lost time), rest and recharge, do some fun things.

Box 8.2. Catherine's Thought Evaluation Worksheet responses to the thought "I'm going to be a disgrace."

spend more time at this." She worked on Thought Evaluation Worksheets for each of these thoughts that decreased her anxiety and helped her stick to a more balanced schedule.

In addition, Catherine collected data on the quantity and quality of her writing with the new schedule versus the old schedule. For the old schedule, she retrospectively calculated the number of manuscript pages she produced. She found that the quantity of her writing was only about 7% less with the new system. She believed that with the new system she had been more creative, she felt more motivated, happier, and was better rested.

After meeting every other week for several months, Catherine and her therapist decided to terminate therapy. However, they planned to have booster sessions, the first of which occurred three months following termination and subsequently occurred every 6 months. During the 2 years after termination, at the time of this writing, she had no depressive episodes. She felt very positive about her changed lifestyle. She continued to work hard but enjoyed friends, recreational activities, and time for just relaxing. Catherine believed that her new approach was conducive to long-term enjoyment of her career and long-term productivity rather than burnout.

Case 8.D (Mary): Guilt, Self-Hatred, and Alcohol Dependence, Precipitated by Son's Accidental Death That Resulted From Her Mistake

Mary's therapist considered two issues to be likely stumbling blocks to therapy: Mary's alcohol dependence and her belief that she deserved punishment and therefore must not let herself be happy. Concurrent with the start of therapy, Mary participated in an outpatient detox program.

Finding Life Meaning

Because of Mary's intense self-hatred and belief that she deserved punishment, her therapist initially was careful not to challenge Mary's belief that she deserved punishment. In fact, he used her belief that she deserved punishment as a starting point for finding healthier strategies to deal with her pain. Unbeknownst to Mary, the type of "punishment" that the therapist guided her toward was designed to help her begin to forgive herself by having her engage in activities that made a positive contribution to others and gave her life purpose. The therapist presumed that finding such activities might also begin to help Mary reestablish relationships, interests, and attachments that could substitute for what had been lost. According to Klerman et al. (1984), the process of reengaging in people and the world is essential in working through grief.

Therapist: If you don't mind, I'd like to share with you my view on punishment. Let's use prison as an analogy. Society generally likes prison to cause prisoners to suffer. Ideally, prison also helps reform or otherwise improve the offender's behavior.... I'll ask you an obvious question first. Do you feel like you have been suffering since your mistake that led to your son's death?

Mary: Yes, I have been suffering a great deal and deserve every bit of it!

Therapist: OK. So in that regard the punishment has been doing what it's supposed to .... What about the other function of punishment? Would you agree that your punishment has *not* improved your behavior?

Mary: Well, yes. I've been a mess.

Therapist: Mary, the way I see it, you've chosen an ineffective punishment.... Would you be willing to consider other types of punishment that could help you repay your debt to society in some way?

Mary: Let's hear what you have in mind.

Therapist: I don't really have anything in particular in mind. If you're interested, you could think more about the issue. What could you do to repay your debt to society, other people in your life, or to children?.... If you think about this, I'll be very interested in hearing what you come up with.

Mary took these questions very seriously. The next week she indicated to the therapist that she felt some relief that perhaps there was a way out of her guilt and grief. After a couple weeks, she decided that a more effective punishment that would benefit others would be to talk to various groups about the importance of water safety. Her rationale for doing so was that she might help save other children from drowning, honor her own son, and subject herself to public humiliation and scorn, which she felt she deserved. Finally, being an advocate of water safety might give hope to her husband that she was willing to move on with her life.

Mary and her therapist decided that she would be a more persuasive speaker if she waited for a couple months. During that time, she could gain greater control over her consumption of alcohol and perhaps she could begin to work through some of her feelings about her son's death. This helped motivate her to attend AA meetings and take them seriously. She began attending two meetings each week. She also learned all she could about water safety (relating to bathtubs, boating, and swimming) from the Coast Guard Reserves, who had extensive educational programs on this topic.

The therapist also convinced Mary that if her intense self-loathing was detected by her audiences, her message would be lost to many people. He also convinced her that she could not adequately hide her intense negative feelings about herself. Therefore, she reluctantly agreed to work on trying to modify to some degree how she felt about herself.

Grief Work

Therapy followed the guidelines of Klerman et al. (1984) for helping clients with unresolved grief. More specifically, Mary's therapist encouraged her, in a nonjudgmental atmosphere, to feel and think about all aspects of her son's death. The therapist reassured Mary that after a loved one dies, it is natural and often healing to experience a wide range of feelings—including anger at oneself, guilt, shame, fear, anger at the deceased, sadness, and longing. The therapist guided Mary to think and feel about her deceased son and her relationship with him. In addition, he encouraged her to remember the sequence of events before, during and after the death, the consequences of the death, and the meaning of the death. Staying with and accepting these feelings rather than escaping through alcohol or food permitted her to begin to work through the feelings. Mary's therapist was particularly encouraging when Mary began to express feelings other than guilt, anger at herself, and shame. This is because Mary had experienced these latter three feelings to excess. In contrast, Mary had not allowed herself to have other feelings that could have helped her work through her grief.

After several months Mary and her therapist agreed that she was ready to begin talking to groups. She had been abstinent from alcohol for 2 months. She also was beginning to feel slightly less hatred toward herself for making the error that allowed her son to drown. Mary spoke to various groups including scouts, PTAs, churches, synagogues, and schools. After several months of this, she felt positive about this activity. She believed that the groups that she talked to were very interested and attentive and therefore she concluded that the message was getting through to them. Her belief that she deserved punishment began to lessen slightly. She continued to attend AA meetings. After several PTA meetings, she discovered that most parents were grateful to her for her willingness to deliver her message and moved by her story.

As Mary's hatred for herself began to lessen, she began to experience a variety of new feelings. Briefly, she felt anger toward her son for not being more careful in the pool when he died. He had dived into the plastic pool from a stepladder, hit his head and lost consciousness resulting in his drowning. Subsequently, the anger faded, and she felt intense sadness and longing for her lost son. Because of the intensity of these feelings, she took a hiatus from her speaking engagements. However, after several months, she was able to resume speaking to groups.

After 1½ years of therapy, she continued to feel sadness about her son's death. However, she felt less self-hatred, guilt and anger at herself. Other positive changes included feeling good about her community service, becoming closer with her husband, abstaining from drinking, and developing some friendships. She no longer believed at all that she deserved further punishment for her mistake and in fact had developed empathy for herself for experiencing such enormous losses. At this point, she and her therapist terminated therapy.

SUMMARY

This chapter discussed the assessment, case conceptualization, and treatment of individuals with chronic or recurrent major depressive disorder. Several case examples were provided that demonstrated how cognitive case conceptualizations could be effectively used to address potential obstacles to therapy, deactivate depressive responses, and modify depressogenic beliefs. Interventions that were demonstrated with depressed clients included: activity scheduling, the cost-benefit analysis, the Motivation Worksheet, cognitive restructuring, expressing emotion exercises, finding life meaning, grief work, and behavioral experiments.

Appendix: Blank Forms

CASE CONCEPTUALIZATION SUMMARY FORM

Identifying Information:
Presenting Problem:
Precipitant(s):
Exhaustive List of Problems, Issues, and Therapy-Relevant Behaviors:

1.	6.
2.	7.
3.	8.
4.	9.
5.	10.

Relevant Beliefs:

1.	5.
2.	6.
3.	7.
4.	8.

Origins of Core Beliefs:

WORKING MODEL

VICIOUS CYCLES / MAINTAINING FACTORS:

TREATMENT:

Goals:

1.
2.
3.
4.
5.
6.

Possible Obstacles to Treatment:

1.
2.
3.

Plan:

1.
2.
3.
4.
5.
6.
7.

THOUGHT EVALUATION WORKSHEET (side 1)

Name:
Date:
Time:

TRIGGERING SITUATION (objective description of environment or events; who, what where, when, how, but not why)

EMOTIONS (Rate intensity of each, 0-100)

AUTOMATIC THOUGHTS: What is/was going through my mind when I felt that emotion?

Please make sure there are thoughts or images corresponding to each emotion. Also, be sure there are emotions that correspond to each thought.

Are there Automatic Thoughts that account for the intensity of the emotions? If not, search for and record other Automatic Thoughts that may be present and causing the emotion. Rate how much you believe each thought is true (0-100%).

Select one key Automatic Thought above that you want to work on. Select the above Emotion that corresponds to the key Automatic Thought. Write these on the reverse side of the page and use the questions for evaluating the automatic thought.

THOUGHT EVALUATION WORKSHEET (side 2)

AUTOMATIC THOUGHT:

EMOTION:

1. **Is this a thought that I can DISREGARD without further consideration (e.g., is it absurd or is a thought one I've already worked through effectively)?**

2. **Underline any DISTORTIONS that apply to the key thought:**
   All-or-Nothing; Over-Generalization; Mental Filter; Discounting Positives; Mind-Reading; Fortune-Telling; Emotional Reasoning; Magnification/Minimization; "Should's"; Labeling; Personalization

3. **What's the EVIDENCE FOR the Automatic Thought?**

   What's the EVIDENCE AGAINST the Automatic Thought?

4. **What are ALTERNATIVE PERSPECTIVES of the situation?**

   What would I tell a FRIEND if s/he were having the thought in the situation?

5. **What's the WORST that could happen given the situation?**

Could I live through it?
What's the likelihood that this will happen (0-100%):
What would happen over time?

What's the BEST that could happen given the situation?

What's MOST LIKELY to happen given the situation?

6. **What are the ADVANTAGES, if any, of having the Automatic Thought?**

What are the DISADVANTAGES of having the Automatic Thought?

7. **What constructive PLANS can I make given the situation?**

8. **After re-reading answers to questions 1-7, please CIRCLE numbers of the above questions that were most convincing.**
RE-RATE Belief in key Automatic Thought (0-100):
RE-RATE Key Emotion (0-100):

HISTORICAL TEST FOR MODIFYING A CORE BELIEF
(adopted with permission from McKay & Fanning, 1991[1])

Self-Defeating Core Belief: ______________________________

"Evidence" For the Core Belief Plus Challenges	Any Other Evidence Against the Core Belief

[1]McKay and Fanning. (1991). *Prisoners of Belief.* New Harbinger Publications, Oakland, CA 94605; www.harbinger.com.

PROGRESSIVE-RELAXATION MONITORING FORM

Date	Time	Anxiety (Before)	Tension (Before)	Anxiety (After)	Tension (After)	Comments

All ratings are on a scale of 0-10, where 0 = None at All, 5 = Moderate, and 10 = Extreme.

PANIC DISORDER CONCEPTUALIZATION WORKSHEET

Client's Name:

PANIC SCENARIOS

TRIGGERING STIMULI	BENIGN PHYSICAL SENSATIONS	CATASTROPHIC MISINTERPRETATION OF SENSATIONS	SUBTLE OR GROSS SAFETY-SEEKING BEHAVIOR
External:			
Internal:			

AVOIDED SITUATIONS OR INTERNAL STATES

OTHER PROBLEMATIC SCENARIOS

TRIGGERING STIMULI	COGNITIONS	EMOTIONS	BEHAVIORS

OBSESSIVE-COMPULSIVE DISORDER CONCEPTUALIZATION WORKSHEET

Client's Name:

OCD SCENARIOS

TRIGGERING STIMULI	INTRUSIVE COGNITIONS	PATHOLOGICAL INTERPRETATION OF INTRUSIONS	OVERT OR COVERT COMPULSIONS

AVOIDED SITUATIONS OR INTERNAL STATES

OTHER PROBLEMATIC SCENARIOS

TRIGGERING STIMULI	COGNITIONS	EMOTIONS	BEHAVIORS

CASE CONCEPTUALIZATION WORKSHEET FOR DEPRESSION

Client's Name:

TRIGGERING STIMULI	COGNITIONS (CORE BELIEFS CAPITALIZED)	EMOTIONS	BEHAVIOR (Disorder-Maintaining or Adaptive)

References

Abramowitz, J. S. (1997). Effectiveness of psychological and pharmacological treatments for obsessive-compulsive disorder: A quantitative review. *Journal of Consulting and Clinical Psychology, 65,* 44–52.

Abramson, L. Y., Alloy, L. B., & Metalsky, G. I. (1995). Hopelessness depression. In G. M. Buchanan & M. E. P. Seligman (Eds.), *Explanatory style* (pp. 113–134). Hillsdale, NJ: Lawrence Erlbaum Associates.

Abramson, L. Y., Garber, J., Edwards, N. B., & Seligman, M. E. P. (1978). Expectancy changes in depression and schizophrenia. *Journal of Abnormal Psychology, 87,* 49–74.

Abramson, L. Y., Metalsky, G. I., & Alloy, L. B. (1989). Hopelessness depression: A theory-based subtype of depression. *Psychological Review, 96,* 358–372.

Alford, B. A., & Gerrity, D. M. (1995). The specificity of sociotropy-autonomy personality dimensions to depression versus anxiety. *Journal of Clinical Psychology, 51,* 190–195.

Allen, N. B., de L Horne, D. J., & Trinder, J. (1996). Sociotropy, autonomy, and dysphoric emotional responses to specific classes of stress: A psychophysiological evaluation. *Journal of Abnormal Psychology, 105,* 25–33.

American Psychiatric Association. (1994). *The diagnostic and statistical manual of mental disorders* (4th ed.). Washington, DC: Author.

Arntz, A., & van den Hout, M. (1996). Psychological treatments of panic disorder without agoraphobia: Cognitive therapy versus applied relaxation. *Behaviour Research and Therapy, 34,* 113–121.

Azrin, N. H., McMahon, P. T., Donohue, B., & Besalel, V. A. (1994). Behavior therapy for drug abuse: A controlled treatment outcome study. *Behaviour Research and Therapy, 32,* 857–866.

Bandura, A. (1973). *Aggression: A social learning analysis.* Englewood Cliffs, NJ: Prentice-Hall.

Bandura, A. (1986). *Social foundations of thought and action: A social cognitive theory.* Englewood Cliffs, NJ: Prentice-Hall.

Bandura, A., Blanchard, E. D., & Ritter, B. (1969). Relative efficacy of desensitization and modeling approaches for inducing behavioral, affective, and attitudinal changes. *Journal of Personality and Social Psychology, 12,* 173.

Bandura, A., & Cervone, D. (1983). Self-evaluative and self-efficacy mechanisms governing the motivational effects of goal systems. *Journal of Personality and Social Psychology, 45*, 1017–1028.
Barlow, D. H. (1988). *Anxiety and its disorders.* New York: Guilford.
Barlow, D. H., & Cerny, J. A. (1988). *Psychological treatment of panic.* New York: Guilford.
Beck, A. T. (1963). Thinking and depression: 1, Idiosyncratic content and cognitive distortions. *Archives of General Psychiatry, 9*, 324–333.
Beck, A. T. (1967). *Depression: Clinical, experimental, and theoretical aspects.* New York: Hoeber.
Beck, A. T. (1987). Cognitive models of depression. *Journal of Cognitive Psychotherapy, 1*, 2–27.
Beck, A. T. (1988). *Love is never enough.* New York: Harper & Row.
Beck, A. T. (1991). Cognitive therapy: A 30–year retrospective. *American Psychologist, 46*, 368–375.
Beck, A. T. (1996). Beyond belief: A theory of modes, personality, and psychopathology. In P. M. Salkovskis (Ed.), *Frontiers of cognitive therapy* (pp. 1–25). New York: Guilford.
Beck, A. T., Brown, G., Berchick, R. J., Stewart, B. L., & Steer, R. A. (1990). Relationship between hopelessness and ultimate suicide: A replication with psychiatric outpatients. *American Journal of Psychiatry, 147*, 190–195.
Beck, A. T., & Clark, D. A. (1997). An information processing model of anxiety: Automatic and strategic processes. *Behaviour Research and Therapy, 35*, 49–58.
Beck, A. T., Emery, G., & Greenberg, R. L. (1985). *Anxiety disorders and phobias: A cognitive perspective.* New York: Basic Books.
Beck, A. T., Epstein, N., Harrison, R. P., & Emery, G. (1983). *Development of the Sociotropy-Autonomy Scale: A measure of personality factors in psychopathology.* Unpublished manuscript, Center for Cognitive Therapy, University of Pennsylvania Medical Center, Philadelphia.
Beck, A. T., Freeman, A., Pretzer, J., Davis, D. D., Fleming, B., Ottaviani, R., Beck, J., Simon, K. M., Padesky, C., Meyer, J., & Trexler, L. (1990). *Cognitive therapy of personality disorders.* New York: Guilford.
Beck, A. T., Kovacs, M., & Weissman, A. (1979). Assessment of suicidal intention: The Scale for Suicide Ideation. *Journal of Consulting and Clinical Psychology, 47*, 343–352.
Beck, A. T., Riskind, J. H., Brown, G., & Steer, R. A. (1988). Levels of hopelessness in *DSM–III* disorders: A partial test of content-specificity in depression. *Cognitive Therapy and Research, 12*, 459–469.
Beck, A. T., Rush, A. J., Shaw, B. F., & Emery, G. (1979). *Cognitive therapy of depression.* New York: Guilford.
Beck, A. T., Sokol, L., Clark, D. A., Berchick, R., & Wright, F. (1992). Focused cognitive therapy of panic disorder: A crossover design and one year follow-up. *American Journal of Psychiatry, 149*, 778–783.
Beck, A. T., Steer, R. A., Ball, R., & Ranieri, W. F. (1996). Comparison of Beck Depression Inventories–IA and –II in psychiatric outpatients. *Journal of Personality Assessment, 67*, 588–597.

Beck, A. T., Steer, R. A., Epstein, N., & Brown, G. (1990). The Beck Self-Concept Test. *Psychological Assessment: A Journal of Consulting and Clinical Psychology, 2*, 191–197.

Beck, A. T., Weissman, A., Lester, D., & Trexler, L. (1974). The measurement of pessimism: The Hopelessness Scale. *Journal of Consulting and Clinical Psychology, 72*, 861–865.

Beck, A. T., Wright, F. D., Newman, C. F., & Liese, B. S. (1993). *Cognitive therapy of substance abuse.* New York: Guilford.

Beck, J. S. (1995). *Cognitive therapy: Basics and beyond.* New York: Guilford.

Becona, E., & Garcia, M. P. (1995). Relation between the Tolerance Questionnaire (nicotine dependence) and assessment of carbon monoxide in smokers who participated in treatment for smoking. *Psychological Reports, 77*, 1299–1304.

Bettelheim, B. (1975). *The uses of enchantment: The meaning and importance of fairy tales.* New York: Vintage Books.

Blagden, J. C., & Craske, M. G. (1996). Effects of active and passive rumination and distraction: A pilot replication with anxious mood. *Journal of Anxiety Disorders, 10*, 243–252.

Blatt, S. J., Quinlan, D. M., Pilkonis, P. A., & Shea, M. T. (1995). Impact of perfectionism and need for approval on the brief treatment of depression: The National Institute of Mental Health Treatment of Depression Collaborative Research Program revisited. *Journal of Consulting and Clinical Psychology, 63*, 125–132.

Booth, R. J., Petrie, K. J., & Pennebaker, J. W. (1997). Changes in circulating lymphocyte numbers following emotional disclosure: Evidence of buffering? *Stress Medicine, 13*, 23–29.

Bouchard, S., Gauthier, J., LaBerge, B., French, D., Pelletier, M., & Godbout, C. (1996). Exposure versus cognitive restructuring in the treatment of panic disorder with agoraphobia. *Behaviour Research and Therapy, 34*, 213–224.

Boulougouris, J. C., Rabavilas, A. D., & Stefanis, C. (1977). Psycho-physiological responses in obsessive-compulsive patients. *Behaviour Research and Therapy, 15*, 221–230.

Bowlby, J. (1980). *Loss, sadness, and depression.* New York: Basic Books.

Brown, J. D. (1990). Evaluating one's abilities: Shortcuts and stumbling blocks on the road to self-knowledge. *Journal of Experimental Social Psychology, 26*, 149–167.

Brown, R. W. (1973). *A first language: The early stages.* Cambridge, MA: Harvard University Press.

Brown, G. K., Beck, A. T., Newman, C. F., Beck, J. S., & Tran, G. Q. (1997). A comparison of focused and standard cognitive therapy for panic disorder. *Journal of Anxiety Disorders, 11*, 329–345.

Burns, D. D. (1980). *Feeling good: The new mood therapy.* New York: William Morrow.

Burns, D. D. (1989). *The feeling good handbook.* New York: William Morrow.

Burns, D. D., & Auerbach, A. (1996). Therapeutic empathy in cognitive-behavioral therapy: Does it really make a difference? In P. M. Salkovskis (Ed.), *Frontiers of cognitive therapy* (pp. 135–164). New York: Guilford.

Burns, D. D., & Nolen-Hoeksema, S. (1992). Therapeutic empathy and recovery from depression in cognitive-behavioral therapy: A structural equation model. *Journal of Consulting and Clinical Psychology, 59,* 305–311.

Campbell, J. (1972). *Myths to live by.* New York: Bantam Books.

Carey, M. P., Flasher, L. V., Maisto, S. A., & Turkat, I. D. (1984). The a priori approach to psychological assessment. *Professional Psychology: Research and Practice, 15,* 515–527.

Chambless, D. L., Caputo, G. C., Bright, P., & Gallagher, R. (1984). Assessment of fear of fear in agoraphobics: The body sensations questionnaire and the agoraphobic cognitions questionnaire. *Journal of Consulting and Clinical Psychology, 52,* 1090–1097.

Chambless, D. L., Caputo, G. C., Jasin, S. E., Gracely, E. J., & Williams, C. (1985). The mobility inventory for agoraphobia. *Behaviour Research and Therapy, 23,* 33–44.

Chambless, D. L., Foa, E. B., Groves, G. A., & Goldstein, A. J. (1982). Exposure and communications training in the treatment of agoraphobia. *Behaviour Research and Therapy, 20,* 219–231.

Chambless, D. L., & Hope, D. A. (1996). Cognitive approaches to the psychopathology and treatment of social phobia. In P. M. Salkovskis (Ed.), *Frontiers of cognitive therapy* (pp. 345–382). New York: Guilford.

Chomsky, N. A. (1965). *Aspects of the theory of syntax.* Cambridge, MA: MIT.

Clark, D. A., & Beck, A. T. (1991). Personality factors in dysphoria: Psychometric refinement of Beck's Sociotropy-Autonomy Scale. *Journal of Psychopathology and Behavioral Assessment, 13,* 369–388.

Clark, D. A., Beck, A. T., & Brown, G. K. (1992). Sociotropy, autonomy, and life event perceptions in dysphoric and nondysphoric individuals. *Cognitive Therapy and Research, 16,* 635–652.

Clark, D. A., & Oates, T. (1995). Daily hassles, major and minor life events, and their interaction with sociotropy and autonomy. *Behaviour Research and Therapy, 33,* 819–823.

Clark, D. A., Ross, L., Beck, A. T., & Steer, R. A. (1995). Psychometric characteristics of Revised Sociotropy and Autonomy Scales in college students. *Behaviour Research and Therapy, 33,* 325–334.

Clark, D. A., & Steer, R. A. (1996). Empirical status of the cognitive model of anxiety and depression. In P. M. Salkovskis (Ed.), *Frontiers of cognitive therapy* (pp. 75–96). New York: Guilford.

Clark, D. A., Steer, R. A., Haslam, N., Beck, A. T., & Brown, G. K. (1997). Personality vulnerability, psychiatric diagnoses, and symptoms: Cluster analyses of the Sociotropy-Autonomy Subscales. *Cognitive Therapy and Research, 21,* 267–283.

Clark, D. M. (1986). A cognitive approach to panic. *Behaviour research and therapy, 24,* 461–470.

Clark, D. M., Salkovskis, P. M., Hackmann, A., Middleton, H., Anastasiades, P., & Gelder, M. (1994). A comparison of cognitive therapy, applied relaxation and imipramine in the treatment of panic disorder. *British Journal of Psychiatry, 164,* 759–769.

Clum, G. A., Broyles, S., Borden, J., & Watkins, P. L. (1990). Validity and reliability of Panic Attack Symptoms and Cognitions Questionnaires. *Journal of Psychopathology and Behavioral Assessment, 12,* 233–245.

Csikszentmihalyi, M. (1990). *Flow: The psychology of optimal experience.* New York: Harper & Row.

Davey, G. C. (1992). An expectancy model of laboratory preparedness effects. *Journal of Experimental Psychology: General, 121,* 24–40.

Davey, G. C. (1995). Preparedness and phobias: Specific evolved associations or a generalized expectancy bias? *Behavioral and Brain Sciences, 18,* 289–325.

Davidson, G. C., & Neale, J. M. (1994). *Abnormal psychology* (6th ed.). New York: Wiley.

Dobson, K. S. (1989). A meta-analysis of the efficacy of cognitive therapy for depression. *Journal of Consulting and Clinical Psychology, 57,* 414–419.

D'Zurilla, T. J. (1988). Problem-solving therapies. In K. S. Dobson (Ed.), *Handbook of cognitive-behavioral therapies* (pp. 85–135). New York: Guilford.

Edwards, S., & Dickerson, M. (1987). On the similarity of positive and negative intrusions. *Behaviour Research and Therapy, 25,* 207–211.

Egan, G. (1982). *The skilled helper: A model for systematic helping and interpersonal relating.* Monterey, CA: Brooks/Cole.

Ekman, P. (1993). Facial expression and emotion. *American Psychologist, 48,* 384–392.

Ellis, A. (1977a). Fun as psychotherapy. *Rational Living, 12,* 2–6.

Ellis, A. (Speaker). (1977b). *A garland of rational humorous songs* (cassette recording). New York: Institute for Rational-Emotive Living.

Ellis, A. (1981). The use of rational humorous songs in psychotherapy. *Voices, 16,* 29–36.

Ellis, A., & Dryden, W. (1987). *The practice of rational emotive therapy.* New York: Springer.

Emmelkamp, P. M., & Beens, H. (1991). Cognitive therapy with obsessive-compulsive disorder: A comparative evaluation. *Behaviour Research and Therapy, 29,* 293–300.

Emmelkamp, P. M., van Linden van den Heuvell, C., Ruphan, M., & Sanderman, R. (1989). Home-based treatment of obsessive-compulsive patients: Intersession interval and therapist involvement. *Behaviour Research and Therapy, 18,* 61–66.

Emmelkamp, P. M., & Wessels, H. (1975). Flooding in imagination vs. flooding in vivo: A comparison with agoraphobics. *Behaviour Research and Therapy, 13,* 7–16.

Epstein, M. (1995). *Thoughts without a thinker.* New York: Basic Books.

Erikson, E. (1950). *Childhood and society* (2nd ed.). New York: W. W. Norton.

Evans, M. D., Hollon, S. D., DeRubeis, R. J., Piasecki, J. M., Garvery, M. J., Grove, W. M., & Tuason, V. B. (1992). Differential relapse following cognitive therapy, pharmacotherapy, and combined cognitive-pharmacotherapy for depression. *Archives of General Psychiatry, 49,* 802–808.

Fabry, J. (1988). *Guideposts to meaning.* Oakland, CA: New Harbinger.

Fabry, J. (1998). The calls of meaning. In P. T. P. Wong & P. S. Fry (Eds.), *The quest for human meaning* (pp. 295–305). Hillsdale, NJ: Lawrence Erlbaum Associates.

Fairburn, C. G., Marcus, M., & Wilson, G. T. (1993). Cognitive-behavioral therapy for binge eating and bulimia nervosa. In C. G. Fairburn & G. T. Wilson (Eds.), *Binge eating: Nature, assessment and treatment* (pp. 361–404). New York: Guilford.

First, M. B., Gibbon, M., Spitzer, R. L., Williams, J. B., & Benjamin, L. (1997). *Structured Clinical Interview for* DSM–IV, *Axis II Personality Disorders, Clinician Version.* Washington, DC: American Psychiatric Association.

First, M. B., Spitzer, R. L., Gibbon, M., & Williams, J. B. (1997). *Structured Clinical Interview for* DSM–IV, *Axis I Disorders, Administration Booklet.* Washington, DC: American Psychiatric Association.

Fischer, J., & Corcoran, K. (1994). *Measures for clinical practice: A sourcebook* (2nd ed.). New York: The Free Press.

Fiske, S. T. (1993). Social cognition and social perceptions. *Annual Review of Psychology, 44,* 155–194.

Fiske, S. T., & Taylor, S. E. (1984). *Social cognition.* Reading, MA: Addison-Wesley.

Fiske, S. T., & Taylor, S. E. (1991). *Social cognition* (2nd ed.). New York: McGraw-Hill.

Foa, E. B., & Goldstein, A. (1978). Continuous exposure and complete response prevention of obsessive-compulsive neurosis. *Behavior Therapy, 9,* 821–829.

Foa, E. B., McNally, R. J., Steketee, G. S., & McCarthy, P. R. (1991). A test of preparedness theory in anxiety-disordered patients using an avoidance paradigm. *Journal of Psychophysiology, 5,* 159–163.

Foa, E. B., & Steketee, G. S. (1987). Behavioral treatment of phobics and obsessive-compulsives. In N. S. Jacobson (Ed.), *Psychotherapists in clinical practice: Cognitive and behavioral perspectives* (pp. 78–120). New York: Guilford.

Foa, E. B., Steketee, G. S., & Milby, J. B. (1980). Differential effects of exposure and response prevention in obsessive compulsive washers. *Journal of Consulting and Clinical Psychology, 48,* 71–79.

Folstein, M. F., Folstein, S. E., & McHugh, P. R. (1975). Mini-mental state: A practical method for grading the cognitive state of patients for clinicians. *Journal of Psychiatric Research, 12,* 189.

Ford, M. E. (1992). *Motivating humans: Goals, emotions, and personal agency beliefs.* Newbury Park, CA: Sage.

Frankl, V. E. (1959). *The doctor and the soul.* New York: Vintage.

Frankl, V. E. (1984). *Man's search for meaning.* New York: Simon & Schuster. (Original work published 1959)

Freeman, A., & Leaf, R. C. (1989). Cognitive therapy applied to personality disorders. In A. Freeman, K. M. Simon, L. E. Beutler, & H. Arkowitz (Eds.), *Comprehensive handbook of cognitive therapy* (pp. 403–433). New York: Plenum.

Freeman, A., & Reinecke, M. A. (1993). *Cognitive therapy of suicidal behavior: A manual for treatment.* New York: Springer.

Freeman, A., & Simon, K. M. (1989). Cognitive therapy of anxiety. In A. Freeman, K. M. Simon, L. E. Beutler, & H. Arkowitz (Eds.), *Comprehensive handbook of cognitive therapy* (pp. 347–365). New York: Plenum.

Freeman, A., & White, D. M. (1989). Cognitive therapy of suicidal behavior. In A. Freeman, K. M. Simon, L. E. Beutler, & H. Arkowitz (Eds.), *Comprehensive handbook of cognitive therapy* (pp. 321–346). New York: Plenum.

Freeston, M. H., & Ladouceur, R. (1993). Appraisal of cognitive intrusions and response style. Replication and extension. *Behaviour Research and Therapy, 31,* 181–191.

Freeston, M. H., Rhéaume, J., & Ladouceur, R. (1996). Correcting faulty appraisals of obsessional thoughts. *Behaviour Research and Therapy, 34,* 433–446.

French, S. A., Jeffery, R. W., & Wing, R. R. (1994). Sex differences among participants in a weight-control program. *Addictive Behaviors, 19,* 147–158.

Frost, R. O., Marten, P., Lahart, C., & Rosenblate, R. (1990). The dimensions of perfectionism. *Cognitive Therapy and Research, 14,* 449–468.

Frost, R. O., & Steketee, G. (1997). Perfectionism in obsessive-compulsive disorder patients. *Behaviour Research and Therapy, 35,* 291–296.

Gambrill, E. D., & Richey, C. A. (1975). An assertion inventory for use in assessment and research. *Behavior Therapy, 6,* 550–561.

Garcia, J., & Koelling, R. A. (1966). The relation of cue to consequence in avoidance learning. *Psychonomic Science, 4,* 123–124.

Gelder, M. G., Bancroft, J. H., Gath, D. H., Johnston, D. W., Mathews, A. M., & Shaw, P. M. (1973). Specific and non-specific factors in behaviour therapy. *British Journal of Psychiatry, 123,* 445–462.

Gibbs, N. A. (1996). Nonclinical populations in research on obsessive-compulsive disorder: A critical review. *Clinical Psychology Review, 16,* 729–773.

Goodman, W. K., Rasmussen, S. A., Price, L. H., Mazure, D., Heninger, G. R., & Charney, D. S. (1989). The Yale-Brown Obsessive Compulsive Scale: I. Development, use, and reliability. *Archives of General Psychiatry, 46,* 1006–1010.

Gottman, J. (1994). *Why marriages succeed or fail.* New York: Simon & Schuster.

Grayson, J. B., Foa, E. B., & Steketee, G. (1982). Habituation during exposure treatment: Distraction vs attention-focusing. *Behaviour Research and Therapy, 20,* 323–328.

Grayson, J. B., Nutter, D., & Mavissakalian, M. (1980). Psychophysiological assessment of imagery in obsessive-compulsives: A pilot study. *Behaviour Research and Therapy, 18,* 590–593.

Greenberg, L. S., Rice, L. N., & Elliott, R. (1993). *Facilitating emotional change.* New York: Guilford.

Greenberg, P. E., Stiglin, L. E., Finklestein, S. N., & Berndt, E. R. (1993). The economic burden of depression in 1990. *Journal of Clinical Psychiatry, 54,* 405–418.

Gupta, P., Banerjee, G., & Nandi, D. N. (1989). Modified Masters Johnson technique in the treatment of sexual inadequacy in males. *Indian Journal of Psychiatry, 31,* 63–69.

Hammen, C., Ellicott, A., Gitlin, M., & Jamison, K. R. (1989). Sociotropy/autonomy and vulnerability to specific life events in patients with unipolar depression and bipolar disorders. *Journal of Abnormal Psychology, 98,* 154–160.

Hastie, R. (1981). Schematic principles in human memory. In E. T. Higgins, C. Herman, & M. Zanna (Eds.), *Social cognition: The Ontario symposium on personality and social psychology* (Vol. 1). Hillsdale, NJ: Lawrence Erlbaum Associates.

Hauri, P., & Linde, S. (1990). *No more sleepless nights.* New York: Wiley.

Hawton, K., & Kirk, J. (1989). Problem solving. In K. Hawton, P. M. Salkovskis, J. Kirk, & D. M. Clark (Eds.), *Cognitive behaviour therapy for psychiatric problems: A practical guide* (pp. 406–426). New York: Oxford University Press.

Hewitt, P. L., & Flett, G. L. (1990). Perfectionism and depression: A multidimensional analysis. *Journal of Social Behavior and Personality, 5,* 423–438.

Hewitt, P. L., & Flett, G. L. (1991a). Dimensions of perfectionism in unipolar depression. *Journal of Abnormal Psychology, 100,* 98–101.

Hewitt, P. L., & Flett, G. L. (1991b). Perfectionism in the self and social contexts: Conceptualization, assessment, and association with psychopathology. *Journal of Personality and Social Psychology, 60,* 456–470.

Hewitt, P. L., & Flett, G. L. (1993). Dimensions of perfectionism, daily stress, and depression: A test of the specific vulnerability hypothesis. *Journal of Abnormal Psychology, 102,* 58–65.

Hewitt, P. L., Flett, G. L., & Ediger, E. (1996). Perfectionism and depression: Longitudinal assessment of a specific vulnerability hypothesis. *Journal of Abnormal Psychology, 105,* 276–280.

Hewitt, P. L., Mittelstaedt, W. M., & Flett, G. L. (1990). Self-oriented perfectionism and generalized performance importance in depression. *Individual Psychology: Journal of Adlerian Theory, Research and Practice, 46,* 67–73.

Hillenberg, J., & Collins, J. (1982). A procedural analysis and review of relaxation training research. *Behaviour Research and Therapy, 30,* 251–260.

Hodgson, R. J., & Rachman, S. (1977). Obsessive-compulsive complaints. *Behaviour Research and Therapy, 15,* 389–395.

Hodgson, R. J., Rachman, S., & Marks, I. M. (1972). The treatment of chronic obsessive-compulsive neurosis: Follow-up and further findings. *Behaviour Research and Therapy, 10,* 181–189.

Hoffart, A. (1995). A comparison of cognitive and guided mastery therapy of agoraphobia. *Behaviour Research and Therapy, 33,* 423–434.

Hollon, S. D., DeRubeis, R. J., Evans, M. D., Wiemer, M. J., Garvery, M. J., Grove, W. M., & Tuason, V. B. (1992). Cognitive therapy and pharmacotherapy for depression: Singly and in combination. *Archives of General Psychiatry, 49,* 774–781.

Hollon, S. D., Shelton, R. C., & Davis, D. D. (1993). Cognitive therapy for depression: Conceptual issues and clinical efficacy. *Journal of Consulting and Clinical Psychology, 61,* 270–275.

Hollon, S. D., Shelton, R. C., & Loosen, P. T. (1991). Cognitive therapy and pharmacotherapy for depression. *Journal of Consulting and Clinical Psychology, 59,* 88–99.

Honeybourne, C., Matchett, G., & Davey, G. C. (1993). Expectancy models of laboratory preparedness effects: A UCS-expectancy bias in phylogenetic and ontogenetic fear-relevant stimuli. *Behavior Therapy, 24,* 253–264.

Hornsveld, R. J. J., Kraaimaat, F. W., & van Dam-Baggen, R. M. J. (1979). Anxiety/discomfort and handwashing in obsessive-compulsive and psychiatric control patients. *Behaviour Research and Therapy, 17,* 223–228.

Hugdahl, K., & Johnsen, B. H. (1989). Preparedness and electrodermal fear-conditioning: Ontogenetic vs. phylogenetic explanations. *Behaviour Research and Therapy, 27,* 269–278.

Izard, C. E. (1971). *The face of emotion.* New York: Appleton-Century-Crofs.

Jacobson, E. (1938). *Progressive relaxation* (Rev. ed.). Chicago: University of Chicago.

Jacobson, N. S., Dobson, K. S., Truax, P. A., Addis, M. E., Koerner, K., Gollan, J. K., Gortner, E., & Prince, S. E. (1996). A component analysis of cognitive-behavioral treatment for depression. *Journal of Consulting and Clinical Psychology, 64,* 295–304.

Kabat-Zinn, J. (1990). *Full catastrophe living: Using the wisdom of your body and mind to face stress, pain, and illness.* New York: Dell Publishing.

Kabat-Zinn, J. (1994). *Wherever you go, there you are.* New York: Hyperion.

Kabat-Zinn, J., Lipworth, L., & Burney, R. (1985). The clinical use of mindfulness meditation for the self-regulation of chronic pain. *Journal of Behavioral Medicine, 8,* 163–190.

Kabat-Zinn, J., Massion, A. O., Kristeller, J., & Peterson, L. G. (1992). Effectiveness of a meditation-based stress reduction program in the treatment of anxiety disorders. *American Journal of Psychiatry, 149,* 936–943.

Kaelber, C. T., Moul, D. E., & Farmer, M. E. (1995). Epidemiology of depression. In E. E. Beckham & W. R. Leber (Eds.), *Handbook of depression* (2nd ed., pp. 3–35). New York: Guilford.

Kagan, J. (1984). *The nature of the child.* New York: Basic Books.

Kandel, E. R., & Schwartz, J. H. (1985). *Principles of neural science* (2nd ed.). New York: Elsevier.

Kanfer, F. H., & Gaelick, L. (1986). Self-management methods. In F. H. Kanfer & A. P. Goldstein (Eds.), *Helping people change* (3rd ed., pp. 283–345). New York: Pergamon.

Kanfer, F. H., & Schefft, B. K. (1987). Self-management therapy in clinical practice. In N. S. Jacobson (Ed.), *Psychotherapists in clinical practice: Cognitive and behavioral perspectives* (pp. 10–77). New York: Guilford.

Kasvikis, Y., & Marks, I. M. (1988). Clomipramine, self-exposure and therapist-accompanied exposure in OCD: Two-year follow-up. *Journal of Anxiety Disorders, 2,* 291–298.

Kaplan, H. S. (1989). *How to overcome premature ejaculation.* New York: Brunner/Mazel.

Kiesler, D. J. (1979). An interpersonal communication analysis of relationship in psychotherapy. *Psychiatry, 42,* 299–311.

Kirk, J. W. (1983). Behavioural treatment of obsessional-compulsive patients in routine clinical practice. *Behaviour Research and Therapy, 21,* 57–62.

Klerman, G. L., Weissman, M. M., Rounsaville, B. J., & Chevron, E. S. (1984). *Interpersonal psychotherapy of depression.* New York: Basic Books.

Kolenberg, R. J., & Tsai, M. (1987). Functional analytic psychotherapy. In N. S. Jacobson (Ed.), *Psychotherapists in clinical practice: Cognitive and behavioral perspectives* (pp. 388–444). New York: Guilford.

Kozak, M. J., Foa, E. B., & Steketee, G. (1988). Process and outcome of exposure treatment with obsessive-compulsives: Psychophysiological indicators of emotional processing. *Behavior Therapy, 19,* 157–169.

Kruglanski, A. W., & Mayseless, O. (1990). Classic and current social comparison research: Expanding the perspective. *Psychological Bulletin, 108,* 195–208.

Lacks, P. (1987). *Behavioral treatment for persistent insomnia.* New York: Pergamon.

Ladouceur, R., Leger, E., & Rhéaume, J. (1995). Cognitive treatment of compulsive checkers. *Behaviour Research and Therapy, 34,* 767–774.

Ladouceur, R., Rhéaume, J., & Aublet, F. (1997). Excessive responsibility in obsessional concerns: A fine-grained experimental analysis. *Behaviour Research and Therapy, 35,* 423–427.

Layden, M. A., Newman, C. F., Freeman, A., & Morse, S. B. (1993). *Cognitive therapy of borderline personality disorder.* Nedham Heights, MA: Allyn & Bacon.

Lazarus, A. A. (1977). *In the mind's eye: The power of imagery for personal enrichment.* New York: Guilford.

Lazarus, A. A., & Lazarus, C. N. (1991). *Multimodal Life History Questionnaire* (2nd ed.). Champaign, IL: Research Press.

Lelliott, P. T., Noshirvani, H. F., Marks, I. M., & Monteiro, W. O. (1987). Relationship of skin conductance activity to clinical features in obsessive-compulsive ritualizers. *Psychological Medicine, 17,* 905–914.

Lepore, S. J. (1997). Expressive writing moderates the relation between intrusive thoughts and depressive symptoms. *Journal of Personality and Social Psychology, 73,* 1030–1037.

Lewinsohn, P. M., & Gotlib, I. H. (1995). Behavioral theory and treatment of depression. In E. E. Beckham & W. R. Leber (Eds.), *Handbook of depression* (2nd ed., pp. 352–375). New York: Guilford.

Lewinsohn, P. M., Sullivan, J. M., & Grosscup, S. J. (1980). Changing reinforcing events: An approach to the treatment of depression. *Psychotherapy: Theory, Research, and Practice, 47,* 322–334.

Libet, J., & Lewinsohn, P. M. (1973). The concept of social skill with special reference to the behavior of depressed persons. *Journal of Consulting and Clinical Psychology, 40,* 304–312.

Liese, B. S., & Franz, R. A. (1996). Treating substance use disorders with cognitive therapy: Lessons learned and implications for the future. In P. M. Salkovskis (Ed.), *Frontiers of cognitive therapy* (pp. 470–508). New York: Guilford.

Linehan, M. M. (1993a). *Cognitive-behavioral treatment of borderline personality disorder.* New York: Guilford.

Linehan, M. M. (1993b). *Skills training manual for treating borderline personality disorder.* New York: Guilford.

Linehan, M. M., Heard, H. L., & Armstrong, H. E. (1993). Naturalistic follow-up of a behavioral treatment for chronically parasuicidal borderline patients. *Archives of General Psychiatry, 50,* 971–974.

Linehan, M. M., Tutek, D. A., Heard, H. L., & Armstrong, H. E. (1994). Interpersonal outcome of cognitive behavioral treatment for chronically suicidal borderline patients. *American Journal of Psychiatry, 151,* 1771–1776.

Linker, C. A. (1991). Blood. In S. A. Schroeder, M. A. Krupp, L. M. Tierney, & S. J. McPhee (Eds.), *Current medical diagnosis and treatment* (pp. 344–395). Englewood Cliffs, NJ: Appleton & Lang.

Logan, F. A. (1965). Decision making by rats: Delay versus amount of reward. *Journal of Comparative and Physiological Psychology, 59,* 1–12.

Lopatka, C., & Rachman, S. (1995). Perceived responsibility and compulsive checking: An experimental analysis. *Behaviour Research and Therapy, 33,* 673–684.

Lovibond, P. F., Siddle, D. A., & Bond, N. W. (1993). Resistance to extinction of fear-relevant stimuli: Preparedness or selective sensitization? *Journal of Experimental Psychology: General, 122,* 449–461.

MacPhillamy, D. J., & Lewinsohn, P. M. (1975). *Pleasant Events Schedule.* University of Oregon.

Magraf, J., & Schneider, S. (1991, November 26). *Outcome and active ingredients of cognitive-behavioral treatments for panic disorder.* Paper presented at the Annual Conference of the Association for Advancement of Behavior Therapy, New York.

Marchione, K. E., Michelson, L., Greenwald, M., & Dancu, C. (1987). Cognitive behavioral treatment of agoraphobia. *Behaviour Research and Therapy, 25,* 319–328.

Markowitz, J., Weissman, M., & Quellette, R. (1989). Quality of life in panic disorder. *Archives of General Psychiatry, 46,* 984–992.

Marks, I. M., Boulougouris, J., & Marset, P. (1971). Flooding versus desensitization in the treatment of phobic patients. *British Journal of Psychiatry, 119,* 353–375.

Marks, I. M., Hodgson, R., & Rachman, S. (1975). Treatment of chronic obsessive-compulsive disorder by in vivo exposure: A two-year follow-up and issues in treatment. *British Journal of Psychiatry, 127,* 349–364.

Marks, I. M., & Mathews, A. M. (1979). Brief standard self-rating for phobic patients. *Behaviour Research and Therapy, 17,* 263–267.

Masters, W. H., & Johnson, V. E. (1988). *Human sexuality* (3rd ed.). Boston: Little Brown.

Mathews, A. M., Johnston, D. W., Lancashire, M., Munby, D., Shaw, P. M., & Gelder, M. G. (1976). Imaginal flooding and exposure to real phobic situations: Treatment outcome with agoraphobic patients. *British Journal of Psychiatry, 129,* 362–371.

Maxmen, J. S., & Ward, N. G. (1995). *Psychotropic drugs: Fast facts* (2nd ed.). New York: W. W. Norton.

McCabe, M. P. (1992). A program for the treatment of inhibited sexual desire in males. *Psychotherapy,* 29, 288–296.

McCranie, E. W., & Riley, W. T. (1992). Hopelessness and persistence of depression in an inpatient sample. *Cognitive Therapy and Research. 16,* 699–708.

McGinn, L. K., & Young, J. E. (1996). Schema-focused therapy. In P. M. Salkovskis (Ed.), *Frontiers of cognitive therapy* (pp. 182–207). New York: Guilford.

McKay, M., & Fanning, P. (1991). *Prisoners of belief.* Oakland, CA: New Harbinger.

Michelson, L. K., Marchione, K. E., Greenwald, M., Testa, S., & Marchione, N. J. (1996). A comparative outcome and follow-up investigation of panic disorder with agoraphobia: The relative combined efficacy of cognitive therapy, relaxation training, and therapist-assisted exposure. *Journal of Anxiety Disorders, 10,* 297–330.

Michelson, L. K., Mavissakalian, M., & Marchione, K. E. (1985). Cognitive and behavioral treatments of agoraphobia: Clinical, behavioral, and psychophysiological outcomes. *Journal of Consulting and Clinical Psychology, 53,* 913–925.

Miller, J. J., Fletcher, K., & Kabat-Zinn, J. (1995). Three-year follow-up and clinical implications of a mindfulness meditation-based stress reduction intervention in the treatment of anxiety disorders. *General Hospital Psychiatry, 17,* 192–200.

Moore, R. G., & Blackburn, I. M. (1994). The relationship of sociotropy and autonomy to symptoms, cognition and personality in depressed patients. *Journal of Affective Disorders, 32,* 239–245.

Morin, C. M., Culbert, J. P., & Schwartz, S. M. (1994). Nonpharmacological interventions for insomnia: A meta-analysis of treatment efficacy. *American Journal of Psychiatry, 151,* 1172–1180.

Morrow, J., & Nolen-Hoeksema, S. (1990). Effects of responses to depression on the remediation of depressive affect. *Journal of Personality and Social Psychology, 58,* 519–527.

Nathanson, D. L. (1992). *Shame and pride.* New York: Norton.

Nolen-Hoeksema, S. (1987). Sex differences in unipolar depression: Evidence and theory. *Psychological Bulletin, 101,* 259–282.

Nolen-Hoeksema, S. (1991). Responses to depression and their effects on the duration of depressive episodes. *Journal of Abnormal Psychology, 100,* 569–582.

Nolen-Hoeksema, S., & Morrow, J. (1991). A prospective study of depression and distress following a natural disaster: The 1989 Loma Prieta earthquake. *Journal of Personality and Social Psychology, 61,* 105–121.

Nolen-Hoeksema, S., & Morrow, J. (1993). Effects of rumination and distraction on naturally-occurring depressed mood. *Cognition and Emotion, 7,* 561–570.

Nolen-Hoeksema, S., Morrow, J., & Fredrickson, B. L. (1993). Response styles and the duration of episodes of depressed mood. *Journal of Abnormal Psychology, 102,* 20–28.

Nolen-Hoekseman, S., Parker, L. E., & Larson, J. (1994). Ruminative coping with depressed mood following loss. *Journal of Personality and Social Psychology, 67,* 92–104.

Öhman, A., Fredrikson, M., Hugdahl, K., & Rimmo, P. (1976). The premise of equipotentiality in human classical conditioning: Conditioned electrodermal responses to potentially phobic stimuli. *Journal of Experimental Psychology: General, 105,* 313–337.

Öst, L., Fellenius, J., & Sterner, O. (1991). Applied tension, exposure in vivo, and tension-only in the treatment of blood phobia. *Behaviour Research and Therapy, 29,* 561–574.

Öst, L. G., & Westling, B. (1995). Applied relaxation vs. cognitive therapy in the treatment of panic disorder. *Behaviour Research and Therapy, 33,* 145–158.

O'Sullivan, G., Noshirvani, H., Marks, I. M., Monteiro, W., & Lelliott, P. (1991). Six-year follow-up after exposure and clomipramine therapy for obsessive compulsive disorder. *Journal of Clinical Psychiatry, 52,* 150–155.

Padesky, C. (1996). Developing cognitive therapist competency: Teaching and supervision models. In P. M. Salkovskis (Ed.), *Frontiers of cognitive therapy* (pp. 266–292). New York: Guilford.

Panksepp, J. (1982). Toward a general psychobiological theory of emotions. *The Behavioral and Brain Sciences, 5,* 407–468.

Pavlov, I. P. (1960). *Conditioned reflexes.* (G. V. Anrep, Trans.). New York: Dover. (Original work published 1927)

Pennebaker, J. (1997). Writing about emotional experiences as a therapeutic process. *Psychological Science, 8,* 162–166.

Pennebaker, J. W., Colder, M., & Sharp, L. K. (1990). Accelerating the coping process. *Journal of Personality and Social Psychology, 58,* 528–537.

Persons, J. B. (1989). *Cognitive therapy in practice: A case formulation approach.* New York: Norton.

Piaget, J. (1952). *The origins of intelligence in children.* (M. Cook, Trans.). New York: International Universities.

Pinker, S. (1994). *The language instinct: How the mind creates language.* New York: Morrow.

Pyszcynski, T. A., Greenberg, J., & LaPrelle, J. (1985). Social comparison after success and failure: Biased search for information consistent with a self-serving conclusion. *Journal of Experimental Social Psychology, 21,* 195–211.

Rachman, S. (1990). *Fear and courage* (2nd ed.). New York: W.H. Freeman.

Rachman, S. (1993). Obsessions, responsibility, and guilt. *Behaviour Research and Therapy, 31,* 149–154.

Rachman, S. (1997). A cognitive theory of obsessions. *Behaviour Research and Therapy, 35,* 793–802.

Raush, H. L., & Bordin, E. S. (1957). Warmth in personality development and in psychotherapy. *Psychiatry, 20,* 351–363.

Regan, M., & Howard, R. (1995). Fear conditioning, preparedness, and the contingent negative variation. *Psychophysiology, 32,* 208–214.

Rhéaume, J., Ladouceur, R., Freeston, M., & Letarte, H. (1994). Inflated responsibility in OCD II. Psychometric studies of a semi-idiographic measure. *Journal of Psychopathology and Behavioral Assessment, 16,* 265–276.

Rhéaume, J., Ladouceur, R., Freeston, M., & Letarte, H. (1995). Inflated responsibility in OCD I: Validation of a theoretical definition of responsibility. *Behaviour Research and Therapy, 33,* 159–169.

Rholes, W. S., Riskind, J. H., & Neville, B. (1985). The relationship of cognitions and hopelessness to depression and anxiety [Special Issue: Depression]. *Social Cognition, 3,* 36–50.

Rijken, H., Kraaimaat, F., deRuiter, C., & Garssen, B. (1992). A follow-up study on short-term treatment of agoraphobia. *Behaviour Research and Therapy, 30,* 63–66.

Rogers, C. (1953). A research program in client-centered therapy. *Nervous and Mental Disorders, 31,* 106–113.

Rogers, C. (1957). The necessary and sufficient conditions of therapeutic personality change. *Journal of Consulting Psychology, 21,* 95–103.

Rogers, C. (1961). *On becoming a person.* Boston: Houghton Mifflin.

Roper, G., & Rachman, S. (1976). Obsessional-compulsive checking: Experimental replication and development. *Behaviour Research and Therapy, 14,* 25–32.

Roper, G., Rachman, S., & Hodgson, R. (1973). An experiment on obsessional checking. *Behaviour Research and Therapy, 11,* 271–277.

Roszak, T., Gomes, M. E., & Kanner, A. D. (Eds.). (1995). *Ecopsychology: Restoring the heart, healing the mind.* San Francisco: Sierra Club.

Rush, A. J., & Beck, A. T. (1988). Cognitive therapy of depression and suicide. In S. Lesse (Ed.), *What we know about suicidal behavior and how to treat it* (pp. 283–306). Northvale, NJ: Aronson.

Sacco, W. P., & Beck, A. T. (1995). Cognitive theory and therapy. In E. E. Beckham & W. R. Leber (Eds.), *Handbook of depression* (2nd ed., pp. 329–351). New York: Guilford.

Saddler, C. D., & Sacks, L. A. (1993). Multidimensional perfectionism and academic procrastination: Relationships with depression in university students. *Psychological Reports, 73,* 863–871.

Salkovskis, P. M. (1985). Obsessional-compulsive problems: A cognitive-behavioural analysis. *Behaviour Research and Therapy, 25,* 571–583.

Salkovskis, P. M. (1989). Cognitive-behavioural factors and the persistence of intrusive thoughts in obsessional problems. *Behaviour Research and Therapy, 27,* 677–682.

Salkovskis, P. M. (1996). The cognitive approach to anxiety: Threat beliefs, safety-seeking behavior, and the special case of health anxiety and obsessions. In P. M. Salkovskis (Ed.), *Frontiers of cognitive therapy* (pp. 48–74). New York: Guilford.

Salkovskis, P. M., & Campbell, P. (1994). Thought suppression induces intrusion in naturally occurring negative intrusive thoughts. *Behaviour Research and Therapy, 32,* 1–8.

Salkovskis, P. M., Clark, D. M., & Gelder, M. G. (1996). Cognitive-behaviour links in the persistence of panic. *Behaviour Research and Therapy, 34,* 453–458.

Salkovskis, P. M., & Harrison, J. (1984). Abnormal and normal obsessions—A replication. *Behaviour Research and Therapy, 22,* 549–552.

Salkovskis, P. M., & Kirk, J. (1989). Obsessional disorders. In K. Hawton, P. M. Salkovskis, J. Kirk, & D. M. Clark (Eds.), *Cognitive behaviour therapy for psychiatric problems: A practical guide* (pp. 129–168). New York: Oxford University Press.

Salkovskis, P. M., & Westbrook, D. (1989). Behaviour therapy and obsessional ruminations: Can failure be turned into success? *Behaviour Research and Therapy, 27,* 149–160.

Salkovskis, P. M., Westbrook, D., Davis, J., Jeavons, A., & Glenhill, A. (1997). Effects of neutralizing on intrusive thoughts: An experiment investigating the etiology of obsessive-compulsive disorder. *Behaviour Research and Therapy, 35,* 211–219.

Sanderson, W. C., & Wetzler, S. (1993). Observations on the cognitive behavioral treatment of panic disorder: Impact of benzodiazepines. *Psychotherapy, 30,* 125–132.

Schneider, W., & Shiffrin, R. M. (1977). Controlled and automatic human information processing. I. Detection, search and attention. *Psychological Review, 84,* 1–66.
Seligman, M. E. P. (1971). Phobias and preparedness. *Behavior Therapy, 2,* 307–320.
Seligman, M. E. P., Abramson, L. Y., Semmel, A., & von Baeyer, C. (1979). Depressive attributional style. *Journal of Abnormal Psychology, 88,* 242–247.
Sharp, D. M., & Power, K. G. (1996). Fluvoxamine, placebo, and cognitive behavior therapy used alone and in combination in the treatment of panic disorder and agoraphobia. *Journal of Anxiety Disorders, 10,* 219–242.
Shaver, P., Schwartz, J., Kirson, D., & O'Connor, C. (1987). Emotion knowledge: Further explorations of a prototype approach. *Journal of Personality and Social Psychology, 52,* 1061–1086.
Shiffrin, R. M., & Schneider, W. (1977). Controlled and automatic human information processing. II. Perceptual learning, automatic attending, and a general theory. *Psychological Review, 84,* 127–190.
Skinner, B. F. (1953). *Science and human behavior.* New York: The Free Press.
Snyder, M., Tanke, E. D., & Berscheid, E. (1977). Social perception and interpersonal behavior: On the self-fulfilling nature of social stereotypes. *Journal of Personality and Social Psychology, 35,* 656–666.
Soares, J. J., & Öhman, A. (1993). Preattentive processing, preparedness and phobias: Effects of instruction on conditioned electrodermal responses to masked and non-masked fear-relevant stimuli. *Behaviour Research and Therapy, 31,* 87–95.
Sokol, L., Beck, A. T., Greenberg, R. L., Wright, F. D., & Berchick, R. J. (1989). Cognitive therapy of panic disorder: A nonpharmacological alternative. *Journal of Nervous and Mental Disease, 177,* 711–716.
Spera, S. P., Buhrfeind, E. D., & Pennebaker, J. W. (1994). Expressive writing and coping with job loss. *Academy of Management Journal, 37,* 722–733.
Spitzer, R. L., Williams, J. B. W., Kroenke, K., Linzer, M., deGruy, F. V., Hahn, S. R., & Brody, D. (1994). The utility of a new procedure for diagnosing mental disorders in primary care: The PRIME–MD 1000 Study. *Journal of the American Medical Association, 272,* 1749–1756.
Stekette, G., & Foa, E. B. (1985). Obsessive-compulsive disorder. In D. Barlow (Ed.), *Clinical handbook of psychological disorders* (pp. 69–144). New York: Guilford.
Stekette, G., & Shapiro, L. J. (1993). Obsessive-compulsive disorder. In A. S. Bellack & M. Hersen (Eds.), *Handbook of behavior therapy in the psychiatric setting* (pp. 199–227). New York: Plenum.
Stern, R. S., & Marks, I. M. (1973). Brief and prolonged flooding: A comparison in agoraphobic patients. *Archives of General Psychiatry, 28,* 270–276.
Tart, C. T. (1994). *Living the mindful life.* Boston: Shambhala.
Teasdale, J. D., Segal, Z., & Williams, J. M. G. (1995). How does cognitive therapy prevent depressive relapse and why should attentional control (mindfulness) training help? *Behaviour Research and Therapy, 33,* 25–39.
Timberlake, W. (1984). An ecological approach to learning. *Learning and Motivation, 15,* 321–333.
Tobi, M. (1996). *The art of positive parenting.* Columbus, OH: Greyden.

Tomkins, S. S., & McCarter, R. (1964). What and where are the primary affects? Some evidence for a theory. *Perceptual and Motor Skills, 18,* 119–158.

Trevarthen, C. (1993). An infant's motives for speaking and thinking in culture. In A. H. Wold (Ed.), *The dialogical alternative: Towards a theory of language and mind* (pp. 99–137). Oslo, Norway: Scandinavian University Press.

Trinder, P., & Salkovskis, P. M. (1994). Personally relevant intrusions outside the laboratory: Long-term suppression increases intrusion. *Behaviour research and therapy, 32,* 833–842.

Tulving, E. (1985). How many memory systems are there? *American Psychologist, 40,* 385–398.

Turner, S., & Beidel, D. (1988). *Treating obsessive compulsive disorder.* New York: Pergamon.

Turkat, I. D. (1990). *The personality disorders: A psychological approach to clinical management.* New York: Pergamon.

Vaillant, G. (1993). *The wisdom of the ego.* Cambridge, MA: Harvard University Press.

van Balkom, A. J., de Beurs, E., Koele, P., & Lange, A. (1996). Long-term benzodiazepine use is associated with smaller treatment gain in panic disorder with agoraphobia. *Journal of Nervous and Mental Disease, 184,* 133–135.

van den Hout, M., Arntz, A., & Hoekstra, R. (1994). Exposure reduced agoraphobia but not panic, and cognitive therapy reduced panic but not agoraphobia. *Behaviour Research and Therapy, 32,* 447–451.

van Oppen, P., & Arntz, A. (1993). Cognitive therapy for obsessive-compulsive disorder. *Behaviour Research and Therapy, 32,* 79–87.

van Oppen, P., De Hann, E., Anton, A. J., Spinhoven, P., Hoogduin, K., & van Dyck, R. (1995). Cognitive therapy and exposure in vivo in the treatment of obsessive-compulsive disorder. *Behaviour Research and Therapy, 33,* 379–390.

Watts, F. N. (1979). Habituation model of systematic desensitization. *Psychological Bulletin, 86,* 627–637.

Weishaar, M. E. (1993). *Aaron T. Beck.* London: Sage.

Weishaar, M. E. (1996). Cognitive risk factors in suicide. In P. M. Salkovskis (Ed.), *Frontiers of cognitive therapy* (pp. 226–249). New York: Guilford.

Weissman, A., & Beck, A. T. (1978). *Development and validation of Dysfunctional Attitude Scale: A preliminary investigation.* Presented at the annual meeting of the American Educational Research Association, Toronto, Ontario.

Willerman, L., & Cohen, D. B. (1990). *Psychopathology.* New York: McGraw-Hill.

Williams, S. L., & Falbo, J. (1996). Cognitive and performance-based treatments for panic attacks in people with varying degrees of agoraphobic disability. *Behaviour Research and Therapy, 34,* 253–264.

Wincze, J. P., & Carey, M. P. (1991). *Sexual dysfunction: A guide for assessment and treatment.* New York: Guilford.

Wolpe, J. (1982). *The practice of behavior therapy* (3rd ed.). New York: Pergamon.

Wong, P. T. P. (1998a). Implicit theories of meaningful life and the development of the personal meaningful profile. In P. T. P. Wong & P. S. Fry (Eds.), *The quest for human meaning* (pp. 111–140). Mahwah, NJ: Lawrence Erlbaum Associates.

Wong, P. T. P. (1998b). Meaning-centered counseling. In P. T. P. Wong & P. S. Fry (Eds.), *The quest for human meaning* (pp. 395–435). Mahwah, NJ: Lawrence Erlbaum Associates.

Wong, P. T. P. (1998c). Spirituality, meaning, and successful aging. In P. T. P. Wong & P. S. Fry (Eds.), *The quest for human meaning* (pp. 359–394). Mahwah, NJ: Lawrence Erlbaum Associates.

Wong, P. T. P., & Fry, P. S. (Eds.). (1998). *The quest for human meaning*. Mahwah, NJ: Lawrence Erlbaum Associates.

Wright, J. H., Thase, M. E., Beck, A. T., & Ludgate, J. W. (Eds.). (1993). *Cognitive therapy with inpatients: Developing a cognitive milieu*. New York: Guilford.

Yalom, I. (1980). *Existential psychotherapy*. New York: Basic Books.

Young, J. E. (1990). *Cognitive therapy of personality disorders: A schema approach*. Sarasota, FL: Professional Resource Exchange.

Zeiss, A. M., & Lewinsohn, P. M. (1979). Nonspecific improvement effects in depression using interpersonal skills training, pleasant activity schedules, or cognitive training. *Journal of Consulting and Clinical Psychology, 47*, 427–439.

Author Index

D

E

F

G

H

I

J

K

L

S

T

V

W

Y

Z

Subject Index

A

D

W

X